AMC'S BEST BACKPACKING IN NEW ENGLAND

D0754280

WELCOME TO THE AMC

What Is the Appalachian Mountain Club?

Since 1876, the Appalachian Mountain Club has been promoting the protection, enjoyment, and wise use of the mountains, rivers, and trails of the Northeast outdoors. We are the nation's oldest outdoor recreation and conservation organization.

Join Us!

Members support our mission while enjoying great AMC activities, our award-winning AMC Outdoors magazine, and special discounts. Join online, or call 800-372-1758 for more information.

People

We are nearly 90,000 members in 12 chapters, 20,000 volunteers, and over 450 full time and seasonal staff. Our chapters reach from Maine to Washington D.C.

Outdoor Fun

We offer over 8,000 trips each year, from local chapter activities to major excursions worldwide, for every ability level and outdoor interest – from hiking and climbing to paddling to snowshoeing and skiing.

Great Places to Stay

We serve over 140,000 guests each year at our AMC Lodges, Huts, Full-Service Camps, Cabins, Shelters and Campgrounds – each AMC Destination is a model for environmental education and stewardship.

Opportunities for Learning

We teach people the skills to be safe outdoors and care for the natural world around us, through programs for children, teens and adults, as well as outdoor leadership training.

Caring for Trails

We maintain over 1,700 miles of trails throughout the Northeast, including nearly 350 miles of the Appalachian Trail in five states.

Protecting Wild Places

We advocate for land and riverway conservation, monitor air quality, and work to protect alpine and forest ecosystems through the Northern Forest and Highlands regions.

Engaging the Public

We seek to educate and inform our own members and an additional 1.5 million people annually through AMC Books, our website, our White Mountain visitor centers, and AMC Destinations.

AMC'S BEST BACKPACKING IN
NEW ENGLAND

A Guide to Thirty-Three of the Best Multi-Day Trips from Maine to
Connecticut

MATT HEID

Appalachian Mountain Club Books
Boston, MA

The AMC is a non-profit organization and
sales of AMC books fund our mission of
protecting the Northeast outdoors. If you appreciate our
efforts and would like to make a donation to the AMC,
contact us at
Appalachian Mountain Club,
5 Joy Street, Boston, MA 02108.
www.outdoors.org/publications/books/

Distributed by the Globe Pequot Press, Guilford, Connecticut.

Published by the Appalachian Mountain Club. No part of this publication may be reproduced or
transmitted in any form or by any means, electronic or mechanical, including photocopying and
recording, or by any information storage or retrieval system, except as may be expressly permitted by
the 1976 Copyright Act or in writing from the publisher.

Front-Cover Photograph: © Jerry and Marcy Monkman/Ecophotography.com
Back-Cover Photographs: © Matt Heid
Unless noted, all interior photographs are the author's

Library of Congress Cataloging-in-Publication Data

Heid, Matt, 1975-
   AMC's best backpacking in New England : a guide to 33 of the best multi-day trips from Maine to
Connecticut / By Matt Heid. -- 1st ed.
   p. cm.
   Includes bibliographical references.
   ISBN 978-1-929173-74-7
   1. Backpacking--New England--Guidebooks. 2. Hiking--New England--Guidebooks. I. Title. II.
Title: Best backpacking in New England.
   GV199.42.N38H45 2007
   796.510974--dc22

                                                                               2007037317

The paper used in this publication meets the minimum requirements of the
American National Standard for Information Sciences-Permanence of
Paper for Printed Library Materials, ANSI Z39.48-1984. ∞

**Due to changes in conditions, use of the information
in this book is at the sole risk of the user.**

Printed in the United States of America.

Printed on recycled paper.

10 9 8 7 6 5 4 3 2 1

TRIP LOCATOR MAP

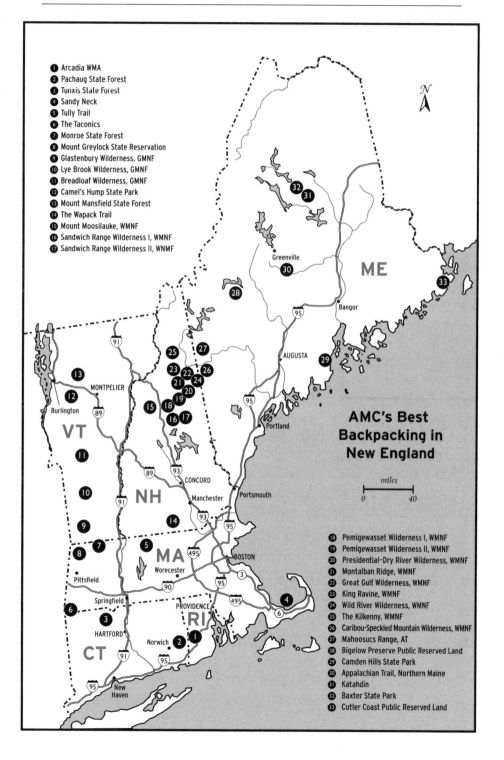

1. Arcadia WMA
2. Pachaug State Forest
3. Tunxis State Forest
4. Sandy Neck
5. Tully Trail
6. The Taconics
7. Monroe State Forest
8. Mount Greylock State Reservation
9. Glastenbury Wilderness, GMNF
10. Lye Brook Wilderness, GMNF
11. Breadloaf Wilderness, GMNF
12. Camel's Hump State Park
13. Mount Mansfield State Forest
14. The Wapack Trail
15. Mount Moosilauke, WMNF
16. Sandwich Range Wilderness I, WMNF
17. Sandwich Range Wilderness II, WNMF

ME

Greenville

Bangor

AUGUSTA

MONTPELIER

Burlington

VT

NH

CONCORD

Manchester Portsmouth

Pittsfield

Worcester

BOSTON

Springfield

PROVIDENCE

RI

HARTFORD

Norwich

CT

New Haven

Portland

AMC's Best Backpacking in New England

miles

0   40

18. Pemigewasset Wilderness I, WMNF
19. Pemigewasset Wilderness II, WMNF
20. Presidential-Dry River Wilderness, WMNF
21. Montalban Ridge, WMNF
22. Great Gulf Wilderness, WMNF
23. King Ravine, WMNF
24. Wild River Wilderness, WMNF
25. The Kilkenny, WMNF
26. Caribou-Speckled Mountain Wilderness, WMNF
27. Mahoosucs Range, AT
28. Bigelow Preserve Public Reserved Land
29. Camden Hills State Park
30. Appalachian Trail, Northern Maine
31. Katahdin
32. Baxter State Park
33. Cutler Coast Public Reserved Land

CONTENTS

BACKPACKING TRIPS

1 SOUTHERN NEW ENGLAND: MASSACHUSETTS, CONNECTICUT, AND RHODE ISLAND

4 MAINE

FOREWORD

WELCOME TO THE TOTAL NEW ENGLAND BACKCOUNTRY EXPERIENCE. This guidebook tours the wildest, least touched landscapes in a region known for its dramatic terrain, majestic forests, and exhilarating mountaintops. The 33 featured trips range in length from less than a mile to 100 miles. They visit nine wilderness areas, eight state forests, four state parks, two national forests, and a variety of other protected landscapes. Though many can be completed as day hikes, all of them provide opportunities for overnight adventure. Most are two- to three-day trips, perfect for a weekend outing.

Trips were selected based on two criteria:

- They are loop hikes.
- They do not cross roads.

Loop hikes are convenient, do not revisit scenery, and avoid the hassle of arranging a car shuttle. Road crossings detract from the wilderness experience and are avoided whenever possible. There are a few exceptions, most notably the 100-Mile Wilderness, a one-way hike through the wild heart of Maine and the longest trip featured in this book.

So what are you waiting for? Go discover. Go explore. The wilds of New England beckon.

ACKNOWLEDGMENTS

THIS BOOK TOOK FOUR YEARS TO PRODUCE. Now, after nearly 100 days of field research, more than 500 miles of hiking, and countless hours of butt-numbing computer sessions, it is done. But it would not have been possible without the unwavering support and love of those around me.

Twenty people joined me on at least one research excursion. Their company was much appreciated, their patience even more so as they put up with my constant positioning requests for photos. Thanks goes first to Pete Ingraham, who joined me on a half-dozen overnight hikes, and whose enthusiasm and knowledge of the region's natural history was a constant pleasure. Here's to many more extra-cheesy meals in the backcountry, Pete. Stewart Anderson wanted me to tell passing hikers that I was doing field research on his special hiking style, but I instead dragged him out of his bunk at 4 a.m. to climb Katahdin, joined by his adventurous fiancée, Blair Beakley, and Karen Finogle, who we wrapped in a bivy sack on the mountaintop. John and Maria Capello accompanied me to the top of Camel's Hump, Maria enthusing along the way, "It's like eating ice cream with your head!" Kalev Freeman and Monique McHenry waited patiently as the clouds rolled in on top of Mount Greylock and I ran down the far mountainside. Ben Shelton and Regan Brooks successfully cajoled their dog Otter through Mahoosuc Notch after I took them into the challenging boulder maze. Katie Holden didn't complain when I unexpectedly led her into the ice-covered alpine zone below Mount Adams in late October. And though I never did convince him to go on a research hike with me, thanks also to Brian Drohan, who has joined me on many other outdoor adventures in the past few years.

My love and appreciation goes to my parents, who have provided caring and unwavering support for my outdoor pursuits over the years. And to my extended family—Karen, Steve, Krissy, and Beth Ela—for their enthusiasm and excitement (and bravery on scary bridges) during our overnight adven-

Bunchberry in flower

tures to Royalston Falls and Monroe State Forest. My brother and sister-in-law, John and Analise, were troopers on our "death march" around the Dry River Valley, and I look forward to many more outdoor adventures with them in the years to come (though they seem to have grown increasingly wary of my hiking invitations . . .).

Thank you to all my coworkers at the Appalachian Mountain Club, both past and present, whose support and flexibility allowed me to gather the materials for this book. Thank you Beth Krusi for signing me up to do this title in the first place, Kevin Breunig for providing the flexibility I needed to get it done, and Bryan Davidson for shepherding this project through to completion. To all my coworkers at *AMC Outdoors*, it's been one hell of a ride. Special thanks to Katharine Wroth, Ed Winchester, and Kelly Powers for making it such a fun place to work, even in times of (constant) adversity.

But my greatest thanks, love, and appreciation go to my wife, Gretchen. For the past four years, she has been an integral part of this seemingly interminable project, joining me on myriad trips and patiently supporting me as this book consumed my free time. In some ways, this book marks the beginning of a much greater adventure for us—we married midway through this marathon project. Thank you, Gretchen. Here's to a lifetime of adventure together.

Matt Heid
July 15, 2007

HOW TO USE THIS BOOK

FOR THE PURPOSES OF THIS BOOK, NEW ENGLAND is divided into four geographic areas—Southern New England, Vermont, New Hampshire, and Maine. Trips are listed in separate sections in that regional order. Locator maps are included at the beginning of each section to help you identify trip locations. Each hike uses a standard format, described in greater detail later.

To prepare for your adventure, first read the section *Safety, Gear, and the Leave-No-Trace Ethic*. Those unfamiliar with the outdoor world of New England or unsure about where to go should consult the section *Where Should I Go?* For those looking for a specific feature, the hikes are grouped by theme starting on page xxiv. Otherwise just flip through the pages and evaluate each adventure based on the standard information provided.

BACKPACKING TRIPS
Each backpacking trip is described using a standard, easily understood template. The template is divided into two parts: The Header and Hike Description.

THE HEADER
Title. Something fun to intrigue the reader, most hike titles are the author's creation and will not appear on maps, signs, or be known to those not holding this book.

Location. The location identifies the area or specific destination visited by the hike.

Highlights. What makes the trip special, unique, and impossible to resist.

Distance. The total mileage of the hike. For point-to-point hikes, the one-way distance is listed.

Total Elevation Gain/Loss. The amount of climbing and descending on the hike, measured in vertical feet. It can be significantly greater than the difference between the hike's lowest and highest points.

Trip Length. This is the recommended number of days for the trip. A range of days may be listed, depending on your desired pace. It is important to be aware of your physical capabilities and limitations when selecting a hike. As a general rule of thumb, a reasonably fit hiker can expect to cover 2–3 miles per hour over level ground and on gradual descents, 1–2 miles per hour on gradual climbs, and only about 1 mile—or 750–1000 feet of elevation—per hour on the steepest ascents.

Difficulty. This book uses a five-star rating system.

★ *Easy.* Short and level, these hikes can be done by nearly anybody and have less than 500 feet of elevation gain.

★★ *Moderate.* Longer hikes with 500–3,000 feet of total elevation gain per day along good, easy-to-follow trails. Suitable for any reasonably fit hiker.

★★★ *Strenuous.* Difficult hikes with 1,000–3,000 feet of elevation gain per day on more challenging trails. Good fitness required.

★★★★ *Challenging.* A very strenuous hike involving considerable elevation gain and loss on challenging trails. Higher mileage can also increase the difficulty to this rating.

★★★★★ *Epic.* Extended adventures with considerable and constant elevation gain and loss, often in remote regions on challenging trails. Experienced backpackers only. Maine's 100-Mile Wilderness (Trip 30), the Pemigewasset Wilderness in New Hampshire (Trip 19), and Baxter State Park (Trips 31 and 32) are the only destinations featured in this category.

Recommended Maps. Some hikes can be completed using only the maps in this book, but greater safety and enjoyment comes with more detailed and comprehensive knowledge—especially on lesser-known hikes that venture into more remote areas. It is strongly recommended that you aquire a good map of the area; the best are listed here, followed by publisher if applicable.

HIKE DESCRIPTION

The hike description is broken down into five main sections:

Hike Overview

A general overview of the hike, discussing trail highlights and route, including whether dogs are allowed.

Overnight Options

A detailed description of established campsites, lean-tos, and other overnight options, including mileages, natural setting, and amenities. Information about reservations and crowds is included in this section.

It's a small world. A red-spotted newt explores Tully Trail.

To Reach the Trailhead

Concise driving directions to the trailhead. This book assumes you have a basic highway map of New England. Every car's odometer is different, so please note that mileages may vary slightly between those listed here and in your vehicle.

Hike Description

A detailed narrative of the hike itself. Parenthetical notations such as (3.2/1,450) are included in the text at all trail junctions and important landmarks. The first number represents the total distance traveled from the trailhead in miles, the second identifies the elevation of the location in feet. Occasional notations of peaks such as (3,849) indicate elevation in feet.

Information

Address, phone number, and website for the best source of information about the hike.

THE MAPS IN THIS BOOK

A basic reference map is included with each hike description to help readers plan their trips. Important landmarks are featured using a standard series of symbols—including trailheads, designated camping areas, summits, and bodies of water—but these maps are not intended for navigation purposes. You are strongly encouraged to purchase the recommended maps highlighted at the beginning of each trip, which will include detailed topographic information and other elements crucial for a safe and enjoyable trip in the backcountry.

WHERE SHOULD I GO HIKING?

NEW ENGLAND GEOGRAPHY

New England is a jigsaw of mountain ranges, a rumpled world of outdoor adventure. From the low-lying terrain of Massachusetts, Connecticut, and Rhode Island, north to the mountainscapes of New Hampshire, Vermont, and Maine, the region offers an inspiring diversity of landscapes, ecosystems, and backpacking excursions.

Southern New England (Trips 1–8)

Rhode Island, Connecticut, and Massachusetts compose southern New England. The region can roughly be divided into three sections, which become increasingly mountainous as you go from east to west.

The east region, which includes Rhode Island and the east third of Massachusetts and Connecticut, is a densely populated landscape dimpled by hills and small parcels of open space. Backpacking opportunities are limited, though a large swath of protected land is located in southwest Rhode Island (Arcadia Wildlife Management Area, Trip 1) and southeast Connecticut (Pachaug State Forest, Trip 2). In Massachusetts, the long spit of Cape Cod protrudes into the Atlantic Ocean, providing a rare seaside backpack along Sandy Neck in the mid-Cape region (Trip 4).

The central portion of southern New England includes central Massachusetts and Connecticut east of the Connecticut River. Here, the landscape begins to rumple and roll, defined by a low-lying collection of hills and small mountains. Elevations climb above 1,000 feet in many locations, capped by the prominent bulge of 2,006-foot Mount Wachusett in north-central Massachusetts. Open space begins to increase, though it remains a patchwork of small parklands. Nevertheless, a sense of wildness begins to grow. The population density is low in many areas. Moose live in the region, some as far south as Tunxis State Forest (Trip 3) in north-central Connecticut. In north-central Massachusetts, the 22-mile Tully Trail (Trip 5) explores a multitude of conservation lands through the lush forest that blankets most of the region.

The west portion of southern New England encompasses west Connecticut and Massachusetts, including the Berkshires and Taconic Range. The terrain becomes more mountainous and starts to exceed 2,000 feet. Lush and diverse forest cloaks ridges and valleys. In Massachusetts, the Berkshires rise west of the Connecticut River, a hilly range highlighted by several stands of old-growth forest. Monroe State Forest (Trip 7) protects one of the most remarkable. Near the state line, the Berkshires drop into deep valleys bordered to the west by the older peaks of the Taconic Range. The Appalachian Trail (AT) weaves between the two ranges, running along a unique high-elevation plateau in northwest Connecticut and southwest Massachusetts (Trip 6) and later clambering over the singular massif of Mount Greylock (Trip 8)—the highest point in Massachusetts—in the state's northwest corner.

Vermont (Trips 9–13)

Vermont is defined by the Green Mountains, a linear mountain range that spans the length of the state on a north-south axis. The 272-mile Long Trail runs along the Green Mountain spine for its entire length, and is the state's primary hiking and backpacking artery.

Elevations in the Green Mountains generally rise above 2,000 feet, and exceed 3,000 feet in many locations. Forest veils most of the range, and hiking here is defined more by woodlands than by dramatic above-treeline views. The Green Mountain National Forest protects much of the southern Green Mountains and is divided into two sections. The southern portion is less mountainous and less traveled than points farther north. At 3,748 feet, Glastenbury Mountain (Trip 9) crowns the southern region, protected within the Glastenbury Mountain Wilderness. A high-elevation plateau rolls north of Glastenbury, dissected by streams and ponds, and is the site of the Lye Brook Wilderness (Trip 10). The northern portion of Green Mountain National Forest is more rugged, though still densely forested. Breadloaf Wilderness (Trip 11) epitomizes the experience.

The Greens continue north past the national forest to the Canadian border, marked by two landmark peaks: Camel's Hump and Mount Mansfield. The summits of both protrude above the surrounding forest, offering alpine views in all directions. Camel's Hump (Trip 12) is the highest peak with an undeveloped summit in the state. Mount Mansfield (Trip 13)—the state's tallest peak—is composed of a long alpine ridge with wild trails.

The landscape east of the Green Mountains is lined with ridges, incised by valleys, and flush with pastoral scenery. Backpacking options, however, are essentially nonexistent.

New Hampshire (Trips 14–25)

The White Mountains define New Hampshire's backpacking scene. Protected within the 700,000-acre White Mountain National Forest in the north-central portion of the state, they are a rugged collection of peaks laced by hundreds of miles of trails. Forty-eight summits exceed 4,000 feet. Five designated wilderness areas protect vast swaths of the landscape. Hiking and backpacking opportunities are almost without limit.

A variety of smaller ranges compose the overall topography. The Sandwich Range (Trips 16 and 17) rises as the White's southern front, one of the area's most accessible—yet least traveled—collection of trails. To the west, the isolated massif of Mount Moosilauke (Trip 15) looms, another easily accessed destination. North of the Sandwich Range is the 45,000-acre Pemigewasset Wilderness, the largest in New England. Ringed by peaks, including fifteen taller than 4,000 feet, it is drained by the Pemigewasset River and offers some of the deepest and longest adventures in this book (Trips 18 and 19). The most remote summit in the Whites—Bondcliff—can be found here, more than 10 miles from the closest trailhead.

Then there is the Presidential Range. Capped by 6,288-foot Mount Washington—the highest mountain in New England—the Presidential Range boasts miles upon miles of above-treeline travel. Its extensive alpine zone stretches for more than a dozen miles and is the largest alpine area east of the Rocky Mountains.

Deep valleys score the mountain flanks. The Great Gulf (Trip 22) is the wildest chasm, curving below the northern Presidentials to terminate at a 2,000-foot headwall beneath Mount Washington. The Dry River Valley (Trip 20) drains the southern Presidentials, a significant watershed hemmed to the east by little-traveled Montalban Ridge and the Davis Path (Trip 21). Beyond Mount Washington are the towering peaks of the northern Presidentials: Mounts Jefferson, Adams, and Madison. Their northern flanks are dissected by streams, deep valleys, and a remarkable density of trails. King Ravine (Trip 23) is the deepest gorge, a sheer bowl gouged from the mountainside.

The Wild River Wilderness (Trip 24), the newest wilderness area in the White Mountains, is located east of the Presidential Range and encompasses most of the Wild River watershed. It is a self-contained world of forest, streams, and few people.

The White Mountains also include two outlying areas. The first is the Pilot Range (Trip 25), located north of the Presidential Range and disjunct from the rest of the national forest. A mountain range in miniature, it is capped by 4,170-foot Mount Cabot. The second is Speckled Mountain (Trip 26), just over the state line in Maine and protected within the Caribou–Speckled Mountain Wilderness.

Outside of the White Mountains, the state boasts multitudes of smaller ranges and summits, but backpacking opportunities become more limited. An exception can be found at the state's southern edge, where the diminutive Wapack Range (Trip 14) straddles the Massachusetts–New Hampshire border.

Maine (Trips 26–33)

Maine is larger than the five other New England states combined. A mountainous backbone runs northeast from the White Mountains in New Hampshire to the north-central portion of the state. The AT travels the length of it—more than 280 miles—passing over a collection of peaks and small ranges en route to its terminus atop Katahdin in Baxter State Park.

After leaving the White Mountain National Forest in New Hampshire, the AT travels across the Mahoosuc Range—arguably the most rugged ridgeline in New England. In the middle of it is Mahoosuc Notch (Trip 27), a boulder-strewn cleft rightly dubbed the hardest mile on the AT. A hundred miles later, the AT travels across the Bigelow Range (Trip 28), a prominent east-west mountain ridge capped with exceptional views.

Near its end, the AT enters the 100-Mile Wilderness (Trip 30), the most remote section of the entire trail. The route does not cross a paved road for 99.4 miles as it visits open ridgelines, massive lakes, and rushing rivers on a grand tour of the Maine backcountry.

Baxter State Park borders the 100-Mile Wilderness to the northeast. Its centerpiece is 5,268-foot Katahdin. The ice sheet of the last Ice Age failed to overtop this granite monolith, though alpine glaciers gouged its flanks. The result is New England's only true arête: the Knife Edge. This narrow mile-long ridge crowns a headwall rising more than 2,000 feet above placid Chimney Pond (Trip 31). Crowds tend to congregate around Katahdin, but there is a vast landscape of lakes and hills to its north that receives much less use, centered around Russell Pond (Trip 32).

Most backpacking opportunities in Maine center around the AT, rather than along its sinuous coastline, though there are two exceptions. The low-lying Camden Hills (Trip 29) bulge above Penobscot Bay, a few miles from the ocean. And at the farthest end of the Maine coast, the soggy Cutler Coast Preserve (Trip 33) protects a rare example of maritime forest.

BEATING THE CROWDS

Hikers in New England are attracted to views like moths to a flame—areas above treeline are usually heavily traveled. In Vermont, the summits of Camel's Hump and Mount Mansfield are visited annually by tens of thousands of hikers. In New Hampshire, Franconia Ridge and the Presidential Range are often chock-a-block with the booted masses. In Maine, Katahdin swarms with summiteers.

These areas are popular for a reason—the scenery is exceptional—and shouldn't be skipped just because of the crowd factor. Avoid weekends and visit mid-week to enjoy them with a modicum of solitude, or plan a trip after mid-September when hiking traffic markedly diminishes.

Many of the hikes in this book also travel portions of the AT. A pulse of thru-hikers moves north as the summer progresses, filling trailside shelters and campsites. In Massachusetts and Vermont, June and July are peak travel times. In New Hampshire, July and August. In Maine, August, September, and early October.

In the White Mountains, a disproportionate number of hikers head to the Pemigewasset Wilderness and Presidential Range. Areas outside of these regions receive much less visitation, particularly the Sandwich Range (Trips 16 and 17), Kilkenny Range (Trip 25), and Speckled Mountain (Trip 26). In the Presidential Range, the Dry River watershed (Trip 20) and Montalban Ridge (Trip 21) provide the best opportunities for solitude.

A SEASON-BY-SEASON PLAYBOOK

This is a three-season guide and is designed to cover the period from spring through fall (April–October). The trips can be completed in the winter months as well, but this guide does not describe how snow and ice conditions may affect trails or camping areas. Be prepared and know what you're doing if you head out between November and March!

April. It's springtime in southern New England. Let the hiking season begin! The snow is gone in southern areas. Although trees are bare and leafless, plants in the understory begin to emerge by the middle of the month. The season's first wildflowers bloom in Arcadia Wildlife Management Area in

Rhode Island (Trip 1) and adjacent Pachaug State Forest in Connecticut (Trip 2). The beaches of Sandy Neck (Trip 4) warm up for the first time, and don't have summer crowds. The weather remains fickle and highly variable. Expect anything from freezing temperatures to comfortable sunny days that can reach into the 60s and even 70s, depending on location.

May. Spring creeps northward and upward. Wildflowers are at their peak. Painted trillium and hobblebush flower prolifically in northern New England forests, peaking around Memorial Day. In southern New England, trees have fully leafed out and hiking season is in full swing. It is an ideal time for mid-elevation hikes such as the Wapack Trail (Trip 14), the Tully Trail (Trip 5), the Tunxis Trail (Trip 3), Monroe State Forest (Trip 7), the Taconics (Trip 6), and Camden Hills (Trip 29). In northern New England, April and May are also known as Mud Season, when the ground is soggy underfoot and trails are easily damaged—some locations close their trails entirely during this period. This is also the time of year when black flies swarm. Depending on the season, snow may linger at higher elevations well into May. Wait until the end of the month before heading north. Crowds are minimal until Memorial Day weekend, at which point they pick up markedly.

June. By the middle of the month, the last trees in northern New England leaf out and summer arrives across the region. Kids remain in school until around the middle of the month, which keeps the traffic factor low. It's hard to go wrong when selecting a destination, though black flies and mosquitoes can be fierce, especially in wet and low-lying areas.

July–August. July and August are perhaps the two most similar months of the year. Temperatures and humidity are at their peak, with many sweltering days. Summer crowds are at their maximum, and thousands of people visit the backcountry. It is the time of year for swimming holes and lesser-traveled destinations. Soak your sweaty self in the Dry River (Trip 20) or Wild River watershed (Trip 24). Beat the crowds by visiting the Sandwich Range (Trips 16 and 17), Speckled Mountain (Trip 26), or Vermont's southern Green Mountains (Trips 9–11). This is also a good time of year to tour the alpine zones of the Presidential Range (Trips 21–23), when you're more likely to enjoy hospitable weather.

September. In September, fall foliage erupts in northern New England and marches south over the next four to six weeks. Colors first appear early in the month. High-elevation paper birch are the first to go, followed by the northernmost regions of New England. By late September, the Kilkenny (Trip 25), Mahoosucs (Trip 27), and Baxter State Park (Trips 31 and 32) peak in a radiance of color, followed in short order by Mount Mansfield

(Trip 13), Camel's Hump (Trip 12), and the Bigelow Range (Trip 28). Temperatures begin to cool and below-freezing nights return later in the month. Expect warm crisp days and cool nights.

October. Fall completes its sweep across southern New England. Peak foliage occurs in early October at most locations and then rapidly moves south. Peak foliage times vary year to year, but as a rule, you should head for the White and Green Mountains during the first and second weeks of the month. Lye Brook Wilderness (Trip 10) and the Pemigewasset Wilderness (Trips 18 and 19) are particularly nice. Color lingers at lower elevations and farther south through the third week of October, but by month's end, the leaves are down across the region. Expect cool days and cold nights. The season's first snowfall usually dusts the higher elevations by the end of the month. Hiking season winds down, the days get short, and soon it's winter.

NEW ENGLAND NATURAL HISTORY

The forests of New England can be roughly divided into four categories, each of which occurs within a different range of elevation.

Oak-Pine Forest is common throughout southern New England and at low-elevation sites farther north. It typically grows on rolling terrain with dry, rocky soil. The primary constituents of this assemblage are red oak and white pine. Recognize *red oak* by its large lobed leaves, which have spiny tips at their points; by its acorns, which have a relatively small, shallow cap; and by the distinctive red coloration that often appears in cracks on its main trunk. *White pine* is easily recognized by its long needles, which always occur in clusters of five, and the 6- to 8-inch-long pendulous cones that often litter the forest floor.

Other common trees in this forest type are *eastern hemlock*, a lacy, short-needled evergreen usually found in moister locations; *white ash*, another water-loving tree that features a distinctive diamond-shaped pattern on its bark; *white oak*, whose leaves lack spiny tips and are more deeply lobed than those of red oak; and *black birch*, which has finely serrated leaves and a generally smooth dark trunk. *Blueberry* and *huckleberry* bushes are common in the open understory, though they seldom grow fruit unless exposed to direct sunlight. Look for the large fronds of *interrupted* and *cinnamon ferns* in damp and shady locations, and keep an eye out for the delicate blossoms of *pink lady's slipper* orchids in late spring.

Northern Hardwood Forest is the most widespread forest type in New England. It predominates between 1,000 and 3,000 feet in elevation and features several common and easily recognized trees. *Yellow birch* is the key marker for this ecosystem and can be easily spotted by its golden bark, which peels in thin ribbons. (Older specimens develop a much gnarlier trunk; look upward to spot the telltale bark higher in the canopy.) *Paper birch* is quickly identified by its white bark, which peels in much wider sheets than yellow birch. *Quaking* and *big-tooth aspen* prefer recently disturbed sites with ample sunshine. Their fluttering leaves make them easy to identify, though the leaf shape differs between the two species: quaking has smooth margins, whereas the leaves of big-tooth are indeed toothed. The white bark of these trees can be confused with that of paper birch, but does not peel. *Sugar maple* occurs in northern hardwood forest but is a less common species, preferring less acidic soils at the lower end of the elevation spectrum.

The understory of northern hardwood forest is usually a tangled collection of *hobblebush*, a shrubby plant easily recognized by its large dinner-plate-sized leaves, which extend in pairs down the stem. Also common is *blue-bead lily* (also known as *yellow clintonia*). It extends a small stalk above a pair of large glossy basal leaves; in spring and early summer, yellow flowers cap the stem and transform into a cluster of (non-edible) blue berries later in the season.

Spruce-Fir Forest is the highest elevation forest type and occurs between roughly 3,000 feet and treeline, which varies between 4,000 and 5,000 feet, depending on location. It is composed of relatively few species. *Balsam fir*, the only fir species in New England, features flat splays of needles with pale undersides and notched tips. Its cones grow upright from the uppermost branches. *Red spruce* can be recognized by its spiny needles, which grow continuously around the twigs, and by the feathery 1- to 2-inch cones, which hang down from the branches. (*Black spruce* also occurs, especially at the uppermost elevations, but is difficult to distinguish from red spruce.)

Balsam fir and red spruce extend downward into the northern hardwood forest in limited numbers, but above 3,000 feet, they form thick and continuous stands. Dense moss often blankets the highly acidic forest floor where only a handful of other species survive. Among them is *bunchberry*, a diminutive member of the dogwood family. In early summer, dainty white flowers emerge from its ground-hugging four-leaved whorls, changing to clusters of small red berries in fall.

One of the more unusual features of spruce-fir forest is a *fir wave*, which occurs when a portion of a balsam fir stand becomes exposed to the elements. When clustered together, the trees shelter each other from the high winds and ice that occur at higher elevations. But when exposed directly to these harsh elements, they rapidly succumb and die. This then exposes their neighbors, which perish in turn. This moving line of tree death slowly migrates up the mountainside, moving an average of one meter per year. Recognize an active fir wave by the bleached snags of dead fir trees overhead and the thick and bushy young trees filling in beneath them.

The Alpine Zone occurs when the elements become too harsh for trees to survive. The precise boundary can vary more than 1,000 feet in elevation, depending on the terrain, prevailing wind direction, and a host of other factors, but typically occurs somewhere around 4,500 feet. Plant life becomes adapted to extreme cold and wind, and closely hugs the ground to avoid exposure to the elements.

The grassy stems of *Bigelow's sedge* extend a foot or so off the ground, lending a lawn-like appearance to portions of the alpine zone. *Diapensia* grows in dense, kidney-like clumps, extending clusters of small white flowers in May and June. *Labrador tea* features small leaves with curled-under margins and hairy undersides. *Alpine cranberry* burnishes the ground with bright red berries in late summer.

A multitude of other species manage to survive in this harsh environment, but keep in mind that they are all extremely fragile and easily damaged by the boots of wayward hikers. When in the alpine zone, always travel on durable surfaces, do not step on the plants, and stick to the established trails whenever possible.

TRIPS BY THEME

Numbers here refer to the Trip numbers in the text

DAY HIKABLE

1 Arcadia
2 Pachaug State Forest
3 Tunxis State Forest
4 Sandy Neck
7 Monroe State Forest
8 Mount Greylock
12 Camel's Hump
13 Mansfield
15 Mount Moosilauke
23 King Ravine
25 The Kilkenny
26 Speckled Mountain
28 Bigelow Range
29 Camden Hills
31 Chimney Pond
33 Cutler Coast

WATERFALLS

5 Tully Trail
6 The Taconics
8 Mount Greylock
10 Lye Brook Wilderness
15 Mount Moosilauke
18 Pemigewasset Wilderness
19 Pemigewasset Wilderness

20 Dry River
22 The Great Gulf
23 King Ravine
26 Speckled Mountain
30 100-Mile Wilderness

SWIMMING HOLES

5 Tully Trail
10 Lye Brook Wilderness
18 Pemigewasset Wilderness
19 Pemigewasset Wilderness
20 Dry River
22 The Great Gulf
24 Wild River
26 Speckled Mountain
28 Bigelow Range
30 100-Mile Wilderness
32 Big Baxter

NEAT SHELTERS

2 Pachaug State Forest
8 Mount Greylock
12 Camel's Hump
13 Mount Mansfield
17 Sandwich Range (Mount Chocorua)

23 King Ravine
30 100-Mile Wilderness
31 Chimney Pond
32 Big Baxter

UNUSUAL FOREST

4 Sandy Neck
6 The Taconics
7 Monroe State Forest
8 Mount Greylock
28 Bigelow Range
29 Camden Hills
33 Cutler Coast

SWEEPING 360-DEGREE VISTAS

6 The Taconics
8 Mount Greylock
9 Glastenbury Wilderness
12 Camel's Hump
13 Mansfield
14 Wapack Trail
15 Mount Moosilauke
16 Sandwich Range
17 Sandwich Range
18 Pemigewasset Wilderness
19 Pemigewasset Wilderness
20 Dry River
21 Montalban Ridge
22 The Great Gulf
23 King Ravine
24 Wild River
25 The Kilkenny
26 Speckled Mountain
27 Mahoosucs
28 Bigelow Range
30 100-Mile Wilderness
31 Baxter State Park
32 Baxter State Park

LAKES AND PONDS

5 Tully Trail
6 The Taconics
10 Lye Brook Wilderness
19 Pemigewasset Wilderness
25 The Kilkenny
27 Mahoosuc Range
28 Bigelow Range
30 100-Mile Wildernes
31 Baxter State Park
32 Big Baxter
33 Cutler Coast

STREAMS

1 Arcadia
3 Tunxis Trail
5 Tully Trail
6 The Taconics
7 Monroe State Forest
8 Mount Greylock
10 Lye Brook Wilderness
11 Breadloaf Wilderness
15 Mount Moosilauke
18 Pemigewasset Wilderness
19 Pemigewasset Wilderness
23 King Ravine
24 Wild River
25 The Kilkenny
26 Speckled Mountain
30 100-Mile Wilderness
31 Baxter State Park
32 Big Baxter

MAJOR RIVERS

18 Pemigewasset Wilderness
19 Pemigewasset Wilderness
20 Dry River
22 The Great Gulf
24 Wild River

SAFETY, GEAR, AND THE LEAVE-NO-TRACE ETHIC

SAFETY

Venturing into the outdoors entails a degree of risk. Preparation, fitness, and knowledge help mitigate this risk.

WILDLIFE HAZARDS

Moose. As a general rule, New England's largest land animal poses little threat on the trail, and you should consider yourself fortunate if you see one in the backcountry. They avoid people for the most part, and in most close encounters, your best view will be of the animal fleeing the scene. But they are not harmless either. Bull moose can act aggressively during the fall mating season, and a female moose will defend her young if she feels they are threatened.

Learn to recognize the signs of an agitated moose: Its ears are laid back, the hair on its back stands on end, it kicks or stomps the ground, walks directly at you, makes threatening noises, or licks its lips. In such situations, give the moose a wide berth—at least 100 feet—and do not try to scare it off. If it does charge, you should run, jump out of the way, or get behind a tree or other large object. Do not stand your ground. Moose are interested primarily in scaring you off. Once it perceives that you are no longer a threat, it will leave you alone.

Black Bears. Black bears are common in New England—wildlife biologists estimate that there are about 30,000—but the odds of seeing one in the backcountry are remote. (The author did not see a single bear while researching this book.) Most bears live in Maine (roughly 21,000), though New Hampshire and Vermont also have healthy populations—New Hampshire's

White Mountain National Forest is thought to have one bear for every 1.1 square mile.

Black bears feed mostly on nuts, berries, dead animals, and other plants, and rarely kill anything themselves. They almost never attack humans and usually flee at the first sight of an approaching hiker. If a bear does confront you, do not run. Make yourself look as large as possible and slowly back away. A loud noise—a whistle, banging pots, or shouting—can help scare off the animal. Always avoid a mother with her cubs. At night, hang your food from a tree branch at least 8 feet off the ground (or place it in a bear box if available). Never keep food in the tent with you.

Ticks. These parasites love brushy areas and are common throughout southern New England until the season's first hard freeze. Always perform regular body checks when hiking through tick country. If you find a tick attached to you, *do not* try to pull it out with your fingers or pinch the body; this can inject tick fluid under the skin and increase the risk of infection. Using an appropriate tool, gently pull the tick out by lifting upward from the base of the body where it is attached to the skin. Pull straight out until the tick releases and do not twist or jerk as this may break the mouth parts off under your skin. A small **V** cut in the side of a credit card works well for this operation, as do a pair of tweezers.

Ticks are known for transmitting *Lyme disease*, but only one tick species found in New England is capable of transmitting it—the diminutive deer tick. The deer tick has a two-year life cycle and ranges in size from a pinhead to a poppy seed, depending on its age. It is typically dark-colored, though adult females appear brick red. An infected tick must be attached for a minimum of six hours to transmit the disease. Caused by a spirochete bacteria, Lyme disease can be life threatening if not diagnosed in its early phases. Common early symptoms include fatigue, chills and fever, headache, muscle and joint pain, swollen lymph nodes, and a blotchy skin rash that clears centrally to produce a characteristic ring shape 3 to 30 days after exposure. If you fear that you have been exposed to Lyme disease, consult a doctor immediately. Note that most people infected with Lyme disease never see the tick that bit them.

Giardia. *Giardia lamblia* is a microscopic organism occasionally found in backcountry water sources. Existing in a dormant cyst while in the water, the critter develops in the gastrointestinal tract upon being consumed and can cause diarrhea, excessive flatulence, foul-smelling excrement, nausea, fatigue, and abdominal cramps. Although the risk of contraction is slight, the potential consequences are worth preventing. All water taken from the backcountry should be purified with a filter, a chemical treatment, or by boiling for 1 to 3 minutes. Be especially vigilant about water sources near shelters, camping areas, and other heavily used locations.

Raccoons, Skunks, Porcupines, Mice, and Foxes. Although not a threat to humans, these mostly nocturnal varmints are a major hazard for food supplies and have learned that lean-tos and campsites are prime locations for free meals. Never leave your food unattended and always store it somewhere safe at night. Food lockers are occasionally provided at established camping areas; otherwise hang it from a nearby tree or on a mouse-proof line (these common shelter accessories usually feature a small can or other obstacle that prevents mice from shimmying down the line). Bringing food inside the tent with you is not a good idea.

Black Flies, No See 'Ums, and Mosquitoes. These biting insects aren't dangerous, but they certainly can be aggravating. The wet landscape of New England provides ideal breeding grounds, and bugs flourish in the millions, especially during May and June. Avoid low-lying and wet areas during this period if possible. Use an insect repellent as needed. DEET is the most effective; only a small amount is needed for it to work. Concentrations of 20 to 30 percent provide four to six hours of coverage. Consider carrying a head net if the bugs are severe or your tolerance is low.

PLANT HAZARDS

Poison Ivy. If you learn to recognize only one plant, it should be this one. Poison ivy grows throughout southern New England and is abundant anywhere there is adequate sunshine, such as meadows, field margins, open trail corridors, and abandoned pastureland. A low-lying shrub or climbing vine, its glossy leaves grow in clusters of three and turn bright red in the fall before dropping off in the winter. Other key identification marks are its terminal leaf, which always has a stem, and its hairy vines, which climb trees and other structures. Both the leaves and branches contain urushiol oil, which causes a strong allergic reaction in most people and creates a maddening and long-lived itchy rash. Wash thoroughly with soap after any exposure, and clean clothing that may have come in contact with the plant. Residual oil on pets, pants, and other clothing can often be a culprit as well.

Danger Berries. Berries are abundant in New England, and many of them— blackberries, blueberries, cranberries, raspberries, and huckleberries —provide delightful trailside snacks. But many other berry species are poisonous and potentially dangerous. Be 100 percent sure before you start snacking.

PHYSICAL DANGERS

Hypothermia. This occurs when your core body temperature begins to drop. Typically caused by exposure to the elements, hypothermia is a life-threatening condition whose initial symptoms include weakness, mental confusion, slurred speech, and uncontrollable shivering. Cold, wet, and windy weather poses the greatest hazard—conditions commonly encountered above treeline in New England. Fatigue reduces your body's ability to produce its own heat, wet clothes conduct heat away from the body roughly 20 times faster than dry layers, and wind poses an increased risk because it quickly strips away warmth.

Immediate treatment is critical and entails raising the body's core temperature as quickly as possible. Get out of the wind, take off wet clothes, drink warm beverages, eat simple energy foods, and take shelter in a warm tent or sleeping bag. *Do not* drink alcohol because this dilates the blood vessels and causes increased heat loss.

Heat Stroke. The opposite of hypothermia, this occurs when the body is unable to control its internal temperature and overheats. Usually brought on by excessive exposure to the sun and accompanying dehydration, symptoms include cramping, headache, and mental confusion. Treatment entails rapid, aggressive cooling of the body through whatever means available—cooling the head and torso is most important. Stay hydrated and have some

Hobblebush flowers in late May

type of sun protection for your head if you expect to travel along a hot, exposed section of trail.

Sunburn. The New England sun can fry you quickly, even if the sky is overcast with light fog or clouds. Always wear sunscreen of sufficiently high SPF and consider regularly wearing a hat or visor to shield your face from the sun. An SPF of 30 or more filters out virtually all of the sun's damaging rays.

Rivers. Be careful crossing rivers and streams and be selective when choosing a spot to ford. Look for broad, slower-moving shallow sections and remember that any current reaching above your thighs will wash you off your feet. When crossing, undo your waistbelt so that your pack won't drag you under in the event of a fall. Trekking poles or a walking stick are invaluable aids for river crossings.

HIKING SAFETY

Leave an Itinerary. Always tell somebody where you are hiking and when you expect to return. Friends, family, rangers, and visitor centers are all valuable resources that can save you from a backcountry disaster when you fail to reappear on time.

Know your limits. Don't undertake a hike that exceeds your physical fitness or outdoor abilities.

Avoid hiking alone. A hiking partner can provide the margin between life and death in the event of a serious backcountry mishap.

GEAR

Always have the following survival essentials with you:

- **Water.** Carry at least one liter of water (preferably two), drink frequently, and have some means of purifying backcountry sources (chemical treatment or filter).
- **Fire and Light.** Waterproof matches for starting an emergency fire, Vaseline-coated cotton balls for kindling, headlamp or flashlight in case you are still hiking after the sun goes down.
- Survival Gear. Heavy-duty garbage bags and a whistle.
- **First Aid Kit.** At a minimum this should include an over-the-counter painkiller/swelling reducer (ibuprofen is always good); a 2- to 4-inch wide elastic (ACE) bandage for wrapping sprained ankles, knees, and other joints; and the basics for treating a bleeding wound: antibiotic ointment, sterile gauze, small bandages, medical tape, and large band-aids. Prepackaged kits are readily available at any outdoor equipment store.

- **Map and Compass.** To find your way home. Even the simplest compass is useful.
- **Knife.** A good knife can be invaluable in the event of a disaster. Pocket-knives and all-in-one tools have many other useful features as well.
- **Extra Clothes and Food.** Warm clothing can be critical in the event of an unexpected night out or a developing fog. A few extra energy bars can make a huge difference in morale and energy level if you are out longer than expected.
- **Other Good Ideas.** A whistle is a powerful distress signal and can save your life if you become immobilized. Sunscreen and sunglasses protect you from blazing sun.

FOR YOUR FEET

Your feet are your most important piece of gear. Keep them happy, and you will be even more so. Appreciate them. Care for them.

Footwear. The appropriate hiking footwear provides stability and support for your feet and ankles while protecting them from the abuses of the environment. Most trails in New England are rough, rocky, and root-crossed. Even though a pair of lightweight boots or trail running shoes may be adequate for hikers with strong ankles, most people will want to opt for stiffer mid-weight hiking boots.

When selecting footwear, keep in mind that *the most important feature is a good fit*—your toes should not hit the front while going downhill, your heel should be locked in place inside the boot to prevent friction and blisters, and there should be minimal extra space around your foot (although you should be able to wiggle your toes freely). When lacing, leave the laces over the top of your foot (instep) loose but tie them tightly across the ankle to lock the heel down. Stability over uneven ground is enhanced by a stiffer sole and higher ankle collar. All-leather boots last longer, have a good deal of natural water resistance, and will mold to your feet over time. Footwear made from synthetic materials or a combination of fabric and leather are lighter and cheaper, but less durable. Many boots include Gore-Tex, a waterproof-breathable layer, recommended for the wet conditions found on many New England trails. Be sure to break-in new boots before taking them on an extended hike—simply wear them around as much as possible beforehand.

Socks. After armpits, feet are the sweatiest part of the human body. Unfortunately, wet feet are much more prone to blisters. Good hiking socks will wick moisture away from your skin and provide padding for your feet. Avoid cotton socks as these become quickly saturated, stay wet inside your shoes, and take a long time to dry.

Most outdoor socks are a confusing mix of natural and synthetic fibers. *Wool* provides warmth and padding and, although it does absorb roughly 30 percent of its weight in water, is effective at keeping your feet dry. If regular wool makes your feet itch, try softer *merino wool*. *Nylon, polyester, acrylic*, and *polypropylene* (also called *olefin*) are synthetic fibers that absorb very little water, dry quickly, and add durability. *Liner socks* are a thin pair of socks worn underneath the principal sock and are designed to more effectively wick moisture away—good for really sweaty feet.

Blister Kit. As everybody knows, blisters suck. They are almost always caused by friction from foot movement (slippage) inside the shoe. Prevent blisters by buying properly fitting footwear, taking a minimum of 1 to 2 weeks to break them in, and wearing appropriate socks. If the heel is slipping and blistering, try tightening the laces across the ankle to keep the heel in place. If you notice a blister or hotspot developing, stop immediately and apply adhesive padding (such as moleskin) over the problem spot. Bring a lightweight pair of scissors to cut the moleskin.

OUTDOOR CLOTHING

Get dressed and go! The following information is useful for staying warm and dry in camp or on the trail.

The Fabrics. *Cotton* is a lousy fabric for outdoor activity and should be avoided. It absorbs water quickly and takes a long time to dry, leaving a cold wet layer next to your skin and increasing the risk of hypothermia. Jeans are the worst. *Polyester* and *nylon* are two commonly used, and recommended, fibers in outdoor clothing. They dry almost instantly, wick moisture effectively, and are lighter weight than natural fibers. Fleece clothing (made from polyester) provides good insulation and will keep you warm even when wet. Synthetic materials melt quickly, however, if placed in contact with a heat source (camp stove, fire, sparks, etc.). *Wool* is a good natural fiber for hiking. Despite the fact that is retains up to 30 percent of its weight in water, it still insulates when wet.

Raingear/Windgear. Three types are available: waterproof/breathable, waterproof/nonbreathable, and water-resistant. *Waterproof/breathable* shells contain Gore-Tex or an equivalent fabric and effectively keep liquid water out while allowing water vapor (i.e., your sweat) to pass through. They keep you marginally more comfortable in the rain but are generally bulky and more expensive. *Waterproof/nonbreathable* shells are typically coated nylon or rubber and keep water out but hold all your sweat in. Seams must be taped for them to be completely waterproof. Although wearing these on a strenuous hike is a hot and sticky experience, they are cheap and often very lightweight. *Water-resistant* shells are typically lightweight nylon windbreakers coated with a water repellent that wears away with use. The seams will not be taped. They will often keep you dry for a short period but will quickly soak through in a heavy rain. All three are good in the wind.

Keeping Your Head and Neck Warm. The three most important parts of the body to insulate are the torso, neck, and head. Your body will strive to keep these a constant temperature at all times. Without any insulation, the heat coursing through your neck to your brain radiates out into space and is lost. Warmth that might have been directed to your extremities is instead spent replacing the heat lost from your head. A thin balaclava or warm hat and neck gaiter are small items, weigh almost nothing, and are more effective at keeping you warm than an extra sweater.

Keeping Your Hands Warm. Hiking in cold and damp conditions will often chill your hands unpleasantly. A lightweight pair of synthetic liner gloves will do wonders.

BACKPACKING EQUIPMENT

Backpack. For overnight trips, a pack with 3,000 cubic inches is generally necessary. For longer trips, a pack with 4,000 cubic inches or more is recommended. When shopping for a pack, remember that, just like footwear, the most important feature is a good fit. A properly fitting backpack allows you to carry most of the weight on your hips and lower body, sparing the easily fatigued muscles of the shoulders and back.

When trying on packs, loosen the shoulder straps, position the waist belt so that the top of your hips (the bony iliac crest) is in the middle of the belt, attach and cinch the waist belt, and then tighten the shoulder straps. The waist belt should fit snugly around your hips, with no gaps. The shoulder straps should rise slightly off your body before dipping back down to attach to the pack about an inch below your shoulders—no weight should be resting on the top of your shoulders, and you should be able to shrug them freely. Most packs will have load stabilizer straps that attach to the pack behind your ears and lift the shoulder straps upwards, off your shoulders. A sternum strap links the two shoulder straps together across your chest and prevents them from slipping away from your body.

Load your pack to keep its center of gravity as close to your middle and lower back as possible. Heaviest items should go against the back, becoming progressively lighter as you go outward and upward. Do not place heavy items at or below the level of the hip belt—this precludes the ability to carry that weight on the lower body and is one of the main reasons internal frame packs have their sleeping bag compartments in that location.

Sleeping Bag. Nighttime temperatures in New England vary dramatically depending on weather and seasons. In July and August, it is not uncommon to have overnight temperatures in the 50s or even 60s. In May, early June, mid- to late-September, and October, freezing temperatures can occur at any time, especially at higher elevations. A sleeping bag rated to 20 degrees is recommended for all-purpose use, though a model rated to 0 degrees is often a better option in the colder seasons or for people who are always cold at night (keep in mind that manufacturer's temperature ratings are highly subjective). During the sweltering height of summer, a lightweight bag rated to 35 degrees or higher is often adequate and helps reduce pack weight.

Down sleeping bags offer the best warmth-to-weight ratio, are incredibly compressible, and will easily last 5 to 10 years without losing much of their warmth. However, down loses all of its insulating ability when wet and takes forever to dry—a concern during long rainy spells. Synthetic-fill sleeping bags retain their insulating abilities even when wet and are che-

The forest has eyes—tread lightly

aper, but weigh more and are bulkier. Polarguard 3D, Polarguard Delta, and Primaloft are currently the lightest weight synthetic fills, but other synthetic options are often significantly cheaper (though heavier and bulkier). Keep in mind that synthetic-fill bags lose some of their loft and warmth after a few seasons of use.

Sleeping Pad. Sleeping pads offer vital comfort and insulation from the cold ground. Inflatable, foam-filled pads are the most compact and comfortable to sleep on, but expensive and mildly time-consuming to inflate and deflate. Basic foam pads are lightweight, cheap, and virtually indestructible. Comfort makes the call.

Tent. A lightweight, three-season tent is usually recommended, though you can get by without one during spells of good weather or by staying at established lean-tos. These days, the weight for a two-person backpacking tent hovers between 4 and 6 pounds. As a general rule, the lighter they get, the less space they have inside. A rain fly that extends to the ground on all sides is critically important for staying dry. Leaks are typically caused by water seeping through unsealed seams or contact between a wet rainfly and the tent body. Seal any untaped seams that are directly exposed to the rain or to water running off the fly—pay close attention to the floor corners of the tent body. Pitch the tent as tautly as possible to keep a wet and saggy rain fly away from the tent body. Although most trail camps offer good shelter from the wind, a few do not. Stability in wind is enhanced by pole intersections—the more poles and the more times they cross, the stronger the tent will be in blustery conditions. Placing a tarp between the tent floor and the ground will protect the floor from ground moisture, wear and tear, and will increase the lifespan of your tent. Most tents these days have an optional footprint that exactly matches the floor—a nice accessory.

Cooking Equipment. A stove is necessary if you want hot food on the trail. Two types are available. *Canister stoves* run on a butane/propane blend pressurized in a metal canister. Simply attach the stove burner to the canister, turn the knob, and light. Such stoves are simple, safe, cheap, and have an adjustable flame. However, the canisters can be hard to purchase outside of outdoor equipment stores, are more expensive, hard to recycle, do not work below freezing, and heat very slowly when less than a quarter full. Their safety and simmer-ability make them a good choice for summer backpacking. *Liquid fuel* stoves run on white gas contained in a self-pressurized tank or bottle. White gas is inexpensive, burns hot, is widely available around the world, and works in extremely cold conditions. However, you must work directly with liquid fuel to prime the stove, adding an element of danger. They're also prone to flaring up, may not have an adjustable flame, and are more expensive. Liquid fuel stoves are a good choice for those interested in winter camping or international travel.

A simple 2-to-3 quart pot is all that is usually needed for backcountry cooking. Add a small frying pan if necessary. A black, or blackened, pot will absorb heat more quickly and increase fuel efficiency. A windscreen for the stove is invaluable in breezy conditions. The only dish needed is a plate with upturned edges, which can double as a broad bowl—a Frisbee or gold pan work well. Don't forget the silverware! Lastly, bring an insulated mug to enjoy hot drinks.

Other Good Stuff. A length of *nylon* cord is useful for hanging food, stringing clotheslines, and guying out tents. A simple *repair kit* should include needle, thread, and duct tape. A plastic *trowel* is nice for digging crapholes. *Insect repellent* will keep the bugs away. A pair of *sandals* or *running shoes* for around camp are a great relief from hiking boots. A *pen* and *waterproof notebook* allow you to record outdoor epiphanies on the spot. Extra *Ziplocs* or *garbage bags* always come in handy. *Compression stuff sacks* will reduce the bulk of your sleeping bag and clothes by about a third.

Fun Equipment. Make sure your *camera* is ready for outdoor abuse and keep it safe from dirt and moisture. A good protective camera bag costs much less than a new camera. A polarizing filter is good for taking outdoor pictures of sky, water, or fall foliage. Shady forests are challenging to photograph when the sun is out—wait for foggy or overcast days and carry a small tripod and shutter-release cable for shooting in the low-light conditions. An *altimeter* is a fun toy for tracking your progress and identifying your location. With *binoculars*, you can see more, and with a *hacky sack, Frisbee,* or *cards* you can play more.

THE LEAVE-NO-TRACE ETHIC

To preserve the New England outdoors for future generations, follow some simple guidelines to leave no trace of your passage:

- **Do Not Scar the Land.** Do not cut switchbacks. Stay on the trail. Leave rocks, plants, and other natural objects as you find them.
- **Camping.** Camp only at established sites. Do not dig ditches around your tent. Keep your camp clean and never leave food out. Contain activities to where vegetation is absent.

- **Fires.** Campfires, where allowed, should always be made in a fire ring. Collect only dead or downed wood. Make sure the fire is completely out before leaving.
- **Sanitation.** When Nature calls, choose a spot at least 200 feet away from trails, water sources, and campsites. Dig a cat hole six inches deep, make your deposit, and cover it with the soil you removed. Do not bury toilet paper.
- **Washing.** To wash yourself or your dishes, carry water 200 feet away from streams or lakes. Scatter strained dishwater. Avoid the use of soap if possible; otherwise use only small amounts of biodegradable soap.
- **Garbage.** Carry out all garbage and burn only paper. Thoroughly inspect your site for trash and spilled food before leaving.
- **Group Size.** Keep groups small to minimize impact.
- **Animals.** Do not feed wildlife. Observe only from a distance.
- **Meeting Horses on the Trail.** Move off the trail on the downhill side and stand still until the animals pass by.
- **Noise.** Be respectful of other wilderness users. Listen to the sounds of Nature.

1

SOUTHERN NEW ENGLAND: MASSACHUSETTS, CONNECTICUT, AND RHODE ISLAND

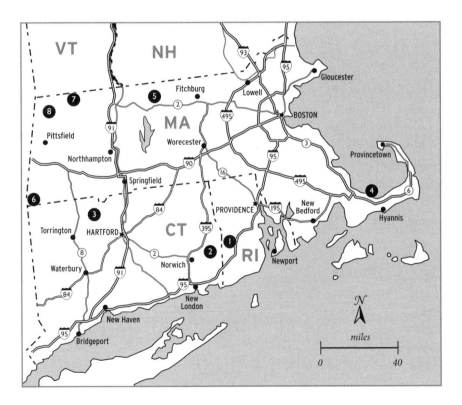

TRIP 1
THE RHODE LESS TRAVELED

Location: Arcadia Wildlife Management Area
Highlight: A quiet backcountry base camp in Rhode Island's largest protected landscape
Distance: 0.6 mile round-trip
Total Elevation Gain/Loss: 50/50
Trip Length: 1–2 days
Difficulty: ★
Recommended Map: Arcadia WMA Reference Map, northwest section (www.dem.ri.gov/maps/wma.htm)

In the southwest corner of Rhode Island lies a vast rolling landscape of streams, forests, ponds, open fields, wildflowers—and few people. As the only backpacking option in Rhode Island, 13,817-acre Arcadia Wildlife Management Area beckons with more than 30 miles of trail and provides an ideal early-season destination for those chomping at the spring bit.

The hike visits the Falls River, a tributary of the trout-filled Wood River, one of the state's best examples of a scenic and wild river. Animal life is healthy in the surrounding woods. Fox and mink hunt cottontails. White-tailed deer and grey squirrels skitter through the trees. Birdlife includes ruffed grouse, wild turkey, ring-necked pheasant, and bobwhite, some of which are stocked for hunting in the fall. Fish can also be found in several warm-water ponds scattered throughout the property, including trout, bass, and pickerel. Frosty Hollow Pond, near the main park entrance, is stocked with trout and managed for youth (under fourteen) fishing only.

HIKE OVERVIEW

To call this hike a backpacking trip is a bit of a stretch—the designated camping area is only a quarter mile from the trailhead—but the site feels surprisingly remote and isolated, and provides an ideal base camp for exploring the network of trails that lace the park. The short hike is also a pleasant stroll through lush and diverse forest along one of the most pristine waterways in the state. Dogs are allowed.

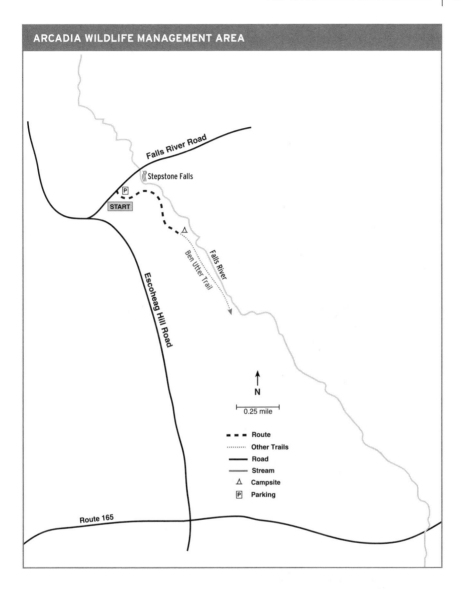

ARCADIA WILDLIFE MANAGEMENT AREA

OVERNIGHT OPTION

Stepstone Falls Backpack Area is located in the northwest corner of the park, perched on forested slopes just above murmuring Falls Brook. The broad area features a large open-air shelter, plus a clearing beneath red maple and white pines suitable for numerous tents. Reservations are required and can be made by calling 401-539-2356; you'll need to pick up your permit at the park office before heading out. The site is free and open year-round. Campers are limited to a three-day stay, with a minimum seven-day break between visits. Water is available from Falls Brook and another nearby stream.

TO REACH THE TRAILHEAD
Take Exit 5A from I-95 and turn right on Route 102 south. Go 0.1 mile and continue straight to follow Route 3 south for 1.2 miles to Route 165. Turn right (west) and drive 5.3 miles to Escoheag Hill Road, located 2 miles past the main park entrance on the right. Turn right on Escoheag Hill Road, proceed

Skunk Cabbage, Arcadia Wildlife Management Area

2.4 miles on an increasingly rough road, and turn right on unpaved Falls River Road. In 0.6 mile, look for the small parking area by the creek, signed for the Tippecansett and Ben Utter trails.

HIKE DESCRIPTION

Near the parking area, sugar and red maples, white pine, hickory, and the triangular leaves of gray birch overshadow tumbling Falls River, which quickly drops over Stepstone Falls, a 3-foot-high curtain dropping off a large rock slab. From the trailhead (0.0/290), yellow and blue blazes indicate your route along the double-track Ben Utter Trail. Smooth-barked beech trees line the trail, which almost immediately passes a path on the left that leads down to an open rocky area by the creek. Continue straight, following yellow and blue blazes across a rivulet and away from the stream.

Hazel and false Solomon's seal can be spotted in the understory, and beech and some large red oaks rise overhead. The path rises gently and traverses along the slope to reach an old red shelter by a large fire pit and small trickling brook. Welcome to the Stepstone Falls Backpacking Area, which includes a large area around the shelter (0.3/260). The Ben Utter Trail continues for another mile past this point, passing through a lush and diverse forest along murmuring Falls Brook.

INFORMATION

Division of Forest Environment, Arcadia Headquarters, 260 Arcadia Road, Hope Valley, RI 02832, 401-539-2356, www.dem.ri.gov/maps/wma.htm

TRIP 2
THE QUIET CORNER

Location: Pachaug State Forest
Highlights: A hidden shelter, Connecticut's backpacking potential
Distance: 0.8 mile round-trip
Total Elevation Gain/Loss: 160/160
Trip Length: 1–2 days
Difficulty: ★
Recommended Map: *Connecticut Walk Book East*, Connecticut Forest and Park Association

More than 700 miles of trail lace through Connecticut, a vast hiking network encompassing the full spectrum of the state's diversity. Known as the Blue-Blazed Trails, they consist of 15 long-distance pathways and many other shorter trails scattered throughout the state. Speckled among them are a handful of designated overnight backpack areas. In southeast Connecticut, 23,000-acre Pachaug State Forest shelters one of the nicest, and provides a tempting introduction to the state's backpacking potential.

Few settlers considered the rocky landscape of southeast Connecticut to have potential for farming and agriculture and consequently the land was never extensively developed. During the Great Depression, the federal and state government bought out many of the private landowners here as part of an economic relief effort, relocating them to more productive farming land elsewhere. The Civilian Conservation Corps then moved in, creating a network of roads, trails, and facilities. The landscape then passed on to the state as a working forest. Today Pachaug State Forest includes more than 50 miles of trails and roads, two campgrounds, several large ponds, and four backpacking areas.

HIKE OVERVIEW

This short out-and-back hike visits the Dry Reservoir Backpack Area, a secluded site tucked within rustling beech-hickory forest, which serves as a backcountry base camp for exploring the adjoining Pachaug and Nehantic trails. It makes an excellent early- or late-season excursion. At the trailhead, a short climb leads you atop Mount Misery for a view of the forested landscape that characterizes this region of Connecticut.

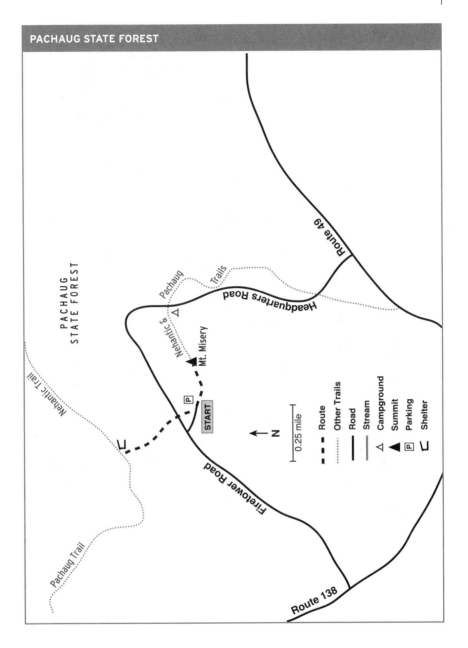

PACHAUG STATE FOREST

PACHAUG STATE FOREST

Route 49

Pachaug
Trails
Headquarters Road
Nehantic & Pachaug
Mt. Misery
Nehantic Trail
START
Firetower Road
Pachaug Trail
Route 138

0.25 mile
N

Route
Other Trails
Road
Stream
Campground
Summit
Parking
Shelter

Dry Reservoir Shelter, Pachaug State Forest

OVERNIGHT OPTION

Dry Reservoir Backpack Area features a small lean-to, a large fire ring, and numerous spots for tenting beneath the surrounding beech, hickory, and red oaks. Located at 400 feet elevation, a short distance from the closest trail, this quiet spot is unposted and all but invisible if you don't know where to look.

The Connecticut Department of Environmental Protection (DEP) manages the free site. Advance reservations are required, which can only be made through the mail or by fax (860-344-2941). To make a reservation, send a letter of application at least two weeks before your visit to DEP—Eastern District Headquarters, Attn: Backpack Camping, 209 Hebron Road, Marlborough, CT 06447. The request needs to include the following: (1) camping area (Dry Reservoir), (2) date of planned visit, (3) name and address of trip leader, and (4) number and ages of people in the group. Overnight stays are limited to one night only. Campfires are permitted. Pets are not. For more information, or to check availability, call 860-295-9523.

TO REACH THE TRAILHEAD

From the North. Take Exit 88 from I-395 and follow Route 14A east for 3.5 miles. Turn right (south) on Route 49, proceed 8 miles, and turn right at the Pachaug State Forest entrance. Follow the park road for 0.3 mile, go left at the fork, and left again 0.5 mile farther by the Mount Misery Brook Picnic Area. Cross over the brook and bear left at the next fork. The road becomes unpaved and passes by the entrance to Mount Misery Campground on your left. Continue straight on signed Cutoff Road for 0.3 mile and then turn left on signed Firetower Road. Proceed 0.7 mile to the road's end at a large loop.

From the South. Take Exit 85 from I-395 and follow Route 138 east for 6.5 miles to Route 49. Turn left (north) on Route 49, proceed 0.6 mile to the state forest entrance, and turn left. Continue as in directions from the north.

HIKE DESCRIPTION

From the trailhead (0.0/350), take a few minutes to dash up Mount Misery. To tag its 441-foot summit, follow the blue blazes upslope from the parking area, quickly curving right over rocky outcrops before reaching the summit at an open ledge. Views look east over the seemingly endless forests of southeast Connecticut and west Rhode Island.

To head to the shelter from the trailhead (0.0/350), briefly follow the blue blazes back down the road beneath white and red oak. Hay-scented and bracken fern grow in the understory. The well-blazed route—here the combined Nehantic and Pachaug trails—cuts left off the road and narrows to single-track. The trail soon reaches an open area with stumps and other evidence of past logging activity and then drops down a slope beneath beech and oak trees. As you descend, look for polypody fern sprouting from a moss-covered boulder by the trail. You then encounter a T-junction with a wider path (0.1/290).

Go right, passing a shagbark hickory on the left (its name obvious), across the trail from the lacy needles of a hemlock. The tiny blue-white flowers of bluets dot the trail in spring as you approach a gurgling brook, where witch hazel, black birch (also known as sweet birch), and skunk cabbage appear. Cross the stream, noting the false Solomon's seal and Christmas and cinnamon ferns that grow in the lush surroundings. The diamond-patterned bark of white ash—a water-loving tree—also appears. The forest becomes somewhat older past the stream, with some nice beech and red oaks, and you reach the posted junction where the Pachaug and Nehantic trails split (0.4/370). The large embankment in front of you was once a dam, but today holds nothing but a dry reservoir.

Go right on the Nehantic Trail, crossing a bridge over a small outlet stream emerging from beneath the old dam. Spicebush, jack-in-the-pulpit, yellow birch, and red maple grow in the damp streambed. Approximately 50 feet past the bridge, look for faint and unposted spur trails heading off to the right, which lead a short distance to the otherwise invisible Dry Reservoir Shelter and camping area (0.4/400).

INFORMATION

Pachaug State Forest, Route 49, P.O. Box 5, Voluntown, CT 06384, 860-376-4075, www.dep.state.ct.us/stateparks/forests/pachaug.htm

TRIP 3
CONNECTICUT WILD

Location: Tunxis State Forest
Highlight: Woodlands so wild even moose live here
Distance: 9.8 miles one-way
Total Elevation Gain/Loss: 1,650/1,500
Trip Length: 2 days
Difficulty: ★★
Recommended Map: *Connecticut Walk Book West*, Connecticut Forest and Park Association

There's a wild landscape in north-central Connecticut, a forest so substantial that even moose have taken up residence. Located adjacent to the Massachusetts border and protecting the rumpled terrain and crashing streams above Barkhamsted Reservoir, Tunxis State Forest is one of the state's least visited parcels of protected land. In its east section, a long portion of the Tunxis Trail travels through a wooded landscape of solitude and quiet natural highlights.

HIKE OVERVIEW

The trip is a point-to-point journey on a 10-mile section of the Tunxis Trail. The route undulates along a high plateau that rises parallel to out-of-sight Barkhamsted Reservoir below to the west. The area is particularly nice in May and June, when abundant laurel blooms. Although the hike can be completed in either direction, the following description goes south to north, which involves less overall elevation gain.

You'll need two cars or a bike to shuttle between the trailheads. Dogs are allowed.

OVERNIGHT OPTION

There is a designated overnight camping area 2.8 miles from the trailhead, about a quarter of the way along the trail. Situated on either side of tumbling Roaring Brook, it offers several good tentsites beneath the shade of young hemlocks and white pine. A fire pit is available and water can be taken from the stream. There is no privy. The site operates on a first-come, first-served basis; no reservations are required. Camping is prohibited elsewhere in the forest.

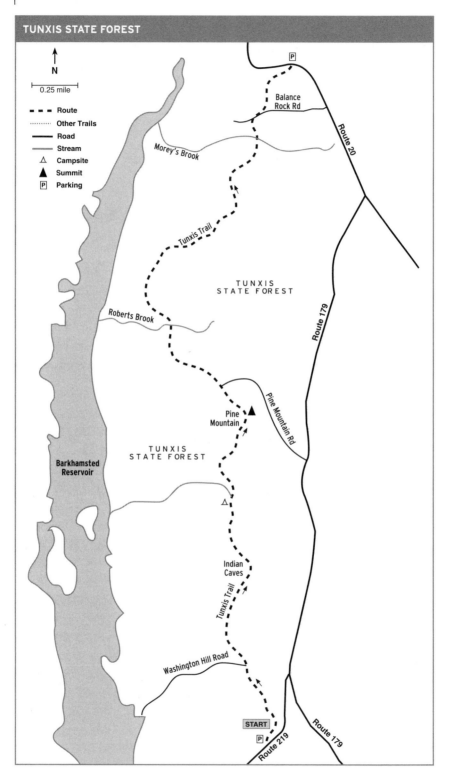

TUNXIS STATE FOREST

N

0.25 mile

- - - Route
.... Other Trails
—— Road
—— Stream
△ Campsite
▲ Summit
P Parking

Balance Rock Rd

Route 20

Morey's Brook

Tunxis Trail

TUNXIS STATE FOREST

Route 179

Roberts Brook

Pine Mountain ▲

Pine Mountain Rd

TUNXIS STATE FOREST

Barkhamsted Reservoir

△

Indian Caves

Tunxis Trail

Washington Hill Road

START

P

Route 219

Route 179

TO REACH THE TRAILHEAD

To Reach the Southern (Starting) Trailhead. Head to the Route 219/179 junction in the town of Barkhamsted. Proceed south on Route 219 for 0.9 mile to a small dirt parking area on the left, signed for the Tunxis Trail.

To Reach the Northern (Ending) Trailhead. Take Route 20 to the Route 179/20 junction in north Granby. Continue on Route 20 north for 1.4 miles to a small parking area on the right, signed for the Tunxis Trail.

HIKE DESCRIPTION

From the southern trailhead (0.0/950), cross the busy road and follow the blue-blazed trail up into hardwood forest. Look for the pointy leaves of red oak and the telltale red fissures in their trunks that identify them. Also watch for the distinctive diamond-patterned trunks of white ash, the smooth boles of beech trees, the lacy evergreen foliage of hemlocks, and a few scattered paper and yellow birch, unusual so far south. Laurel fills the understory, blooming profusely from late May through June.

Roots protrude in the initially faint trail, which quickly crosses a woods road and passes through a thicket of witch hazel. Coarse-grained boulders bulge from the ground in spots, and you soon cross a stone wall guarded by a massive white oak nearly 4 feet in diameter. Note the rounded lobes of its leaves, which distinguish the tree from the more common red oak. One side of the tree has calved off and lies crumpled on the ground. Old spreading trees such as these are known as *wolf trees*, left uncut along stone walls by early settlers to provide shade for grazing livestock. Left in open sunlight, their branches spread outward unencumbered by surrounding vegetation.

The trail slowly rises, passing blueberry bushes as it winds past a mix of white and red oaks. Chestnut oak also appears in abundance as you traverse along a rocky hilltop, a less common species that can be identified by its extremely knobby bark and wavy leaf margins. The trail then bends right and drops slightly, traversing through dense laurel. The route steepens and curves left in a semi-open clearing of three types of birch. Paper birch is known by its white bark, which peels in large sheets; yellow birch by its silvery-golden bark peeling in thin ribbons; and black birch by its dark smooth bark, fissuring into large plates with age. From here, you slowly descend, cross Kettle Brook in the shade of hemlock and white oaks, and reach Washington Hill Road (1.1/890), lined with some large and gnarled sugar maples.

Cross the road, travel a short distance through dense white pines and past thickets of invasive barberry and reach a woods road by a substantial creek. Turn right on the road, walk about 50 feet, bear right at the fork in the road, and then take an immediate left to continue on the single-track trail. Navigate carefully—splotches of confusing blue paint are everywhere.

As you resume climbing through open oak woodland, a beaver pond and dam can be spotted below to the right. You cross another woods road and make a slow curving rise to the left, winding past thick laurel to top out at a small ledge with limited views west. The trail runs along solid rock outcrops and passes an overlook with views of a pond down below. You've reached the top of the pleasantly isolated Indian Council Caves—there's no sign of humanity. Drop steeply past a 40-foot high overhanging rock face and take time to explore the extensive cracks and crevices in this giant boulder pile (2.2/1,050).

Beyond the caves, you soon reach another woods road by an inactive beaver pond (gnawings are evident). Turn left on the road to head through an area of past settlement. Rock walls, stone enclosures, cellar holes, and large gnarly sugar maples by the roadside all provide evidence of past human lives. The road forks by another cellar hole (2.5/1,040). The route bears left here—watch for the blazes. After passing another swampy field and former beaver habitat, you reach Roaring Brook and the designated backpacking area (2.8/990).

The trail rock-hops the brook and curves right, passing the bog outlet and then a small stream flowing into the swampy area. The trail now follows a woods road—the southern end of Pine Mountain Road—through an open forest of ash, black cherry, and increasing oaks. You next encounter a clearing marked with orange placards and arrows where the road widens markedly. Remain on the now-drivable road as it steadily climbs past young red oaks and paper birch. As the road crests, the route turns right on a single-track path (3.6/1,220). Evidence of forestry activity surrounds you as the trail briefly climbs and then runs level over bedrock outcrops to emerge into a clearing—a false summit of Pine Mountain offering a few glimpses of ridges to the east. The trail then drops briefly before rising to a small clearing on the actual summit (4.2/1,391), which offers a view east-northeast toward Springfield, Massachusetts.

From the peak, descend past oaks and hemlocks through an actively logged area. After crossing Pine Hill Road (4.6/1,250), you soon cross a smaller woods road and then almost immediately turn left on another. The easy-going road winds slowly downward and eventually forks (5.1/1,160)—bear right on the lesser-traveled option. After a long steady cruise past extensive hemlocks, the trail passes some large beech trees and then drops more steeply to cross Roberts Brook, a pleasant stream murmuring over rocks and boulders (5.6/1,100).

The route follows the stream downward past small pools and whispering waterfalls. The trail then narrows to single-track and curves left—keep an

Cascade on Roaring Brook

eye out for the arrows and blazes—before descending into a hemlock ravine and crossing a small brook. The faint trail winds along the lip of dripping stones above steepening slopes. You gain a sense of depth of Roberts Creek gorge. Extensive downed wood indicates the relative maturity of the surrounding forest.

The trail next travels along the state forest boundary, indicated by yellow paint and some occasional rusting barbed wire. For the first time, the reservoir is faintly visible through the trees more than 500 feet below. After making a slow rise, the route crosses a stone wall and undulates along a ridgeline cloaked with young beech. The well-blazed but faint trail crosses a small creek

(7.1/1,080) and enters a dense hemlock grove. A half mile farther you reach a sign that exemplifies a problem common throughout southern New England: WHITE PINES ARE BEING FAVORED IN ANTICIPATION OF HEMLOCKS SUCCUMBING TO THE WOOLLY ADELGID, RECENTLY DISCOVERED IN THE AREA.

The microscopic woolly adelgid is an invasive insect that feeds at the base of hemlock needles, slowly defoliating the tree and killing it over time. Common in southern New England, it is slowly marching north, though there is some debate about whether the increasingly cold winter temperatures farther north will prevent it from establishing a foothold.

Past the sign, the trail heads left and follows a woods road that soon curves right through a mixed hardwood forest. The trail bears left at a fork—watch for blazes—then quickly crosses old Route 20, paved but in disrepair (8.0/980). The trail next follows a flat woods road, immediately passes over a brook, turns right, then bears left at a well-signed fork. The trail returns to single-track and passes some nice red maples as it descends into the Morey's Brook drainage. Once you reach the pleasant stream (8.7/1,000), take a moment to appreciate the murmuring water as it rushes over rocks and boulders; some pleasant cascades are just upstream.

The trail resumes climbing, ascending some rock steps past pleasant little falls. You parallel the stream briefly, then bear left and climb to reach young, recently cut woods. After some level cruising, the trail next encounters unpaved Balance Rock Road (9.1/1,150). Go right to follow the road about 50 yards, then turn left in a grassy clearing—a blazed rock marks the spot. On the final stretch, the trail crosses several small brooks and winds through dense hemlock stands. After one final quick descent, you cross a stream and reach the Route 20 parking area (9.8/1,100).

INFORMATION
Tunxis State Forest, 960-379-2469

TRIP 4
SANDY NECK

Location: Barnstable, Cape Cod
Highlight: Dune camping
Distance: 7.9 miles round-trip
Total Elevation Gain/Loss: 50/50
Trip Length: 1–2 days
Difficulty: ★
Recommended Map: *Map of Sandy Neck,* Town of Barnstable

A 6-mile-long spit of dunes lines the south shore of Cape Cod Bay. A broad sandy beach stretches along the northern margin of the 1,500-acre peninsula. Beach grass and twisted pitch pines nestle inland between rolling swales of sand, separated from the mainland by a large saltwater marsh. And a small backcountry camping area nestles in the middle of it all.

HIKE OVERVIEW

The hike loops around the west half of Sandy Neck, traveling first along the beach, then inland past the camping area before returning along the marsh via the wide Marsh Trail. (You can also return on the beach, which reduces the round-trip journey by 1.3 miles.) Trails continue all the way to the east end of Sandy Neck, located 3 miles past the camping area.

Vehicles are allowed on the beach during the summer, and dozens of RVs and truck campers set up shop for multiday stays along its entire length, which can detract from the wilderness experience. A number of small cottages are also speckled throughout Sandy Neck, mostly on the south side. Vehicle access to these weather-worn structures (residents only) is along the Marsh Trail, which can become flooded during wet periods. Dogs are prohibited on Sandy Neck from May 15 to September 15, and in the camping area year-round.

OVERNIGHT OPTION

Camping is permitted only at the designated tenting area, which consists of four small sites in a grove of twisted pitch pine, located just inland from the beach. (Camping elsewhere on Sandy Neck is punishable by a $100 fine.) A privy is available. Sites cost $20 and are available on a first-come, first-served basis from the Sandy Neck gatehouse, where you must obtain a permit before

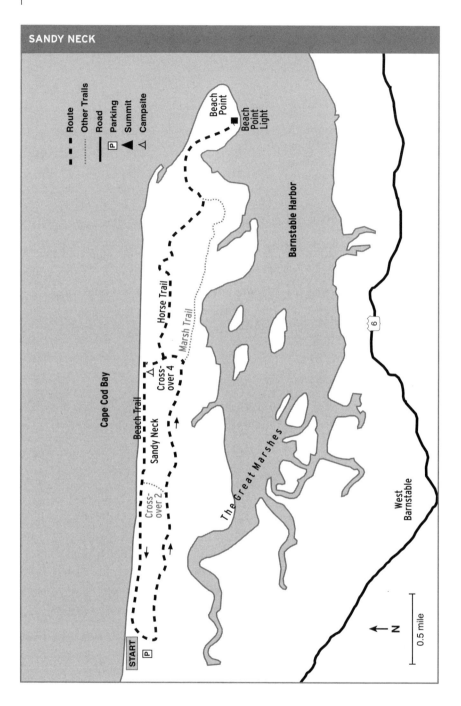

January at Sandy Neck

heading out (open Memorial Day–Labor Day, 8 a.m.–9 p.m.; Labor Day–Mid-October, 9 a.m.–4 p.m.). Arrive as early as possible to secure a site and parking spot, especially during the height of summer.

The park provides five gallons of water for each site per night; no water is otherwise available at the tenting area. Campfires are prohibited within the camping area, though open fires are permitted on the nearby beach. Park staff will even deliver wood for a small fee. The sites are open year-round, though you will need to call in advance during the off-season to arrange a permit.

TO REACH THE TRAILHEAD

Take Route 6 to Exit 5, turn left (north) onto Route 149, and follow it to Route 6A. Turn left and follow Route 6A for 2 miles to Sandy Neck Road. Turn right on Sandy Neck Road and follow it 0.9 mile to the gatehouse; the main parking lot is 0.3 mile farther by a snack stand and bath house.

HIKE DESCRIPTION

From the parking lot (0.0/20), descend to the beach and start heading east down the sandy waterfront. Views northwest look up the Massachusetts coast toward Plymouth, Marshfield, Scituate, and beyond. Footing is generally good along the sandy beach, lined with tire tracks and speckled with rounded cobbles of all colors and sizes.

Sandy Neck, like all of Cape Cod, was bulldozed into position by the massive ice sheet that smothered New England during the last Ice Age. As the glacier's snout moved southward, it pushed massive piles of sand and stones before it. Streams and rivers poured from its face, adding to the sediment. It then stopped advancing and receded, leaving an arc of sand that marks its farthest reach south—today's Cape Cod. (Nantucket, Martha's Vineyard, and Long Island were also formed in similar fashion.)

The scenery changes little as you progress down the dune-backed strand. Please remain on the beach; the adjoining dunes may be tempting to explore but are fragile and easily damaged. Crowds start to diminish as you gain distance from the parking area, though vehicles continue intermittently along the shore. You pass the posted Connector Trail 2 on the right (1.6/10) and continue along the unchanging beach, eventually reaching the signed Connector Trail 4 on the right (3.2/10).

Turn inland on Trail 4, which immediately enters the dunes and encounters a mature stand of pitch pine. Easily recognized by their twisted architecture and needles in clusters of three, these gnarly trees are well adapted to survive in dry soil (or sand) environments. Small black oaks complete the unusual forest mosaic. The tenting area is just ahead (3.3/20). Please heed the signs and stay off the surrounding dunes.

Continue inland past the camping area, quickly reaching the Horse Trail on the left (3.4/30). (The Horse Trail heads east to reach the Marsh Trail, which then proceeds out to the (off-limits) lighthouse near the end of Sandy Neck. The round-trip excursion to the lighthouse is about 6 miles.) Bear right to remain on Trail 4 as it winds through a rolling dunescape and reaches the

Marsh Trail (3.6/10). The Marsh Trail also heads east toward the lighthouse, but you turn right to begin your return journey to the trailhead.

The trail is a wide sandy road. It occasionally passes dense woods on the right, populated by white and black oak, juniper, and holly trees. To the left are the open wetlands of the Great Marshes, a large estuary that divides Sandy Neck from the Cape Cod mainland. Cottages appear intermittently on your right as you proceed. Eventually you encounter a house perched in the nearby dunes, just before the inland junction with the Connector Trail 2 (5.6/10).

Trees diminish past this point and the route begins rolling through a sandier landscape. Walking becomes tiresome in the loose sand. A few more cottages pass by; the final one sits on a small promontory in the marsh. You pass Connector Trail 1 on the right (7.1/10), the Marsh Trail soon transforms into a dirt road, and you can see an osprey platform in the marshes to your left. You reenter a dune oak forest and soon emerge adjacent to the gatehouse (7.6/30). Turn right and follow the road back to the parking area (7.9/20).

INFORMATION

Sandy Neck, Town of Barnstable, 1189 Phinney's Lane, Centerville, MA 02632, 508-362-8300, http://town.barnstable.ma.us/SandyNeck/default.asp

TRIP 5
THE FULL TULLY

Location: Tully Trail
Highlight: The surprising wilds of north-central Massachusetts
Distance: 20.6 miles round-trip
Total Elevation Gain/Loss: 3,300/3,300
Trip Length: 2 days
Difficulty: ★★
Recommended Map: *Tully Trail Map*, Trustees of Reservations

A region of exceptional conservation land exists in north-central Massachusetts. Small mountains bulge above the landscape, crystalline streams tumble over bedrock, and numerous ponds shimmer within a vast and continuous forest. The area, known as North Quabbin country, is located in the ten-town region located between the Quabbin Reservoir and the New Hampshire border. This is one of the least densely populated parts of the state, home to 94,000 acres of protected parkland. The Tully Trail was completed in 2001 as the first project of the North Quabbin Regional Landscape Partnership—a collection of state agencies, local land trusts, and environmental groups working to protect and promote the North Quabbin Region—and was designed to tour some of the region's highlights. Today it is managed by the Trustees of Reservations.

HIKE OVERVIEW

The hike makes a broad loop through a mix of conservation land, visiting three Trustees properties, three state forests, two state wildlife management areas, and property managed by the Army Corps of Engineers. The hike's low elevation makes it an attractive early- or late-season option, and is particularly good for fall foliage. Several natural gems can be found on the hike—including Royalston Falls and the summit of Tully Mountain—but the primary appeal is its proximity to Boston and the light use much of the trail receives. But overall, the total hike experience ranks low on the wilderness factor. Although some sections follow remote single-track, many other portions travel along wide woods roads and one long stretch follows a paved secondary road.

The hike begins from Tully Lake Campground and follows the loop counter-clockwise. On day one—the shorter of the two—you'll follow the East

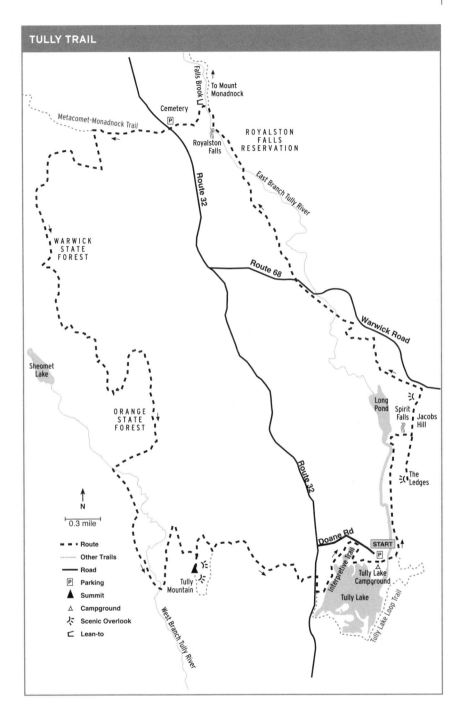

TULLY TRAIL

To Mount Monadnock

Falls Brook

Cemetery

P

Metacomet-Monadnock Trail

Royalston Falls

ROYALSTON FALLS RESERVATION

East Branch Tully River

Route 32

Route 68

Warwick Road

WARWICK STATE FOREST

Sheomet Lake

ORANGE STATE FOREST

Long Pond

Spirit Falls

Jacobs Hill

The Ledges

Route 32

N

0.3 mile

Doane Rd

START

P

Interpretive Trail

Tully Lake Campground

Tully Lake

Tully Lake Loop Trail

Tully Mountain

West Branch Tully River

- - - Route
.... Other Trails
—— Road
P Parking
▲ Summit
△ Campground
⅄ Scenic Overlook
⊏ Lean-to

Branch of the Tully River north, climbing above it to visit pattering Spirit Falls and a pair of viewpoints. The watershed narrows as you follow Falls Brook, a tributary, into Royalston Falls Reservation, past its namesake falls, and reach Royalston Falls Shelter. Day two takes you through undulating forested terrain along a mix of single-track trails, woods roads, and a 1.5-mile section along paved Warwick Road. The final highlight is near journey's end atop 1,163-foot Tully Mountain, which offers the hike's best views.

OVERNIGHT OPTIONS

The hike offers only one overnight option: Royalston Falls Shelter. Camping is prohibited elsewhere, though Tully Lake Campground is available for drive-up use at the trailhead.

Royalston Falls Shelter is located at 960 feet in a grove of hemlock and young beech, a short distance above Tully Brook. The cabin-like structure features a sheltered porch, four double bunks, and a loft, and can hold as many as 12 people. The free shelter is first-come, first-served, and receives light use. Camping is permitted around the shelter, though the sloped terrain provides limited options. Tully Brook provides water, though it is usually brown and tannin-soaked. Campfires are allowed in the fire ring in front of the shelter. There is no privy.

Tully Lake Campground sits along the shore of its namesake lake and features 33 drive-up sites. The only campground managed by the Trustees, it is open daily from late May through early September, weekends only through mid-October. Hot showers and canoe rentals add enticements to this pleasant location. Reservations are recommended for any weekend visit (978-248-9455, www.tullylakecampground.org).

TO REACH THE TRAILHEAD

Take Route 2 to Exit 17 in Athol and follow Route 32 north for 6.4 miles. Be watchful for highway signs as the route meanders substantially. Turn right on Doane Road (signed for Tully Lake Campground) and proceed 0.8 mile to the campground entrance on your right. Park in the free outer lot and let campground staff know you're leaving your car there.

HIKE DESCRIPTION

From the outer area (0.0/680), head back toward Doane Road and look for the purple Tully Trail signs that indicate your route, which initially bears right to cross over the sluggish Tully River. After passing a boat launch and parking area on your left, bear left on the Tully Trail at the yellow gate. Initially marked by a combination of yellow (hiking route) and orange (biking route) blazes, the broad trail begins in young hardwood forest. Around you is a classic southern New England mix of white pine, red maple, beech, hemlock, and red oak. In the understory, blueberries, hazel, witch hazel, and royal, interrupted, and sensitive ferns fill the forest with lush greenery.

The trail parallels the Tully River, glimpsed nearby to your left, and soon passes a red house on the right labeled WHISPERING WILDERNESS. Past the building, the route curves left and closer to the adjacent wetlands. Undulating briefly, the trail leaves the Army Corps of Engineers property, enters the Trustees' Jacobs Hill parcel, and heads toward the south end of Long Lake (1.4/640). Views look north to the nearby hills. After passing another lakeside clearing, the trail curves right, narrows to single-track, and crosses a brook on a small bridge.

Here the Tully Trail turns right and begins climbing past white pines and yellow birch. After crossing a stone wall, the path drops briefly toward the brook and stops by Spirit Falls, a little slider that spatters 20 to 30 feet down the rocks. The route now ascends a rock staircase along the hissing creek and reaches an unposted four-way junction (1.6/970).

The Tully Trail turns left here, but consider dropping your pack for a moment and heading right to check out the Ledges, one of the hike's best views. The 0.5-mile side-trip undulates along an increasingly narrow trail through a ridge-top community of beech and paper birch. From the aptly named viewpoint, Tully Lake is visible to the south, the round hump of Tully Mountain rises to the southwest, and 1,621-foot Mount Grace appears on the west horizon.

Back at the junction, follow the Tully Trail as it winds along a rocky, hemlock-topped ridge and passes a brief view west to Mount Grace. Continue straight at the posted junction (2.0/1,110), climbing to the forested summit of Jacobs Hill and a three-way junction. To reach another pleasant view, head straight and briefly follow circle blazes to reach an overlook of Long Pond, Mount Tully, and Mount Grace.

Return to the three-way junction and follow the Tully Trail's square blazes, which soon lead down to a wide dirt road. Turn left and immediately cross a power line corridor. Bear left on the far side and follow the power lines downhill through a brushy corridor, filled with blackberry vines and head-high rhododendrons. The route soon crosses a dirt access road and steepens. The path becomes difficult to discern as it drops through goldenrod and young birch trees, with loose footing in places. The route generally remains on the right (north) side of the corridor, but crosses over to the opposite side shortly before reaching the bottom. Keep an eye out for a few blazes and small cairns that indicate your route, but use your best judgment in finding the easiest way down. At the bottom, you reach a posted junction for the bike path on the left (2.6/680). Turn right to remain on the Tully Trail.

You now enter moist woods, cross a stone wall, and pass by fern carpets in a red maple swamp to your left. The trail briefly parallels and then crosses a frog-loaded brook, before reaching extensive sweet ferns and an old building foundation on the right. The route winds down to Boyce Brook and crosses it on a boardwalk (3.0/690). You next pass through a sunny area marked by past beaver activity and dead trees and then abruptly reach a wide woods road. Turn right to immediately reach another major woods road near some residences. Paved Warwick Road is visible roughly 10 yards ahead to the right, but bear left to follow the signed trail.

The wide grassy trail passes through young forest and crosses the East Branch of the Tully River on a rickety bridge (3.5/620). The river flows here through another old beaver area; most trees to the right have been killed by beaver-induced flooding. Just beyond this spot, you pass the final junction with the bike path, which splits off to the left. Remain on the Tully Trail, cross a yellow gate, and reach paved Warwick Road (3.9/690). Turn left, follow the road briefly, and then turn right just before the next curve to continue on the Tully Trail—watch for signs and faded blazes. You quickly encounter a wide woods road and curve right. Several other woods roads join in—keep going straight. The route crosses a small brook and passes by young conifers, cruising for a while on a more overgrown road. You eventually descend to the upper reaches of the Tully River; here it has become Falls Brook, a nice gravelly stream. Cross it on a rustic bridge (5.6/710) then immediately ascend along a single-track trail in a small hemlock-shaded ravine.

The trail climbs steeply, then makes a traverse on a rocky and root-laced trail. Nearby Royalston Falls becomes audible as the trail navigates past boulders bulging from the hillside. You then drop down to reach a fence-protected view of Royalston Falls (6.1/850), which sheets downward into an inaccessible grotto.

The trail continues past the falls and along the now-placid creek. You pass a dark pool fed by a diminutive cascade, travel along the stream, and reach the junction with the white-blazed Metacomet-Monadnock (M-M) Trail (6.5/940), a 114-mile long-distance trail that runs from the Connecticut border to Mount Monadnock in southern New Hampshire. Turn left to cross the brook on a basic bridge and reach Royalston Falls Shelter (6.5/960).

For the next 1.4 miles, the Tully Trail overlaps with the M-M Trail. The double-track trail departs the shelter, curving uphill to the left. After a brief drop, it begins a steady rise through a more mature forest punctuated by large standing snags and old yellow birch trees. The gradient eases near the top and a gently rising traverse leads you to the Royalston Falls parking area on Route 32 (7.0/1,180).

Turn right on Route 32, follow it about 20 feet, and then turn left to follow the single-track trail. The level route passes a few boulders and makes a slow undulation through young hardwoods. The faint but well-blazed trail quickly passes through a grove of red pine plantation, the trees readily recognized by their 4- to 6-inch needles in bunches of two.

You pass through a swampy area, cross a stone wall, and reach unpaved Bliss Hill Road by a driveway (7.9/1,180). The M-M Trail continues up the driveway, but you turn left, following the road and soon reaching the property boundary for Warwick State Forest (8.3/1,130). A hundred yards farther, the trail turns right off Bliss Hill Road and onto another broad woods road. Rounded river stones litter the route as it descends past a man-made pond on the left and reaches a fork—proceed straight. As you continue, note how the woods on the right feature an open understory and intact overstory of red oak and red and sugar maple, whereas the area on the left is a more cluttered world of young trees. Foresters have thinned the woods on the right to allow fewer trees to obtain more sunlight, producing a larger and more economically valuable forest.

The road passes a massive red maple as you slowly descend through hardwoods to reach the power line corridor you traversed earlier in the hike (9.9/930). Cross the corridor and bear right at the next woods road (10.1/930). The trail winds past a swampy area and underneath white pines as it parallels stone walls and NO TRESPASSING signs on the right. Watch for blazes as the route next turns left onto a smaller woods road (10.2/920). The grassy road soon crosses a small stream and climbs past increasing beech and oaks on a traversing ascent of Bliss Hill. A palpable sense of height culminates at a ledge with a narrow view west to Mount Grace (11.0/1,090).

The blazes here can be confusing. The path to the ledge is only a side trail; the main route forks left uphill just before reaching the viewpoint. The continuing trail narrows and becomes faint as it climbs past paper and black birch and curves right. You crest the hill by a wall of flat rocks (11.2/1,180). The trail

Looking east from Tully Mountain

wraps around the wall and begins a steep descent. After a steady drop, the gradient eases and you pass among thick hemlocks to reach the battered pavement of Bliss Hill Road (11.7/960).

Cross the road and climb briefly to reach another woods road by an old rusting vehicle frame. Turn right to immediately reach a four-way junction—go straight, parallel to the rock wall on your left. The trail returns to thin single-track, tours an area rife with stone walls, and climbs over a small rise, which offers glimpses east. The forest composition changes here, and white oaks and hickories become common.

The trail now makes its steepest drop yet, curving left near the bottom to join an overgrown woods road. The trail immediately bears right off the road and enters the small hemlock-shaded gorge of Fish Brook. The route curves down to reach the rushing stream (12.5/850), a mossy rocky stream-bed lined by a stone wall. The darkness and seclusion make this one of the trail's highlights.

The route follows an overgrown woods road upstream and soon turns away from the brook on a single-track path, climbing briefly to cross a small feeder brook before returning to the main stream. The trail crosses the brook by some pleasant riffles on a plank bridge (13.1/960) and climbs again on a thin trail, which soon levels out and begins descending along another stone wall. The traversing drop is occasionally steep, but soon the gradient eases and you reach unpaved Butterworth Road (14.2/700).

Go right and follow the road past roughly a dozen houses. Just before you reach paved Warwick Road (14.8/610), you pass a nice view of Tully Mountain—your continuing route—beyond somebody's backyard. Turn left on Warwick Road and follow it for the next 1.5 miles. Vehicles zip by, but focus instead on the intermittent views across the Tully River to Tully Mountain, and watch for a roadside rock engraved with a 2002 dedication to the establishment of the North Quabbin Bioreserve, another recognition of the region's ecological value. You pass Creamery Hill Road on the right after 1.3 miles and a short distance later the road crosses over the Tully River on a bridge. On the opposite side, the Tully Trail immediately cuts left on a grassy woods road (16.3/580).

The wide trail runs level, offering glimpses to the right of adjacent Tully Mountain's steep slopes. The grass disappears as the trail begins winding along the mountain's lower slopes and climbs through denser forest. The trail then cuts sharply away from the road to the right (16.9/600) and makes a rising traverse through a young hemlock-beech forest that is being actively managed as a woodlot; cuttings and stumps are apparent.

The trail gains 250 feet of elevation, switchbacks left, passes some nice boulders, and then wraps around the ridge to reach a posted junction (17.5/1,030). The Tully Trail goes left here to Tully Lake, but you'll want to turn right to make the 0.1-mile side-trip to the summit. To reach the best view of the hike, climb along the double-track trail through dense hemlock and cross the forested summit, then descend a short distance to reach several ledges with unrestricted views east.

Tully and Packard Ponds are apparent nearby to the southeast, and Tully Lake is visible to the east. The Wapack Range (Trip 14) lines the east-northeast horizon. The summit of Mount Wachusett peaks over the horizon to the east-southeast. But most glamorous of them all is Mount Monadnock, which punctuates the landscape to the northeast in full profile.

Return to the earlier junction and continue on the Tully Trail as it traverses gently downward. The trail becomes more of a woods road as it descends to reach another posted junction (17.9/790). Go left to continue toward Tully Lake (right leads to a trailhead parking area for Tully Mountain). The trail returns to thin single-track, descends through even-aged white pines, and crosses a dribbling brook. It continues straight across a grassy woods road, makes a brief climb, and then curves right to begin a traverse. After winding past some car-sized boulders, the route crosses another woods road, drops briefly to cross a rock-strewn stream, and then heads through a brushy corridor to reach yet another woods road. Turn right here and drop down to reach Royalston Road (19.1/660). Turn left and follow the road, which becomes paved just before reaching Route 32. Turn right and follow the highway about 50 yards to a parking area by Tully Lake on the left (19.4/680).

From the parking area, the trail follows a root-covered single-track path toward the lakeshore. Curving left, the route runs parallel to the lakeshore about 30 feet inland and reaches the posted junction for the Interpretive Loop, signed as the STORY TRAIL. Continuing straight, you soon pass a second junction for the Story Trail on the left. You then cross a small brook and undulate over some rocky terrain on a well-trod single-track trail.

Winding around a small inlet, the route passes several unmarked spurs leading down toward the water. The trail crosses a brook, approaches within 5 feet of Doane Road, and then curves right to travel along a berm separating a wetlands area from the lake. More spurs run to a small peninsula in the lake, but the trail turns left to cross the wetlands outflow on a small plank bridge. Green circle blazes appear, the path cuts left and widens, and soon you emerge at the campground parking area and hike's end (20.6/680).

INFORMATION

Trustees of Reservations, 572 Essex St., Beverly, MA 01915-1530, 978-249-4957 (seasonal), 978-840-4446 (year-round), www.thetrustees.org

TRIP 6
THE TACONICS

Location: Appalachian Trail, Northwest Connecticut, Southwest
Massachusetts
Highlights: Summits, ravines, waterfalls, vistas, old-growth forest
Distance: 16.9 miles one-way
Total Elevation Gain/Loss: 4,600/4,450
Trip Length: 2–3 days
Difficulty: ★★★
Recommended Maps: *Official Map to the Appalachian Trail in Massachusetts
& Connecticut: Map 4, Massachusetts Section 10, Connecticut Section 1,* Appa-
lachian Trail Conservancy

The Appalachian Trail (AT) travels atop the ancient bedrock prow of
the Taconic Range for nearly 17 miles without crossing a single road.
Touring a broad swath of wildland in a far corner of New England, the
hike visits the highest peak in Connecticut, the second-highest in Massachusetts, old-growth hemlock forest, bonsai'd pitch pines, waterfalls,
and nine different places to spend the night.

Located near the triple junction of Massachusetts, New York, and
Connecticut, the Taconic Range contains some of New England's most
ancient rocks. A half billion years ago, a tectonic collision occurred.
A chain of volcanic islands hit North America, mashing the sand and
calcium-rich coral layers of an ancient sandbed against the continent.
Over the ensuing eons, pressure transformed these jumbled layers into
calcium-rich marble and erosion-resistant schist, and the schist layer
was thrust over the marble to form a hard cap in some locations. Over
time, the exposed marble eroded away to form the flat valley of the Housatonic River, whereas the erosion-resistant schist layer withstood time
to form the hard backbone of today's Taconic Range. Where the schist
cap ends, steep slopes have formed, an abrupt boundary that defines the
topography of this range.

The calcium-rich soils produced by marble are rare in New England.
This less acidic soil provides habitat for a variety of trees and plants
uncommon elsewhere in the region. The area's ecological diversity is
remarkable, and includes an unusual pitch pine–bear oak forest along
the ridgelines.

THE TACONICS

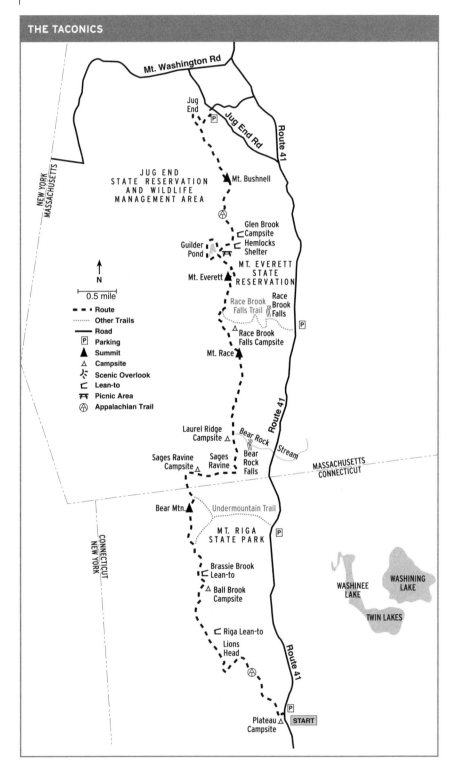

Mt. Washington Rd

Jug End

Route 41

Jug End Rd

P

NEW YORK
MASSACHUSETTS

JUG END
STATE RESERVATION
AND WILDLIFE
MANAGEMENT AREA

Mt. Bushnell

Glen Brook
Campsite
Hemlocks
Shelter

Guilder
Pond

MT. EVERETT
STATE
RESERVATION

Mt. Everett

N

0.5 mile

- - - Route
.... Other Trails
——— Road
P Parking
▲ Summit
△ Campsite
Scenic Overlook
Lean-to
Picnic Area
Appalachian Trail

Race Brook
Falls Trail

Race
Brook
Falls

P

Race Brook
Falls Campsite

Mt. Race

Route 41

Laurel Ridge
Campsite △

Bear Rock
Stream

Sages Ravine
Campsite △

Sages
Ravine

Bear
Rock
Falls

MASSACHUSETTS
CONNECTICUT

Bear Mtn. ▲

Undermountain Trail

MT. RIGA
STATE PARK

P

CONNECTICUT
NEW YORK

Brassie Brook
Lean-to

△ Ball Brook
Campsite

WASHINEE
LAKE

WASHINING
LAKE

TWIN LAKES

Riga Lean-to

Lions
Head

Route 41

P

Plateau △
Campsite

START

HIKE OVERVIEW

This point-to-point trip travels the AT from Highway 41 in Salisbury, Connecticut, to its next road crossing at Jug End Reservation in the town of Mount Washington, Massachusetts. The route ascends Lion's Head, passes over Bear Mountain (Connecticut's highest peak), drops into the old-growth haven of Sages Ravine, clambers atop the cliffs of Mount Race, climbs to the top of Mount Everett, and then undulates north through a lightly traveled landscape to reach its terminus.

Route 41 runs parallel to the hike for most of its distance, down in the valley to the east a thousand feet below. Several trails access the AT from along the highway, providing options for shorter trips. To return to your starting point, you'll need to shuttle vehicles, leave a bicycle at your exit point, or hitchhike back. Although it is possible to hike the route in either direction, the following description goes from south to north—the most common direction for travel. The area receives moderate use and finding an available campsite is seldom a problem. Dogs are permitted on the trail.

OVERNIGHT OPTIONS

There are nine designated overnight areas; four offer shelters, eight have tentsites. With a few exceptions (noted later), water is readily available from nearby streams. Campfires are permitted only at Race Brook Falls, Hemlocks Shelter, and Glen Brook Shelter. No camping is allowed outside of designated areas.

Black bears are common in the area and have become food-swiping nuisances in several locations. Hang your food securely at night or use the bear boxes that have been installed in Sages Ravine and at a few other locations.

Plateau Campsite. Located 0.2 mile from the trailhead, this site occupies a level clearing on steep slopes. Red oak, beech, and black birch shade the central area, and upslope, a small hemlock glade shelters a more secluded site. The traffic on Highway 41 is audible, though the forest hides it from view. A thin trickling spring provides water; a pump is recommended for collecting it. Because of the proximity of several private residences, there is a designated quiet period from 8 a.m.–8 p.m.

Riga Shelter, Mile 3.4. This area perches just below the ridgeline and features an east-facing shelter that offers a restricted overlook of the Housatonic River Valley—the only overnight location to offer a view. Three adjacent tentsites and one large tentsite are located nearby. A nearby spring provides reliable water.

Ball Brook Campsite, Mile 4.0. Two tentsites are located within earshot of rushing Ball Brook. Two large group sites cluster nearby around a large split boulder beneath young hardwoods. A basic privy serves the sites, offering 360-degree forest views. Obtain water from easily accessible Ball Brook.

Brassie Brook Lean-to, Mile 4.6. A large shelter and five tentsites occupy the slopes 50 feet above musical Brassie Brook, a reliable water source. The surrounding woods support lush carpets of ferns and wildflowers.

Sages Ravine Campsite, Mile 6.8. Located just over the state line in Massachusetts, this large camping-only area is spread along the slopes above rushing Sawmill Brook, in close proximity to old-growth hemlock forest. Eight numbered sites and one group site are dispersed along a wide loop. Half the sites offer tent platforms. Sites 6, 7, and 8 are located farthest from the campground entrance and offer the most seclusion. Water is readily available from the brook or from a nearby spring popular with frogs. Bears have become a nuisance in this area—please use the metal bear boxes to store your food at night.

Laurel Ridge Campsite, Mile 8.7. Laurel Ridge replaced Bear Rock Falls Campsite, which was located near its namesake falls but became severely impacted by overuse. Laurel Ridge provides five tentsites and one group site dispersed on a steep and shady hillside among maple, oak, and laurel. The sites are small, a few resembling rocky nests, but they are all nice and private. A nearby brook provides water.

Race Brook Falls Campsite, Mile 11.6. Located 0.4 mile off the AT on the Race Brook Falls Trail, this spread-out area is shaded by dense hemlock and beech forest. Three tent platforms and many adjacent sites are available. A small spring trickles by the campsite; Race Brook is also nearby and readily accessible. Campfires are permitted.

Hemlocks Shelter, Mile 13.4. This capacious shelter, the newest along this hike, perches beneath its namesake trees. Water is readily available from an adjacent creek. Campfires are permitted. Tent camping is prohibited.

Glen Brook Shelter, Mile 13.5. Hidden downslope and out-of-sight from the AT, this small shelter offers good opportunities for seclusion. The shelter is older and considerably more rustic than nearby Hemlocks Shelter, but the surrounding understory is open, the site perches on the edge of steeper slopes, and several tent platforms and other good tentsites are available.

TO REACH THE TRAILHEAD

To Reach the Northern (Ending) Trailhead. Take Route 41 south from Great Barrington through South Egremont. Remain on Route 41 as Route 23 splits right, and then in 0.1 mile, bear right on Mount Washington Road. In 1.0 mile, turn left on Avenue 0-35 and proceed 0.6 mile to a three-way junction with Jug End Road. Proceed straight on the dirt road for 0.3 mile and look for the AT crossing. A pull-out on the right side of the road provides parking.

To Reach the Southern (Starting) Trailhead (and Other Access Trails). Remain on Route 41 where Mount Washington Road splits right. Continue south, passing the Berkshire School on the right, and then 1.9 miles later the parking area for the Race Brook Falls Trail on the right. The Undermountain Trail parking area—usually the most packed—is on the right 4.5 miles past the Race Brook Falls turn-off. Continue 2.5 miles past the Undermountain Trailhead to reach the southern AT trailhead on the right. The small parking area is hidden and easy to miss—watch for the sign indicating a "hikers crossing."

HIKE DESCRIPTION

Sugar maples and white pines shade the trailhead (0.0/710). Heading out, you immediately pass an outhouse on the right and begin climbing, passing a large red oak on the right—note the flat disk-shaped acorn caps littering the ground. Soon after, the spur trail to Plateau Campsite (0.2/830) splits left by another substantial red oak and a patch of cinnamon ferns.

The AT traverses upslope, steadily rising as it passes beneath a diverse forest of beech, white oak, hemlock, and white ash. Also common is invasive Japanese barberry, a thorny shrub proliferating in the understory. As the trail ascends the flanks of the Taconic Range, the route passes over marble bedrock. Marble produces calcium-rich soil, which is more hospitable for sugar maple—many of which line the trail. Other species are only found in such calcareous soils. One of these is the delicate maidenhair fern, which can be spotted here—identify it by its lacy, finger-like fronds with black stems.

The trail becomes rockier and begins an undulating traverse. Mountain laurel soon appears, indicative of a change in bedrock—the plant thrives in the more acidic soils produced by the underlying schist. As you pass several stone walls, look for large red oaks growing next to them. Known as "wolf trees," they were likely left for shade by early field-clearing settlers. Unencumbered by surrounding trees, they grew tall with wide-spreading branches and are easily recognized among the younger narrower trees.

The trail crosses several small creeks and encounters low-lying blueberry bushes, another indicator of acidic soil. The broad hump of 1,738-foot Lion's Head appears through the trees to the west. Curving left, the trail steepens, switchbacks, and enters an increasingly thick forest of red oak and striped maple. Soon you reach the Lion's Head Trail on the left (2.5/1,480), which leads south to a nearby trailhead. Bear right to remain on the AT.

Abundant mountain laurel accompanies you as the trail attains the ridge-line for the first time. Turning north, the trail resumes climbing and soon reaches a hemlock-shaded clearing where the Lion's Head Bypass Trail splits left (2.6/1,690), rejoining the AT in 0.2 mile. The forested bypass skirts the summit to the west and is lined with numerous pink lady's slipper orchids in early summer, but unless the weather is horrible, remain on the AT and quickly clamber to the summit of Lion's Head (2.7/1,738).

On the summit, an outcrop provides open views south and east. To the east, expansive vistas look across the hummocky terrain of the Housatonic River Valley, with the Twin Lakes—Washining and Washinee—clearly visible. To the southeast, 1,461-foot Mount Prospect is located in the distance past a closer hilly complex and marks the AT's continuing southbound route. Views west encompass the unbroken forest of the Wachocastinook Creek watershed.

Look closely at the rock under your feet. Heavily metamorphosed—note the taffy-like banding caused by intense heat and pressure—it is pocked by numerous small red garnets. This semi-precious stone forms as the surrounding rock partially melts and then recrystallizes in small pockets.

Pitch pine and bear oak grow around you, common denizens of rocky ridgelines and other poor soils. Recognize pitch pine by its scraggly form, three-needle clusters, and numerous small cones—the summit sign here is nailed to a 10-foot-tall specimen. Identify shrubby bear oak by its distinctive leaves, which are white underneath and split into two pointed lobes at their ends with no terminal point.

Descending north from the summit and past the second junction for the Bypass Trail, you reach an expansive vista north overlooking the ridgeline spine of your upcoming route. The rounded summit of 2,316-foot Bear Mountain is next; to its right is the long ridge of Mount Race. Between the two lies the deep gully of Sages Ravine. The prominent hump of Mount Greylock (Trip 8)—the highest point in Massachusetts—rises on the distant north-northeast horizon 45 miles away. Directly in line with Greylock is the distinctive profile of Monument Mountain near Great Barrington.

After dipping into a younger forest of sugar maple, paper birch, and red oak, the trail rises to reach the spur to Riga Camping Area (3.4/1,620). Continuing, you pass through a fern-filled forest of laurel and hobblebush, whose large dinner-plate sized leaves make it hard to miss. Ubiquitous throughout the mountains of northern New England, hobblebush is uncommon south of Massachusetts.

Next up are junctions for Ball Brook Group Campground (4.0/1,700), followed in short order by an easy rock-hop over Ball Brook and the main Ball

Brook Campsite. Past the campsite, the mostly level trail winds past the fuzzy leaves of azalea—flowering in May—and more mountain laurel. Tantalizing views east peek regularly through the trees as you proceed to the junction for Brassie Brook Shelter (4.6/1,730).

Brassie Brook flows just beyond the junction, lined by yellow birch, red maple, ash, and hemlock. The trail rock-hops the stream's multiple channels and undulates gently through young forest corridors of mountain laurel. The laurel, along with blueberries and tiny bunchberry (the smallest dogwood species), indicate high soil acidity.

Upon reaching the Riga Trail (5.1/1,850), the AT abruptly widens to begin a heavily trafficked section. As the state's highest summit, Bear Mountain is one of Connecticut's most popular day-hiking destinations. Thousands walk the 5.6-mile summit loop from Highway 41 on the Undermountain and Paradise Lane trails.

The forest becomes younger as you continue, evidenced by small gray birch trees. A short-lived species that pioneers regenerating fields and other disturbed areas, gray birch is shade-intolerant and quickly disappears from the forest once overtopped. Its white bark appears similar to paper birch, but it does not peel. The tree's distinctive triangular shaped leaves make it easy to recognize.

After passing an unmarked spur on the left, the trail becomes rocky and starts rapidly ascending. The vegetation diminishes in height, and soon the route follows a thin ribbon of quartz-veined bedrock. The shrubby growth steadily shrinks and a few boulders protrude from the hillside to offer scramble-accessible views south toward Lion's Head and the headwaters of Brassie Brook.

A massive rock pile greets you upon reaching the summit (6.0/2,316), the highest mountaintop in Connecticut. (The state's highest *point* is found a few miles to the northwest on the flanks of Mount Frissell, whose summit is in Massachusetts.) The view east includes the boggy curves of Schenob Brook below and the Twin Lakes, just north of which is the state line. Peering north, the Taconic Ridge marches toward the horizon. Your journey next heads into Sages Ravine, which slices east-west in a deep cut below Bear Mountain, and then heads north over Mount Race and the rounded summit of Mount Everett.

Sandy glades of pitch pine surround the rocky summit as you proceed onward, soon dropping down the steepest section of the entire hike. The trail plummets more than 300 feet, and scrambling is required to navigate the large rock outcrops. The trail enters shady beech forest and then abruptly levels for a short distance. Carpets of hay-scented fern fill the understory and you soon resume the descent, crossing the unmarked state line and reaching the junction with the Paradise Lane Trail (6.7/1,800).

The sounds of rushing Sawmill Brook infuse the forest as you drop into Sages Ravine. Hemlocks predominate as you finish the descent to the crystalline stream and reach the junction for Sages Ravine Campsite (6.8/1,550), located on the opposite side of the stream and accessible via a log bridge.

The acidic carpet of decomposing hemlock needles prevents other plants from gaining a foothold, leaving an open understory. Past the campsite, the trail travels adjacent to the rushing brook as it sluices downward. Look closely and you may spot brook trout in the stream's crystalline pools. A few holes are large enough for a refreshing dip.

A series of tumbling tributaries feed Sawmill Brook; one picturesque flow falls 8 feet directly into it. The canyon becomes increasingly gorge-like as the trail descends on wooden steps and soon rock-hops the brook. Depending on conditions, the crossing can be easy or a challenging ford. Past the crossing, the trail resumes climbing and quickly reenters a forest of beech and oak, punctuated by the appearance of young chestnut oak. As the trail slowly curves north, it leaves the ravine behind on a steady traverse and reaches the junction for Laurel Ridge camping area (8.7/1,710).

A short distance past Laurel Ridge, the sound of thundering Bear Rock Falls fills the forest. The former location of Bear Rock Falls Campsite is evident downslope to your right just before you cross Bear Rock Stream. A short distance below, the cascade pours 150 feet down in a sheet of foaming water. There is no good view of the cascades in their entirety; opt instead for the open views east from the rock ledge on the stream's northern edge.

Past Bear Rock Stream, the rocky trail begins climbing the long ridge of Mount Race. Grass grows in the less-traveled trail and intermittent views peek through the trees to the right. After briefly topping out, the trail descends and then climbs to reach a dramatic open viewpoint. Here your route unfolds to the south, from the round dome of Bear Mountain to Lion's Head. Most remarkable are the sheer escarpments of the plateau's east edge, now visible soaring above Route 41 below.

The view marks the beginning of a dramatic stretch. The trail winds along the rocky edge of a cliff, offering continuous views east. Traveling over exposed bedrock, the trail also looks north to the distinctive profile of Mount Greylock and beyond to the distant mountains of southern Vermont. Head-high pitch pines appear, intermixed with extensive ground-hugging blueberry bushes. You ascend a gray quartz-streaked hunk of schist—like scrambling up an arching whale's back—and reach the summit of Mount Race (10.5/2,365).

From the summit, your next destination comes into view, the humping hulk of Mount Everett, the state's second highest peak. Vistas west also open up, and you can identify the prominent notch of Bish Bash Falls where it clefts the Taconic Range beyond the forested valley of Mount Washington. Alander Mountain and Mount Frissell dimple the terrain due west. As you marvel at the old-growth pitch pine forest around you, twisted and bonsai'd by the elements, take time to also look beneath your feet. Notice the striations in the rock running against the grain of the rock bands—marks left by the glaciers as they ground over and rounded off these peaks.

From the summit, the trail drops back into the trees, leaving pitch pines behind, and makes a mellow descent to the boggy saddle between Mounts Race and Everett. Entering a grove of stately hemlocks, the trail encounters trickling Race Brook and the Race Brook Trail (11.6/1,920). To descend to Race Brook Falls Campsite, bear right and follow the triangular blue blazes through a hummocky hemlock forest for 0.4 mile. From there, you can descend 750 feet to visit the trail's namesake series of falls. There are two cascades. The upper falls shoot through a narrow seam, splattering on a large boulder field. The lower falls pour down in a curtain of spray into a field of car-sized rocks flanked by downed oak and birch trees.

Back on the AT, you start your ascent of Mount Everett. The rocky trail becomes progressively steeper, and soon begins following solid bedrock through a more stunted forest. At 2,300 feet, pitch pine reappears alongside bear oak. Blueberries, bracken fern, and azalea line the trail. The surrounding trees steadily shrink in stature and intermittent views begin looking south toward the peaks behind you. To the west, you can spot structures on the shore of nearby Plantain Pond. The trail moderates as it approaches the top, entering dense 10-foot high woods before emerging on the shrubby summit (12.3/2,602).

The concrete footings of an old fire tower pock the summit, cloaked with small mountain ash and gray birch. Views look south and southwest. Bear right to continue on the AT, ignoring the large TO YOUR CAR sign and yellow arrow painted on the rocks, which leads to an alternate trailhead.

Descending, you quickly reach an open ledge with views east and north to Mount Greylock; the prominent drainage of the Hoosic River is apparent east of Greylock. Slabbing downward, the trail passes several more open views east and then curves north to cross a wide unmarked trail. From here, the rocky forest transforms into a world of black and yellow birch with a glowing understory of ferns. The AT crosses the old dirt service road to the summit, cuts left, and then descends to emerge at a grassy field and picnic area (13.0/2,100).

Visitors used to be able to drive up Mount Everett Road to this spot, but the road has been closed for many years. Now this is a strangely quiet picnic area complete with BBQ pits, picnic tables, and a privy. From here, the AT bears right along a wide woods road and reaches the Guilder Pond Trail on the left (13.1/2,080). Plastic blue triangles indicate the route of this side-trip as it makes an 0.8-mile loop around the lake and passes some good swimming spots on the northeast shore. This is the highest pond in Massachusetts. Mount Everett can be seen rising above the water in spots. Also look for evidence of beaver activity, including a dam and lodge.

Back on the AT, you travel on a wide level path beneath hemlocks and soon reach an east-flowing stream. Descending, you reach the junction for the Hemlocks Shelter at the bottom of a long staircase (13.4/1,950). The AT crosses the brook and immediately encounters the spur for Glen Brook Shelter on the right (13.5/1,940). Beyond this point, the trail feels considerably less traveled as it winds downhill through young forest and reaches the junction with the Elbow Trail on the right (14.1/1,800), which descends east to reach a trailhead at the Berkshire School.

Continuing north, the AT undulates through dense forest and past mountain laurel. After a brief climb, the trail winds along the rocky ledges of Mount Bushnell, which offer occasional views east and north. Zigzagging along a rocky spine, you pass through continuous pitch pine community and reach a good vista south from the top of Mount Bushnell (14.6/1,834). To the west, radio towers atop Mount Darby can be spotted beyond the watershed of Fenton Brook. Mount Everett is visible to the south, and views northeast look toward the broad rise of East Mountain State Forest and the continuing route of the AT.

Sporadic views continue as you proceed along the ledgy trail. At the end of the ridge, the first view entirely north opens up. From here, the trail drops steeply, making one last rise to a rock outcrop. The trail switchbacks right and steadily traverses downward past chestnut oak, fern-coated rocks, and more views. A few final switchbacks lead to a level area and an enormous boulder. The nice dirt trail then slowly descends past a large clearing to emerge on Jug End Road and the end of your journey (16.9/860).

INFORMATION

www.nature.org/wherewework/northamerica/states/berkshire/

TRIP 7
MIGHTY MONROE

Location: Monroe State Forest
Highlight: Old-growth forest
Distance: 2.0 miles round-trip
Total Elevation Gain/Loss: 300/300
Trip Length: 1–2 days
Difficulty: ★
Recommended Map: *Monroe State Forest Map*, Massachusetts Department of Conservation and Recreation

Dunbar Brook flows through some of the most isolated terrain in Massachusetts. Steep, boulder-pocked slopes rise above the stream as it drops into the deep gorge of the Deerfield River. Loggers found the topography too difficult to penetrate, and today Monroe State Forest boasts some of the finest old-growth forest in southern New England.

Established in 1924 with the purchase of 1,600 acres, Monroe State Forest has since grown to more than 4,000 acres with 9 miles of trails. The forest straddles an ecological divide between northern and southern New England, and shelters trees common to both regions. The resulting diversity is remarkable. Nearly every tree in New England is represented, from balsam fir, red spruce, yellow and paper birch, and striped maple—more common farther north and at higher elevations— to big-tooth aspen, black birch, white ash, and red oak, more frequent in southern regions and lower elevations. Hemlock, beech, and red and sugar maple complete the forest mosaic. These woods are a haven for wildlife, including moose and bear. But most remarkable of all is the 150 acres of old growth.

HIKE OVERVIEW

This is a short and easy hike and a good introduction for novice backpackers. It also makes a great day hike. You journey up the Dunbar Brook Trail, winding along the slopes and waters of its namesake stream. Two designated campsites and a shelter are located within a mile of the trailhead. Two other shelters—Ridge and Smith Hollow—can be found along the Smith Hollow Trail, 1.3 and 2.2 miles from the trailhead, respectively. Monroe's 9 miles of trail provide additional hiking opportunities from an established base camp.

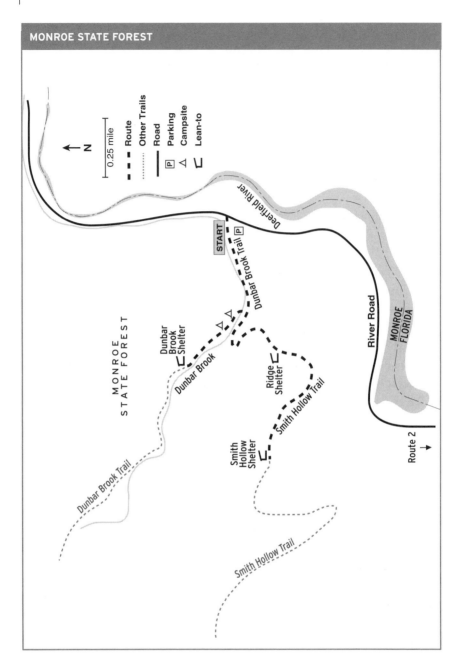

The area is lightly used, and crowds tend to be minimal. Campfires and dogs are permitted.

OVERNIGHT OPTIONS

Camping is permitted only at Monroe's three designated shelters and a pair of campsites. All overnight sites are first-come, first-served; no registration is required. There are no fees.

Dunbar Brook Campsites are located adjacent to the Dunbar Brook Trail 0.7 mile from the trailhead. Shaded by towering white pines, both sites offer ample space for tents. The first, closer site is the better of the two; the second is located closer to the trail. Water is readily obtained from the brook.

Dunbar Brook Shelter is situated between Dunbar and Haley brooks in peaceful forest, washed by stereophonic stream sounds. Past settlers recognized this as a good site—an old cellar hole can be found nearby. Haley Brook is more accessible, but you can also reach bouldery Dunbar Brook via a steep slope. At least one pool is deep enough for a refreshing sit-and-soak.

Ridge Shelter perches up the valley slopes at 1,700 feet, 1.3 miles from the trailhead. Small and somewhat dilapidated, the shelter is located in quiet hemlock forest next to a thin trickle of water—a filter is necessary. A fire ring is available.

Smith Hollow Shelter is located in the adjacent Smith Brook watershed at 1,750 feet, 2.2 miles from the trailhead. Shaded by large beech, yellow birch, and other hardwoods, it is a small little-used facility. A fire ring is present, but the lack of an obvious nearby water source is a drawback.

TO REACH THE TRAILHEAD

Follow Route 2 to the Deerfield River crossing, located 1.5 miles west of the Route 2/8A South junction. Head north on River Road, which splits off Route 2 on the east side of the Deerfield River bridge. Follow the sinuous road as it curves up the deep valley. In 2.5 miles, you reach the junction of River and Rowe roads—go left to remain on River Road. After crossing under railroad tracks, the road returns to the river and continues 8.7 miles to reach the Dunbar Brook Trailhead, which abruptly appears on the left. Look for the DUNBAR BROOK trail sign, posted by USGen New England.

HIKE DESCRIPTION

From the trailhead parking lot (0.0/1,050), begin up the dirt road on the left (the trail on the right leads down to a small dam that impounds lower Dunbar Brook).

Tree-huggers love old-growth white pines

After walking approximately 50 yards, bear right to follow the single-track trail that heads off to the right. The trail immediately enters shady forest and passes the scaly bark of a black cherry tree on the left. Marked by blue blazes and plastic skier signs, the narrow trail passes above the dammed waters of Dunbar Brook and soon enters a stately grove of large hemlock trees. The plate-sized leaves of hobblebush—ubiquitous farther north but unusual here in Massachusetts—appear in the understory.

Dunbar Brook soon comes alive below in rushing flow. The arcing branches of yellow birch frame the broad stream as it tumbles over boulders. A large ash soon appears, marking the edge of the old-growth stand. As you proceed, keep an eye on the right for the deep furrowed bark of two large big-toothed aspens, their brain-like bark a marked contrast to the smooth boles of younger trees.

The trail descends toward the creek and travels close to it, passing trillium, striped maple, and sarsparilla in the understory. Soon you reach the unposted junction with the Smith Hollow Trail on the left (0.7/1,170). The blue blazes continue left on the Smith Hollow Trail (see later), but you should bear right to pass over the creek on a long wooden bridge.

The route continues upstream and soon encounters the journey's first white pine, an impressive specimen roughly 2.5 feet in diameter. White pines are common today throughout New England, largely because of their tendency to proliferate in abandoned fields. In historic times, however, their natural habitat was considerably more limited. Shade-intolerant, they were more commonly found in the sunny openings along streams and rivers like this setting here.

The trail passes the first Dunbar Brook campsite on the right, and 50 yards later encounters the second site. Passing by another enormous white pine (the biggest yet), the trail then ascends the slopes beneath numerous paper birch. As you approach Haley Brook, bear left at the unsigned fork to cross it on a topsy-turvy bridge. Just beyond is Dunbar Brook Shelter (1.0/1,280).

SIDE-TRIP TO DUNBAR BROOK TRAIL

After setting up camp, consider touring some of the forest's other trails. Past Dunbar Brook Shelter, the Dunbar Brook Trail continues another 1.8 miles to Monroe's northern entrance at Raycroft Road. Closely following the stream and then exploring the hillside, a round-trip on this section of trail from the shelter includes 700 feet of elevation gain and loss. En route, it passes more massive white pines near a power line corridor, visits bulging boulders, and then emerges at unpaved Raycroft Road (high-clearance vehicle required), where Dunbar Brook races through a series of small cascades below large rock slabs.

SIDE-TRIP TO SMITH HOLLOW TRAIL The forest's most dramatic section is along the Smith Hollow Trail. To see it, return to the earlier junction on the west side of Dunbar Brook, and follow the blue blazes uphill into the heart of Monroe's old-growth forest. Quickly passing a huge shaggy sugar maple on the right, the trail ascends a boulder-pocked slope. Trees of all ages grow overhead, predominantly ash, sugar maple, and beech.

Soon the sentinel of the forest comes into view upslope: an enormous white ash. It is the state champion, the largest of its species in Massachusetts. Past this mega-tree, the trail continues uphill, makes a big S-turn, and then begins a more direct ascent, leaving the old-growth behind. The trail enters hemlock forest and soon reaches Ridge Shelter at 1,700 feet, 0.6 mile from the trail junction.

Past the shelter, the trail widens to become a woods road and climbs to reach unpaved Raycroft Extension road. The route turns right, follows the road for 0.4 mile, and passes by second-growth red oaks of considerable stature. The trail next bears left off the road—watch for the offset blue blazes—and proceeds straight on a ski trail, soon encountering an unmarked junction. Bear left to quickly reach Smith Hollow Shelter, 0.3 mile from Raycroft Extension Road.

INFORMATION

Monroe State Forest, Tilda Hill Road, Monroe, MA 01350; 413-339-5504, www.mass.gov/dcr/parks/western/mnro.htm

TRIP 8
HAVE A GREY DAY

Location: Mount Greylock State Reservation
Highlight: The highest mountain in Massachusetts
Distance: 11.0 miles roundtrip
Total Elevation Gain/Loss: 3,050/3,050
Trip Length: 1–2 days
Difficulty: ★★★
Recommended Map: *AMC Northern Berkshires Map*, AMC Books

**In the rolling hillscape of west Massachusetts, 3,491-foot Mount Grey-
lock stands alone, an isolated massif carved by deep valleys and awash
in a sea of diversity. A loop around the peak, from base to summit, experiences the full range of the mountain, including old-growth forest,
spattering waterfalls, and soaring vistas.**

HIKE OVERVIEW

The hike makes a complete circuit of the mountain. From the mountain's west
base, you enter a broad ravine known as the Hopper, which scoops deeply into
the west flanks of the mountain. The journey travels along a burbling stream,
climbs among massive red oaks, passes the 60-foot cascade of Money Brook
Falls, and then reaches Wilbur Clearing Shelter near the summit ridge. Here
you join the Appalachian Trail as it follows the wooded ridgeline over the
developed summit, passing several side trails that plummet eastward to reach
two other overnight options: Bellows Pipe and Gould Brook shelters. The
journey then returns to the Hopper, descending to the trailhead through an
old-growth forest of sugar maple and white ash. Dogs are permitted, but must
be leashed at trailheads, the summit, and in the Sperry Road campground.

OVERNIGHT OPTIONS

Camping is permitted only at designated shelters and in a dispersed camping area near the Hopper trailhead. Shelters are free, operate on a first-come,
first-served basis, and all feature adequate tentsites. Campfires are permitted
only at the designated fire rings in front of the shelters. Usage of the sites varies
markedly, based largely on their distance from the AT.
Hopper Brook Dispersed Camping Area. Several large grassy fields provide excellent tenting close to Hopper Brook, only a short distance (0.3 mile) from

MOUNT GREYLOCK STATE RESERVATION

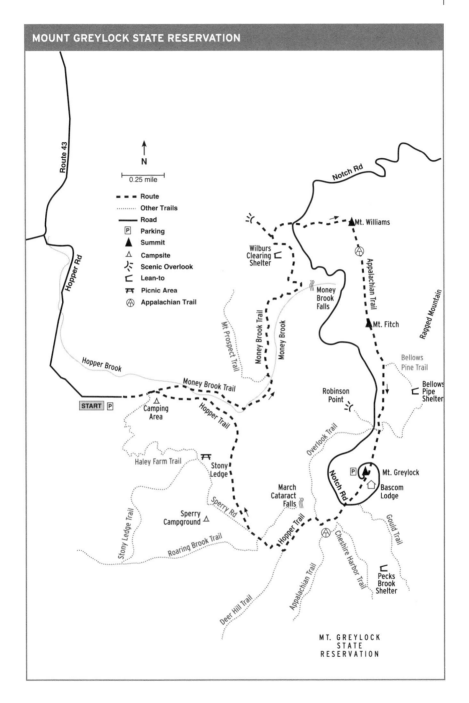

N

0.25 mile

- - - Route
.... Other Trails
—— Road
P Parking
▲ Summit
△ Campsite
⚡ Scenic Overlook
⊏ Lean-to
⊓ Picnic Area
🄰 Appalachian Trail

Route 43

Notch Rd

Hopper Rd

Mt. Williams

Wilburs
Clearing
Shelter

Money
Brook
Falls

Appalachian Trail

Ragged Mountain

Mt. Prospect Trail

Money Brook Trail

Money Brook

Mt. Fitch

Bellows
Pine Trail

Hopper Brook

Money Brook Trail

Robinson
Point

Bellows
Pipe
Shelter

START P

Camping
Area

Hopper Trail

Overlook Trail

Haley Farm Trail

Stony
Ledge

March
Cataract
Falls

Notch Rd

P ▲ Mt. Greylock

⌂ Bascom
Lodge

Sperry
Campground △

Sperry Rd

Stony Ledge Trail

Roaring Brook Trail

Hopper Trail

Gould Trail

Appalachian Trail

Cheshire Harbor Trail

Pecks
Brook
Shelter

Deer Hill Trail

MT. GREYLOCK
STATE
RESERVATION

the trailhead. The area allows for an evening arrival and an early start on the trail the next morning. The location is lightly used, sites are abundant, and no reservation or registration is required. Camping is limited to only one night. No campfires are permitted. A privy is available.

Wilbur Clearing Shelter. Located 3.3 miles from the trailhead at 2,200 feet, Wilbur Clearing is the first lean-to encountered on this hike. The surrounding forest is grand, with mature yellow birch and red oak adjacent to the shelter, and large sugar maple interspersed throughout. Two tent platforms provide camping space and water is readily accessible from an adjacent brook. Located only 0.2 mile from the AT, the shelter receives heavy use, especially during thru-hiker season in mid-summer.

Bellows Pipe Shelter. Located 7.4 miles from the trailhead at 2,250 feet along the Bellows Pipe Trail, this shelter sits on Greylock's east side. Accessing the shelter from this hike requires a 1.1-mile drop of nearly a thousand feet from the ridge and the AT, but its distance from the main hiking thoroughfare means that it's much less used. The basic structure sits in pleasant maple-ash forest with an adjacent stream for water. Ample level sites surround the area for camping. A night here adds 2.2 miles to the overall journey.

Pecks Brook Shelter. Pecks perches 8.3 miles from the trailhead at 2,400 feet along the Gould Trail, and necessitates a 1.0-mile detour 700 feet down the mountainside. Located near its namesake stream, which features a thin nearby waterfall, the shelter area features good tentsites in shady forest.

TO REACH THE TRAILHEAD

Take Route 27 south from its junction with Route 2 in central Williamstown. In 1.6 miles, turn left on Hopper Road at a distinctive rock bridge. Remain on Hopper Road as it forks left in 1.3 miles and becomes a moderately rough dirt road (still easily navigated by low-clearance vehicles). A parking area is located 0.8 mile farther at road's end across from a picturesque barn.

HIKE DESCRIPTION

From the kiosk at the head of the parking area (0.0/1,090), look for the wooded summit of 2,690-foot Mount Prospect rising over the barn—your route climbs below its east flanks. Heading out, the trail follows an old road through a gate and alongside open fields, passing a gnarled basswood tree on the right. Signs soon welcome you to The Hopper and the trail follows a classic woods road flanked by stone walls and lined with sugar maples and black cherry trees. The Hopper Loop Trail quickly splits left (0.1/1,130).

The level fields here are situated on old lake terraces. As the glaciers of the last Ice Age retreated northward roughly 10,000 years ago, a large body of water known as Bascom Lake briefly filled the valleys west and north of Greylock. Sediment deposited along its ancient shoreline created level terraces that today ring the slopes at roughly 1,100 feet.

At the head of the last field, the Hopper Trail (your return route) splits right (0.2/1,130). Continue straight on the blue-blazed Money Brook Trail.

You now leave the terrace behind for steeper topography as the trail descends to reach the Hopper Dispersed Camping Area. Numerous woods roads crisscross the young forest here, indicative of its recent agricultural past. A grassy field on the left boasts an old snag-top sycamore tree, recognized by its distinctive mottled bark and large leaves. You pass two more camping fields (the second sports an outhouse), reenter shady forest, and descend to Hopper Brook.

The trail winds through young northern hardwood forest, running parallel to the creek as both a woods road and single-track path. The shallow brook offers a few waist- to chest-deep pools for a quick soak. After crossing Money Brook, a tributary of Hopper Brook, you reach the Cutoff Trail to Sperry Campground and the Hopper Trail on the right (1.1/1,250). Remain on the Money Brook Trail as it begins a steady climb, passing several nice hemlocks and rock-hopping two small creeks.

Watch for the first appearance of hobblebush along this section, a low-lying shrub with large dinner-plate leaves. Ubiquitous in northern New England, it is relatively uncommon in Massachusetts. The trail crosses Money Brook on a more challenging rock-hop, passes the Mount Prospect Trail on the left (1.7/1,430), and then ascends above the streamcourse on a rising traverse.

At this point, you begin journeying through mature red oak forest. As a young tree, red oak grows at roughly the same rate as other tree species. But most trees slow down their vertical expansion upon reaching heights of around 40 feet. Red oak, however, continues to grow vigorously, forming an umbrella-like canopy above the mature forest and attaining heights of 80 feet or more in good sites. Red oak is readily identified by its leathery lobed spiny-tipped leaves, furrowed bark, and a distinctive reddish tinge that often appears in the cracks of the bark. Though common in southern New England, red oak rarely occurs in such mature stands, or predominates so dramatically as it does here. Large white ash join the oaks in places.

The trail makes a brief but steep drop to cross a rushing tributary, heads up the increasingly narrow gorge, and encounters the spur to Money Brook Falls on the right (2.8/1,950). A short 0.1-mile side-trip leads to the falls, where

Bellows Pipe Shelter

Money Brook cascades in a pattering sheet over a steep bedrock ledge and then gurgles through a boulder field.

Continuing, the Money Brook Trail steadily traverses upward and then switchbacks right to briefly climb along a ridgeline. The gradient eases, you pass a cutoff trail to nearby Notch Road on the right (3.2/2,190), and then encounter the short spur to Wilbur Clearing Shelter (3.3/2,220).

Continuing, the Money Brook Trail winds beneath stately red spruce, which rise overhead straight as arrows. These woods are one of the most southerly examples of spruce-fir forest in New England. Large snags on the forest floor indicate the forest's age and maturity. You next reach the junction with the AT (3.5/2,270); its white blazes head off in both directions.

Your continuing route turns right (north), but for one of the mountain's better views, you should drop your packs and briefly head left. This side-trip quickly ascends 220 feet to the shoulder of Mount Prospect, where an open ledge looks north and west. To the west, the long ridge of the Taconics traces along the New York-Massachusetts border. North, the rolling rise of Vermont's Glastenbury Mountain (Trip 9) marks the horizon as the second peak visible north. The pastoral landscape of Williamstown lies below.

Back at the earlier junction, head north on the AT through young spruce forest. This area was once Wilbur's Clearing, an open agricultural field roughly a century ago. Cross paved Notch Road (3.6/2,330) and continue past a spur on the right that leads to a nearby day-use parking area. The AT now ascends Mount Williams, making several switchbacks before turning directly uphill to attain the summit (4.5/2,951). Restricted views look out to the north and northeast—Glastenbury Mountain is again visible.

Continuing north, you travel through a forest of twisted beech and yellow birch that obscures all views. Descending to the saddle between Mount Williams and Mount Fitch, the trail encounters a four-way junction (4.7/2,780); right leads to Notch Road, the Bernard Farm Trail descends to the left to meet Notch Road lower down.

Remain on the AT as it winds among thick and crusty yellow birch, bonsai'd by the elements to heights no greater than 30 feet. After gently rising over Mount Fitch (5.5/3,110), you reach a restricted view west—the only vista on the AT between the summits of Williams and Greylock. The knobby spine of Ragged Mountain parallels the ridge below, sheltering the isolated valley of Notch Brook.

After traveling through a corridor of young spruce, you next reach the Bellows Pipe Trail (6.3/3,080). To reach Bellows Pipe Shelter, turn left here and plummet 800 feet down the Bellows Pipe Trail in 1.1 miles. The route follows a wide, curving ski trail, leveling out near the bottom as it passes nice hardwoods at the base of an overgrown field.

Continue on the AT to skip this bonus exercise, immediately passing the adjoining Thunderbolt Ski Trail. Built in the early 1930s, the Thunderbolt Ski Trail was once considered the most difficult ski run in the country and was the site of numerous races during the first half of the twentieth century. For a sense of its severe slopes, which have a maximum gradient of 35 degrees, follow the Thunderbolt Trail a short distance to the top of its first major drop. While marveling at the descent, take in decent views west as well.

Past this junction, the AT quickly reaches a signed spur to Notch Road and Robinson's Point, a worthwhile 0.3-mile side-trip. The trail drops 300 feet down a narrow path to reach a protruding boulder, which offers deep views into the northern section of the Hopper. The rounded summit of Mount Prospect is visible to the northwest.

Back heading north on the AT, a wide blackberry-lined trail corridor soon ascends to the developed summit area (6.8/3,480). Take some time to wander around the maze of roads, paths, parking areas, and pavement that crown the peak. Rest inside the nearby Thunderbolt Cabin Warming Hut, built in 1934 by the Civilian Conservation Corps. Check out the myriad viewpoints in the area, many of which include signs identifying landmarks along the skyline. Climb up the War Memorial for a 360-degree view. Stop in at Bascom Lodge to warm up and buy some snacks.

Once you've had your fill of humanity, continue north on the AT, crossing the road once again and passing a humming building below the radio tower. After a steep rocky drop through spruce-fir forest, the trail emerges at a three-way road intersection (7.3/3,200). The Gould Trail splits left from the far side to descend to the Pecks Brook Shelter, but your continuing route on the AT crosses the intersection and bears right back into the woods. You pass by a small pond and old pump house and reach the Hopper Trail (7.5/3,150).

Bear right on the Hopper Trail, which you'll follow from here back to the trailhead. The forest quickly transitions back to yellow birch and beech and passes the Cheshire Harbor Trail on the left. Wide and rocky, the Hopper Trail briefly parallels the road above, touches it momentarily, and then curves right to pass the Overlook Trail on the right (7.7/2,900).

Traversing downward, the trail crosses several rivulets, passes the Deer Hill Trail on the left (8.2/2,630), and then drops to reach unpaved Sperry Road (8.3/2,470). Turn right and follow Sperry Road 0.1 mile past the campground entrance station to the March Cataract Trail on the right, which leads to its thin namesake falls in 0.8 mile. Just beyond on the right is the well-signed turn-off for the Hopper Trail.

Follow the Hopper Trail as it traverses downward and passes through magnificent forest. Calcium-rich outcrops have enriched the soils here, and the hand of man has little disturbed the forest for more than a century. The result is a large, beautiful, and mature forest of sugar maple and white ash, joined by impressive red oaks and occasional basswood trees.

The Hopper Trail passes the Cutoff Trail to the Money Brook Trail on the right (9.4/1,600), and then curves to the west. The gradient eases and before long the forest abruptly diminishes in size and age. Invasive barberry plants line the trail corridor, which soon becomes a woods road and winds around a field to reach the junction with the Money Brook Trail (10.8/1,130). Turn left and return to the trailhead (11.0/1,090).

INFORMATION
Mount Greylock State Reservation, P.O. Box 138, Lanesborough, MA 01237; 413-499-4262, www.mass.gov/dcr/parks/western/mgry.htm

2

VERMONT

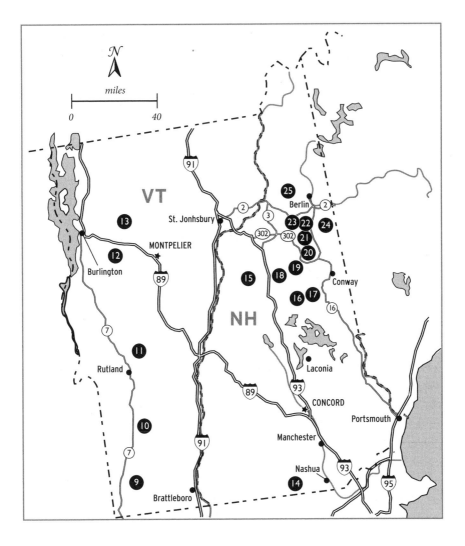

TRIP 9
DEEP IN THE GREENS

Location: Glastenbury Wilderness, Green Mountain National Forest
Highlight: The most remote summit in the Green Mountains
Distance: 22.9 miles round-trip
Total Elevation Gain/Loss: 4,700/4,700
Trip Length: 2 days
Difficulty: ★★
Recommended Map: *The Long Trail Guide*, Green Mountain Club

Deep in the southern Green Mountains, 3,748-foot Glastenbury Mountain rises above a vast sea of uninterrupted woodland. A fire tower crowns the summit, offering 360-degree views over some of Vermont's wildest terrain. Miles of easy-cruising solitude surround it. But to reach the peak, you've got to earn it. Other than the exceptional view on top, most of the hike travels through an unchanging hardwood forest that offers little in the way of scenic variety.

HIKE OVERVIEW

The trip loops counter-clockwise along the southern ridges of Glastenbury Mountain, traveling first along the Long Trail and then returning via the little-traveled West Ridge Trail. The summit and nearby Goddard Shelter are located at the hike's midpoint, neatly dividing the hike into two days. A 1.9-mile road walk separates the starting and ending trailheads. Campfires and dogs are permitted.

OVERNIGHT OPTIONS

Dispersed camping is permitted throughout this hike, and you'll pass numerous potential sites along the level terrain. But water is scarce—the hike travels almost entirely along dry ridgelines. The only reliable sources are located near the beginning of the hike (at the trailhead, Manheim Shelter, and Hell Hollow Brook), and adjacent to the Goddard Shelter.

Manheim Shelter is located at 2,450 feet, 1.6 miles from the trailhead. It would
    be a good option for starting the hike late in the day and making it a two-
    night journey. (You could also camp 0.1 mile from the trailhead on the
    far side of City Creek.) Surrounded by extensive blackberry bushes, the
    basic eight-man shelter features four double sleeping platforms and a nice

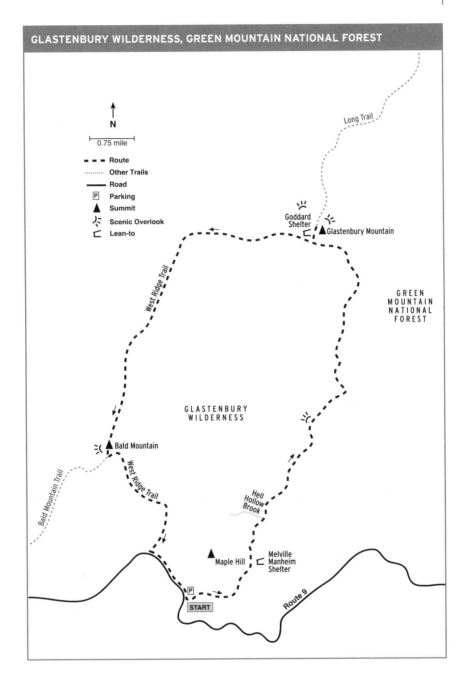

GLASTENBURY WILDERNESS, GREEN MOUNTAIN NATIONAL FOREST

N

0.75 mile

- - - Route
.... Other Trails
—— Road
P Parking
▲ Summit
Scenic Overlook
Lean-to

Long Trail

Goddard
Shelter
▲ Glastenbury Mountain

GREEN
MOUNTAIN
NATIONAL
FOREST

West Ridge Trail

GLASTENBURY
WILDERNESS

▲ Bald Mountain

West Ridge Trail

Bald Mountain Trail

Hell
Hollow
Brook

Maple Hill

Melville
Manheim
Shelter

P

START

Route 9

nearby tenting area. Fire rings, a picnic table, and privy are available. Water is available nearby, though a filter may be necessary to collect it from the thin flowing source.

Goddard Shelter is located at 3,560 feet, 10.1 miles from the trailhead. Renovated by the Green Mountain Club in 2005, it perches in an open clearing facing due south and offers views of distant Mount Greylock. An adjacent spring provides reliable water. Several tentsites are located along the Long Trail just north of the shelter.

TO REACH THE TRAILHEAD

Follow Route 9 west past the Route 8/9 junction in Searsburg for 9 miles. The trailhead is located on the right—keep an eye out for the hiker sign. Approaching from the west, the trailhead is located 5 miles from the Route 7/9 intersection in downtown Bennington.

The hike ends at the West Ridge Trailhead, where parking is sketchy. To find it, head 1.1 miles west past the main trailhead and turn right on unpaved Harbour Road. Proceed 0.8 mile to a large round black water tank, located adjacent to a private residence. The almost invisible trailhead is located about 50 yards up the driveway on the left.

HIKE DESCRIPTION

From the trailhead (0.0/1,400), head out on the Long Trail past a large information sign. Blackberry and thimbleberry vines line the trail, which quickly passes a privy in front of a large aspen. The route briefly follows rocky City Stream and then crosses it on the William D. MacArthur footbridge. A few streamside tentsites can be found on the far side. Head upstream, hiking parallel to the creek beneath red maple, beech, and striped maple.

The route quickly turns uphill on a rocky path and ascends slabs and steps. The trail switchbacks twice and starts a steep climb through a young forest punctuated by sugar maples and a few older yellow birch—one striking specimen sprouts two enormous burls from its trunk. The trail switchbacks right, straightens, and passes two enormous boulders split in half. The diamond-patterned trunks of white ash soon join the forest mosaic as the trail traverses slowly upward. The route crosses two old woods roads and then reaches a trickling stream and the spur to the Manheim Shelter (1.6/2,440), located a short distance uphill to the right.

Continuing, you resume your gradual ascent and quickly pass a tentsite by the creek. A power line corridor soon appears through the trees on your left, and after a short distance, the trail crosses the open swath (1.9/2,610). The electric lines trace east toward 3,420-foot Haystack Mountain. The trail rises to pass near the forested summit of Maple Hill (2,690), where it begins a rockier descent. Mature yellow birch dot the forest as you drop past a trickling brook and make a level traverse to tumbling Hell Hollow Brook (3.2/2,350), where two small tentsites are located.

Cross the stream on a bridge, bear right, and slowly climb. You now travel for the first time through sections of spruce-fir forest. The route attains the ridge, travels along the ridgeline, and soon reaches a restricted view southeast (4.4/2,810). The Searsburg wind turbines are visible in the distance, smaller Hagar Hill in the foreground, and Haystack Mountain in between. There is a nice (but dry) campsite here.

The trail now begins a long undulating journey along the ridge, passing numerous small campsites tucked in thick beech woods. The beech trees are heavily afflicted by the nectria fungus, which creates the canker-like sores you see on their trunks. Over the course of many years, the fungus disrupts the tree's nutrient flow, weakens the trunk, and ultimately leads to the tree's demise.

Spruce, fir, and mountain ash appear regularly as you ascend past 3,000 feet. Some restricted views pass by, including one spot (7.6/2,920) that looks toward the rounded dome of Glastenbury Mountain and its prominent fire tower. As the route approaches the summit, it curves left off the ridge and abruptly enters pure spruce-fir forest, one of the southernmost examples of this forest type in New England. After a steady rising traverse, aided in places by nice rock steps, the trail levels and reaches a spring immediately before the Goddard Shelter (10.1/3,560).

The blue-blazed West Ridge Trail splits left from the far side of the shelter; the Long Trail continues uphill. To head toward the summit, follow the Long Trail as it climbs a series of nice wooden steps past several campsites. A 50-foot tower crowns the summit of Glastenbury Mountain (10.4/3,748), renovated in 2005 by the Green Mountain Club. Clamber up the metal staircase to the open-air lookout, but be prepared to linger—the view encompasses one of the largest contiguous swaths of wildland in Vermont.

Begin your survey by looking south over your approach route—the cradling arms of both your ascent ridge and returning West Ridge are visible. You can spot the twin peak profile of Mount Greylock (Trip 8) in the distance; more of the Berkshire hills dimple the horizon beyond it.

Turn west to admire the rugged peaks of the Taconic Range, which run parallel to the Green Mountains. Just north of Glastenbury's West Ridge is West Mountain, separated from adjacent Grass Mountain by Dry Brook Hol-

Looking north from Glastenbury Mountain

low. Below Grass Mountain is the Batten Kill drainage; Red Mountain looms above the northern side of the watershed. Moving north, next up is the prominent massif of Mount Equinox (3,672)—the highest peak in Vermont outside of the Green Mountains—readily identified by the deep cleft of Cook Hollow slicing its west flank (a keen eye can also spot the summit buildings). Mount Aeolus (3,230) and adjacent Owls Head are the final Taconic peaks visible north. Separating the Taconics from the Green Mountains is the deep cleft traced by Route 7. Marble underlies the valley, an easily eroded bedrock that has weathered faster than the rocks of the neighboring mountains.

To the north, the Long Trail continues over hilly terrain toward Stratton Mountain (3,936), the prominent peak rising almost due north. The forested landscape of the Lye Brook Wilderness (Trip 10) cascades down its flanks to the west. On the more distant northern horizon, Pico and Killington are both visible. To the northeast and east is Somerset Reservoir, the dammed headwaters of the Deerfield River. Haystack and the Searsburg wind turbines can be spotted southeast.

Wipe your chops clean after so much savory viewin' and return to the shelter (10.7/3,560). Head out on the blue-blazed West Ridge Trail, located to the right of the privy. This lightly traveled path begins a slow descending traverse, quickly leaving spruce-fir forest to return among beech. The trail then makes a long level cruise, drops to cross an old woods road, and reaches an abandoned beaver lodge and lakebed in a boggy saddle (12.6/3,020).

An enormous lodge sits here empty, its once underwater entryway exposed by the diminished lake. But the animal's effects are evidenced by the dead trees that protrude from the former pond area like drowned matchsticks. A rerouted section of trail skirts the old shore to the north; the original trail crosses the lakebed and continues on the opposite side past some old rotting puncheon—a quicker option in dry conditions.

Beyond beaverland, the trail crosses another woods road and curves around to the north side of the ridge. Old scaly yellow birch punctuate this section, and encroaching blackberries and other undergrowth narrow the trail. You return to the ridge and make a steady descent to a broad saddle. From here, the route slowly rises and falls over a high point along the ridge, passing several campsites (all dry) and a few restricted views west. You then make a gradual ascent of Bald Mountain; a few switchbacks lead you to the summit (18.4/2,840).

After so much continuous beech forest, the distinctive white rocks and scrubby evergreens atop Bald Mountain are a refreshing change. The summit also offers the best views since Glastenbury Mountain, which is now visible to the north. The trail descends 0.1 mile along the ridge and encounters the junction with the Bald Mountain Trail, which heads southwest down the mountain toward Bennington. Bear left to remain on the West Ridge Trail. The trail immediately leaves the ridge, drops steeply via several switchbacks, and reaches the posted sign for Bear Wallow spring, a marginal water source located a short distance to your left.

The trail passes through some thick spruce-fir stands sheltering an abundance of pink lady's slippers—blooming in late May and June—but the forest soon transitions back to hardwoods. After a steady and steep descent, you cross a flowing creek in nice sugar maple forest where the trail gradient eases. As the hike approaches the bottom, the trail turns sharply left and then follows a dirt road to emerge on Woodland Hollow Road (21.0/1,270). To return to your starting trailhead, turn right, walk downstream along the road for 0.8 mile to Route 9, turn left, and walk east for 1.1 miles along the highway (22.9/1,400).

INFORMATION

Green Mountain National Forest, Manchester Ranger District, 2538 Depot Street, Manchester, VT 05255, 802-362-2307, www.fs.fed.us/r9/gmfl

TRIP 10
NICE LYE

Location: Lye Brook Wilderness, Green Mountain National Forest
Highlights: Streams, ponds, Prospect Rock, the state's highest waterfall
Distance: 15.3 miles round-trip
Total Elevation Gain/Loss: 2,500/2,500
Trip Length: 2 days
Difficulty: ★★★
Recommended Map: *The Long Trail Guide*, Green Mountain Club

An 18,000-acre parcel of glowing woodlands, the Lye Brook Wilderness perches atop a high-elevation plateau in the southern Green Mountains. Its west front drops steeply into the broad marble valley of Manchester. Century-old forest swathes the slopes and lakes shimmer on the plateau. It is a classic Green Mountain destination and an outstanding hike in the fall.

HIKE OVERVIEW

The hike uses the Lye Brook, Branch Pond, and Long trails on a loop through the west portion of the wilderness. The journey first ascends the Lye Brook Trail for 7 miles to reach Bourne Pond and good camping options. Along the way, you pass Lye Brook Falls, the state's highest. The hike then heads north across flat terrain on the Branch Pond Trail, reaching Douglas Shelter just before encountering the Long Trail. The route briefly follows the Long Trail to an open view from Prospect Rock, and then follows a dirt road back down to pavement. A 1.4-mile road-walk returns you to the trailhead. Because this hike uses paths other than the Long Trail, it is much less traveled than other nearby areas. Some tricky stream crossings and several (very) boggy sections increase the hike's overall difficulty. Campfires and dogs are permitted.

OVERNIGHT OPTIONS

Dispersed camping is permitted throughout this hike. The terrain is often level, but the dense woods can make finding a good tentsite difficult outside of the three established overnight areas.

Bourn Pond Tenting Area is located at 2,570 feet, 7.6 miles from the trailhead. It features a large open area for tenting, plus several nice sites along the pond's west and south shores. The South Bourne Pond Shelter still appears

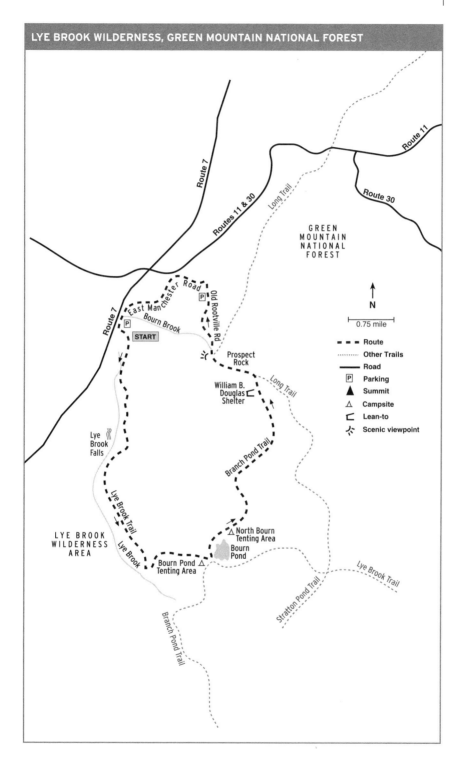

LYE BROOK WILDERNESS, GREEN MOUNTAIN NATIONAL FOREST

Route 7

Route 11

Routes 11 & 30

Long Trail

Route 30

GREEN
MOUNTAIN
NATIONAL
FOREST

N

0.75 mile

East Manchester Road

Old Rootville Rd.

Route 7

Bourn Brook

START

Prospect
Rock

William B.
Douglas
Shelter

Long Trail

Lye
Brook
Falls

Branch Pond Trail

Lye Brook Trail

LYE BROOK
WILDERNESS
AREA

Lye Brook

North Bourn
Tenting Area

Bourn
Pond

Bourn Pond
Tenting Area

Stratton Pond Trail

Lye Brook Trail

Branch Pond Trail

- - - Route
.... Other Trails
——— Road
P Parking
▲ Summit
△ Campsite
⊏ Lean-to
⋏ Scenic viewpoint

on some maps, but it burned down and no longer exists. Campfires are permitted and there is a large central fire ring for group gatherings. Water is available from a nearby stream.

North Bourn Tenting Area is located 0.5 mile from the Bourn Pond Tenting Area by the pond's north shore. It features a large central area with a massive fire ring. Additional tentsites are scattered in the surrounding forest. Paths to the lake are few, though there's a nice overlook of the water at the main access point.

The William B. Douglas Shelter is located at 2,230 feet, 11.1 miles from the trailhead, just before the junction of the Branch Pond Trail with the Long Trail. Built in 1956, it was renovated in 2005 and now features a new roof and other improvements. A small spring provides reliable water; out-of-sight Bourn Brook also rushes audibly nearby. Young sugar maples shade the six-person shelter, which opens south for excellent mid-day sun. There are a few tenting areas in the nearby trees.

TO REACH THE TRAILHEAD

Take combined Route 11/30 east from Route 7 in Manchester for 2 miles to East Manchester Road. Turn right and follow East Manchester Rd for 1.1 miles to Glen Road. Turn left, follow Glen Road about 100 feet, and then continue straight on the Lye Brook access road (signed), which dead-ends at the trailhead parking area in 0.4 mile.

HIKE DESCRIPTION

From the trailhead (0.0/800), strike out on the rocky double-track trail to immediately reach a sign indicating upcoming mileages. A large red maple stands sentinel across the trail. Just past the sign is an access point for wide, tannin-soaked Lye Brook, which is shaded by the lacy branches of hemlocks. Access to the brook becomes difficult beyond this point.

The rocky route winds by black cherry trees—look for their dark scaly bark—and soon levels out to begin its journey along a former railroad bed. Nearly all of the Lye Brook Wilderness was logged in the early twentieth century—most of this hike follows the old railroad beds used to extract timber.

Steep cutbanks hem in the water below as the route parallels the brook and crosses into the Wilderness area at a boundary sign (0.5/930). The trail rock-hops a flowing tributary, briefly becomes single-track as it makes a steep climb, and then returns to the railroad bed. The route quickly makes a long curving switchback left, and then gradually bears back right. Hemlock, beech, and red maple predominate in the surrounding hardwood forest, joined by oc-

**Bog-hopping New
England style**

casional paper birch. You can hear the brook rushing below as the trail gently traverses across steep, boulder-pocked slopes and reaches the posted spur on the right for Lye Brook Falls (2.0/1,580).

The side-trip to the falls slowly descends a single-track path to emerge near the hissing base. The multitiered waterfall falls in a curtain of spray over sheer rock faces, a display of rushing droplets. The main upper fall is the tallest and most vertical; the waterfall in its entirety tumbles about 100 feet. Steep use paths lead to multiple viewpoints—the best is located halfway up the falls.

Back on the main trail, continue steadily upward on the railroad bed, passing some large red maples. Roughly 0.3 mile past the falls junction you cross the stream that feeds it (2.3/1,850). The trail levels, crosses a few small brooks, and winds past tangles of hobblebush. The trail soon resumes a steady ascent and then levels at 2,300 feet in a land of hobblebush, paper birch, beech, and endless red maple.

Next up is a heart-pumping stream crossing (3.7/2,470) that can be challenging in higher water. Once across, the rocky trail returns to single-track and makes a long level cruise through damp hardwoods. In fall, it's a soft rainbow of color. The path becomes increasingly faint—watch closely for blazes—as you undulate along, crossing a small brook as you go. Then you abruptly enter spruce-fir forest.

Let the bog-hopping begin! The final section of the Lye Brook Trail passes through a notoriously swampy area. Slow careful movement and delicate hops are required to pass through without overtopping your boots. After the initial bog-hop, the trail crosses the marshy outflow of a nearby meadow and then curves around to cross the inflow as well. You soon pass a second meadow, bog-hop another section, and then briefly descend to emerge at the clearing and former site of the South Bourn Pond Shelter (7.6/2,570) A red maple is visibly charred, marking the location where the shelter burned down.

Bear right at the clearing to reach the signed junction for the West Branch Trail by a flowing stream. (If you head left from the clearing, a small stone staircase also leads to the West Branch Trail.) Turn left and start cruising north on the West Branch Trail, initially following a section of wide railroad bed. You soon diverge on well-trod single-track, which curves around a boggy area and crosses a flowing brook. Immediately past the brook on the right is a lakeside campsite offering ready shore access and views across the water to Stratton Mountain and its summit fire tower. The lakeshore is generally sandy and muddy in spots, and swimming is a tempting possibility. A mix of evergreens and hardwoods ring the pond.

Another good campsite appears to your right as you continue onward, this one featuring marble rocks protruding from the shore. Past here, the wet trail passes a few more lake views before curving away from the water to reach the posted spur to the North Bourn Tenting area (8.1/2,560), located 0.2 mile away to the right.

Continuing, the easy-walking trail tours spruce-fir forest and encounters Bourn Brook, which drains the pond. You now curve left onto single-track and begin to parallel the out-of-sight stream; you'll follow its general course for the remainder of the hike. The railroad bed returns underfoot and slowly descends near the audible brook. Yellow and paper birch snags jut into the surrounding forest. You then curve right off the railroad bed and gentle drop to reach the brook. Crossing the shin- to knee-deep stream requires another exciting rock-hop, and you can only pine for the bridge that used to be here, evidenced by the small remaining footings. Century-old red maples and yellow birches rise overhead as you steadily descend, bog-hopping a few sections as you go.

The trail returns to the creek, now rockier and faster flowing. When you next encounter it, the rushing waters are nearly river-like, with boulders protruding from a 10- to 20-foot wide streambed. The route returns to the railroad bed, which parallels the out-of-sight stream as it descends. Sugar maples slowly increase as you approach the William B. Douglas Shelter (11.1/2,230), located directly by the trail.

Past the shelter, the hike continues on the railroad bed and immediately encounters the first puncheon of the hike—hooray! The trail now becomes more of an old road, lined with beech and sugar maple. The going is easy over extensive puncheon, and you quickly reach the junction with the Long Trail/AT (11.6/2,310). This marks your departure from the Lye Brook Wilderness. Bear left on the Long Trail to immediately cross a bridge over a small tributary. Turn left on the opposite side to follow the route downstream; an arrow on a rusting machinery wheel indicates the way.

The wide trail soon begins journeying on an unpaved drivable road, which travels high above the rushing stream below. The easy-walking road steadily descends past sugar maple, beech, black cherry, and red maple to reach a locked gate. White ash has appeared as well—you can identify one to the left of the gate, marked with a blaze.

Soon thereafter, you reach Prospect Rock (12.5/2,020), an open outcrop located to the left by an obvious clearing. From here, a grand view peers west and north. Below you, Bourn Brook rushes out-of-sight through a deep ravine. Mount Equinox (3,672) and its neighboring peaks of the Taconic Range dominate the west horizon. Downtown Manchester is visible north, and the Valley of Vermont narrows as it recedes into the distance.

Just past Prospect Rock, the Long Trail/AT turns right off the road on a narrower footpath, but you remain on the road, which drops steeply and becomes increasingly rocky. The road forks at one point—bear right to follow the main route. As you approach the bottom, the road begins a steep, quad-tensing drop next to a small stream on the right. Marble boulders appear intermittently in the surrounding forest. Grayish-white in color, they can be recognized by their lack of banding and tendency to fracture at right angles.

The road crosses the stream, the young forest becomes more lush, and hemlocks appear. You cross the forest boundary (13.9/1,150) and then reach Rootville Road by a water tank. Two small lots provide limited parking.

To return to the trailhead, follow Rootville Road 0.6 mile down past several residences. Turn left on Manchester Road, follow it 1.0 mile, and then turn left to return to the trailhead (15.3/800).

INFORMATION

Green Mountain National Forest, Manchester Ranger District, 2538 Depot Street, Manchester, VT 05255, 802-362-2307, www.fs.fed.us/r9/gmfl

TRIP 11
LOAF AROUND

Location: Breadloaf Wilderness, Green Mountain National Forest
Highlight: Forested heart of the Green Mountains
Distance: 12.4 miles round-trip
Total Elevation Gain/Loss: 3,500/3,500
Trip Length: 1–2 days
Difficulty: ★★★
Recommended Map: *The Long Trail Guide*, Green Mountain Club

The Breadloaf Wilderness is a classic slice of the Green Mountains. Its 25,000 acres include 27 miles of the Long Trail and a chain of rugged 3,000-foot peaks. Views are precious in this forested region, but the streams, forests, trails, and shelters are a microcosm of the Green Mountains. Plus, there aren't many people.

HIKE OVERVIEW
The hike uses the Cooley Glen, Long, and Emily Proctor trails to loop clockwise around the headwaters of the New Haven River near the center of the wilderness area. Along the way you visit melodious streams, climb over the presidential summits of Mounts Cleveland (3,482), Roosevelt (3,528), and Wilson (3,745), and enjoy a few excellent views southeast. Dogs are permitted.

OVERNIGHT OPTIONS
The hike passes two shelters, each of which has adjoining tentsites. Dispersed camping is permitted throughout the hike, though finding a level location to pitch a tent is difficult at best. Campfires are permitted.

Cooley Glen Shelter is located 3.2 miles from the trailhead at 3,100 feet. Spruce-fir woods surround the basic shelter, which features several nice tentsites nearby. A large fire ring in front of the shelter is good for evening warmth. Water is available at Cooley Spring, 100 feet down the Cooley Glen Trail.

Emily Proctor Shelter is located 8.9 miles from the trailhead at 3,560 feet. It is similar to Cooley Glen, tucked within spruce-fir forest and providing space for six people. There's a fire ring in front of the shelter, a small stream flows adjacent to the site, and three tent platforms are located uphill on a surprisingly long spur trail.

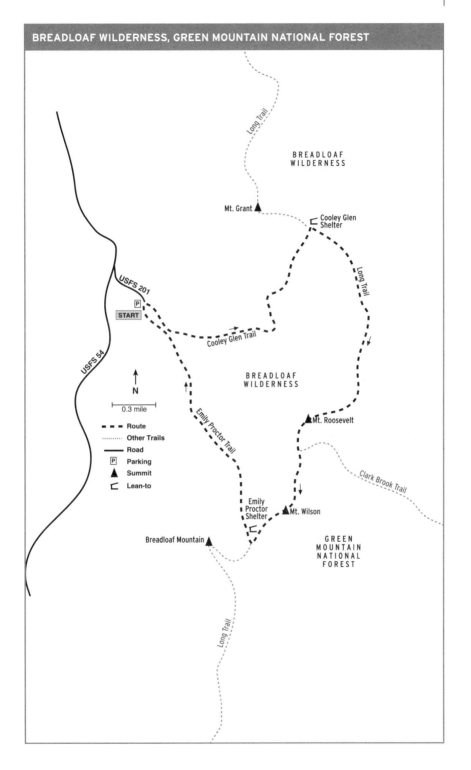

BREADLOAF WILDERNESS, GREEN MOUNTAIN NATIONAL FOREST

Long Trail

BREADLOAF
WILDERNESS

Mt. Grant ▲

Cooley Glen
Shelter

Long Trail

USFS 201

P
START

Cooley Glen Trail

USFS 54

N

0.3 mile

- - - Route
.... Other Trails
—— Road
P Parking
▲ Summit
⊏ Lean-to

BREADLOAF
WILDERNESS

Emily Proctor Trail

▲ Mt. Roosevelt

Clark Brook Trail

Emily
Proctor
Shelter

▲ Mt. Wilson

Breadloaf Mountain ▲

GREEN
MOUNTAIN
NATIONAL
FOREST

Long Trail

TO REACH THE TRAILHEAD

Follow Route 116 1.0 mile south of Bristol to Lincoln Road on the east side of the highway. Turn left and follow Lincoln Road for 4.5 miles, passing through Lincoln center to reach USFS 54. Turn right on USFS 54 and in 1.1 miles bear left on South Lincoln Road. In another 0.8 mile, bear left to remain on USFS 54 and continue for 2.2 miles to USFS 201 on the left. Turn left and continue 0.4 mile to reach the trailhead and small parking area at road's end.

HIKE DESCRIPTION

A sign by the trailhead (0.0/1,610) indicates the Cooley Glen Trail leading off to the left; the Emily Proctor Trail—your return route—comes in from the right. A yellow birch rises behind the sign, readily identified by its thin ribbons of peeling golden bark. Head out on the blue-blazed Cooley Glen Trail, which immediately narrows to single-track and begins paralleling the New Haven River on the left. Over the next 3 miles, the route passes among hardwoods typical of New England's middle elevations (1,000–3,000 feet). Beech and yellow birch are common, joined by the occasional sugar maple, black cherry, and balsam fir. The dinner-plate leaves of hobblebush fill the understory along with the distinctive lined bark of striped maple.

The trail follows an old roadbed, rising above and then alongside the river. The bouldery streambed is readily accessible and offers numerous spots to relax. You soon reach the posted wilderness boundary by a bridge over the river (0.4/1,710); sign in at the trail registry. From here, the trail winds near the river on a slow climb, crosses several small streams, and reaches the confluence of two equal-sized tributaries (1.4/2,020).

The trail rock-hops the north branch and follows the south fork to the right. The gradient increases and you briefly parallel the creek before curving back left to start a more sustained rise. Shortly before the trail levels out, you pass a few limited views north toward Mount Grant. The route contours back into the corridor of the stream's north branch and leads past a monster yellow birch on the right, its ponderous girth extending 30 feet off the ground before diminishing.

The forest now becomes older and punctuated by more mature yellow birch. The trail steadily climbs, crosses the stream twice, and then passes a final trickle that marks the stream's headwaters—Cooley Spring. Here, the forest abruptly transitions to spruce-fir. Just ahead in the saddle is the white-blazed Long Trail (3.2/3,110).

Cooley Glen Shelter is located about 50 yards to the north, but your continuing journey heads south. It has been easy cruising up to this point, but the route now abruptly transforms into a rocky trail challenge more typical of New England hiking. It begins with a direct stair-like ascent of steep rocks and a series of switchbacks to the wooded summit of Mount Cleveland (3.7/3,482).

The trail makes an easier descent down the other side and reaches a saddle (4.4/2,980). The route then steepens and makes several long looping switchbacks to attain the summit of Peak 3348, also known as Little Hans Peak (5.4/3,348). Down the far side you go, making a steady descent via switchbacks. As you cross the next saddle, you pass the first and only water along the ridge, a dribbling rivulet.

A steep traversing rise leads up the east flanks of the ridge, then crosses over to the west side. Occasional views look north. At one point, Mount Abraham (4,006) becomes visible to the south, located just north of Lincoln Gap and framed by Mounts Grant (left) and Cleveland (right). The path briefly

Cooley Glen Shelter, Breadloaf Wilderness

levels, then heads up over rock slabs and a ribbon of exposed bedrock to reach the trip's most dramatic view (6.8/3,530).

Perched just below the summit of Mount Roosevelt, enjoy unrestricted vistas south and southeast. To the south is Mount Wilson, the final peak of your ridge traverse. To the southeast, Highway 100 runs through its creased valley, backed by the long rounded spine of the Braintree Mountains. The range's highest point is 2,750-foot Mount Cushman. On the horizon, you can see the ski mountains of Pico (left) and Killington (right).

The trail now makes a steep and jarring drop, passing the Clark Brook Trail on the left (7.2/3,390). You undulate through another saddle and begin a steady rise to the summit of Mount Wilson (8.0/3,750). Along the way, a few glimpses west reveal the south end of Lake Champlain. Near the summit, a spur trail leads left to another excellent view, similar to that of Roosevelt.

The trail undulates along and then drops toward the Emily Proctor Shelter, passing a spur to the tenting area shortly before reaching the lean-to (8.9/3,560). The Emily Proctor Trail joins here, your return route. Follow it away from the shelter and begin a steep rocky drop, which tapers slowly to a mellow traverse.

The forest transitions from spruce-fir forest as you descend. Yellow birch appear first, followed by beech and striped and sugar maples. The trail crosses several small brooks and becomes increasingly gentle, soon curving left along an old level roadbed. This road likely provided access for selective logging activity. Note how more valuable sugar maples and conifers disappear near the road, leaving behind yellow birch and beech.

The route begins to run parallel to the creek below, and then descends to cross it above a confluence and small soaking hole (10.2/2,020). Past this crossing, the route makes a level traverse, descending occasionally on nice rock staircases. The creek below curves away to the right, red maples appear in increasing abundance, and the occasional glimpse north reveals Mount Grant looming overhead. The trail becomes increasingly road-like and soon makes a steady descent to cross the posted wilderness boundary. Near the end, you pass a beautiful field of hay-scented ferns, bowing softly as they wish you farewell (12.4/1,610).

INFORMATION

Green Mountain National Forest, Middlebury Ranger District, 1007 Route 7, Middlebury, VT 05753, 802-388-4362, www.fs.fed.us/r9/gmfl

TRIP 12
HUMP DAY

Location: Camel's Hump State Park
Highlight: The highest never-developed peak in Vermont
Distance: 7.3 miles round-trip
Total Elevation Gain/Loss: 2,700/2,700
Trip Length: 1–2 days
Difficulty: ★★★
Recommended Maps: *Long Trail Guide,* Green Mountain Club; *Northern Vermont Hiking Trails,* Map Adventures

This bulbous mass of a mountain does indeed resemble its namesake. A hump of solid stone composes the 4,083-foot summit, tufted with a small patch of alpine tundra. Expansive views sweep across the state. A vast protected landscape of 20,000 acres surrounds it. No structure has ever stood upon the summit, making it Vermont's highest undeveloped peak. It's a popular destination—an estimated 30,000 people visit the summit each year—but the scenery and views merit the crowds.

HIKE OVERVIEW
The hike ascends the mountain from the west on the Monroe and Dean trails, passing the Hump Brook Tenting Area midway up the mountain and the Montclair Glen Lodge on the ridgeline. The hike then follows the Long Trail north, clambers over the rocky summit, and descends. The trip is easily completed as a day hike, but spending the night turns it into a more leisurely adventure and provides the opportunity to reach the summit before day hikers arrive en masse. Dogs are permitted but must be leashed above treeline and at designated shelters and camping areas.

OVERNIGHT OPTIONS
The hike loops past a designated camping area and a nice old-school shelter. Green Mountain Club caretakers collect an overnight per person fee at both sites. Dispersed camping is permitted below 2,500 feet throughout the park, but must be at least 200 feet (75 adult paces) away from the any trail or water source; good sites are hard to find on the steep slopes.

Hump Brook Tenting Area spreads out beneath lush hardwoods at 2,400 feet, 1.6 miles from the trailhead, and offers eight tent platforms on a first-come,

CAMEL'S HUMP STATE PARK

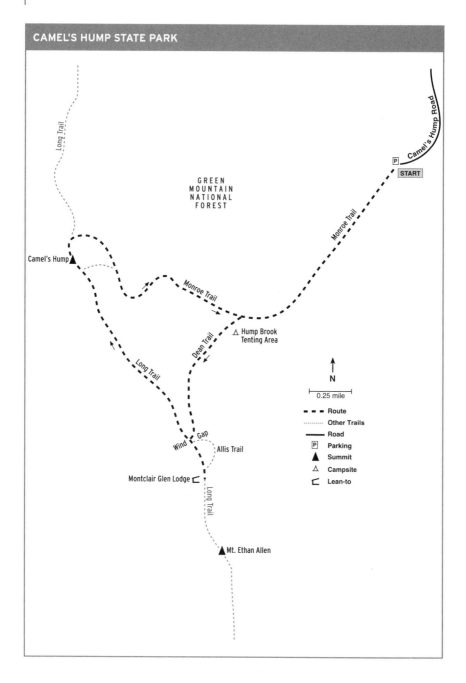

first-served basis. The higher the site number, the quieter the spot. Sites 1–3 sit close to the entrance and each other, but have the only permitted fire ring (fires are prohibited at other sites). Sites 7 and 8 offer the most privacy. Nearby Hump Brook provides water and soothing lullabies at night. A bear line is available for hanging food—always a good idea.

Montclair Glen Lodge is located at 2,770 feet, 2.5 miles from the trailhead. Built in 1948, it is a small cabin with tables and bunks for a maximum of 12 hikers. A nearby brook provides reliable water. The shelter is busy during the July and August thru-hiking season, but otherwise often has space. There are also a few campsites—including a tent platform—nearby. No fires allowed.

Gorham Lodge still appears on some maps, but was removed in 2003 and replaced with a new shelter on Bamforth Ridge, 2.9 miles farther north on the Long Trail and off of the described route. Camping is prohibited at the former shelter site.

TO REACH THE TRAILHEAD

Take Route 100 south from I-89 (Exit 10), and proceed 0.7 mile to Winooski Street, the first right after the railroad bridge. Turn right on Winooski Street, proceed 0.3 mile to River Road, and turn right. In 1.7 mile, River Road becomes a mellow dirt road. After 2.2 miles of unpaved travel, turn left on Camel's Hump Road. In 2.4 miles, continue straight past Scrabble Hill Road where a small brown sign indicates the distance of "Hump" ahead. At 1.8 miles farther, you pass a Camel's Hump Summit Trails sign. A short 0.3 mile after that, you reach the smaller lower parking area; there is a larger (often full) lot 0.1 mile uphill from here.

HIKE DESCRIPTION

The hike begins from the upper lot (0.0/1,520) and heads out on the Monroe Trail. Hardwoods—red maple and paper, gray, and yellow birch—fill the surrounding forest. You immediately pass a plaque honoring the victims of a 1944 airplane crash, when a U.S. Army B-24J bomber hit the mountainside. (You can visit remaining debris later in the hike.) The wide, blue-blazed trail continues past a privy on the right and reaches an information sign.

Sugar maples and beech appear as you continue past the sign, crossing a dry gully on a small bridge. Stone walls line the woods and belie the area's agricultural past. Balsam fir and big-tooth aspen join the forest mosaic as the trail steepens and passes a stand of healthy beech unafflicted by the nectria

Camel's Hump from Wind Gap

fungus—compare their smooth bark with the cankered skin of affected trees. The trail makes a gentle rising traverse, crossing several rivulets and climbing to reach the junction with the Dean Trail (1.3/2,350).

Bear left on the Dean Trail, a narrower and less-traveled pathway. Curve around briefly to cross Hump Brook on a bridge. Savor the crystalline sounds of the rushing stream. The posted spur for Hump Brook Camping Area is just ahead on the left (1.6/2,360).

Past the campground, hobblebush and hardwoods start to transition to spruce-fir forest and its common constituents: mountain ash, blueberry, and tiny bunchberry plants. The trail crosses a small brook and levels out to contour into Wind Gap. Here, a shallow tarn opens north toward the south face of Camel's Hump, a lofty lump lording over the forest. The continuing trail navigates some boggy and slippery sections, passes another small pond, and reaches the Long Trail (2.3/2,870).

Turn left here to head toward Montclair Glen Lodge, located 0.2 mile south. (The continuing hike bears right.) The trail to Montclair Glen passes below a

60- to 80-foot cliff base and immediately reaches the Allis Trail on the left—a short indistinct 0.1-mile spur that rejoins the Long Trail just south of the lodge after passing a memorial bench with views south to nearby Mount Ethan Allen. Past the Allis Trail, the Long Trail drops over rough terrain to reach the junction with the Forest City Trail and Montclair Glen Lodge just beyond.

Back heading north on the Long Trail from the Dean Trail junction (2.3/2,870), you pass a small pond and an overgrown beaver dam. Now the route begins its summit journey. A sign warns of the challenges you'd next face if you attempted this in winter.

The trail quickly steepens. The path climbs rock steps in places and offers occasional views south through the trees toward Mount Ethan Allen. After a switchback right, the route takes a direct line up the mountain that soon eases to make a gradual traverse toward an outcrop with full views east (2.7/3,140). The long prominent ridgeline of the Worcester Range fills the east view; several Green Mountain ridges are visible south.

The trail levels briefly and heads toward a rocky cliff, where a scramble over large boulders leads to more nice vistas. After cutting through a cleft in the rock, you reach an outlook west for the first time. Lake Champlain and the Adirondacks fill the horizon.

The bald pate of the summit looms north as the trail reenters trees and descends past a trickling water source. You slice though spruce-fir woods to reach the final ascent. The summit peeks out ahead as you climb. Dogwood, cherry, hazel, and mountain ash line the trail. You bank left and pass a good view southwest, then head straight up to reach the Alpine Trail (3.8/3,820).

The remains of the crashed bomber await you a few hundred feet down the Alpine Trail. To check it out, head right down the Alpine Trail, which steeply descends, switchbacks right, and then traverses. Views south of Mount Ethan Allen appear shortly before you encounter a 20-foot long section of wing. The old wheel well and landing gear are easily recognized.

Back on the Long Trail, the summit block and cliffs loom ahead. As you clamber up to the base of the crags, views south unveil in their entirety. The trail banks left around the cliff base, reenters diminutive fir forest, and then cuts back right to attain the summit (4.0/4,083).

The 360-degree summit view is delicious. North is the prominent bald hump of 4,393-foot Mount Mansfield (Trip 13)—the state's highest peak—rising above I-89 and the Winooski River Valley. Below to the east, the Camel Brook watershed drains north into the Winooski. South is the Mad River Glen Ski Area and Sugarbush Resort. On a clear day, you can see as far as Killington and Ascutney in the southern Greens and as far east as Franconia Ridge and Mount Washington. Lake Champlain, Burlington, and the Adirondacks beyond line the west horizon.

Be watchful where you step and do not walk on the vegetation. The surrounding alpine tundra is extremely rare in Vermont and easily damaged by wayward boots. A caretaker watches the summit throughout the summer and fall to help protect the fragile ecosystem. The Long Trail heads north from the summit and quickly reenters the forest. The trail traverses downward, at one point dropping steeply over damp rock slabs. The striated, deformed layers in the rock beneath your feet hint at its tectonic history. Heavily transformed from its original state by heat and pressure, the banded rock is shot through with veins of quartzite. This telltale mineral is one of the first to melt and re-form as buried rock heats up. The remainder of this rock deformed like putty, but did not melt. Such clues allow geologists to isolate the conditions in which outcrops formed.

Views north continue intermittently toward the bald knobs along Bamforth Ridge and more distant Mansfield. You next reach the Camel's Hump Hut Clearing and the four-way junction with the Burrows and Monroe Trails (4.2/3,810). A hotel was located here in the nineteenth century, but burned down in 1875.

Bear right on the Monroe Trial to begin your descent to the trailhead. The slick path is muddy in spots. Paper birch reappears as you traverse downward to reach the lower end of the Alpine Trail (4.8/3,330). Remain on the Monroe Trail as it cruises down at a constant grade over rocky terrain. The route crosses a creek, briefly follows it downstream, and then banks left to re-cross it. Increasing paper birch and hobblebush indicate the transition back to hardwood forest.

Down the streamcourse you go, winding into a beech forest as the path traverses left. Black cherry and yellow birch join in abundance and sugar maples speckle the woods as the trail makes a gentle traverse to return to the Dean Trail (6.0/2,350). Bear left to remain on the Monroe Trail and retrace your steps to the trailhead (7.3/1,520).

INFORMATION

Green Mountain Club, 4711 Waterbury-Stowe Road, Waterbury Center, VT 05677, www.greenmountainclub.com, 802-244-7037

TRIP 13
HEAD ABOVE THE REST

Location: Mount Mansfield State Forest
Highlights: The tallest mountain in Vermont, gnarly trails
Distance: 10.6 miles round-trip, plus as many as 3 miles of bonus adventure
Total Elevation Gain/Loss: 3,800/3,800
Trip Length: 1–3 days
Difficulty: ★★★
Recommended Maps: *Long Trail Guide* (Green Mountain Club), *Northern Vermont Hiking Trail* (Map Adventures)

The long alpine spine of Mount Mansfield is said to resemble a human face. He looks upward; the top of his head points south. His features are named promontories—the Forehead, the Nose, the Adam's Apple—but the Chin juts highest, at 4,393 feet the tallest point in Vermont. The Long Trail walks across this craggy visage, touring expansive views of the landscape. A series of wild trails run parallel to the ridgeline, thrilling explorations through the weathered furrows of Mansfield's face.

HIKE OVERVIEW

This hike makes a complete loop around Mansfield's alpine ridgelines. Approaching from Underhill State Park to the west, the journey ascends the open bedrock of Maple Ridge, traverses the mountain's 1.9-mile ridgeline on the Long Trail, and then returns to the trailhead via view-laden Sunset Ridge. Side-trips explore fantastic stuff along the way, including caves, fissures, and giant rocks. Crowds are usually heavy atop The Chin and Forehead, but diminish rapidly away from the main routes.

The journey can be completed as a long day hike, but spending a night (or two) at one of the mountain's three overnight sites allows for more extensive exploration and enjoyment. Note that the mountain's trails are closed during mud season (generally April through mid-May) to prevent erosion. Dogs are allowed.

OVERNIGHT OPTIONS

Overnight use is restricted to three designated sites. The Green Mountain Club (GMC) maintains two lodges on either end of Mansfield's long ridge and a designated camping area is located south of The Forehead. A nice drive-in

MOUNT MANSFIELD STATE FOREST

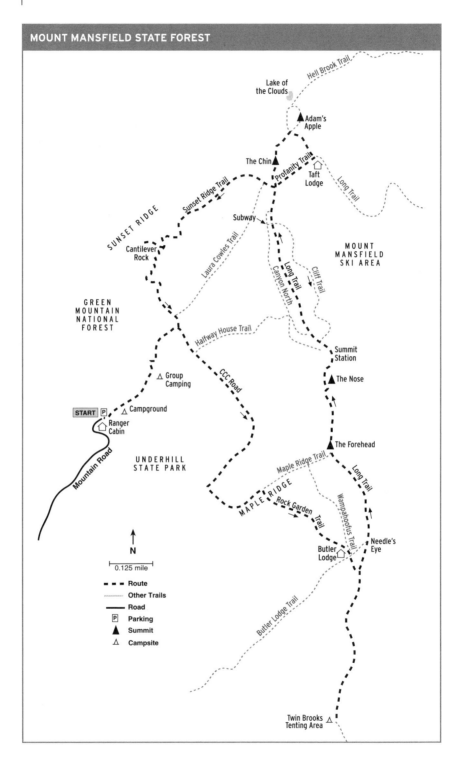

Hell Brook Trail

Lake of
the Clouds

Adam's
Apple

The Chin

Profanity Trail

Taft
Lodge

Long Trail

Sunset Ridge Trail

SUNSET RIDGE

Subway

Cantilever
Rock

Laura Cowles Trail

MOUNT
MANSFIELD
SKI AREA

Long Trail
Canyon North

Cliff Trail

GREEN
MOUNTAIN
NATIONAL
FOREST

Halfway House Trail

Summit
Station

Group
Camping

CCC Road

The Nose

START   P   Campground

Ranger
Cabin

The Forehead

UNDERHILL
STATE PARK

Mountain Road

Maple Ridge Trail

Long Trail

MAPLE RIDGE

Rock Garden

Wampahoofus Trail

Needle's
Eye

Butler
Lodge

N

0.125 mile

Route
Other Trails
Road
P   Parking
▲   Summit
△   Campsite

Butler Lodge Trail

Twin Brooks   △
Tenting Area

campground is available at the trailhead in Underhill State Park, though there is a minimum two-night stay.

Twin Brooks Tenting Area lounges 4.8 miles from the trailhead in pleasant hardwood forest at an elevation of 2,300 feet. Located 1.3 miles south of Butler Lodge, it requires a moderate detour off the main route. It is a tent-only area and receives much less use than the two lodges. Five platforms are scattered about, each nicely private with a fire ring. A five-platform group camping area is also available. The closest water is a quarter mile away in either direction on the Long Trail.

Butler Lodge, 3.5 miles from the trailhead, perches near 3,000 feet less than a mile south of the Forehead. The enclosed cabin overlooks a rolling hillscape toward the south end of Lake Champlain. A reliable water source trickles nearby. Rebuilt in 2000, the lodge sleeps a maximum of fourteen people and is available on a first-come, first-served basis. A caretaker on site collects an overnight per person fee during the summer and fall.

Taft Lodge, 7.0 miles from the trailhead, is located at 3,660 feet almost directly below The Chin. Built in 1920 and renovated in 1996, it tucks against steep forested slopes and is the largest overnight facility on the Long Trail. As many as 24 people can squeeze on two large platforms, available on a first-come, first-served basis. A small deck by the front door offers views east. Water is 50 feet away in a nearby brook. A caretaker is in residence during summer and fall, and collects an overnight per person fee.

TO REACH THE TRAILHEAD

From the East. Take exit 11 off I-89, turn left on Route 2, and proceed 1.7 miles south to a stoplight in Richmond. Turn left onto Jericho Road and proceed 5.0 miles to reach a T-junction. Turn right here and head toward Jericho Corner, reaching Route 15 in 3.4 miles. Turn right on Route 15 and proceed 0.5 mile to River Road on the right, posted for Underhill State Park. Turn right and follow River Road 2.7 miles to Underhill Center, where the road becomes Pleasant Valley Road. In another 1.0 mile, turn right on unpaved (but easily passable) Mountain Road, which heads upward for 2.7 miles to reach the parking area and park entrance. There is a nominal per person entrance fee.

From Burlington and Points West. Take Exit 15 off I-89 and follow Route 15 east for 12.3 miles to the junction with River Road. Proceed as described in the previous paragraph.

HIKE DESCRIPTION

The hike begins on the Eagle Trail, which leaves from the upper parking area by a blue-blazed post (0.0/1,870). The single-track trail starts out among hardwoods—beech, white ash, and yellow and paper birch—and quickly crosses the paved road to the group camping area. Interrupted fern and jack-in-the-pulpit punctuate the understory. The route crosses the road again, widens, and then re-crosses the road at a tantalizing view of Maple Ridge (your route up) to the southeast. Spruce appears in the mix and the Eagle Trail next turns left to travel directly along the road (0.6/2,150).

In 0.1 mile, the road splits. To the right is a large youth group camping area, but your journey heads left on the Sunset Ridge Trail. You initially climb along a woods road, parallel to a rushing creek below, to reach the CCC Road on the right (1.0/2,360). Bear right on the CCC Road, following the wide woods trail as it cruises gently past the Halfway House Trail on the left (1.2/2,440) and then slowly rises past several rivulets.

There is a sense of increasing elevation, and soon you reach a bench with a restricted view northwest (1.8/2,680). Lake Champlain is visible; the Adirondacks rise beyond in the distance. Just past the viewpoint, a two-tiered mini-waterfall marks the road's high point. You now start a gentle descent and reach the Maple Ridge and Teardrop Ski trails (2.2/2,530).

Turn left on the Maple Ridge Trail, which immediately narrows to single-track and starts ascending steeply over roots and rocks. The surrounding forest quickly transitions to spruce-fir forest. Yellow clintonia, hobblebush, and bunchberry appear underfoot, mountain ash rises overhead. The trail clambers up rock slabs and reaches a sunny outcrop surrounded by diminutive spruce. Just past this point, you reach an open ledge with 180-degree views west.

Looking south, the prominent massif of Camel's Hump (Trip 12) is readily spotted; the lumpy terrain of the Green Mountains trails away behind it. North, the long spine of Mount Mansfield terminates at The Chin, where Sunset Ridge joins from the west.

Continuing, you next reach the Frost Trail joining from the right (2.5/2,910). Looking up from here, you can trace rocky Maple Ridge rising to the Forehead. You now begin the ascent along Maple Ridge's open terrain, which provides endless views in all directions. Nearby to the southeast rises 3,371-foot Dewey Mountain. Nebraska Notch sits below it, followed next by Bolton Mountain and then Camel's Hump on the skyline beyond. The Worcester Range serrates the east sky.

Continuing up the rocky ridge, you pass a cleft on the right against a hulking boulder. From here, the trail alternately slabs over open rocks and passes through stands of stunted trees. Watch for the presence of cones on these small but ancient specimens. Next up is the Rock Garden Trail, which joins from the right (2.9/3,120).

Bear right on the Rock Garden Trail to head toward Butler Lodge. (Note that you can also continue on the Maple Ridge Trail to reach The Forehead in 0.7 mile. This shorter variation saves 0.7 mile of effort, but skips Butler Lodge and some radical sections of trail.) The narrow Rock Garden Trail descends into a sheltered forest of paper birch and mountain ash and immediately becomes more challenging. You'll need to scramble as the route winds by small cliffs, passes through a 3-foot-high squeezer cave (you can also climb over), visits a 20-foot high megalith, and then squishes through a narrow crack of stone. You're not done yet! Scramble past small crevasses and through a crack barely 1-foot wide where you'll need to remove your pack to fit. You then pass a few breaks in the trees and reach the Wampahoofus Trail (3.5/3,080). Bear right to head toward Butler Lodge, following the Wampahoofus Trail as it slabs out into a clearing with southerly views and glimpses of the cliffs below The Forehead. Butler Lodge is just ahead.

Named for Michael Taylor Butler, a long-time member of the GMC, the current lodge was rebuilt in 2000. It replaced an original structure that had become so dilapidated chains were needed to hold the bowed front wall in position. Aided by 41 helicopter supply drops, GMC crews raised the new shelter 3 feet off the ground and completed construction in only five weeks. The project used 43 tamarack and spruce logs harvested from state land.

From the shelter, head past the lodge to the Wallace Cutoff Trail, located opposite the privy path. Follow the single-track trail as it climbs up a small ladder and stone staircase to reach the Long Trail (3.6/2,880).

SIDE-TRIP TO TWIN BROOK TENTING AREA

To head to the Twin Brook Tenting Area—located 1.3 miles south—bear right on the Long Trail. The trail runs mostly level, then begins a slow descent. Dewey Mountain appears through the trees ahead as you approach a saddle and then curve down to the right. The forest transitions back to hardwoods. Spruce diminishes and quickly disappears, replaced by sugar maple, beech, striped maple, and yellow birch. The Long Trail levels out briefly by a flowing creek (fill up here if staying at Twin Brooks; this is the last water source) and then crosses a ski trail to resume its downward course. The path levels again and moseys along to reach the spur for Twin Brooks Tenting Area.

To continue your traverse across Mansfield, head north from the Wallace Cutoff junction (3.6/2,880). The Long Trail travels over bog bridging and then a giant pile of rocks, moss, and tree debris. The route steepens. Cliffs loom overhead. You traverse along their base to pass through the Needle's Eye, a passageway between two boulders. On the opposite side, the Forehead Bypass Trail comes in from the right (3.9/3,210), a bad-weather alternative if summit conditions are too gnarly. (It rejoins the Long Trail in 1.2 miles, just before The Nose.)

Remain on the Long Trail as it switchbacks left and starts ascending the cliffs along a hair-raising section of trail. The route follows a series of five ladders to negotiate near-vertical terrain, winding by nerve-wracking gullies and crevasses that would severely punish a misstep. The forest shrinks around you and dead snags increase; intermittent views look south toward Dewey Mountain. You can also spot the roof of Butler Lodge below.

After the final ladder, the trail makes a steady but less wild ascent past trees and more views to reach the Maple Ridge Trail (4.6/3,880). Looking east, you can see across Stowe Valley to the Worcester Range. South you can see Camel's Hump and the central Green Mountains. To the north, equipment and buildings mark the upper border of the Mount Mansfield Ski Area.

Butler Lodge

Hikers on Maple Ridge

Continue north on the Long Trail, ascending slightly to pass near the summit of the Forehead. Enjoy the views before reentering the trees. Abundant trillium, yellow clintonia, and bracken fern fill the understory as the trail cruises along a level, easy-going section through spruce-fir woods. The Forehead Bypass Trail rejoins from the right (4.9/3,880), and you emerge on an unpaved service road.

Antennas, fences, and small buildings pimple Mansfield's Nose, located above you to the right. You can get close to the summit area by turning right on the road here, but it's an eerie place. One sign informs you that RADIO FRE-QUENCY FIELD BEYOND THIS POINT MAY EXCEED THE FCC GENERAL PUBLIC EXPOSURE LIMIT.

Turning left on the service road, you quickly pass the Lakeview Trail on the left. This 0.8-mile loop travels along the slopes through thick krummholz and offers the occasional view, but is not really recommended. A weird humming noise accompanies you along the road, emanating from the multifarious tower equipment. Past the rocky cliffs of The Nose, you reach the Summit Station and its accompanying tower (5.2/3,850). A sign indicates that this is the Mount Mansfield Visitor Center, but it has stood empty for many years.

Views north follow the ridgeline to The Chin; the Adam's Apple is just beyond. The Long Trail continues on the opposite side of the Summit Station, reenters the trees, and then quickly crosses the road to leave the cankered proboscis behind. The trail soon emerges on open slabs with views west and reaches the Halfway House Trail (5.4/3,900).

Remain on the Long Trail as it traverses more rock slabs and passes the final tower. The Chin rises ahead of you. Maple and Sunset ridges extend their arms west. It's a good area for checking out the alpine tundra, but please stay on the trail while you look for ground-hugging plants like bilberry, Labrador tea, mountain sandwort, and creeping snowberry.

You next pass the Amherst Trail (5.5/3,930) by two large boulders. The Long Trail now alternately travels over solid rock and wooden walkways that protect the fragile tundra. Views are excellent. As you approach a high point, you pass a short spur trail on the left that leads to the Canyon North Trail (5.7/3,960). The view then expands east and looks toward the ski area's summer gondola, which ferries less energetic visitors to open views at 3,500 feet. To the northeast, below the Adam's Apple, the green roof of Taft Lodge peeks out; beyond it are the cliffs that hem Smugglers Notch.

Past this view-rich promontory, you undulate toward the Chin and reach the junction with the Cliff and Subway trails (5.9/4,080). A highly recommended and very adventurous side-trip starts from here (see later). A quick and easy excursion left down the Subway Trail provides a taste of it.

Climbing north, you ride the Long Trail along a rock ribbon highway and quickly pass the upper junction for the Subway Trail. Exposed rock intersperses with pockets of fir trees, sheltering Canada mayflower, bracken fern, and bunchberry in their sheltered crevices. Next up is the four-way junction with the Sunset Ridge and Profanity trails (6.2/4,270). Remain on the Long Trail, soon passing a sign for the West Chin Natural Area. Note that off-trail hiking is prohibited to protect the alpine vegetation. You climb upward, reach The Chin, and stand atop the highest point in Vermont (6.4/4,393).

Open views look north for the first time. You can see your next stop ahead, the Adam's Apple and adjacent Lakes of the Clouds. The deep cleft of Smugglers' Notch lies beyond. Beyond the Notch are Madonna Peak and the Smugglers' Notch Ski area, then Sterling Mountain, and the Butternut and Caraway Mountains. On clear days, the Cold Hollow Mountains peek out beyond Sterling. Views south look back over the now familiar features of Mansfield's long face.

The continuing hike now drops to the Adam's Apple and Taft Lodge below it before returning to the Chin for the journey home. (You can skip this 1.1-

mile segment and return directly to the trailhead from the summit via the Sunset Ridge Trail; see later.) Continuing north on the Long Trail, you drop steeply into Eagle Pass—a few sections require scrambling—and reach the saddle between The Chin and Adam's Apple. Here you meet the junction with the Hell Brook and Hope trails (6.6/4,050).

A short 0.4-mile side-loop circuits over Adam's Apple and past Lakes of the Clouds. To check it out, head left on the narrow and occasionally boggy Hell Brook Trail to reach the Adam's Apple Trail. Lakes of the Clouds is just

The Forehead

out-of-sight to your left; The Chin protrudes sharply above you. Turn right up the Adam's Apple Trail, which immediately makes a staircase-like climb to emerge on the open summit. Hop on the apple. A spur leads to a view north into Smugglers Notch.

Back at Eagle Pass, follow the Long Trail north as it descends through a fir corridor. The sloping rock underfoot is treacherous when wet; a small creek flows on or near the path. The trail levels, enters much taller forest, and reaches the Profanity Trail on the right (6.9/3,690). The spur to Taft Lodge is just ahead.

From the lodge, your journey home begins. Return to the Profanity Trail and follow it up the mountainside. The path crosses several rivulets, including the lodge's water source (keep it clean), and soon ascends a flowing creek. You pass a brief view west, then encounter a glade of hellebore and ferns. The trail proceeds along the cascading stream, offering intermittent views east as it continues a sustained climb. You pass bare cliffs on the right as the trail crests, and then traverse down to reach the Long Trail and Sunset Ridge Trail junction (7.4/4,270).

Down the Sunset Ridge Trail you go! An endless parade of vistas begins as you descend, quickly passing the Laura Cowles Trail on the left (7.5/4,230). The route next traverses right, dropping and entering a taller fir forest with some shelter from the elements. Past it, the trail climbs briefly to the ridgeline and the continuation of drool-worthy views. Along the mountain flanks to the north is adjacent Pleasant Ridge, which encloses hidden Thunder Basin to the south.

The route makes a mellow descent, remaining largely in the open with continuous views. Numerous cairns guide you along the way. The skeletal wind-blasted fingers of small fir trees provide mute evidence of winter's fury. Eventually the open rock slabs peter out and you enter a taller forest. The trail cuts left to offer one final view as it winds past blasted trees.

The gradient increases and soon scrambling is required. The forest greens with wood ferns in a lush understory. A series of stone staircases lead you downward. You pass mega-boulders with a passageway around them. Spruce and fir diminish. The trail switchbacks right and traverses briefly to reach the spur to Cantilever Rock (8.9/2,920).

Cantilever Rock is worth a visit. The 0.1-mile spur climbs briefly to reach a seamless mass of solid rock. Wedged within it is a huge finger of stone suspended horizontally from the cliff face. The walls drip with water, paper birch enhance the scene, and you can spot a view of Camel's Hump from surrounding boulders.

Back on the Sunset Ridge Trail, continue your steady descent into hardwood forest. The trail crosses a small brook on a plank bridge, then re-crosses it and slowly descends past extensive birch trees. After crossing another stream—the biggest yet—the path makes a level traverse, hops across another creek, and reaches the Laura Cowles Trail on the left (9.5/2,380). Remain on the Sunset Ridge Trail as it passes over two more streams to return to the CCC Road (9.6/2,350). Turn right and retrace your earlier route to the trailhead (10.6/1,870).

SIDE-TRIP: CLIFFS AND CANYONS LOOP

This 2.6-mile loop tours both sides of the mountain's upper slopes and runs parallel to the ridgeline. It includes some of the craziest sections of trail you'll find in New England, which is saying something. Only the fit and adventurous should attempt this strenuous excursion. Total elevation gain/loss is 1,100/1,100. Expect it to take 2 to 3 hours.

Consider stashing your packs somewhere safe before you head out—you won't fit through some sections with it on. From the four-way junction with the Long, Cliff, and Subway trails (0.0/4,080), strike out east down the Cliff Trail. The path descends steeply below a prominent cliff; notice Cave of the Winds, a large fissure. A path leads to its mouth where you can peer inside at wedged boulders and snow, which lingers into the summer. Light filters through the back of the drip-dripping tunnel.

Scrambling down steep boulder fields, the trail runs along the cliff base and starts to curve south. The Nose appears overhead. You reach the junction for the nearby Gondola (0.3/3,760), located 0.1 mile away to the left. A sign here warns you that THE CLIFF TRAIL IS EXTREMELY DIFFICULT AND IS NOT RECOMMENDED FOR SMALL CHILDREN OR INEXPERIENCED HIKERS. Experienced hikers should continue on the Cliff Trail as it runs below vertical outcrops and soon enters a long dark gash in the mountainside, a 3-foot gap between the cliff face and a two-story boulder. Basic climbing skills are required to descend into this dark pit of dripping walls and then clamber over a large chockstone near the bottom.

Once on the other side, the route descends over more boulders, passes an unsigned spur trail to the Gondola, and then passes close to a ski run. Now you begin a long undulating traverse, narrow and overgrown in spots, and littered with moose droppings. The route makes several steep drops and climbs, dishing up some good views of The Chin and Adam's Apple. Ladders aid you in spots; the last, tallest one marks your final climb to the Amherst Trail (1.1/3,820). Turn left to quickly reach the toll road.

Go right on the paved road, crossing the Long Trail and immediately reaching the Canyon Trail opposite a concrete bunker (1.2/3,850). Follow the Canyon Trail down the side of the mountain. You drop over loose rocks and pass open views west. The trail then goes through a crack in the rocks and enters the Canyon, a narrow cleft between the mountain and a giant section of cracked stone. It's narrow and progress can be difficult with a pack on. You make a spelunking scramble through a tiny passageway, emerging to reach the junction with the Halfway House Trail (1.8/3,700).

The trail now becomes the Canyon North Trail. After a slow rising traverse, you squeeze through another slot and reach a spur junction leading down from the Long Trail. Now the continuing route is called the Canyon North Extension (2.1/3,800).

Climbing, the trail leads past an open 180-degree view west and then heads through another tight cave passage. A rising traverse through a boulder maze takes you to a junction by another large cave passage, marked with a blue "Y" blaze. The Long Trail is only a short distance to your right, but continue straight instead into the deepest chasm yet. A ladder aids in the descent, a gift from a 1989 Eagle Scout Project. Once through, the trail winds upward past giant boulders and great views. It then banks right and quickly rejoins the Long Trail (2.5/4,100). Turn right to quickly return to the earlier junction with the Cliff and Canyon Trails (2.6/4,080).

INFORMATION

Underhill State Park, P.O. Box 249, Underhill Center, VT 05490, 802-899-3022, www.vtstateparks.com/htm/underhill.cfm; Green Mountain Club, 4711 Waterbury-Stowe Road, Waterbury Center, VT 05677, www.greenmountain-club.com, 802-244-7037

3

NEW HAMPSHIRE

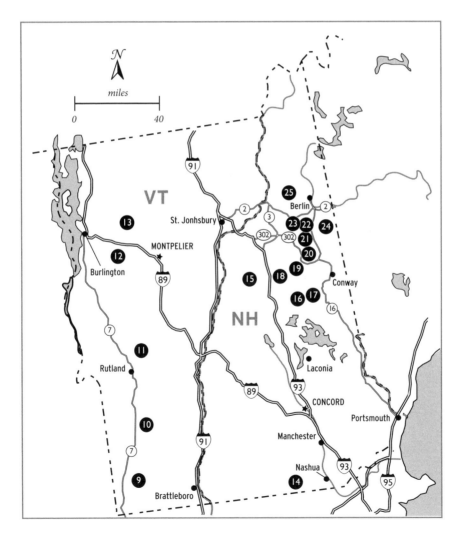

TRIP 14
GET WAPACKING

Location: The Wapack Trail, Southern New Hampshire
Highlight: Ridgeline backpacking less than 50 miles from Boston
Distance: 21.4 miles one-way
Total Elevation Gain/Loss: 5,100/5,030
Trip Length: 2 days
Difficulty: ★★
Recommended Map: *Guide to the Wapack Trail Map*, Friends of the Wapack

The Wapack Range rises above the dimpled landscape of southeast New Hampshire, a mountain range in miniature and the closest backpacking option to the Boston area. It has blueberries and view-rich stretches with few people, and makes an excellent early or late-season foray.

The Wapack Trail runs the length of the range and earns its name from the starting and ending points (Mount WAtatic and PACK Monadnock). When it opened in 1923, it became the first interstate hiking route in the Northeast. Today it is maintained by the nonprofit Friends of the Wapack, which publishes the comprehensive Wapack Trail Guide.

HIKE OVERVIEW

The hike is a point-to-point journey from Mount Watatic in north-central Massachusetts to the trail's terminus at Pack Monadnock in southern New Hampshire. The route connects a series of linear ridges, dipping between them as it goes, and is most commonly done south to north, as is described here. It is a route of intermittent wilderness; the trail often encounters dirt and paved roads. The trip's only overnight options are located 8 miles from the trailhead, dividing the journey into north and south segments of 13 miles and 8, respectively. A car shuttle is required. Dogs are permitted.

OVERNIGHT OPTIONS

The overnight options are located near the hike's midpoint at Windblown Cross-country Ski Area, which maintains two shelters for backpacker use. Reservations are required and can be made by calling 603-878-2869. A fee is charged.

THE WAPACK TRAIL, SOUTHERN NEW HAMPSHIRE

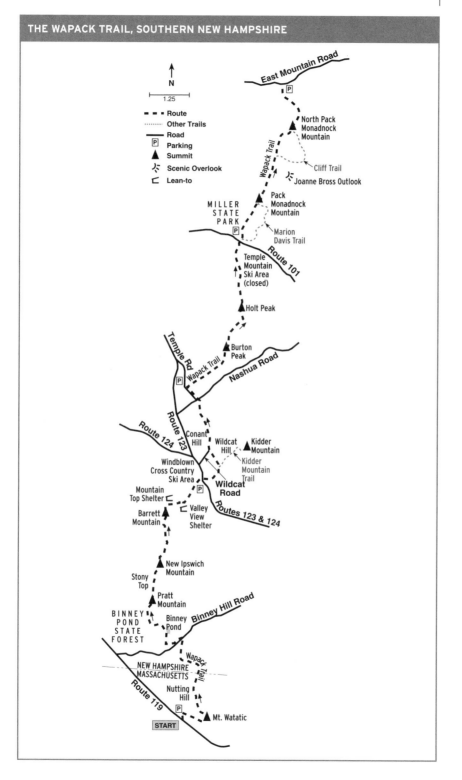

N
1.25

- - - Route
.... Other Trails
——— Road
P Parking
▲ Summit
⚐ Scenic Overlook
⊏ Lean-to

East Mountain Road

P

North Pack
Monadnock
Mountain

Wapack Trail

Cliff Trail

Joanne Bross Outlook

MILLER
STATE
PARK

Pack
Monadnock
Mountain

P

Marion
Davis Trail

Route 101

Temple
Mountain
Ski Area
(closed)

Holt Peak

Temple Rd

Wapack Trail

Burton
Peak

Nashua Road

P

Route 124

Route 123

Conant
Hill

Wildcat
Hill

Kidder
Mountain

Kidder
Mountain
Trail

Windblown
Cross Country
Ski Area

Wildcat
Road

P

Mountain
Top Shelter ⊏

Valley
View
Shelter

Routes 123 & 124

Barrett
Mountain

New Ipswich
Mountain

Stony
Top

Pratt
Mountain

Binney Hill Road

BINNEY
POND
STATE
FOREST

Binney
Pond

Wapack Trail

NEW HAMPSHIRE
MASSACHUSETTS

Route 119

Nutting
Hill

P

START

Mt. Watatic

The Mountain Top Shelter, 7.9 miles from the trailhead, perches at 1,800 feet in a spruce-ringed clearing near the top of a ski run. Views scatter about the area, including glimpses of nearby Kidder Mountain, the rolling hills to the northwest, a profile of Mount Monadnock, and the Boston skyline. Amenities include a fire ring and privy. No water is available nearby; the closest source is down the Wapack Trail near the Barrett's Backbone ski run.

The Valley View Shelter, 8.1 miles from the trailhead, nestles at 1,450 feet in the middle of the cross-country ski area. The shelter features a large deck with rocking chairs, a fire ring and full stack of wood, and an outhouse attached directly to the shelter. A stream flows right below the shelter. Red oak and yellow birch shade the forested dale. There are good tentsites along adjacent ski paths.

TO REACH THE TRAILHEAD

To Reach the Southern (Starting) Trailhead. Follow Route 119 west 1.4 miles past the Route 119/191 junction in Ashburnham. The trailhead parking area is located on the north side of the road; look for the Midstate Trail signs. Approaching on Route 119 from the east, the trailhead is located 1.8 miles past the state line crossing.

To Reach the Northern (Ending) Trailhead. Head to the town of Peterborough and proceed east on Sand Hill Road, located 0.5 mile north of the downtown bridge. In 2.9 miles, Sand Hill Road becomes East Mountain Road. Follow unpaved East Mountain Road for 1.5 miles to the trailhead on the south (right) side of the road. Park by the roadside.

HIKE DESCRIPTION

Throughout the hike, abundant yellow triangle blazes mark the route of the Wapack Trail. A sign at the trailhead (0.0/1,250) indicates upcoming distances in remarkably precise detail. Cross the gate and head down the wide dirt road, immediately passing a pond with signs of past beaver activity. Hemlock, red maple, yellow birch, and red oak shade the rocky road as it climbs slightly to reach a posted junction (0.2/1,270). Turn right to follow the Wapack/Midstate Trail.

Now single-track, the path quickly crosses a bubbling stream and winds between a cloven boulder to reach the base of Mount Watatic's slopes near ash and peeling hop hornbeam. The route begins a rising traversing through hemlock, soon curving left to make a steeper ascent of the boulder-pocked hillside. Black birch and some old gnarly beech can be spotted as you climb. Reaching the base of solid rock slabs, the trail takes a direct line upward to reach the top of the outcrop, where views look south over the rolling Massachusetts landscape.

From here, the trail curves right and runs level along a stone wall. The spiny needles of red spruce join the forest mix. Intermittent views pass by as you follow bedrock and then reach a ledge with more views to the south; nearby Mount Wachusett bulges as the centerpiece. The trail curves back to the left and resumes its climb. It bends right again, leveling out shortly before reaching the remains of an old shelter, more ruins than structure. From here, a brief climb leads you to the open summit (1.2/1,832).

Enjoy the 360-degree view. East is the Boston skyline, south the hump of Mount Wachusett. The nearby ridges and peaks of the Wapack Range run north—your continuing route. Look for the summit tower atop Pack Monadnock, your ultimate destination. Watatic's lower south summit is visible nearby, readily accessible by use paths.

Near the summit marker, a granite monument proclaims the mountain saved. In 2002, developers purchased the mountaintop to install a cell phone tower. The dedicated work of local conservation groups led instead to its protection as parkland.

Continuing north from the summit, the Wapack Trail briefly follows the road that was constructed to service the never-built cell tower. The route quickly splits left off the road and onto single-track, passing hobblebush for the first time. The trail descends past hemlocks and along stone walls, then widens and parallels a wall. The trail reaches a saddle, narrows, and then climbs atop Nutting Hill (1.9/1,610). Cairns mark the open summit, which offers views south toward Watatic's slopes.

Past the peak, the trail widens and quickly reaches the junction with the Midstate Trail on the left. Bear right to remain on the Wapack Trail as it cruises along a wide woods road lined with stone walls and beech-oak forest. You cross the state line at a gap in a stone wall (2.4/1,540), where mileage markers indicate upcoming distances.

As you head into New Hampshire, you pass through an area logged in the recent past. Stumps are evident and, as the road bears left and descends, you pass an old landing area where cut logs where stacked and loaded for shipment. The trail next forks at unpaved Binney Hill Road (3.5/1,380). Bear left and then turn right on a smaller woods road—watch for the double-blaze and sign indicating this turn-off.

You pass an abandoned home surrounded by decrepit sailboats, lawn mowers, old farm equipment, and other treasures. Now rising, the trail encounters the swampy outflow from Binney Pond, enters tiny Binney Pond State Forest, and curves right to wind along the boggy shore, more marsh than pond. The route moseys past oaks and painted trillium—blooming in May—and then traverses the slopes above the water. A posted spring can be found at the far end of the pond, the last quality water source for the next 4 miles.

From here, the trail rises steeply past large sugar maples and oaks on a rocky hillside. Look also for red trillium, jack-in-the-pulpit, and red elderberry—indicators of an enriched soil environment. As you steadily climb, glimpses behind you look toward Binney Pond and Watatic; a posted overlook at the top offers the best vista.

The trail crests atop Pratt Mountain (5.0/1,817), where open ledges look north and west toward your upcoming route, a ridgeline topped by New Ipswich Mountain a few miles ahead. The continuing trail reaches another clearing, this one revealing views of nearby Mount Monadnock in full profile. Twisted oaks, red maples, and blueberries line the trail as it continues over stretches of solid bedrock and past more good views east and west. Stony Top marks the end of this ridge section (5.5/1,770), where an open slab offers unobstructed views west toward Mountain Pond and Monadnock beyond.

The trail descends, returning to forest and reaching the saddle below New Ipswich Mountain. Water trickles in the depression. The orange-blazed Pratt Pond Trail joins from the right. Climbing up New Ipswich, you pass stone walls en route to a small boulder at the viewless summit (6.1/1,884). A brief drop leads past more open ledges to a brief level stretch. The broad dome of approaching Barrett Mountain appears at times; the Pack Monadnocks are visible in the distance. The trail reaches the saddle below Barrett Mountain, where flowing water can be found (6.9/1,600).

The rocky route now resumes climbing, passing the red mottled leaves of trout lilies as it goes. The gradient eases in a spruce grove, and the trail winds over the viewless summit (7.5/1,830). The level duff-covered path heads through stands of dense spruce and soon reaches the boundary of the Windblown Cross-Country ski area (7.8/1,820). Bright yellow signs indicate the East Side Drop on your right; the posted Wapack Trail turns right just beyond. If you're heading to the Mountain Top Shelter, remain on the wide ridge-top trail for another 100 yards.

To continue north, follow the bright yellow Wapack Track sign, which leads down a steep drop. The descent twice crosses the signed Barrett's Backbone ski trail, turns left by a flowing stream, and then drops alongside it to the Valley Trail. The Valley View Shelter is visible to the right. Cross the Valley Trail and head up the opposite slope. The route winds through a maze of trails—watch for blazes—eventually becoming single-track and heading toward Stony Top (the second promontory by that name). The trail climbs briefly to reach the small clearing, which provides views back to Mount Watatic—the old ski runs are apparent from this angle—as well as to the Boston skyline. Watch for the blazes as the trail heads down and crosses numerous paths to reach Route 123/124 (9.1/1,450).

Turn right, follow the pavement a short distance, and turn left onto Old Rindge Road, located across from Wapack Road. A trail sign, blazes, and a small parking area mark the spot. The single-track trail winds below a private residence and edges along a large field. Curving right, you briefly climb to reenter the woods, cruise through young forest, and reach a woods road. Turn left to quickly reach a power line corridor (9.7/1,550). The posted side-trip to Kidder Mountain starts here.

SIDE-TRIP TO KIDDER MOUNTAIN

1,805-foot Kidder Mountain is crowned with abundant blueberries and open views east and south. A side-trip to its summit requires a 1.8-mile round-trip hike with 350 feet of elevation gain and loss. Lowbush blueberries flourish around the ledgy summit area, ripening in early to mid-summer. The route initially follows the power line mud road, then cuts off it to the left and makes a traversing rise. After climbing through hemlock groves, you enter a recently harvested area and then resume a traversing rise over rocky outcrops. Stone walls and cairns line the final section to the top.

From the Kidder Mountain Trail junction, the Wapack Trail follows a gentle woods road and then quickly reaches unpaved Wildcat Road (10.1/1,440), where you turn right. Wildcat Hill Road forks right to become a private driveway (10.4/1,430) but you continue straight on a less-used woods road CLOSED TO MOTORIZED VEHICLES.

The route slowly descends on the overgrown road parallel to a small brook, the last source for the next 6 miles. The route skirts around a beaver pond and then reaches posted Todd Road. Cross the road and follow a nice wide path between stone walls, running next to land owned by the Monadnock Conservancy on the right. To avoid wet sections, the trail occasionally parallels the road on single-track—watch for blazes.

The route rejoins the road, crosses a brook, and then quickly encounters paved Temple and Nashua roads (11.3/1,250). The route continues straight here, following Temple Road for the longest paved section of the journey. You pass numerous homes on your way to the junction of Greenleaf and Temple roads (11.7/1,300); a small parking area sits across from the continuing trail.

The double-track trail heads straight up from here to begin the 2.2-mile stretch known as the Cabot Skyline. A sign and map indicate the origin of the name (Thomas D. Cabot donated a trail easement across these lands). You ascend past an abandoned house on the right and the trail narrows, becomes rockier, and begins to run parallel to a stone wall. You next reach the posted spur to the Roger Myrick Overlook (12.1/1,700), which offers a view south to Barrett and Kidder mountains and Mount Watatic beyond.

You pass another posted overlook with a similar view, then the rocky trail makes its final rise to the ridgeline. Now slowly rising, you pass stunted oak, beech, paper birch, red maple, and abundant cairns. The trail drops briefly through a spruce grove, resumes climbing, parallels a stone wall, and then curves left away from it to reach the Berry Pasture Trail on the left (13.0/1,970). You crest posted Burton Peak (13.1/2,020) and then resume alongside the earlier stone wall, soon crossing it.

The trail undulates along, passes another outlook to the northeast, then comes upon a nice rock with views of Monadnock. The stone wall curves away again, then reappears in the saddle below Holt Peak (13.9/1,940). The route bottoms out, leaves the wall, and climbs steeply past ledgy outcrops to reach the posted viewless summit (14.2/2,045), accessible by a short spur.

Pack Monadnock peeks through the trees north as you descend on the widening trail, which becomes steadily more road-like and soon reaches the first unobstructed view north to Pack Monadnock. Bottoming out in stands of juniper, the trail quickly returns to single-track and enters a sculpture garden of stones. Two head-high mega-cairns hulk on the left, followed by a series of rock piles and other creations, including several chairs.

From here, the trail rises briefly past smaller cairns, then resumes its descent and drops into a spruce-filled saddle. Slowly rising among conifers, the trail reaches a fork—bear left (watch for blazes). You cruise around a cell tower and building, then reach an access road offering full views of Pack Monadnock and route 101 below. The route follows the service road down, and soon bears left at a double blaze (15.5/1,770) to immediately pass the top of a defunct ski lift and the collapsed remains of a shelter. Welcome to Temple Mountain Ski Area, which shuttered operations in 2001. (Efforts are underway to transfer the property to the state park system.)

The route descends an old ski run and then rejoins the service road, losing about 100 feet of elevation before turning left again to descend another ski run. Blazes on small wooden signs and wooden posts help navigate this tricky section. The trail turns right near the bottom (within sight of the lower lift), cuts across old roads and heads to Route 101 (16.0/1,470).

Cross the highway to the large Miller State Park parking area, where the Wapack and Marion Davis trails strike out from the lot. The blue-blazed Marion Davis Trail heads straight and to the right, but your continuing route on the Wapack Trail leads left past nice second-growth red oaks, yellow birch, and beech. You quickly cross the summit access road near the base of rock cliffs and slabs. The trail now ascends steeply over blocky talus, with views of Mount Monadnock and the Temple Mountain ski area behind you.

Climbing Pack Monadnock

You climb through a rock maze, then traverse left through a more forested section before turning steeply uphill again over more loose rock and talus. The trail continues over bedrock, passing a small white pine growing directly out of solid rock. The trail eases above the cliffs and drops into a small gully with trickling water—the first source in 6 miles.

The trail slowly ascends through increasing spruce forest, crosses a stone wall, and steadily rises parallel to the out-of-sight, but audible, summit road. As you approach the summit, you spot the painted red circles of the summit loop (17.3/2,220). The Wapack Trail curves right to join it, follows a wide gravel path, and quickly reaches the often crowded summit complex (17.4/2,280), which includes a parking area, fire lookout tower (closed though you can climb the stairs for a view), picnic tables, air quality station, and an old stone shelter constructed by the Civilian Conservation Corps (CCC).

The view from the tower stairs is excellent. The city of Manchester dots the landscape northeast; the three hills of Pawtuckaway State Park are visible beyond. North is the undeveloped summit of North Pack Monadnock—your final peak. Mount Monadnock stands out in profile to the west-northwest and the mountains of Vermont are visible along the northwest horizon. Looking south, the whole line of the Wapack Range traces your route to this point.

Continuing north, the Wapack Trail initially follows a gravel path past picnic tables and more views and reaches the Raymond Trail on the left. The Wapack Trail then travels along a stretch of solid rock and begins to descend. You cross trickling water and reach a spur to Joanne Bross outlook, which offers another view northeast.

The path drops steadily and makes a few switchbacks. Surrounding spruce woods transition to hardwoods as the descent steepens. Paper and yellow birch appear in abundance. You reach a saddle (17.9/1,730) and shortly afterward cross into The Nature Conservancy's Joanne Bass Bross Preserve. You undulate through dense spruce stands, rising steadily to top out by a cairn, then drop on a root-laced trail to quickly encounter the Cliff Trail entering from the right (19.1/1,860). An indication of the junction is painted on the rocks.

The rocky trail runs level past conifers, encounters a stone wall, then climbs steeply and briefly parallels the wall before curving left to start a rising traverse. You make a slow curving switchback right and continue to rise, then cut left again and climb up solid rock to reach the summit cairn of North

Pack Monadnock (19.8/2,276). Bare rock slabs here provide vistas west and northwest, which include the prominent mass of Mount Kearsarge. If you look closely at the slabs, you'll notice grooves and polished rock along a northwest-southeast line—evidence of the ice sheet that smothered this summit during the last Ice Age.

The trail turns left at the cairn, passes a second summit knob, and then descends directly over solid rock through spruce forest. After a few switchbacks, you resume a steep descent, passing over talus and rock outcrops before leveling out and hiking parallel to a stone wall. White pine and birch reappear, and you encounter more open slabs. A gentle winding descent leads past numerous views north and extensive juniper trees. A final steep drop returns you to a mellow traverse that crosses several small trickles. You then curve right by the most substantial brook yet and descend parallel to it, crossing it shortly before reaching Old Mountain Road and hike's end (21.4/1,320).

INFORMATION

Friends of the Wapack, P.O. Box 115, West Peterborough, NH 03468, info@wapack.org, www.wapack.org

TRIP 15
CHARGE THE MOOSE

Location: Mount Moosilauke, White Mountain National Forest
Highlight: Riveting brookside ascent to an alpine summit
Distance: 3.0 miles round-trip to Beaver Brook Shelter, 7.6 miles round-trip to summit
Total Elevation Gain/Loss: 1,800/1,800 to shelter, 3,100/3,100 to summit
Trip Length: 1–2 days
Difficulty: ★★★
Recommended Map: *AMC White Mountain Guide, Map 4: Moosilauke-Kinsman,* AMC Books

Mount Moosilauke rises alone, the westmost massif of the White Mountains. Isolated from adjoining peaks, hemmed by deep valleys, this 4,802-foot peak offers 360-degree panoramas from an open summit of alpine tundra. Beaver Brook scores the mountain's east flank, tumbling down continuous cascades and providing the most direct route to the summit. The Appalachian Trail (AT) ascends alongside it, climbing the mountain with the aid of 140 wooden steps and more than a dozen metal railings riveted into the rock.

Mount Moosilauke boasts more history than perhaps any peak in the White Mountains save Mount Washington. In 1860, the first building was constructed atop the peak. During the winter of 1869 to 1870, Joseph Huntington and Amos Clough spent two months sheltered inside. The duo were the first to measure above-treeline winter weather conditions in the Whites, including winds in excess of 100 miles per hour, a record at the time.

Between 1899 and 1914, logging operations clear-cut nearly the entire mountain (the little old-growth that remained was demolished by the 1938 hurricane). But following passage of the Weeks Act in 1911, the federal government began purchasing land for the White Mountain National Forest and acquired 7,000 acres on Mount Moosilauke in 1914. In 1920, the Summit House proprietors donated their land holdings to Dartmouth College, including the summit and a broad swatch of land in Jobildunk Ravine on the mountain's southeast side. Dartmouth has acquired additional parcels since, and today owns 4,500 acres. The Dartmouth Outing Club (DOC)—the oldest outdoor club in the nation

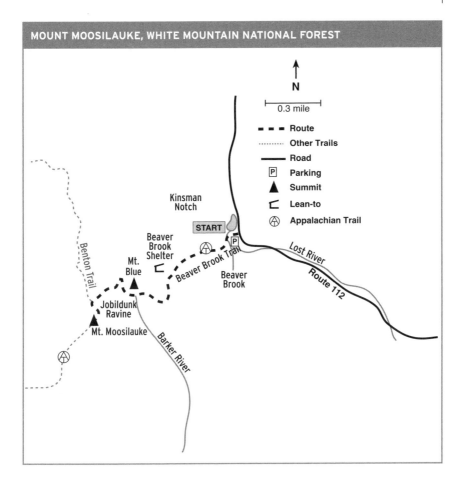

MOUNT MOOSILAUKE, WHITE MOUNTAIN NATIONAL FOREST

maintains trails, posts a summit caretaker during the busy summer months to protect the alpine vegetation, and operates the Ravine Lodge at the base of the mountain.

Most people agree that the name of the mountain comes from the original Algonquin designation—translated it means "bald place"—but pronunciation is a different matter. Whether it's pronounced Moose-a-lock-ee or Moose-a-lock depends on whom you talk to; it's surprising how many people have an opinion.

HIKE OVERVIEW

This short trip is a fun overnighter or an exciting day hike. The route follows the Beaver Brook Trail for its entire length. The first half is very steep—climbing 1,700 feet in 1.2 miles—and travels over wet rock slabs with the aid of wooden steps and hand rails. Descent is a knee-compressing challenge, more difficult in wet conditions—this is not a good rainy day excursion. Beaver Brook Shelter is located at the trip's midpoint. Spending the night here allows you to climb to the summit early before crowds arrive en masse. The trail and summit are popular—come midweek if possible. The Beaver Brook Trail is part of the AT, and consequently receives heavy thru-hiker use in July and early August.

OVERNIGHT OPTION

Beaver Brook Shelter provides the only real overnight option along this hike. Dispersed camping is permitted 200 feet or more away from the trail, but there is essentially no flat ground on the mountain's steep slopes, especially along this trail. Camping is prohibited within 0.25 mile of Route 112.

Beaver Brook Shelter is located 1.5 miles and 1,750 feet above the trailhead. Situated at 3,650 feet, it features a northeast view that stretches as far as Mount Washington. Three shady tentsites are located near the shelter. A small creek dribbles nearby. Campfires are permitted in the shelter fire ring only.

TO REACH THE TRAILHEAD

Take I-93 to Exit 32 in Lincoln. Head west on Route 112 for 6.5 miles. The large trailhead parking lot is on the left. A WMNF parking permit is required.

HIKE DESCRIPTION

Rocky cliffs loom above the parking lot. The Beaver Brook watershed can be seen draining the mountain's flank. A sign warns of the approaching challenge: SECTIONS OF THIS TRAIL ARE STEEP AND CHALLENGING. KNOW YOUR LIMITA-TIONS AND HEED THEM. The white-blazed trail begins at the back of the lot (0.0/1,870), where shrubby pin cherry can be spotted on the right, mountain maple, beech, and paper birch on the left.

The trail immediately bears left at a signed trailhead junction by Route 112 and enters thicker forest. Yellow birch and hobblebush highlight the woods. You quickly rock-hop across a flowing brook and head toward another stream crossing—this one on a solid wooden bridge. After crossing another stream on a bridge, you reach the start of the upcoming climb (0.3/1,890).

Here a sign fashioned by the DOC warns: THIS TRAIL IS EXTREMELY TOUGH. IF YOU LACK EXPERIENCE, PLEASE USE ANOTHER TRAIL. TAKE SPECIAL CARE AT THE CASCADES TO AVOID TRAGIC RESULTS. Taking special care, begin the direct ascent. Soon the sound of rushing water infuses the air and the trail quickly reaches its first waterfall view. Brookside boulders sit below a series of cascades that curtain the rock with spray.

From here, the trail ascends a veritable staircase of rock and wood steps. Rungs drilled into the rock provide handholds as you climb. Beaver Brook flows parallel to the trail on the right, sliding down smooth rock faces. The cascades go on and on. Another beautiful waterfall view opens up; a sheet of water pours down from the forest above, dropping down a long series of falls.

Up and up the trail climbs, rising over sections impossible to climb without the aid of wooden steps. The trail gradient finally eases from its ladder-like angle and passes an overgrown logging road in thick spruce-fir forest.

Beaver Falls

Though less steep, the trail remains very rocky as it curves away from Beaver Brook and banks left up a small tributary gurgling over mossy stones. A steady climb through boulder fields leads to the short spur trail for Beaver Brook Shelter (1.5/3,650).

The summit beckons. From the shelter junction, the trail makes a rising traverse to reach the Asquam Ridge Trail on the left (1.9/3,970). Turn right to remain on the Beaver Brook Trail as it first runs level and then slowly ascends. Views soon open up to the south, peering over the deep valley of Jobildunk Ravine. A glacial cirque, Jobildunk Ravine is reportedly named for three nineteenth-century loggers—Joe, Bill, and Duncan—who worked in the area.

Traversing over rock slabs, the trail then curves right to skirt the 4,529-foot summit of Mount Blue. Views west appear for the first time. The trail drops briefly and then rises to meet the Benton Trail (3.4/4,580). Bear left on the Benton Trail to continue the ascent and soon enter the alpine zone. The open lawn-like terrain of this alpine tundra is tempting to walk on, but stay on the trail as you climb the last hundred feet of elevation to the summit (3.8/4,802).

The stone foundation of the old Summit House (1860–1943) sits almost directly atop the peak, its thick walls providing shelter from the wind. Soak in the 360-degree view. Mount Washington can be spied 31 miles away to the northeast, peeking over the long spine of Franconia Ridge (Trip 18); the pyramidal summit of mile-high Mount Lafayette caps the north ridge. To the southeast, the Sandwich Range (Trips 16-17) fills the horizon and the shimmering waters of Lake Winnipesaukee can be spotted 35 miles away. West, the distant spine of the Green Mountains dimples the horizon—Mount Mansfield (Trip 13) is almost due northwest and the prominent knob of Camel's Hump (Trip 12) a few degrees south of that. After all the fun, return the way you came.

INFORMATION

White Mountain National Forest, Pemigewasset Ranger District, 1171 NH Route 175, Holderness, NH 3245, 603-536-1315, www.fs.fed.us/r9/forests/white_mountain; Dartmouth Outing Club, 113 Robinson Hall, Hanover, NH 03755, 603-626-2429, thedoc@dartmouth.edu, www.dartmouth.edu/~doc

TRIP 16
BASIC SANDWICH

Location: Sandwich Range Wilderness, White Mountain National Forest
Highlights: Sweeping summits, easy access, minimal crowds
Distance: 13.6 miles round-trip
Total Elevation Gain/Loss: 4,750/4,750
Trip Length: 2 days
Difficulty: ★★★★
Recommended Map: *AMC White Mountains Map, Map 3: Crawford Notch-Sandwich Range,* AMC Books

The Sandwich Range rises as the southern front of the White Mountains, a rugged mountain spine uncrossed by any road for more than 25 miles. Lofty summits pierce the sky, including six 4,000-footers. And the wild heart of these mountains is protected within the 36,000-acre Sandwich Range Wilderness. Near its center, Mounts Whiteface and Passaconaway encircle a deep valley known as the Bowl. Exciting ridgeline trails and far-reaching views are the highlights of this ring around the Bowl.

HIKE OVERVIEW

The hike makes a clockwise loop around the Bowl, ascending 4,020-foot Mount Whiteface via the view-rich Blueberry Ledge Trail before circling around on the Rollins Trail to the base of Mount Passaconaway, where a short side-trip leads to summit and views. On the loop's return leg, the route follows the Square Ledge Trail past its namesake outcrop and then follows a burbling brook along the Kelley Trail back to the trailhead. A map of the area reveals myriad other trails that can be used to return to the trailhead, but the described hike reaches the most highlights. Note that water is scarce for long sections. Dogs and campfires are allowed.

OVERNIGHT OPTIONS

There are no officially designated campsites, but three former shelter sites offer good tenting opportunities. Dispersed camping is also permitted, but finding a site outside of these locations is difficult in the steep terrain.

The first two sites are located near the summit of Mount Whiteface. The locations are lofty, with dramatic views only a few strides away, but there is

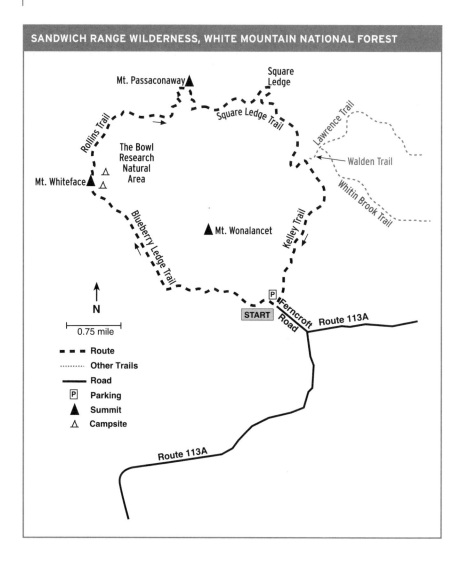

SANDWICH RANGE WILDERNESS, WHITE MOUNTAIN NATIONAL FOREST

Square Ledge

Mt. Passaconaway ▲

Square Ledge Trail

Rollins Trail

Lawrence Trail

The Bowl
Research
Natural
Area

△
△

Walden Trail

Mt. Whiteface ▲

Whitin Brook Trail

Blueberry Ledge Trail

▲ Mt. Wonalancet

Kelley Trail

N

0.75 mile

P

START

Ferncroft Road

Route 113A

Route 113A

- - - Route
.... Other Trails
——— Road
P Parking
▲ Summit
△ Campsite

no reliable water for several miles in either direction. Obtain water near the trailhead or bring it with you from the get-go.

The first, lower, site was once occupied by Camp Shehadi, at 3,900 feet only a short distance from open granite knobs on Whiteface's summit ridge. Located 3.8 miles from the trailhead, the small site is ringed by mountain ash, paper birch, fir, and spruce, and offers space for only a single group. Camp Heermance once perched a short distance past Camp Shehadi, right by the summit. Now an open clearing tucks away in the trees by a large boulder. Tentsites are ample.

The third site is located near the midpoint of the hike at 3,420 feet, 6.6 miles from the trailhead and close to the Passaconaway summit loop trail. The former site of Camp Rich, the substantial clearing is situated by a briskly flowing stream but lacks the dramatic views of the first two sites. Numerous tentsites can be found in a large clearing, along with several others in the trees.

TO REACH THE TRAILHEAD

Take Route 113 north from Highway 25 (the turn-off is located 3.6 miles west of the Route 25/16 junction). In 0.4 mile, turn left to remain on Route 113 and proceed 2.4 miles to reach the junction with Route 113A. Continue straight (north) on 113A, following it for 6.5 miles as it heads northwest and then west through the small community of Wonalancet. Turn right on unpaved Ferncroft Road, located next to the white church, and proceed 0.5 mile to a turn-off on the right for the designated parking area. All of the property around you is private—please respect the landowners and park only in this designated area.

HIKE DESCRIPTION

An information kiosk at the trailhead marks the start of your journey (0.0/1,170). To reach the Blueberry Ledge Trail, follow the signs back down the parking lot road. As you go, enjoy the idyllic view of a nearby farmhouse and Mount Whiteface (left) and the symmetrical dome of 2,780-foot Mount Wonalancet (right). The surroundings here are private property. Your passage is granted through the owners' generosity; please remain on established paths. If you need to obtain water, wait until you reach the Blueberry Ledge Cutoff Trail and its river access a short distance ahead.

Turn right on Ferncroft Road, parallel the Wonalancet River a short distance, and then turn left to cross it on Squirrel Bridge Road (0.3/1,200). Follow the smaller road past several private residences, watching for the trail signs that indicate your route. After passing a final home on the left (#32), your backcountry journey begins.

The forest encroaches around the single-track path. You pass the signed junction for the Pasture Path on the left (0.5/1,210) and then quickly reach the Blueberry Ledge Cutoff Trail (0.6/1,250) on the right. Follow the Cutoff Trail, a slightly rougher but more scenic alternative, which rejoins the Blueberry Ledge Trail in 1.4 mile. The path immediately leads down to the river by the National Forest boundary and then traces along the banks on a narrow path. Moisture-loving white ash and hemlock shade the forest. Granite boulders litter the streambed.

Looking east toward Passaconaway (left) and the distant profile of Chocorua

You pass an unsigned spur on the right that leads to the Dicey's Mill Trail on the far side of the river, then continue on the Cutoff Trail as it turns away from the water and quickly rises above it. Now climbing, the trail passes through a forest of sugar maple and beech and reaches the signed Wilderness boundary (1.5/1,550). The path then ascends past granite boulders to reach the ridgeline and the Blueberry Ledge Trail (2.0/2,140).

Turn right to start heading up the mountain on the Blueberry Ledge Trail. Established in 1899, it is one of the oldest actively used trails in the Whites. The rocky route rises steadily, offering occasional views toward nearby Mount Wonalancet. The surrounding woods gradually transition to spruce-fir and soon the trail steepens markedly. The trail ascends a veritable rock staircase past tantalizing views, and then briefly levels. The summit of Mount White-face looms ahead just before you reach the Tom Wiggins Trail on the right (3.2/3,220).

Remain on the Blueberry Ledge Trail, which briefly eases as it passes through young spruce-fir forest to reach the base of the summit dome. You now begin the final ascent, the most radical section yet. At 3,500 feet, the trail emerges atop the first of many open ledges with exceptional views. Open vistas look southwest to the prominent massif of Sandwich Dome (3,980) and, at the southern edge of the range, the distinctive pyramid of Mount Israel (2,630).

The trail next ascends a very steep slab that may be difficult to negotiate in wet or icy conditions. Holes in the rock used to support steps, but they are no longer present. Scrambling is required to surmount this obstacle and enjoy the reward of a mouth-watering view.

Outstanding views east open up. The Bowl Natural Research Area fills the valley below you. Directly beneath you, the ravine's west slopes harbor old-growth red spruce forest, one of the largest stands in the state. The stature of these untouched trees is apparent even from here. Looming over the Bowl is the distinctive summit of Mount Passaconaway, your upcoming route. In the eastern distance are Mount Paugus (3,198) and the rocky summit profile of Mount Chocorua (3,354)—future destinations on the Super Sandwich hike (Trip 17).

From here, the route navigates a jumbled fortress of rocks, scrambling up slabs and small gullies. Ledge after ledge after ledge offer views, providing ample opportunities to rest and savor the scenery as you progress up the mountain. Most outlooks peer east, but a few look west toward the mountain flanks. Giant rock slabs paste against the mountainside and help give the mountain its name.

The trail crests the summit ridge, reenters the forest, and quickly reaches a spur on the right to the former site of Camp Shehadi (3.8/3,900), which was dismantled in 2002. Just beyond, you reach some open granite knobs where the McCrillis Path enters from the left (3.9/3,920). Far-reaching views south greet you here. The rounded massif of the Ossipee Mountains bulges from the landscape due south. To its right is Lake Winnipesaukee; the Belknap Range can be spotted beyond the water. To the southwest, Red Hill (2,030) separates Squam Lake and Lake Winnipesaukee. Looking southeast, you can see the ocean on a clear day, a distance of more than 60 miles.

Look at the rocks underfoot. Old names are also carved into the rock, including one from 1896, and you can spot the grooves of glacial striations. A mile-high sheet of ice smothered all of New Hampshire during the last Ice Age—even Mount Washington succumbed. The ice left its signature here, too.

Just past this viewpoint is the former site of Camp Heermance. Built in 1912, it was removed in late 2001 as part of the Forest Service's management plan for wilderness areas. Past the shelter site, the trail descends to a small saddle where views west and northwest reveal Mount Osceola (4,340), right, and Mount Tecumseh (4,003), left. The Kate Sleeper Trail joins from the left (4.0/3,890), marking the end of the Blueberry Ledge Trail. Continue straight on the Rollins Trail, which rises to the wooded and viewless summit of Whiteface (4.2/4,020).

The trail now drops, passing a brief view toward Mount Wonalancet and the parking area. As the trail steepens, look for the summit of Mount Washington, which rises north above the distant peaks of the Pemigewasset Wilderness. You pass a spur to another open panorama east and then encounter a view northwest toward the peaks of the nearby Tripyramid massif.

The route now becomes mostly forested and descends steadily over rocky terrain. Leveling out, you next pass among paper birch and hobblebush, and reach the Dicey's Mill Trail on the right (6.4/3,250). This marks the end of the Rollins Trail. Bear left on the Dicey's Mill Trail, which climbs past a seeping spring and then crosses a flowing brook—the first reliable water in 6 miles. You next encounter the East Loop Trail (6.6/3,420). Turn left on the Dicey's Mill Trail to immediately reach the site of former Camp Rich. Also known as Passaconaway Lodge, Camp Rich was built in 1891 by Charles Fay, one of the AMC's founders. It fell into disrepair and collapsed in 2000.

To ascend Passaconaway—a strenuous climb that rewards with a panoramic view north—continue up the Dicey's Mill Trail. (Alternatively you can skip the summit and follow the East Loop for 0.2 mile to the continuing route on the Walden Trail.) The Dicey's Mill Trail ascends switchbacks and rocky terrain, passing an open view northwest just before the summit. The multi-peaked Tripyramids appear once again; Waterville Valley Ski Area can be spotted beyond. The wooded summit (7.5/4,043) offers no views, but don't despair. A short distance past the summit, you'll find a path on the left, posted with a TO VIEW sign. This spur drops 200 feet on an occasionally boggy path to a small outcrop with an exceptional view north.

The mountain slopes fall away beneath you into the Swift River Valley, traced by the Kancamagus Highway. Looking west, North Tripyramid and the Fool Killer loom nearby. Past them and to the right is untracked Mount Kancamagus (3,763). In the northwest distance are Kinsman and Franconia ridges, the latter topped by Mount Lafayette (Trip 18). The bump of Mount Garfield is visible east of Lafayette. Almost due north, the bulging massifs of Mounts Carrigain (4,700) and South Hancock (4,319) guard the east Pemigewasset Wilderness (Trip 19). The distinctive cleft of Carrigain Notch is to the right of Carrigain; Vose Spur and Mount Lowell stand sentinel over the notch to the west and east, respectively. The precipices of Green's Cliff rise in the middle distance, directly in line with Vose Spur. In the distance, just to the right of the notch, the Willey Range hems in hidden Crawford Notch. On a clear day, Mount Washington is visible to the north-northwest; to its right are the even more distant peaks of the Carter Range. A look northeast takes in the Moat Mountains and the mountains of west Maine on the far horizon.

Return to the summit and continue on the Walden Trail. You immediately encounter another excellent view. This one looks east over the entire east Sandwich Range. Below you, the rocky knob of Square Ledge—your next destination—protrudes from the slopes. The trail then plummets down a steep bouldery route to reach the east end of the East Loop Trail (8.1/3,410).

Turn left to remain on the Walden Trail, which drops steeply via rock and log stairs to meet the Square Ledge Trail (8.2/3,320). Bear left and follow the Square Ledge Trail as it begins a long descent from spruce-fir forest into hardwoods. Loose and gritty in spots, the trail parallels an audible, but inaccessible, stream below. You next reach the base of a large open rock slide—a quick scramble reveals a view of Mount Passaconaway looming overheard and Mount Washington in the distance.

Red and sugar maples appear alongside abundant paper birch and the trail soon curves right, away from the stream valley. A brief climb brings you to the Passaconaway Cutoff Trail on the left (8.9/2,550), where a 4-foot high boulder is seemingly supported by a single paper birch, an amusing illusion. Continue on the Square Ledge Trail, rising momentarily to views of nearby Mount Paugus and more distant Mount Chocorua. From here, the trail once again descends, passing through jumbled terrain marked by large spruce and yellow birch. The path becomes indistinct in spots—watch for blazes.

You then abruptly emerge at the base of Square Ledge (9.5/2,400). The route winds along its side, but you can scramble atop this massive stone with some creative gymnastics; a thin path leads to its north end and a view of Mount Passaconaway, Carrigain Notch, and points south. The Square Ledge Trail continues past its namesake stone and soon encounters an impacted level area free of undergrowth. A viewpoint looks down the Oliverian Brook valley and ample tentsites are available, but there is no nearby water source.

From here, the trail turns sharply right and drops into a gully between sheer rock faces. Giant chunks have calved off in places but remain stuck in position overhead, waiting to tumble. Now the route becomes very indistinct—watch closely for blazes—as it remains close to the cliff face. After descending more than 200 feet, the trail enters a thick forest of beech, sugar maple, and yellow birch. Brief glimpses behind you reveal the rocky visage of Square Ledge. Grass grows on this seldom-trod section of trail, which runs levels, crosses a stream, and encounters the Square Ledge Branch Trail on the left (9.9/2,090).

Continue straight on the Square Ledge Trail, passing through an area rich with pink lady's slippers. A single orchid sprouts from their large grooved twin basal leaves in spring and early summer. The narrow trail undulates gently through dense vegetation and reaches the four-way junction with the Walden,

Old Mast Road, Lawrence, and Square Ledge trails (11.0/2,320). Turn left on the Lawrence Trail, gently dipping to reach another four-way junction (11.3/2,220) with the Oliverian Brook, Lawrence, and Kelley trails.

At this point, the route of the Super Sandwich hike (Trip 17) diverges—refer to the next trip for the continuing journey.

The saddle here marks the lowest point along the Sandwich Range divide. Bear right on the Kelley Trail to return to the trailhead. The narrow path descends a wide gully and soon starts to parallel a small trickling creek. The rocky trail soon steepens and descends rock stairs. The stream disappears underground and you begin traveling atop the moss-coated boulders of the dry streambed.

Hemlocks grow in increasing numbers as the creek reemerges from beneath the rocks. Continue to follow the stream, crossing it twice as you descend. Red maple and yellow birch appear as the woods transition back to hardwoods. The trail stays level as the stream abruptly flows downward out-of-sight, then makes a gentle descent to rejoin the creek by a cascade. The ravine broadens here and fills with a pleasantly mature forest of ash, sugar maple, and beech.

The trail brings you to a grassy road (13.0/1,320)—bear right, perhaps stopping to enjoy abundant blackberries if your timing is right. In 0.1 mile, the trail splits left and leaves the road—watch for the sign—to descend to the Old Mast Road (13.3/1,260). Continue straight on the Kelley Trail and follow it through thick hemlock forest, passing the Wonalancet Range Trail on the right immediately before the parking area (13.6/1,170).

INFORMATION

White Mountain National Forest, Pemigewasset Ranger District, 1171 NH Route 175, Holderness, NH 03245, 603-536-1315, www.fs.fed.us/r9/forests/white_mountain; Wonalancet Out Door Club, HCR 61, Box 248, Wonalancet, NH 03897, www.wodc.org

TRIP 17
SUPER SANDWICH

Location: Sandwich Range Wilderness, White Mountain National Forest
Highlights: Rocky peaks, quiet streams, remote mountains
Distance: 26.9 miles round-trip
Total Elevation Gain/Loss: 9,600/9,600
Trip Length: 3–4 days
Difficulty: ★★★★
Recommended Map: *AMC White Mountain Guide Map 3: Crawford Notch-Sandwich Range,* AMC Books

Mount Paugus awaits. Tucked deep within a seldom-trod portion of the Sandwich Range Wilderness, hemmed between the massifs of Mounts Passaconaway and Chocorua, its cliffy visage looms over a hidden watershed. Here, Whitin Brook flows through a valley protected from all humanity, a small wilderness within a wilderness. To the east, the distinctive summit of Mount Chocorua stands sentinel, a pyramid of granite that offers unrestricted views in all directions from a summit of solid stone.

HIKE OVERVIEW
This is an extended variation of the Basic Sandwich hike (Trip 16). After circuiting over Mounts Whiteface and Passaconaway, the hike continues east to ascend Mount Paugus via the challenging Lawrence Trail, then surmounts Mount Chocorua via the Bee Line Trail. Returning west, the hike follows the Brook, Old Paugus, and Whitin Brook trails through a gentle forested landscape—highlighted by Big Rock Cave—before returning home via the Kelley Trail. A look at a trail map will reveal numerous other shorter loops and return options—this hike is designed to maximize scenery and highlights.

OVERNIGHT OPTIONS
Dispersed camping is permitted throughout the Wilderness area, but steep terrain limits the options along the hike's first 11.3 miles (see Trip 16). There are several areas with good camping potential in the Mount Paugus/Whitin Brook area near the hike's midpoint, including the summit of Mount Paugus, near Whitin Brook, and on the west side of the Bolles Trail. Dispersed camping is *not* permitted on and around Mount Chocorua within the designated Mount

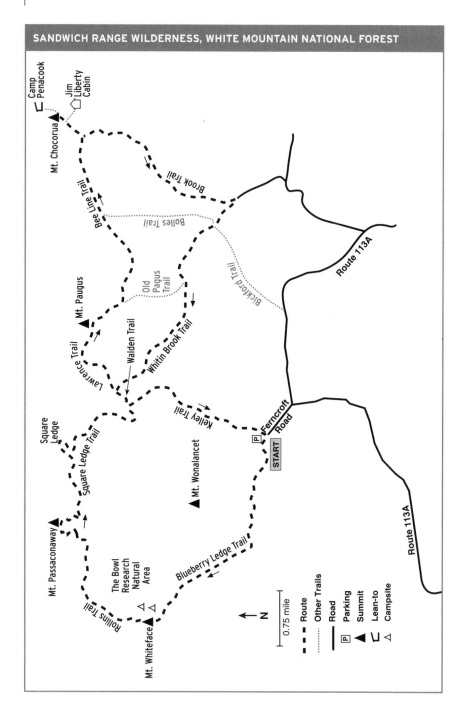

SANDWICH RANGE WILDERNESS, WHITE MOUNTAIN NATIONAL FOREST

Chocorua Scenic Area, which starts on the east side of the Bolles Trail and encompasses most of the mountain. Overnight stays within the scenic area are limited to two designated sites: Jim Liberty Cabin and Camp Penacook.

Jim Liberty Cabin perches at 3,100 feet just below the summit of Chocorua. It is located at the former site of the Peak House Hotel (built 1892), which was literally blown off the mountain by high winds in 1915. Massive chains run over the roof of today's cabin, constructed by The Forest Service in 1932. The cabin is free and provides first-come, first-served space for roughly 10 people. A small unreliable water source is located 130 feet downhill—a filter is necessary. A clearing in front of the cabin provides views of the lower summit cliffs. Camping and fires are prohibited.

Camp Penacook sits at 2,700 feet on the east flanks of Mount Chocorua, a strenuous 3.4-mile round-trip detour with more than a thousand feet of elevation gain and loss. Paper birch and spruce-fir forest surrounds the basic shelter, which offers a few restricted views of the adjacent mountain slopes; Chocorua's summit palpably looms nearby. A fire pit is available as are two tent platforms directly behind the shelter. A diminutive water source is available nearby; you may need a filter to collect it.

TO REACH THE TRAILHEAD

As with Trip 16, take Route 113 north from Highway 25 (the turn-off is located 3.6 miles west of the Route 25/16 junction). In 0.4 mile, turn left to remain on Route 113 and proceed 2.4 miles to reach the junction with Route 113A. Continue straight (north) on 113A, following it for 6.5 miles as it heads northwest and then west through the small community of Wonalancet. Turn right on unpaved Ferncroft Road, located next to the white church, and proceed 0.5 mile to a turn-off on the right for the designated parking area. All of the property around you is private—please respect the landowners and park only in this designated area.

HIKE DESCRIPTION

Follow the hike description in Trip 16 to the four-way junction with the Kelley, Oliverian Brook, and Lawrence trails (11.3/2,220). Continue straight on the Lawrence Trail, climbing briefly to reach the junction with the Cabin Trail (11.6/2,340) on the right—your return route. If you are looking for a campsite at this point, bear right and follow the Cabin Trail 0.5 mile to the Whitin Brook Trail. Turn left and follow the Whitin Brook Trail into the broad valley—and level camping opportunities—around Whitin Brook.

Continuing on the Lawrence Trail, you descend past views of approaching Mount Paugus and drop steeply into beech forest. The gradient eases and views appear southeast down the drainage of Whitin Brook; Lake Ossipee is visible in the distance. The trail bottoms out (11.8/2,140) and then immediately gets radical. The next section is one of the most gnarly of the entire Sandwich Range.

Climbing steeply on loose slopes, you ascend a narrow gully between two large rock slabs. Views look toward Mount Mexico on the southeast side of the Whitin Brook drainage and the more distant Ossipee Mountains. More views follow of the slides and cliffs of Mount Paugus. Clambering upward along the base of dripping rock ledges, the trail then levels out and navigates a boulder field. You ascend another loose gully and pass increasingly distant views southeast; the Belknap Mountains are now visible past slivers of Lake Winnipesaukee. The trail then plummets over slick rocks to cross three small headwater streams of Whitin Brook (12.4/2,400).

The route resumes its steep assault of Mount Paugus, climbing through spruce-fir forest on roots, rocks, and occasional steps. Mounts Passaconaway, Whiteface, and Wonalancet all rise behind you through the trees. The gradient finally eases as you approach the summit plateau of Mount Paugus, crossing a few boggy spots and a flowing stream. After a final climb through dense forest, the trail emerges in a clearing atop a large granite slab (13.1/3,080).

The actual summit is 0.3 mile to the north, but this location offers the best views. Vistas west and southwest take in Squam Lake, Passaconaway, Whiteface, and Sandwich Dome (left of Whiteface). Ragged Mountain and Mount Kearsarge rise in the distance, almost directly in line with Squam Lake. This point also marks the end of the Lawrence Trail and start of the Old Paugus Trail, which continues from the other side of the clearing. Follow the Old Paugus Trail, quickly passing a nice view southeast that features the rocky profile of Chocorua. The path then makes a steep scrambling descent over slick rocks and crosses a creek. After rising briefly, the trail then curves right by an unmarked trail. This turn is easily missed—be watchful!

Dropping over more slick slabs, the trail passes an open ledge with good views south and then cuts right to make yet another scrambling plummet. Beech and yellow birch reappear along the thin overgrown path—proceed carefully to remain on the mostly unblazed route. Mount Chocorua appears through the trees as the trail makes a final descending traverse to reach the Bee Line Trail (13.8/2,450).

Bear left on the Bee Line Trail and begin a sharp descent. Though steep, the path is generally rock-free and more forgiving than previous sections. As you lose elevation, the surrounding beech forest thickens and conifers disappear. The trail eventually curves right, winds past some car-sized boulders, and begins to parallel a hemlock-shaded creek. The trail crosses the rushing stream, cruises level through a marshy area, and reaches the Bee Line Cutoff Trail on the right (14.7/1,300). An abundance of level terrain in the area offers good camping potential.

Go left to remain on the somewhat indistinct Bee Line Trail, which winds through the woods and surmounts a small ridge before dropping to Paugus Brook. Rock-hop the creek to reach a riverside campsite and the four-way junction with the Bolles Trail (14.9/1,300), which marks the east boundary of the Wilderness area.

Remain on the Bee Line Trail and begin climbing on a narrow and rockier path through paper birch forest, flirting with a small creek as you go. The gradient steadily increases. A few rock steps aid your ascent. The trail crosses the creek, climbs briefly, and then returns to the stream to re-cross it. The route curves away to the right and rises past increasing spruce and fir, traversing along bedrock just before reaching the Brook Trail (16.6/2,550).

Bear left on the Brook Trail—your later return route enters from the right—and begin ascending rock slabs. Scrambling is necessary in places. Views west start to appear and you soon reach the open slabs of the summit cone (16.8/2,930). Now the scrambling really begins. Granite outcrops abound as you clamber to the Liberty Trail (17.0/3,120). The rounded summit dome rises above you, a solid mass of granite exfoliating in sheets. To reach the top, continue uphill on the Brook Trail. For Jim Liberty Cabin, bear right and follow the Liberty Trail 0.3 mile, traversing 200 feet downhill over rock slabs to reach the trailside structure.

Heading for the summit on the Brook Trail, you immediately reach the Westside Trail on the left, which curves below the summit to the west. Continue straight on the Brook Trail, climbing up an open ledge and then passing through a stand of dwarf spruce. The Piper Trail joins from the left shortly before the summit (17.1/3,420). Following the yellow blazes, proceed directly up the rock slabs ahead to the summit. Soon you stand upon the small plateau that crowns this peak (17.2/3,500).

The view sweeps 360 degrees across the landscape. Looking west you can trace your previous route over Mounts Whiteface, Passaconaway, and Paugus. The Kancamagus Highway can be seen tracing through the Swift River Valley below you to the north. Mount Washington and the southern Presidential Range (Trip 20) rise in the northern distance; the Carter Range (Trip 24) rises beyond to the right. To the northwest, the peaks of the Pemigewasset Wilderness can be identified. Framing the distinctive V slash of Carrigain Notch are Vose Spur (left) and Mount Lowell (right). Adjacent to Vose Spur is the domed massif of Mount Carrigain, neighbored to the west by South Hancock (Trip 19). On the far northwest horizon, you can make out Franconia Ridge and the west edge of the Pemigewasset Wilderness (Trip 18). Glancing south over the rolling landscape of central New Hampshire, the largest visible body of water is Ossipee Lake; Silver Lake shimmers north of it. Immediately east, at the base of Chocorua, are Whitton Pond (south) and Iona Lake (north). Unless you are headed to Camp Penacook, retrace your steps to the earlier junction of the Bee Line and Brook trails.

SIDE-TRIP TO CAMP PENACOOK

For Camp Penacook, return to the previous junction with the Piper Trail and head north, following the Piper Trail as it traverses along open ledges with endless views. Yellow blazes mark the initially mellow route, which reenters the trees and passes the West Side Trail in 0.5 mile. Remain on the Piper Trail, descending to the Champney Falls Trail at 0.7 mile. Turn right to remain on the Piper Trail and begin a rapid drop down a bouldery ridge. Enjoy views of the summit face and cliffs as you descend, then the route curves right off the ridge and down occasional rock staircases. At 1.5 miles, you reach the posted spur to the shelter, which heads right and ascends 200 feet in 0.2 mile to the shelter.

From the Bee Line–Brook Trail junction (17.8/2,550), bear left to remain on the Brook Trail as it descends into thick spruce forest. You pass some giant slabs with views south before dropping back into hardwood forest. The rocky, lightly used path steadily descends through lush woods and then levels. Rushing Claybank Creek becomes audible, and the trail soon crosses it (18.3/1,880). The route now parallels the creek, which weaves in and out-of-sight, and leaves the Mount Chocorua Scenic Area. The gradient mellows and you cross several rivulets in more gentle terrain—camping would be a possibility along this section. The trail begins a long level stretch, and then turns away from the water to cruise through dense hemlock forest and reach the Bickford Trail (19.8/1,140).

The blue-blazed Bickford Trail heads right and provides the most direct continuation of your hike, but it is faint and hard-to-follow. The recommended—and much easier—option continues straight on the Brook Trail, which becomes a gravel road shortly before its junction with the Bolles Trail (20.7/950). Turn right on the Bolles Trail, which quickly leads to a large campsite by flowing Paugus Brook. Rock-hop the creek and enjoy a level streamside ramble through young hemlock forest with good camping possibilities. The

Old Paugus and Bickford trails enter from the left (21.3/1,010); the continuation of the Bickford Trail turns right off the Bolles Trail 100 yards ahead.

Bear left and follow the Old Paugus Trail as the Bickford Trail immediately splits off to the left. The wide trail quickly reenters the Sandwich Range Wilderness and passes through a stately hemlock grove. Nearby Whitin Brook starts to hiss as the surrounding terrain steepens. You now climb, weaving along the creek then crossing it (21.9/1,200). A gigantic boulder passes on the left as the trail rises to reach the Whitin Brook Trail (22.2/1,410). Continue straight on the Whitin Brook Trail, which climbs briefly to reach the Big Rock Cave Trail on the left (22.4/1,520).

This is your opportunity to visit Big Rock Cave, located 0.1 mile and 200 feet up on the Big Rock Cave Trail. Here, sprouting from the smooth hillside,

Mount Chocorua's summit cone

is a collection of boulders so enormous, they should be called "collosaliths." This jumbled fortress harbors several inviting caves, crevices, and cliffs—an explorer's delight.

Back on the main route, continue on the Whitin Brook Trail as it parallels its namesake stream, climbs briefly, and rock-hops the brook. You then follow a tributary, crossing it twice before curving away to travel through a pleasant forest of beech, sugar and red maple, and yellow birch. There is good camping potential. Mount Paugus peeks through the trees to the right, then the trail curves left to climb steeply through dense conifer forest to reach the Cabin Trail (23.8/2,200).

Turn right and follow the Cabin Trail on a level, root-laced traverse that offers great views of the rocky scars on Mount Paugus. You then return to the earlier junction with the Lawrence Trail (24.3/2,340). Turn left and retrace your steps the short distance to the Kelley Trail (24.6/2,250). The saddle here marks the lowest point along the Sandwich Range divide.

Bear left and head down the Kelley Trail to return to the trailhead. The narrow path descends a wide gully and soon starts to parallel a small trickling creek. The rocky trail soon steepens and descends rock stairs. The stream disappears underground and you begin traveling atop the moss-coated boulders of the dry streambed.

Hemlocks grow in increasing numbers as the creek reemerges from beneath the rocks. You continue to follow the stream, crossing it twice as you descend. Red maple and yellow birch appear as the woods transition back to hardwoods. The trail stays level as the stream abruptly flows downward out-of-sight, then makes a gentle descent to rejoin the creek by a cascade. The ravine broadens here and fills with a pleasantly mature forest of ash, sugar maple, and beech.

The trail brings you to a grassy road (26.3/1,320)—bear right, perhaps stopping to enjoy abundant blackberries if your timing is right. In 0.1 mile, the trail splits left and leaves the road—watch for the sign—to descend to the Old Mast Road (26.6/1,260). Continue straight on the Kelley Trail and follow it through thick hemlock forest, passing the Wonalancet Range Trail on the right immediately before the parking area (26.9/1,170).

INFORMATION

White Mountain National Forest, Pemigewasset Ranger District, 1171 NH Route 175, Holderness, NH 03245, 603-536-1315, www.fs.fed.us/r9/forests/white_mountain; Wonalancet Out Door Club, HCR 61, Box 248, Wonalancet, NH 03897, www.wodc.org

TRIP 18
GIMME THE PEMI I

Location: Pemigewasset Wilderness, White Mountain National Forest
Highlights: Easy cruising, a remote waterfall, 4,000-footers, a long alpine ridgeline
Distance: 25.2 miles round-trip
Total Elevation Gain/Loss: 6,800/6,800
Trip Length: 2–3 days
Difficulty: ★★★
Recommended Map: *AMC White Mountain Guide, Map 4: Moosilauke-Kinsman,* AMC Books

The Pemigewasset Wilderness protects the watershed of the East Branch of the Pemigewasset River, a self-contained world of streams, mountains, cliffs, and views. Ringed by lofty peaks, including sixteen taller than 4,000 feet, it is New England's largest wilderness area with 45,000 acres of protected backcountry. In many ways, it is also one of the friendliest. Many trails follow old railroad beds—wide easy-cruising pathways—deep into the backcountry. The Appalachian Trail (AT) runs along the mountain spine, a well-traveled and rugged footpath. Come ramble by a river, soak by a waterfall, and cruise high above treeline as you take it all in.

HIKE OVERVIEW

This loop hike begins from the Lincoln Woods Trailhead on the Kancamagus Highway and follows the easy-cruising Lincoln Woods and Franconia Brook trails. It passes the sculpted granite slabs of Franconia Falls en route to Thirteen Falls Tentsite and its accompanying cascade. The route then ascends lofty Garfield Ridge and heads south on the AT, passing Garfield Ridge Campsite as it ascends Mount Garfield. You next traverse the length of Franconia Ridge, including 3 miles above treeline, and tag the summits of Mounts Lafayette, Lincoln, Liberty, and Flume. A long, mellow descent on the Osseo Trail returns you to the trailhead.

Note that this hike visits some of New England's most heavily used backcountry. This section of the AT—especially Franconia Ridge—is a hiking highway where you may literally see hundreds of people. Avoid weekends. Dogs are allowed.

PEMIGEWASSET WILDERNESS, WHITE MOUNTAIN NATIONAL FOREST

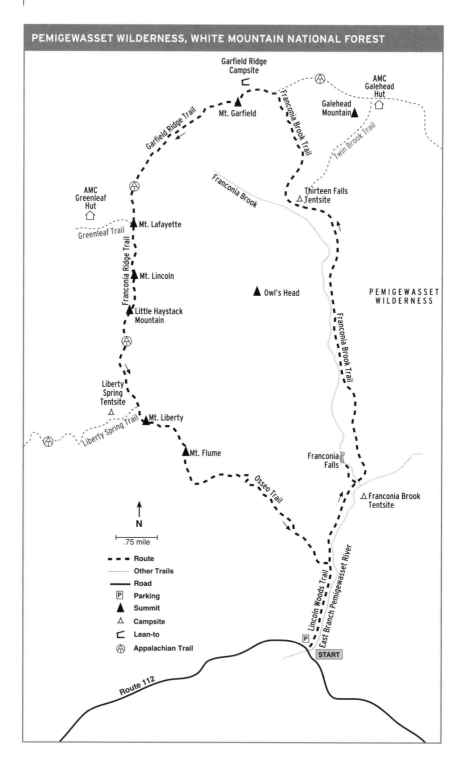

Garfield Ridge
Campsite

Mt. Garfield

Garfield Ridge Trail

Franconia Brook Trail

AMC
Galehead
Hut

Galehead
Mountain

Twin Brook Trail

Franconia Brook

Thirteen Falls
Tentsite

AMC
Greenleaf
Hut

Mt. Lafayette

Greenleaf Trail

Franconia Ridge Trail

Mt. Lincoln

Owl's Head

PEMIGEWASSET
WILDERNESS

Little Haystack
Mountain

Franconia Brook Trail

Liberty
Spring
Tentsite

Mt. Liberty

Liberty Spring Trail

Mt. Flume

Franconia
Falls

Osseo Trail

Franconia Brook
Tentsite

N

.75 mile

Lincoln Woods Trail

East Branch Pemigewasset River

- - - Route
.... Other Trails
——— Road
P Parking
▲ Summit
△ Campsite
⊏ Lean-to
Ⓐ Appalachian Trail

START

Route 112

OVERNIGHT OPTIONS

Dispersed camping is permitted throughout most of the Pemigewasset Wilderness, though there are a number of restrictions in busier areas (see later). The hike visits three designated camping areas. Resident caretakers collect an overnight per person fee from mid-June through Columbus Day, plus a few weekends in October. The funds are used to maintain these heavily used sites.

Thirteen Falls Tentsite, 8.1 miles from the trailhead, hides out in spruce-fir forest at 2,500 feet near the headwaters of Franconia Brook. Eight tentsites perch on boulder terraces resembling rocky nests. The site's namesake falls wash the sites with sound. The falls—and a swimming hole at its base—are accessible. Bear boxes are provided by the entrance. Because of its location away from the AT, Thirteen Falls receives fewer visitors than the other overnight options on this hike.

Garfield Ridge Campsite perches at 4,000 feet on the upper flanks of Mount Garfield, 10.8 miles from the trailhead and near the hike's midpoint. Five large tent platforms and a high-capacity shelter are available. The cave-like shelter faces south and catches good morning sun from the entrance. The trail to the campsite offers far-reaching views to the northeast; there is also a nice bench with a view east. South Twin, Mount Guyot, Mount Bond, West Bond, Bondcliff, and Galehead Hut are all visible. The camping area gets heavy use; expect to share the shelter or tent platform with others. The caretaker posts a current weather forecast each morning.

Liberty Spring Tentsite is located 18.5 miles from the trailhead on the Liberty Spring Trail, 300 feet below Franconia Ridge. Ten numbered tent platforms are dotted within thick spruce-fir woods. Several are nicely private, especially sites 8, 9, and 10. This heavily used location is not an experience in solitude. It fills most summer nights, and you should expect to share tent platforms with other parties. Crowds diminish markedly after the second week of September. Water is available from the site's namesake spring.

Galehead and Greenleaf huts offer alternatives to sleeping outside, 10.8 and 15.8 miles from the trailhead, respectively. Each requires a small detour off the route, but can be blissful experiences in bad weather. Learn more about these pricier overnight options at www.outdoors.org/lodging or call 603-466-2727 for reservations and information. No camping is allowed near the huts.

Franconia Brook Tentsite is located 2 miles from the trailhead along the Pemi East Side Trail and provides an option for your first night if you are starting late in the day. However, it is located on the opposite side of the river from this hike, requiring a moderately challenging (or dangerously difficult, depending on water level) river crossing.

Camping is prohibited within a quarter mile of the East Branch of the Pemigewasset River from the trailhead to Franconia Brook (a distance of 2.6 miles), or at the former Franconia Brook Campsite near Franconia Falls. Camping is also prohibited within 200 feet of Black Pond, the AT, the Liberty Spring Trail, and Franconia Brook from its junction with the East Branch of the Pemi River to the second island above Franconia Brook Falls.

TO REACH THE TRAILHEAD

Follow I-93 to Route 112 in Lincoln (the Kancamagus Highway) and head east for 5.2 miles. The Lincoln Woods Trailhead is signed on the left and features a huge parking area and visitor center (open seven days a week 8:30 a.m.–3:30 p.m.). A WMNF parking permit is required.

HIKE DESCRIPTION

From the parking lot (0.0/1,140), proceed to the visitor center, step inside to pick up a free permit to visit Franconia Falls (see later), and then head out on the Lincoln Woods Trail. Some common trees grow near the building. A red maple stands next to the fence, a yellow birch is just to its right, and a white-barked paper birch grows at the bottom of the stairs. You immediately cross a large suspension bridge over the Pemigewasset River, flowing broadly over thousands of round boulders. Information signs on the opposite side briefly tell the region's history. Twenty-four logging camps and 50 miles of railroad track once laced this portion of the White Mountains—a striking contrast to the area's status today.

Past the signs, you reach one of the old railroad beds—your route for the next 8 miles—and a large mileage sign. Bear right to head out on the wide, easy-cruising Lincoln Woods Trail; look for old railroad ties underfoot. The route initially parallels the river, roughly 20 feet above it. The river is often out-of-sight and usually difficult to access—a scramble down steep embankments is necessary in most spots.

The flanks of Mount Hitchcock are visible east across the river. The surrounding forest is a young and diverse hardwood mosaic of black cherry, beech, yellow and paper birch, hemlock, sugar and red maple, red pine, and white ash. You make an almost imperceptible rise to reach the Osseo Trail on the left (1.4/1,270)—your return route—located in a paper birch grove by a flowing brook.

Approaching Mount Lafayette from the north

The trail narrows to double-track, passes a good river access point, and then widens and travels closer to the river. Views upstream reveal the lower slopes of the Bonds. You then cross Birch Island Brook on a plank bridge and cruise away from the river to reach the Black Pond Trail on the left (2.6/1,360). A sign indicates that this was the former site of the Franconia Brook tenting area, closed because of overuse.

You next reach Franconia Brook and the trail to Franconia Falls on the left (2.8/1,370). This highly recommended 0.4-mile side-trip is so popular that the Forest Service restricts access to no more than 60 people at a time (this is when that free permit comes in handy). Franconia Falls Trail follows a narrow path, briefly ascending before dropping down to reach the falls. An enormous chunk of granite bedrock has been worn smooth by sluicing water, leaving extensive swaths of rock ideal for lounging. Narrow runnels funnel water into several small pools, many of which provide a quality soak. Rock-hop around the falls to your heart's content.

Back on the Lincoln Woods Trail, continue over a wooden bridge atop old railroad trestles and reach the signed wilderness boundary. Just past it, the Wilderness Trail enters from the right and the Franconia Brook Trail splits left (2.9/1,430). Bear left on the Franconia Brook Trail, which narrows and makes a quick rise before leveling out and returning to double-track. You cross and then re-cross a brook as the route becomes increasingly single-track. Root-

Galehead Hut

laced and muddy in spots, the trail curves around, re-crosses the brook, and then climbs up the opposite bank to regain the railroad bed. Now cruising level, you reach the Lincoln Brook Trail on the left (4.6/1,730).

Continue straight on the Franconia Brook Trail, following a level single-track path with views of the lower flanks of nearby Owl's Head. The trail immediately encounters an old beaver pond on the right, which offers limited views of the Bonds. The route continues over the beaver dam, a 50-foot-long structure that requires some delicate footwork.

White pines appear intermittently and the forest encroaches the trail corridor. The trail crosses Hellgate Brook (5.5/1,770) and then continues on its level course, briefly touching Franconia Brook as it goes. The woods slowly transition to spruce-fir forest, brush lines the trail in spots, and you reach Redrock Brook (6.5/1,890). Beyond it, the route has a perceptible upward gradient for the first time and traverses on slopes far above Franconia Brook. Large big-tooth aspens proliferate around you.

The trail slowly rises, crosses a rocky streambed, and makes a level traverse to Twin Brook (7.6/2,090). Crossing the brook, the trail curves northwest and reaches the end of the railroad line by the rushing sheeting waterfall that is

Thirteen Falls. The large and deep swimming hole at its base can be accessed with some scrambling. The trail now turns uphill, abruptly becomes a steeper and rockier route, and quickly meets the Lincoln Brook Trail returning from the left (8.1/2,250). Water sluices over rock slabs here, and there are more views of Owl's Head. Just beyond is the spur to Thirteen Falls Tentsite.

Immediately past the campground, you reach the intersection of the Twin Brook and Franconia Brook trails. The Twin Brook Trail continues straight, leading up 1,500 feet in 2.7 miles to reach the AMC's Galehead Hut, but you continue left on the Franconia Brook Trail. This rocky, root-chocked trail heads upward toward Garfield Ridge; Mount Garfield peeks out above. A much-diminished Franconia Brook, audible but seldom seen, runs parallel below.

The trail levels briefly, the brook rises to meet it, and the water becomes accessible in spots. Paper birch and hobblebush proliferate. You cross over a small brook and some puncheon, pass through an area of open woods, and then climb within a forest of paper birch, hobblebush, and blackberry. The trail parallels a small tributary and at about 3,000 feet elevation enters a predominantly spruce-fir forest. The path gradually rises with an occasional steep section, and soon begins ascending directly up a rocky creek bed—the trickiest portion of trail yet. As you approach the ridge, you cross the posted Wilderness boundary and enter a chaotic stand of spongy spruce-fir forest. Hop through a boggy area and you reach the junction with the AT (10.3/3,430).

Bear left on the white-blazed AT, which has been ground down to bedrock by millions of boot steps. From here on out, the hike is a much rockier journey. The trail climbs steeply, quickly ascends a rock face, then drops, levels briefly, and crosses a small stream flowing north. Brief glimpses of Garfield ahead help motivate you through this rock-o-rama. You surmount another vertical rock staircase and enjoy a restricted view southeast. Water flows down the rock face, the source for the approaching Garfield Ridge Campsite. The spur to the camping area soon splits right (10.8/3,900), immediately crossing the water source before climbing up the rocky slopes.

Fill up your water bottles—this is the last quality source for the next 8 miles. Continuing, the AT ascends a steady staircase of stone and rock steps. The gradient eases just before the Garfield Trail, which enters from the right (11.0/4,250). Remain on the AT as it completes its ascent, reaching the summit via a short spur trail on the left (11.2/4,500). Old tower footings crown the peak, the remains of a fire lookout tower that operated here between 1940 and 1948. The views south are outstanding. The whole line of Franconia Ridge—your continuing route—lies out in front of you. From north to south, the peaks are Mounts Lafayette, Lincoln, Liberty, and Flume. The bulging massif of Owl's Head is below you, and the Sandwich Range (Trips 16 and 17) serrates the horizon—the broad pyramid of Passaconaway is to the left, Tripyramid and Osceola right. The summit of Mount Washington protrudes above North Twin to the east; the northern Presidentials (Trip 23) can be spotted in the distance.

Past the summit, the AT plummets 200 feet down a rocky staircase, then levels and descends more gradually. You next make a radical rock scramble down and resume a steady rocky descent. Eventually the trail reaches a saddle; a trickle of water provides a potential source of refreshment.

The trail crosses some puncheon, climbs again, and then undulates along the forested ridge to the base of Franconia Ridge. The trail rises steadily, passing by the dead snags of a fir wave. The route steepens and continues upward at a constant grade. The trail switchbacks left, travels along a strip of solid bedrock, and then emerges above treeline at 4,500 feet.

You are now in the alpine zone. Grassy tufts of Bigelow's Sedge wave in the wind. Far-reaching views are everywhere. Cairns and painted blazes indicate the route, which soon passes the Skookumchuck Trail on the left (13.9/4,690). The well-marked trail crests a rise at 5,000 feet and for the first time you peer west into Franconia Notch and south along the ridge to the summit of Mount Lafayette. The Greenleaf Trail runs from Greenleaf Hut up the west summit ridge and is often lined with easily spotted hikers. Savor this next quiet section of the AT—it will soon be much busier. A final climb leads you to the summit and accompanying hiker mania (14.7/5,260).

An old foundation crowns the peak, the vestiges of the former Summit House. Greenleaf Hut perches 1,060 feet and 1.1 miles below you via the Greenleaf Trail. Enjoy views south toward Mounts Lincoln, Liberty (just visible), and Flume (the prominent pyramid). Marvel at the hiker super-highway ahead of you. Legions of day hikers often line the ridge from here to the Falling Waters Trail 1.7 miles ahead.

Continue south on the AT toward the saddle between Lincoln and Lafayette, passing views west into the steep drainage of Walker Brook. Climbing again, you top out on a false summit—Greenleaf Hut perches on the mountain's shoulder behind you—and then quickly head to Mount Lincoln's true highpoint (15.7/5,089). Pause once again to savor the far-reaching views.

To the west, Lonesome Lake nestles in the mountainous terrain just south of Cannon Cliffs. To the southeast, Mount Carrigain and North Hancock (Trip 19) define the southeast boundary of the Pemigewasset Wilderness. The Sandwich Range lines the southern horizon; Mount Chocorua is visible for the first time at its east end. Looking east, the cliffs of Bondcliff rise directly past Owl's Head.

Descend to Little Haystack (16.4/4,780), where the hiking masses branch right down the Falling Waters Trail. Remain on the AT as it continues along the ridge and immediately reenters the trees. The duff-covered trail soon leads to another open view west before plummeting toward the broad saddle below Mount Liberty. Occasional glimpses of Mount Liberty entice you along. The path levels out and then slowly rises to reach the Liberty Spring Trail joining from the right (18.2/4,290). To reach Liberty Spring Tentsite—and the first good water source since the Garfield Ridge Tentsite—turn right and descend 300 feet in 0.3 mile.

The AT continues south down the Liberty Spring Trail, but you leave it behind and remain on the blue-blazed Franconia Ridge Trail. A quick rise leads you atop the open summit of Mount Liberty (18.5/4,459). More nice views look east, with Owl's Head and the entire west wilderness area unfolding beneath you. To the north, cliffs rise up the southern flanks of Mount Garfield. Ahead of you to the south, the prominent scar of Flume Slide is apparent on the mountain's flanks.

Dropping off the summit, you scramble over some steep boulders and quickly lose elevation, passing by views of Mount Flume in another fir wave opening. The trail bottoms out in a rocky saddle and then makes a steady climb along a wider footpath, undulating briefly before make the final climb to the summit (19.6/4,328).

The mountaintop is rocky and open, but does not offer a 360-degree view like previous peaks. Instead, it looks west into the deep bowl of Flume Brook, where you can trace the transition between the dark greens of boreal forest and the lighter greens of hardwoods farther down. The Flume—a deep gorge easily accessed from I-93—is located near the bottom of the watershed. Prominent Mount Moosilauke looms to the west, and north you can retrace your route over Mounts Lincoln and Lafayette. East, the Kancamagus Highway heads up the Swift River Valley; Mount Osceola and Scar Ridge guard above it to the south.

From the summit, drop steeply past a few more ledgy outcrops to reach the junction with the Flume Slide and Osseo trails (19.7/4,230). This marks the end of the Franconia Ridge Trail. Head down the Osseo Trail, a pleasant and easy-to-travel trail. Though narrow and less trod than previous paths, the duff-covered path has few rocks. Occasional yellow blazes line the route, increasing as you descend.

The gentle trail initially runs level, then starts slowly down and curves left. There is a palpable sense that you are approaching the edge of a steep drop. Soon it begins, descending a series of long wooden staircases with the occasional view east toward Bondcliff. Equally nice rock steps interrupt the wooden staircases at times, and you soon pass a posted DOWNLOOK on the left (20.6/3,540), which looks northeast past Owl's Head toward the Twins, Mount Guyot, and Mount Bond. The blissful series of wooden steps continues down, ending at a series of tight switchbacks. Paper birch increases and a cliff face peeks out ahead as the trail traverses toward an audible creek. The trail then curves left and begins a steady downhill traverse.

Beech and sugar maple appear as the trail cruises steadily downward. Large yellow birch punctuate the forest. At 2,500 feet, the trail begins curving off its straight course. The creek appears below for the first time; some potential camping areas can be spotted alongside it. Big-tooth aspen and red maple add further diversity to the woods as you next traverse a steep slope of hemlocks. The trail now descends more rapidly, widening to double-track and slowly approaching the stream. Near the bottom, you make a quick drop and hike parallel to the brook, cruising across level terrain. Sounds from the nearby Pemigewasset River start to fill the air just before you reach the earlier junction with the Lincoln Woods Trail (23.8/1,270). Turn right and head back to the trailhead (25.2/1,140).

INFORMATION

Lincoln Woods Visitor Center, Kancamagus Highway, Lincoln, NH 03251, 603-630-5190, www.fs.fed.us/r9/forests/white_mountain, open seven days a week, 8 A.M.–3:30 P.M.

TRIP 19
GIMME THE PEMI II

(Strenuous Version)

Location: Pemigewasset Wilderness, White Mountain National Forest

Highlights: Eight 4,000-footers, Thoreau Falls, and the total White Mountain backcountry experience

Distance: 36.8 miles round-trip, plus 4.8-mile side-trip to the Hancocks

Total Elevation Gain/Loss: 9,500/9,500, plus 2,100/2,100 for Hancock Loop

Trip Length: 4–5 days

Difficulty: ★★★★★

Recommended Map: *AMC White Mountain Guide, Map 2: Franconia-Pemigewasset,* AMC Books

Soaring open summits, rushing waterways, and long easy-cruising sections of trail—this is the total Pemigewasset experience. The hike circles the east half of the Pemigewasset Wilderness, lounges by the rushing Pemigewasset River, scales the Bonds, cruises through moose-rich lowlands, and then climbs over the summit of Mount Carrigain. But if you want it all, you've got to earn it—this grand adventure is not for the faint-of-heart. The total experience also features trail-clogging blowdowns, soggy bog-hopping terrain, and areas where careful route finding is required.

HIKE OVERVIEW

The journey begins from Sawyer River Road near the southeast border of the Pemigewasset Wilderness. The route initially follows the little-used Hancock Notch Trail over blowdowns and through recent logging zones to reach the Cedar Brook Trail. (You can skip this section by starting instead from the Kancamagus Highway, which requires a car shuttle; see later.) A strenuous side-trip leads to the summits of North and South Hancock—the hike's first 4,000-footers. You then descend into the low-lying heart of the wilderness, cross the Pemigewasset River, and ascend the mighty Bonds via the Bondcliff Trail, where Guyot Campsite awaits.

The return portion of the trek briefly follows the Appalachian Trail (AT) before dropping down the Zeacliff Trail toward powerful Thoreau Falls. The route then heads south, passing campsites at Shoal Pond as it follows Shoal Pond Brook to the Desolation Trail, which rises radically to summit Mount

PEMIGEWASSET WILDERNESS, WHITE MOUNTAIN NATIONAL FOREST

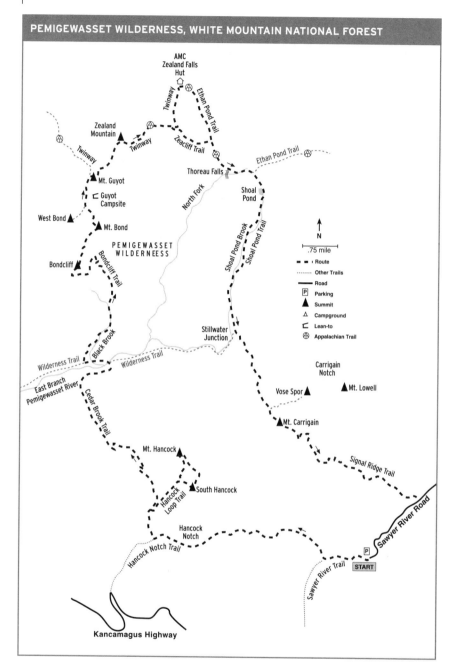

Carrigain. The rocky Signal Ridge Trail returns you to Sawyer River Road. Dogs are allowed.

OVERNIGHT OPTIONS

Dispersed camping is permitted throughout the Pemigewasset Wilderness, though a number of restrictions are in place in areas of heavy use (see later). The only designated overnight area is Guyot Campsite; the recommendations that follow identify other clearly established tentsites. Numerous other options await the intrepid camper elsewhere on the route. Campfires are permitted.

Near the Hancocks, no camping is permitted within 200 feet of the junctions of the Hancock Notch and Cedar Brook trails, or the junction of the Hancock Loop and Cedar Brook trails. There are a few trailside sites along the Cedar Brook Trail between these two restricted areas.

Along the East Branch of the Pemigewasset River, 12.5 miles from the trailhead, good camping options can be found upriver along the Wilderness Trail east of the bridge crossing.

Guyot Campsite, 19.4 miles from the trailhead, perches on the slopes below Mount Bond near 4,000 feet. It offers campsites and a cabin-like shelter with space for roughly a dozen hikers. Six tent platforms—several are double-size—nestle in dense spruce-fir forest. A few overflow sites are located on the ridge. Views are limited, though you can spot Mount Willey to the east from the shelter deck. A caretaker staffs the location from June through mid-October and collects an overnight per person fee. Guyot is the primary overnight option in a popular area, and it's usually a pretty crowded scene. A nearby brook provides reliable water.

Zealand Falls Huts, 24.0 miles from the trailhead, offers an alternative to sleeping outside, and requires a small detour off the main route. Learn more about this pricier overnight option at www.outdoors.org/lodging or call 603-466-2727 for reservations and information. No camping is allowed near the hut, though an established tenting area is located nearby along the Ethan Pond Trail, just outside the limits of the quarter-mile Forest Protection Area boundary.

Shoal Pond, 26.3 miles from the trailhead, has a few decent campsites a short distance from the lakeshore and near a small brook. There are also several sites spread along the Shoal Pond Trail.

The Desolation Trail offers some nice sites near the bottom of Mount Carrigain, 29 miles from the trailhead. A handful of waterless campsites can also be found near the summit.

No camping is permitted at Thoreau Falls, within 200 feet of the East Branch of the Pemigewasset River, or within 200 feet of the Bondcliff Trail from its junction with the Wilderness Trail to the second stream crossing of Black Brook.

TO REACH THE TRAILHEAD

Follow Route 302 east of the Highland Center in Crawford Notch for 10.7 miles to Sawyer River Road on the right. Approaching from the west, the turn-off is 3 miles past Bartlett. Follow Sawyer River Road for 3.8 miles to the parking lot at road's end. A daily WMNF parking fee is required. (To reach the alternate starting trailhead, follow the Kancamagus Highway (Route 112) to the Hancock Notch trailhead, located right at the highway's major hairpin turn.)

HIKE DESCRIPTION

From the Sawyer River Road parking area (0.0/1,710), the hike begins on the Sawyer River Trail. Start down a gated fire road and immediately encounter the Sawyer Pond Trail on the left. Continue straight on the Sawyer River Trail, which quickly forks—go left on the smaller road. A young mixed forest surrounds you. Spruce, fir, white pine, yellow birch, red maple, and mountain ash line the road, and hobblebush, painted trillium, blueberries, and yellow clintonia fill in the understory.

The road crosses the river on a wooden bridge, and 50 yards later, the single-track Sawyer River Trail splits right. Follow the Sawyer River Trail as it parallels the shallow river and crosses a pair of tributaries flowing over granite boulders. The route then briefly turns away from the river and follows a smaller brook. The trail becomes thin and overgrown here, requiring careful navigation as you approach Hayshed Field. The continuing route crosses the brook, then re-crosses it shortly before reaching the open field to regain an obvious footpath. If you find yourself wandering in the field, you've gone too far.

Once back on the trail, you quickly reach a logging road and the junction with the Hancock Notch Trail (1.2/1,760). Bear right on the Hancock Notch Trail. The trail/road returns within sight of the river and then narrows as it passes through a young regenerating forest. The easy-going path soon reaches the first river crossing (2.1/1,850), a precarious rock-hop, and quickly crosses a smaller tributary. Then the path abruptly disappears in a vortex of recent logging activity. Downed trees and ankle-breaking skid roads hide the way. To relocate the trail, curve left to follow the skid road that heads most directly up the river valley. Go left as spur roads branch off in that direction, which eventually returns you to the obvious trail. The trail parallels the main skid road, crosses another tributary, runs closer to the Sawyer River, and then crosses it at the confluence of two equal-sized forks (2.6/1,980).

The trail initially follows the left fork, becomes steeper and rockier, and soon crosses the creek on an easy rock-hop. You now curve over toward the other fork, hiking level through spruce-fir forest. The approaching peaks first peek out here; the rounded humps and cliffs of South Hancock loom to the north and northwest. The trail passes over some boggy spots and then slowly rises through dense second-growth woods to reach the brook and cross it (3.9/2,320)

The trail then bends left as indicated by a small posted arrow and yellow blaze. The hike becomes more challenging now as rocks, blowdowns, and boggy spots increase. You parallel the stream once again, cross it at a confluence (4.5/2,540), and follow the smaller fork left to immediately reach a clearing where you can spot the south summit of South Hancock through the trees. The trail continues along the creek and becomes increasingly faint; faded yellow blazes help keep you on course. You soon find yourself walking directly up the creek bed.

As you approach Hancock Notch, the trail leaves the stream and begins a challenging section that is narrow, overgrown, and blowdown-thick—a real challenge depending on recent maintenance. The trail finally becomes more passable as it enters a flat area, then winds along another narrow section to reach the notch's high point in dense spruce-fir woods (5.4/2,820).

The continuing trail is initially riddled with blowdowns, but quickly becomes easier going. You cross a small stream, rise briefly, and then start a steeper descent. The trail approaches a rushing stream with limited views south and then steadily descends to reach the Cedar Brook Trail (6.3/2,520).

Go right on the Cedar Brook Trail, cross the stream by the junction, and follow the rocky path as it runs near the audible riffles of the North Fork of the Hancock Branch of the East Branch Pemigewasset River (quite the name!). The path approaches the river (6.5/2,630), crosses it, and then immediately re-crosses it. An established camping area can be found near the trail on the opposite side. Continuing, the trail crosses the stream once more, walks over some puncheon, and travels along a mostly level trail. The route crosses the brook twice more and then briefly follows a rocky streambed to reach the Hancock Loop Trail on the right (7.0/2,720).

SIDE-TRIP TO HANCOCKS

Mount Hancock and South Hancock both exceed 4,000 feet and offer restricted views from their summits. To bag 'em, complete the Hancock Loop Trail, a 4.8-mile hike with 2,100 feet of elevation gain and loss. From the junction (0.0/2,720), bear right on the Hancock Loop Trail, a well-trod double-track pathway that immediately crosses the brook and starts climbing rocky slopes. A cascade rushes down the bouldery terrain. The trail rises slowly and South Hancock peeks through the trees above you. The crystalline brook reappears on your left, followed by a muddy section of trail. Now rising steadily, you soon catch glimpses of Mount Hancock's summit for the first time, looking tall and far away. Several slides scar its slopes.

Paper birch is common in the thick spruce-fir forest. The trail then forks to begin its circuit of the two summits (1.1/3,320). Ascending Mount Hancock first allows you to complete the steepest section (1,000 feet in 0.7 mile) going uphill and then descend the less-steep route off South Hancock. Bear left toward Mount Hancock and drop down to the brook, where a well-used campsite is apparent. Climbing again, the trail quickly reaches a rock staircase and then heads almost straight up, gaining almost 200 feet of elevation before curving left to begin a rising traverse. Looser rock fills the path around the 4,000-foot mark, South Hancock becomes visible south, and the trail levels off shortly before reaching the summit (1.8/4,420). An outlook is indicated to the left, located atop three large boulders.

From the outlook, peer south toward the prominent line of Scar Ridge; the Kancamagus Highway runs in the valley below it. Loon Mountain Ski Area is visible west, and Mount Osceola marks a high point on the continuation of Scar Ridge to the east. Greeley Ponds sit in the gap between Osceola to the west and Mount Kancamagus to the east. Trace your eyes further east along the Sandwich Range, and you can spot Tripyramid, and then Mounts Whiteface, Passaconaway, Paugus, and Chocorua (Trips 16 and 17). South Hancock is nearby to the south; Mount Huntington is apparent to its right.

The continuing loop now heads toward South Hancock, winding through a matchstick forest of dense spruce and fir. You follow a nice duff-covered trail down to the long saddle between the two peaks. Mount Carrigain peeks out to the northeast as the trail rises again and undulates through several boggy spots, offering a view behind you toward Mount Hancock. You soon reach the summit of South Hancock (3.2/4,319).

The view here encompasses the landscape to the east and southeast. Mount Carrigain and the long spine of Signal Ridge—your final destination on this hike—loom prominently a few miles away. The distinctive lumpy peak located

Carrigain's Signal Ridge—your final descent

almost due east, just south of Carrigain, is Tremont Peak; the bump of Owls Cliff protrudes on its right. Far below, you can survey your route through Hancock Notch. The rushing Sawyer River is audible even from here.

From the summit, complete the loop on a plummeting trail over roots and smaller rocks. Though steep, it never requires hand-over-hand scrambling. The gradient moderates slightly near the bottom, where the trail begins to feature more soil and less rock, and returns to the earlier fork (3.7/3,320). Turn left to retrace your steps to the Cedar Brook Trail (4.8/2,720).

Continuing on the Cedar Brook Trail, you pass through a nice spruce-fir forest; straight red spruce stand sentinel along the path. The less-traveled trail runs parallel to the stream and passes a few potential campsites. The scenic brook cascades loudly over large boulders. The trail then curves left away from the water, briefly parallels and then crosses a small trickling creek, and follows an increasingly narrow path through encroaching forest. You cross several small streams, pass numerous granite outcrops and boulders, and reach the wilderness boundary at a divide (7.7/3,130). A sign indicates that you're now entering a forest protection area—no camping is permitted within 200 feet of trails and streams.

From the divide, the trail descends slowly through wet sections, at one point heading directly down a flowing stream—the Cedar Brook headwaters. Bedrock and boulders are bleached white in the streambed. Soon the trail mellows, paper birch increase around you, and the slopes of Mount Hancock peek through the trees to your right. The trail becomes rocky again, hops some slick boulders, and then curves right toward the looming flanks of Mount Hancock. Returning again to Cedar Brook, you cross it, turn left to parallel it, and cross several small tributaries as you descend. The lower reaches of the Bonds—your next mountain destination—appear ahead of you.

The stream crossings continue, and you pass over several significant tributaries. The trail becomes increasingly gentle as it parallels audible but out-of-sight Cedar Brook. The route makes a broad curving switchback left, then right, and joins the route of an old railroad bed. Now begins some of the hike's easiest cruising. The presence of striped and red maple marks your return to hardwood forest, joined shortly by black cherry and prolific painted trillium. Beech, yellow birch, and white pine quickly follow. The trail unrolls beneath your feet. Cedar Brook picks up volume as it rushes down a steeper gorge below you to the left.

Watch for railroad relics as you go—metal items occasionally protrude from the trail and chunks of lightweight coal still speckle the ground. You cross numerous small tributaries. Substantial Cedar Brook appears below. The trail eventually cruises down to touch the water (10.4/1,970), but then quickly turns away again. Big-tooth aspen appear in abundance as the trail runs nearly level. Chugging along, you pass through a small clearing with old metal debris—the former site of a logging camp. The path slowly descends, offering up occasional glimpses of the lower Bonds. The audible roar of the East Branch Pemigewasset River infuses the woods, old railroad ties appear in the path, and you reach the Pemi East Side Trail on the left (11.8/1,730).

Bear right to remain on the Cedar Brook Trail, which remains on a wide railroad bed. You cross numerous rivulets and brooks, go over a long stretch of railroad ties, and then curve left to reach the Wilderness Trail (12.4/1,630). Heading right on the Wilderness Trail leads you upstream to an area of good camping opportunities, but your continuing route bears left to follow the Wilderness Trail down to meet the river.

Wide, fast-moving, and seldom deep, the river is accessible via a minor scramble. Explorations both up and downstream can be made with little difficulty, and fishing opportunities are good. There are no major swimming holes in the immediate vicinity, though many spots are deep enough for a sit-and-soak. White pines grow along the banks. Alders populate small islands.

The old railroad bridge footings, built of river stones, still stand in the middle of the river, but today you bounce across the river on a large suspension bridge. Once on the other side, the trail curves left to cruise through hardwood forest and reach an old dilapidated railroad trestle near Black Brook. In case it isn't obvious, the rickety structure is posted as unsafe for climbing. Limited views look south toward your approach route down the Cedar Brook drainage. A hundred yards past the trestle, a bridge crosses Black Brook and takes you to the Bondcliff Trail on the right (13.1/1,590).

Head up the blue-blazed Bondcliff Trail, quickly crossing a small brook. Watch for a 20- to 30-foot section of old railroad track lying to the side. The trail briefly touches Black Brook and then passes an old campsite on the left, where a sign reminds you that overnight use is no longer permitted here. You pass another old site on the right as the single-track trail rises among dense hardwoods. You cross another small creek as you steadily climb. The trail levels briefly and you can see the Hancocks south through the trees.

Contouring level along the slopes, the path now traverses parallel to audible but invisible Black Brook. Wet and boggy in spots, the trail next descends to reach the rushing stream by another no-camping site on the far shore. The rocky route runs up along Black Brook, and soon the woods start to transition back to spruce-fir. You step over a few more streams and then cross Black Brook (14.7/2,500). The gradient now steepens and leads upward at a consistent angle—good for maintaining a steady cruising climb. The trail re-crosses the brook (15.0/2,690) and drops briefly before resuming the ascent parallel to a small tributary. A rock staircase aids your efforts.

The trail levels out again, contours back toward Black Brook, and crosses it once more. Twisted paper birch dot the slopes, framing the bouldery watercourse. A palpable sense of height infuses the trail as it snakes upward, offering intermittent views south of the Hancocks. The trail charges upward, steady and steep, crossing two brooks before curving right and easing as it contours upward. It then curves back left and begins the final long traverse, passing several small springs. The trail curves right again for its final ascent and soon enters the alpine zone, immediately encountering a large outcrop that requires hand-over-hand scrambling. On top is your first unobstructed view of the west Pemigewasset Wilderness.

Look southeast and trace the Pemigewasset River as it drains toward the Kancamagus Highway. Scar Ridge rises on the opposite side. To the west, the long line of Franconia Ridge (Trip 18), topped by Mount Lafayette, towers over the humped massif of Owl's Head.

The trees diminish immediately past this point and you quickly top out on Bondcliff (17.5/4,265). Blocky vertical cliffs give the mountain its name, a jumbled wall of stone that boasts an exceptional view. The whole east half of the Pemigewasset Wilderness rolls out before you. To the south, Mount

Carrigain and the Hancocks bulge upward. Evidence of old logging roads can still be identified on Mount Hancock, and the broad drainage of Cedar Brook is visible to its west. East of Carrigain in order are the red-orange slopes of Mount Lowell, the round hump of Mount Anderson, and then Mount Nancy. Shoal Pond Brook—your return route—flows down the second stream valley to the east. In the southern distance, you can make out Osceola and distinctive Greeley Notch. Scar Ridge and the slopes of Loon Mountain Ski Area are visible to the southwest, and due west is the hulking hump of Owl's Head. Franconia Ridge rises behind it, crenulated by Mounts Lafayette, Lincoln, Liberty, and Flume from north to south. Below you to the northeast is the deep gully of Redrock Brook.

From here, the trail traces visibly up Mount Bond ahead. Prominent fir waves line its upper slopes. The rocky trail travels along the open ridge and past alpine vegetation. Distinctive clumps of diapensia dot the ground in dense rounded mats. You drop briefly, resume climbing up Mount Bond, enter chest-high krummholz, and in short order reach the open summit and its 360-degree views (18.7/4,698).

The view here penetrates farther northeast. You can now spot the bare cliffs of Whitewall Mountain above Zealand Notch. Mount Washington and the Presidential Range are almost directly in line with the cliffs. To the north-northwest is the bald peak of South Twin, but your continuing route heads north over Mount Guyot and Zealand Mountain. Farther east Mount Field

Zealand Falls

and the deep scalloped slopes of Mount Willey hide Crawford Notch from view, located on the other side. Ethan Pond shimmers below Mount Willey.

Past the summit, you return to the trees, hopping along rocks and bog bridging. Intermittent glimpses northwest reveal Mount Garfield. The trail then steepens, offering open views of South Twin, Lafayette, and Guyot, among other peaks. You then reach a spur on the left leading to West Bond (19.2/4,470).

SIDE-TRIP TO WEST BOND

To bag this 4,000-footer (1.0 mile round-trip with 350 feet of elevation gain), turn left on the West Bond Spur and follow the rocky single-track path through dense spruce-fir woods The path drops, then steadily rises and encounters a bouldery section shortly before hitting the rocky summit knob and another excellent view of the west Pemigewasset Wilderness. Mount Bond probably has the better view—views here are blocked toward the east.

Back on the Bondcliff Trail, you drop steeply and soon enter the Forest Protection Area that surrounds Guyot Campsite. Several overflow campsites appear by the trail shortly before it reaches the spur for the camping area (19.4/4,340). Continuing onward, you head toward Mount Guyot. The trail climbs slowly, leaves behind the Forest Protection Area, and levels briefly before descending a short distance. Mount Guyot's broad, bald summit dome appears ahead. A steady uphill climb returns you to the alpine zone, where the path navigates a minor boulder field and then busts out atop the open summit plateau.

The view is good, though Bondcliff and areas south are now obscured by West Bond and Bond. Views east include Mounts Willey and Carrigain; Mount Washington and the smoke from Cog railway are visible in the distance. Dropping from the summit area, you pass briefly among head-high trees and then traverse a slope to reach the Twinway and the AT (20.0/4,510).

Turn right on the Twinway, joining the white-blazed AT, and climb briefly to reach Guyot's actual summit. The trail now quickly reenters head-high trees and leaves the alpine zone. It's a steep and rocky drop—the rockiest yet—and some sections feel like you're hopping down a talus field. The trail moderates and becomes less rocky, though now rooty and boggy, and soon resumes a steady drop. The rounded hump of Zealand Mountain appears ahead shortly before you bottom out in a saddle (21.1/4,020).

Resume climbing, this time over large rocks and stone stairs. You pass a small spring shortly before the trail crests (21.3/4,220), where a short spur leads to the actual (viewless) summit of Zealand Mountain.

The trail now steadily descends, passing through a fir wave marked by numerous bleached snags. A long, gradual downhill leads over forgiving terrain. The trail then levels, follows ribbons of bedrock, and then briefly rises to reach a coarse-grained granite boulder with large crystals of rectangular white feldspar. Ethan Pond is visible from here, as is Shoal Pond for the first time. Carrigain Notch frames Mount Chocorua to the southeast. Look east to spot Mount Washington, Mount Jefferson, and beyond to Mount Hale in the Carter Range (Trip 24).

The route now plummets over solid rock, a ladder, and some steep staircase-like drops. It mellows shortly before reaching a spur on the right to swampy—and tent-unfriendly—Zeacliff Pond (22.5/3,760). Continuing, the trail momentarily rises, cruises along, and breaks out at another good view east of Mount Willard and the Presidentials beyond. The junction for the Zeacliff Trail is just ahead (22.9/3,740).

SIDE-TRIP TO ZEACLIFF AND ZEALAND FALLS HUT.

The described route turns right to descend the Zeacliff Trail, but if you continue straight on the Twinway for 0.2 mile, you'll reach the top of Zeacliff—one of the classic views of the White Mountains. You can continue onward past the view for another 1.1 miles, dropping rapidly to reach the AMC's Zealand Falls Hut. From there, head south for 1.6 miles via the fast-walking Ethan Pond Trail to rejoin the described route at the lower Zeacliff Trail junction. This longer variation adds 1.5 miles to the hike. There is a much-used camping area along the Ethan Pond Trail a short distance south of Zealand Falls Hut.

Turn right and head down the narrow Zeacliff Trail, which immediately crosses back into the Pemigewasset Wilderness. Paper birch increases as you descend sharply past bouldery outcrops and views of Mount Carrigain. After negotiating a challenging drop over solid granite slabs, the trail contours left and passes some bulging stones. The super-plummet soon resumes. A staircase of roots and rocks soon leads you down the middle of a small, flowing creek.

The trail bends left, curves right, and offers a tempting view of the prominent cliffs of Whitewall Mountain. Looming above Zealand Notch, the cliff was laid bare by the large-scale wildfires that followed extensive logging in the early twentieth century. The trail next enters a serene grove of paper birch, where the going gets easier. Blackberry vines, bracken ferns, and trillium punctuate a dense understory of hobblebush—a beautiful flowering scene in late May and early June.

The trail briefly traverses before resuming a plummeting trajectory downward. The trail descends through continuing paper birch forest and then cuts left to drop into a conifer grove. As you approach the bottom, yellow birch, mountain maple, and red trillium (wake robin) appear in increasing abundance. One final drop along a rocky streambed deposits you at the banks of Whitewall Brook.

Rock-hop the burbling stream to reach a pleasant camping area on the opposite bank. Look for fresh beaver activity in the area. The trail then climbs a boulder field to emerge in a swath of talus, created during construction of the old railroad bed above you. Follow the blazes to reach the former railroad route (24.3/2,520), today the Ethan Pond Trail, and turn right.

The Ethan Pond Trail runs totally level and passes a diverse assemblage of flora. A watchful eye will notice almost all the common constituents of the northern hardwood forest along this section: hobblebush, red maple, mountain ash, yellow clintonia, red spruce, fir, yellow and paper birch, sugar maple, Solomon's seal, wake robin, hazel, and quaking aspen. Zealand Falls Hut is visible up the valley behind you as the trail cruises alongside massive talus fields. The cliffs of Whitewall Mountain tower overhead; giant boulders overhead look like they could fall at any moment. Increasingly dense spruce-fir forest surrounds the trail as you continue, reaching a brook dotted with the large veined leaves of false hellebore and then rising slightly to reach the Thoreau Falls Trail on the right (25.1/2,450).

SIDE-TRIP TO THOREAU FALLS

This short detour is well worth it. Located only a few minutes' walk down the Thoreau Falls Trail, this zigzagging cascade roars over polished slabs, dropping 70 feet in sheets of foaming white. A head-deep swimming hole fills a pool at the base of the falls, but requires careful scrambling to reach. The continuing Thoreau Falls Trail provides no access.

Continue on the wide Ethan Pond Trail, hiking closer to the increasingly audible North Fork of the East Branch Pemigewasset River. The trail narrows to single-track and runs along the waterway before crossing it on a wooden footbridge. You parallel the stream on the opposite side and pass at least one established tentsite; the area has good potential for camping, with abundant level ground and a relatively open forest. The trail next encounters the Shoal Pond Trail on the right (25.6/2,520)—watch for the double-white blazes to indicate its approach.

Turn right on the Shoal Pond Trail and leave the AT behind. The blue-blazed trail immediately thins. Moose frequent the area; look for fresh tracks in the mud. The level path reaches shallow Shoal Pond (26.3/2,580). The pond's one established campsite is located midway down the pond on the left side of the trail, just past a small creek. A nicer site can be found on the rise adjacent to the obvious trailside site.

The pond can be accessed in several spots, but the shore is generally boggy with few good spots for lounging. Small larch trees and carnivorous pitcher plants grow in the surrounding area. Mount Carrigain can be seen from the north end of the pond, Whitewall, Zeacliff, and Zealand mountains are visible from the south end. Spring peepers and fish are abundant; moose are in the vicinity. Fishing is catch-and-release; only single barbless hooks are allowed.

Past the pond, the Shoal Pond Trail parallels the tannin-brown outlet stream, soon crosses it, and then leaves it behind. The path travels over old puncheon and then widens as it returns to a railroad bed. Puncheon increases as you proceed through dense forest, at one point following a flowing stream-bed. The trail descends slightly and re-crosses Shoal Pond Brook (27.2/2,400), now a rocky stream. Your journey now tours long stretches of puncheon, nar-row overgrown sections, rock-hoppin' boggy bits, and occasional dry spots. You cross a rocky tributary and then return to Shoal Pond Brook, which now requires a trickier rock-hop to cross (28.0/2,260). A small campsite nestles on the opposite bank. The trail turns downstream to the left (not up and out) and becomes thinner, brushier, and more difficult to follow. After a narrow traverse above the water, the trail then descends a rock staircase to return near the stream. The route returns to the railroad bed and passes a few sections of old railroad ties and at least one piece of rail. A few small campsites pass on the left, one near a swimming hole and rock sluice.

The route now sticks to the railroad bed, traveling at times along a raised berm. After a long stretch of easy cruising, you pass some metal debris near a small open field—another former logging camp. The trail next cuts right, dropping off the berm to return to the brook. You pass some potential camping areas and rock-hop across the stream (29.0/2,190). Once across, you quickly regain the berm and fire up your boilers for a long stretch of easy chugging down a straight and flat thoroughfare. You next reach Anderson Brook, where there is another established campsite (29.6/2,080). The trail turns left along the shin-deep brook and then crosses it by old railroad bridge footings. Rock-hopping is not an option—you'll need to ford it.

Once on the other side, bear left on the yellow-blazed Carrigain Notch Trail to head through spruce-fir chaos forest. Mount Carrigain looms ahead through the trees. After a slow rise, you reach rushing Carrigain Branch. A number of nice campsites line the bouldery stream. The trail curves left and follows a smaller tributary to reach the Desolation Trail (30.0/2,250).

Bear right on the Desolation Trail. Cross Carrigain Branch (your last reliable water for the next 3.5 miles), walk along some rotten puncheon, and start ascending. The easy-to-follow trail is in good shape and steadily ascends over dirt and roots through a pleasant forest. The trail briefly traverses to the left, curves straight uphill, and then makes a rising traverse to the right. Distant mountains peek through the trees and there's a feeling of growing elevation. Paper birch increases as the gradient increases and the trail starts traversing up a steep slope to the left. Carrigain Branch rushes far below, and the occasional vista looks northeast to Mount Washington and the Presidentials.

The trail becomes rockier around 3,300 feet. By 3,600 feet, you're ascending the first section of rock and talus. Then the trail heads directly uphill on a radical talus staircase that requires hand-over-hand scrambling. You soon reach the trail's best view thus far, encompassing the Webster Cliffs above Crawford Notch, the Presidentials beyond, and much of the east Pemigewasset Wilderness, including Zeacliff, Mount Hale, Whitewall Mountain, and the Shoal Pond Brook drainage.

Past this point, the trail becomes somewhat less vertical. Up and up you go. As you near the top, the trail traverses left and levels. You then bank right and complete the final climb to the summit lookout tower (31.9/4,700).

The view from the Carrigain lookout is one of the best in New England. You can see most of your backpacking route, from the Hancocks to the west, to the Bonds, to the AT route over Zealand and down Zeacliff, including a great view of U-shaped Zealand Valley. Shoal Pond and the dark green conifer corridor of Shoal Pond Brook trace your most recent passage. Farther west are Owl's Head and all of Franconia Ridge. East is a grand view of the Presidentials and the Dry River watershed that drains its southern tier (Trip 20). In the eastern distance are the Carter Range and more distant Baldface Range that hem in the Wild River watershed (Trip 24). The whole Sandwich Range fills the southern vista; you can make out Ossipee Lake to the right of pyramidal Mount Chocorua. Below you to the south is the rocky spine of Signal Ridge, which drops down into the Sawyer River drainage toward Hancock Notch.

Several established campsites are located just below the summit, including a large clearing with a fire ring and nice hammock-style swing. Head down the Signal Ridge Trail, immediately descending a rock staircase into mature spruce-fir forest. The rocky trail switchbacks left and then contours past another campsite before resuming its descent. Another slow traversing descent deposits you on open Signal Ridge, which offers up views—your last!—into Carrigain Notch below, including the scarred flanks of Mount Lowell on its far side.

You rise briefly along the ridge to its high point (32.4/4,500) and then resume a sharp descent. A minefield of rocks fills the trail for the remainder of the descent. The trail switchbacks right, makes a slow descending curve back left, levels out, and then drops more gradually. After another switchback right, the sinuous trail curves back and forth and then at about 4,000 feet takes a more direct line down. Paper birch reappears. Several small switchbacks lead you down the ridge, and you curve right on a mile-long traverse that passes a series of flowing springs—the first significant water since Carrigain Branch.

The trail makes a long steady drop, encounters another spring, and then steepens further. Striped maple and hobblebush appear around 3,000 feet, and you soon pass through a pleasant grove of paper birch. The Mount Lowell cliffs can be glimpsed to the left as the trail cuts left, switchbacks right, and passes sugar and mountain maple for the first time. The trail continues on a rocky, rocky traverse. By 2,500 feet, beech and yellow birch appear. The trail switchbacks left by a nice yellow birch. By the time the route switchbacks right again the transition to northern hardwood forest is complete.

You parallel above Carrigain Brook, passing through a mature swath of woods with substantial sugar maples and yellow birch. The trail drops to the brook, crosses it, and finally becomes less rocky. The trail descends near the brook, crossing it twice, and then reaches the main stem. Cross the larger stream and reach the Carrigain Notch Trail on the left (35.2/1,880). Continue straight on the wide Signal Ridge Trail.

A few hundred yards past the junction, an old logging road branches off to the right. Unsigned, it looks more like a path than a road and is blocked with some minor debris. It represents your quickest return to the starting trailhead. Turn right off the main trail to follow this road. (You can also continue on the Signal Ridge Trail for another 1.7 miles, which deposits you on Sawyer River Road two miles from your starting point.)

Initially overgrown, the road makes a brief rise along a cut-over area to your right. A quarter mile past the junction, the overgrown road abruptly becomes a dirt access road. It steadily drops, makes one final rise, and then descends to cross Carrigain Brook on a bridge and reach Sawyer River Road (36.5/1,700). Turn right and follow Sawyer River Road back to your car (36.8/1710). Your total experience is complete.

INFORMATION

Lincoln Woods Visitor Center, Kancamagus Highway, Lincoln, NH 03251, 603-630-5190, www.fs.fed.us/r9/forests/white_mountain, open seven days a week, 8 a.m.–3:30 p.m.

TRIP 20
DRY AND HIGH

Location: Presidential Range–Dry River Wilderness, White Mountain National Forest
Highlights: A wild watershed, the alpine peaks of the southern Presidentials
Distance: 16.5 miles round trip
Total Elevation Gain/Loss: 5,800/5,100
Trip Length: 2 days
Difficulty: ★★★★
Recommended Maps: Bradford Washburn's *Mount Washington and the Presidential Range* Appalachian Mountain Club; *AMC White Mountain Guide, Map 1: Presidential Range,* AMC Books

The Dry River pours south from Mount Washington through one of the wildest and least traveled regions in the Presidential Range. Come travel the length of this rocky waterway, from its confluence with the Saco River to its very headwaters in Oakes Gulf, then cruise south high above it along the heavily trod alpine ridge of the southern Presidentials. It's a bonanza of stimulation—rapids, waterfalls, summits, views, solitude, and people mania—all rolled into one adventure.

HIKE OVERVIEW

This trip is a study in contrasts. The first half tours a peaceful river valley with limited views and few people. The second half winds along an open ridgeline with continuous views and hikers.

The first 9.6 miles travel along the Dry River Trail, closely following the river with regular access for swimming and fishing. Spend your first night at either the Dry River Shelter #3 or at one of the handful of designated campsites spread along the trail (see later). Note that the Dry River is notorious for flooding during periods of snowmelt and heavy rain—avoid this area during such times.

You next ascend the headwall of Oakes Gulf to meet the Crawford Path— part of the Appalachian Trail (AT)—at the AMC's Lakes of the Clouds Hut. From here, it's a long ridgeline traverse over the southern Presidentials and the summits of Mounts Monroe, Eisenhower, and Pierce. You then descend to the Highland Center at Crawford Notch, passing near Mizpah Spring Hut and adjacent Nauman Tentsite en route. You'll need to leave a bike, hitchhike, or

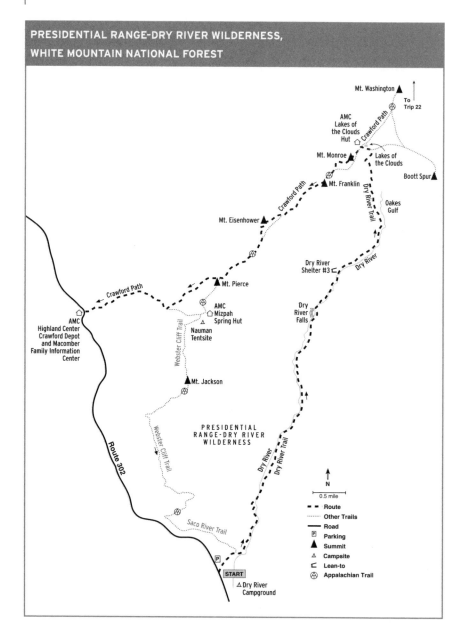

PRESIDENTIAL RANGE-DRY RIVER WILDERNESS,
WHITE MOUNTAIN NATIONAL FOREST

shuttle cars to return to your starting trailhead 5 miles away. Dogs are allowed except at the AMC huts.

OVERNIGHT OPTIONS

Dispersed camping is permitted throughout the Presidential Range–Dry River Wilderness and the Forest Service has established a series of six designated sites along the Dry River Trail. Only one designated site is located past the Dry River Shelter #3, however, where steep and boggy terrain makes good tentsites hard to find. Camping is prohibited above treeline, and once on the ridge your only overnight options are Lakes of the Clouds Hut, Mizpah Springs Hut, and the Nauman Tentsite. Campfires are permitted at designated campsites.

Dry River Shelter #3 is located 6.3 miles from the trailhead by the Dry River at 3,100 feet. It is one of only three remaining shelters in the wilderness, and the only one along the Dry River Trail. (In keeping with wilderness management guidelines, the United States Forest Service removes rather than renovates shelters in wilderness areas as they fall into disrepair.) The lightly used shelter is in good condition, has a capacity of eight, and features some well-used tenting areas behind it. There is no fee.

Designated Campsites have been established by the United States Forest Service (USFS) in an effort to focus use and minimize impact. Posted with small brown tent signs, the six sites are located 2.1, 2.9, 3.6, 4.5, 4.9, and 8.8 miles from the trailhead, respectively. They are bold-faced in the following hike description.

Lakes of the Clouds Hut perches a mile high near the midpoint of the hike, 9.6 miles from the trailhead. This more expensive overnight option is located in a dramatic alpine setting with great dining room views of the northern Presidentials. Lakes is the most popular hut in the system and is full most weekends. Book far ahead if possible (603-466-2727, www.outdoors.org/lodging).

Mizpah Spring Hut is located 2.6 miles from Crawford Notch (14.3 miles from the trailhead) at 3,777 feet, and is a good option if you are interested in extending the trip another day. Tucked within dense woods, it receives much less traffic than Lakes of the Clouds and often has better availability.

Nauman Tentsite is located adjacent to Mizpah Hut, and provides seven tent platforms within thick spruce-fir forest. An AMC caretaker is in residence between Memorial Day and Labor Day, plus most fall weekends, and collects an overnight per person fee. As one of the few designated camping areas in the Presidentials, it receives steady use.

TO REACH THE TRAILHEAD

Follow Route 302 south of the Highland Center in Crawford Notch for 5.4 miles. Coming from the south, follow Route 302 approximately 10 miles north from Bartlett; the trailhead is 0.3 mile north of the Dry River Campground entrance. The small parking area is along the side of the road and signed for the Dry River Trail.

HIKE DESCRIPTION

From the trailhead (0.0/1,200), strike out beneath the overhanging branches of beech and yellow birch, passing a FOOT TRAVEL WELCOME sign posted to a wooden barrier. Note the lacy foliage of a hemlock, the first conifer on your left. Proceed past an information sign and travel through a typical northern hardwood forest; watch for sugar maple, white ash, and an understory of false Solomon's seal, trillium, elderberry, wild oats, and sarsparilla. At this low elevation, a few red oaks mix in as well.

The level single-track trail soon enters more mature forest, where larger yellow birch and sugar maple shade an open understory. The Saco River Trail comes in from the left (0.5/1,290) and a trail splits right toward the campground, but you continue straight to remain on the Dry River Trail. A spur soon leads right toward the Dry River, 30 feet wide and full of rounded rocks of all shapes and sizes.

You cross into the wilderness area (0.7/1,340). The audible river rushes just out-of-sight nearby. You then approach a boulder-choked stream, where the trail bears left as indicated by an arrow sign. The route steepens and becomes rockier as it climbs the slopes and parallels the Dry River about 30 feet below. Climbing steadily, the narrow trail passes some impressive hemlock, drops briefly, and then makes a steep and abrupt rise past numerous hemlocks. As you crest this section, keep an eye out for a brief view. Through a break in the trees, you can peer up the length of the river valley to Mount Washington and Mount Monroe.

The trail then descends to reach the site of the Dry River Bridge (1.7/1,600), which was heavily damaged by flooding in 2005 and scheduled for replacement in September 2007. The river is readily accessible in both directions. Just upstream is a mellow pool, and downstream is a deeper spot better for a full-body dunk. Small brook trout are abundant.

Once on the opposite shore, the trail climbs a pair of switchbacks and contours above the river 10 to 30 feet below. You next reach a posted sign for the first designated **campsite**, located near the river (2.1/1,780). From here the trail winds past extensive hobblebush, travels away from and then back toward the river, turns upslope, and then proceeds along a long level section to reach the Mount Clinton Trail on the left (2.9/1,930). Another designated **campsite** is located here in a flat clearing of sugar maple and paper birch. The nearby river is audible as you continue, rock-hopping a substantial tributary as you go. The trail rises gently for a long section, then encounters another designated **campsite** by a small tributary (3.6/2,150). Two sites are available beneath spruce, fir, and paper birch. Slivers of views look south toward distant peaks.

As you proceed, the surrounding forest begins its transition to spruce-fir. Sugar maple and yellow birch remain, but increasing hobblebush, striped maple, clintonia, red spruce, and balsam fir indicate the shift. The trail climbs steadily, at one point turning upslope to rise steeply and reach its highest point above the rushing river. You then make a steady traverse back toward the water; as you go, enjoy brief glimpses up the river toward the head of the valley. Along the way, you pass another designated **campsite** (4.5/2,500) in a clearing of fir and paper birch. The river is readily accessible and close to the site. Just upstream is another (undesignated) campsite by a pretty tributary. Continuing, the trail encounters a stream with pleasant cascades, follows it a short distance upstream, and then crosses it to reach the Isolation Trail entering from the right (4.9/2,600).

Remain on the Dry River Trail and immediately reach another designated **campsite** on the left, a clearing perched on the edge of the river canyon. Though audible, the river is neither visible nor accessible—the tributary is the only water source. From here, the trail travels through thick young forest. The path becomes faint in spots; a scattering of yellow blazes help you remain on course. You next reach the Mount Eisenhower Trail on your left (5.2/2,680). Bear right to remain on the Dry River Trail, climbing briefly up a steep and trickling path. As the path levels again, the hissing roar of Dry River Falls begins to infuse the air.

To reach the falls (5.4/2,800), watch for an unmarked spur on the left, which drops 70 feet to the river on a scrambling descent. The reward is a 20-foot curtain of water falling into a deep pool. Above the falls is a circular bowl carved into bedrock, fed by two small cascades. Flat outcrops line the pool. The falls also act as a natural fish barrier. Dozens of small brook trout inhabit the pool below the falls, but none live above it, unable to surmount the tumbling obstacle.

Back on the main trail, you pass through thick spruce-fir forest with an occasional glimpse ahead of Mount Monroe and the alpine ridge. You then return to the Dry River and cross it (5.6/2,850). Though considerably diminished, the river must still be forded or crossed on a delicate rock-hop. Watch for the arrow signs that indicate the designated crossing point. Once on the other side, the trail continues upcanyon, becoming narrow and muddy in spots as it stays close to the river. You cross a small tributary along the way to the Dry River Shelter #3, located adjacent to the trail (6.3/3,100).

Dry River Falls

Past the shelter, the trail briefly follows a tributary, rock-hops across it, and then leaves the Dry River behind for good. Yellow blazes help identify the route as it next crosses a rivulet, curves left to re-cross it, and starts climbing a small rocky streamcourse. The faint trail clambers over mossy boulders, and then enters the hike's boggiest section. Super-thick spruce-fir forest surrounds you; trees sprout from a lumpy understory of wood ferns, sorrel, and moss.

The trail briefly approaches the Dry River, where a spur leads down to access it by an undesignated campsite (7.3/3,600). Now the path becomes extremely boggy as it rises upward into Oakes Gulf. At one point, the trail levels out and offers views of Boott Spur to the east. As you crest 4,000 feet, the trail levels and provides intermittent views of the approaching headwall and flanks of Mount Monroe. The route then curves left and clambers up a steep rocky section. You pass the final designated **campsite** on the right (8.8/4,150), a large clearing 30 feet down from the trail.

The steep climb continues. You quickly cross a stream, then crest briefly and descend. Increasingly dramatic views peek through the trees. Views become increasingly open as you resume your ascent; an avalanche path is evident below Boott Spur. You pass a nice water source and then encounter views south for the first time. The distinctive pyramid of Mount Chocorua in the Sandwich Range is visible (Trip 17).

Now the trail gets radical and climbs exposed rocks that survey the landscape. Stunted fir and paper birch accompany you, as does a rushing nearby tributary on the right—the uppermost headwaters of the Dry River. As you crest 4,700 feet, the views become almost continuous. To the east, the long spine of Montalban Ridge and the Davis Path (Trip 21) can be seen tracing south.

Now the trail becomes nothing but loose rocks, the route indicated by cairns and yellow blazes. Curving right as indicated by a sign, you make the final ascent. Burning lungs provide ample persuasion to stop and admire views. The bald hump of Mount Monroe rises above you; the long alpine plateau of the southern Presidentials extends south. Look for the distinctive patterns of fir waves in the valley below. The trail contours briefly, heads up a rock slide, and crosses the posted wilderness boundary (9.4/5,100). Go a few steps farther and nearby Mount Washington heaves into view. You then reach the divide and complete your traverse of the entire Dry River watershed.

Lakes of the Clouds Hut now appears a short distance ahead. Dropping along the west shore of the small namesake lake (no swimming allowed), you quickly reach the Crawford Path and the end of the Dry River Trail. Head over to the hut for a snack, view, water, or bottomless bowl of soup (9.6/5,012).

From here, you follow the white-blazed Crawford Path (part of the AT) south. Immediately past the hut, the Ammonoosuc Ravine Trail joins from the right. A short distance farther, a spur splits right to tag the summit of Mount Monroe. Bear right to head to the top, at first aided by rock stairs. A more direct ascent up solid bedrock then leads to the summit (10.0/5,372). (You can also continue around the summit on the Crawford Path, which saves a few hundred feet of climbing.)

The view from Monroe is the best of the hike. North are Mounts Washington, Jefferson, Adams, and Madison, marching in that order to the horizon in all their rockpile glory. To the east and south, stare down the entire Dry River drainage. The prominent pyramid of Chocorua appears farther south; the Sandwich Range runs to its west (Trips 16 and 17). Lake Winnipesaukee peeks out to Chocorua's right; the even more distant Belknap Range can be spotted above the lake's south shore. Down below to the west are the Mount Washington Hotel and Bretton Ridge Ski Area. The spine of Franconia Ridge lies out in the western distance (Trip 18), and the peaks of Vermont's Green Mountains dot the horizon.

After soaking up the view, head down the far side of Monroe on a steep and rocky path. At one point, you almost reconnect with the Crawford Path below, but bear right instead to clamber over a small rise. You then abruptly drop off the ridge around some large boulders and rejoin the Crawford Path (10.4/5,070).

The Crawford Path is bordered with rocks, both to highlight the path and discourage off-trail wanderings in the fragile alpine vegetation. Stunted spruce and fir appear intermittently in the tundra-scape. Endless views make watching your footing difficult. Behind you, Mount Washington peeks through a gap above Monroe. The trail next encounters a short spur on the left that leads to the top of Mount Franklin (10.6/5,001), a small promontory on the ridge.

From here, the trail runs mostly level and then descends toward the col below Mount Eisenhower. You soon enter the first head-high forest since attaining the ridge, which hides the mountains from view. Rock slabs lead you down toward the col and the Mount Eisenhower Trail (11.6/4,490), which climbs out of the Dry River Valley to the left. Remain on the Crawford Path as it briefly descends and then climbs, making a quick switchback right and reaching the four-way junction with the Edmands Path (right), Crawford Path (left), and the Eisenhower Loop to the summit straight ahead (11.8/4,450). The swampy puddle of Red Pond is nearby to the left.

In inclement weather or tired leg conditions, remain on the Crawford Path to traverse through head-high forest around the south flanks of Mount Eisenhower. In all other conditions, ascend Eisenhower for the view. Mount Washington and the northern Presidentials reappear as you begin your ascent. A steep and rocky climb interspersed with the occasional switchback leads you to the rounded summit dome, then a gradual rise deposits you at the giant pile of rocks and 15-foot-diameter stone ring that mark the top (12.2/4,760). The views are tremendous once again, the last 360-degree mega-view of the hike. Enjoy.

Descending from the summit, the trail traverses down and to the right before cutting left on a switchback. Dropping steeply at times, it returns to head-high conifers shortly before rejoining the Crawford Path (12.6/4,440), which enters from the left. Follow the Crawford Path south, passing through open, slabby terrain near treeline. The trail passes through corridors of 8-foot high trees with occasional boggy bits. Mount Eisenhower is the only peak still visible.

You cross a flowing creek—the first water since Lakes of the Clouds Hut—in a stand of larger trees. Other constituents of the spruce-fir mélange reappear, including mountain ash, yellow clintonia, and bunchberry. After tra-

Above Oakes Gulf

versing a wet and boggy section over rotten puncheon, the trail starts a slow rise toward Mount Pierce. Views behind you reappear of Mounts Monroe, Washington, and then Jefferson. You then reach the Webster Cliff Trail on the left (13.4/4,290).

Direct Route to the Ending Trailhead. From here, your most direct route out is via the Crawford Path, a 3.1-mile descent to Crawford Notch. (See later for the slightly longer variation via Mizpah Spring Hut.) The trail descends steadily at moderate grades, crossing several rivulets before reaching the Mizpah Cutoff on the left (14.6/3,530). Remain on the Crawford Path, continuing your descent through increasingly lush forest. Yellow birch appears, and soon Gibbs Brook becomes audible to your right. Paper and yellow birch increasingly predominate along the lush trail corridor. The well-graded trail descends parallel to the brook, which eventually comes into view at about 2,400 feet. Shortly past this point, a posted spur leads right to Gibbs Falls, a narrow cascade that drops 30 feet down a rocky runnel (15.9/2,280).

From here, the route runs alongside the creek to reach the Crawford Connector (16.3/2,100), which heads right to a trailhead parking area on the

Mount Clinton Road. Remain on the Crawford Path, winding past hemlocks and sugar maples to reach the ending trailhead by Route 302 in Crawford Notch (16.5/1,900).

Trailhead via Mizpah Spring Hut. To head toward Mizpah Spring Hut and Nauman Tentsite from Mount Pierce, bear left on the Webster Cliff Trail. You immediately climb to an open plateau just below the forested summit of Mount Pierce. It's your last full view of the Presidentials. Looking north down the spine of the mountains and over into the Dry River Valley, you can trace almost your entire route. Past the viewpoint, you quickly reenter forest and soon pass a spur that leads left to another view.

Descend through the woods, passing over rock slabs. The trail initially undulates and passes a pair of open areas, one with views north to Washington, the other south to the Sandwich Range. Soon the trail descends over slabs, switchbacks left, and then plummets directly down a rocky corridor. A Forest Protection Area sign indicates your proximity to Mizpah Spring Hut. Several switchbacks lead through dense forest and deposit you at the hut and adjacent camping area (14.3/3,780).

To return to the Crawford Path, continue past the hut on the Webster Cliff Trail for approximately 200 feet to the Mizpah Cutoff and turn right. Dense woods continue along the Mizpah Cutoff, which runs level along a rocky path before slowly dropping. Extensive cobblestones and rock and log steps aid your descent back to the Crawford Path (15.0/3,530). Turn left and proceed down the Crawford Path as described earlier to Crawford Notch (16.9/1,900).

INFORMATION

White Mountain National Forest, Saco Ranger District office, 33 Kancamagus Highway, Conway, NH 03818, 603-447-5448, www.fs.fed.us/r9/forests/white_mountain; Pinkham Notch Visitor Center, 603-466-2725, open daily 6:30 a.m.–10 p.m.

TRIP 21
GONE ON MONTALBAN

Location: Montalban Ridge, Presidential Range–Dry River Wilderness, White Mountain National Forest
Highlight: The least-traveled ridge in the Presidential Range
Distance: 17.7 miles one-way
Total Elevation Gain/Loss: 7,100/6,100
Trip Length: 2 days
Difficulty: ★★★★
Recommended Maps: Bradford Washburn's *Mount Washington and the Presidential Range,* Appalachian Mountain Club; *AMC White Mountain Guide, Map 1: Presidential Range,* AMC Books

Montalban Ridge runs due south from Mount Washington for 15 miles. The Davis Path runs along its spine, one of the longest and most remote sections of trail in the Whites—remarkable given its location in the heavily trod Presidential Range. Crowds gravitate to the alpine peaks of the southern Presidentials, which runs parallel to the west, but Montalban Ridge boasts three exceptional summits of its own. Located near the geographic center of the Whites, they offer 360-degree views of jagged mountainous horizons.

HIKE OVERVIEW

The hike is a point-to-point journey from the Davis Trail trailhead on Route 302 to the Glen Boulder trailhead on Route 16 and requires a car shuttle or some other means of returning to your starting point. (You can make it into a nearly complete loop by combining it with portions of Trip 20, or lengthen it to a longer point-to-point journey over the northern Presidentials by adding sections of Trip 23.)

You earn it early on the Davis Path, ascending nearly 2,000 feet in the first 2 miles to reach open ledges and remarkable views from the summit of Mount Crawford. From here, it's a long cruise along a forested ridgeline, punctuated by two distinctive landmarks: Resolution Shelter, one of the most vintage in the Whites, and Stairs Mountain, a ledgy promontory. The hike next visits more excellent views atop Mounts Davis and Isolation and then ascends into the alpine zone to reach Boott Spur on Mount Washington's southeast flank.

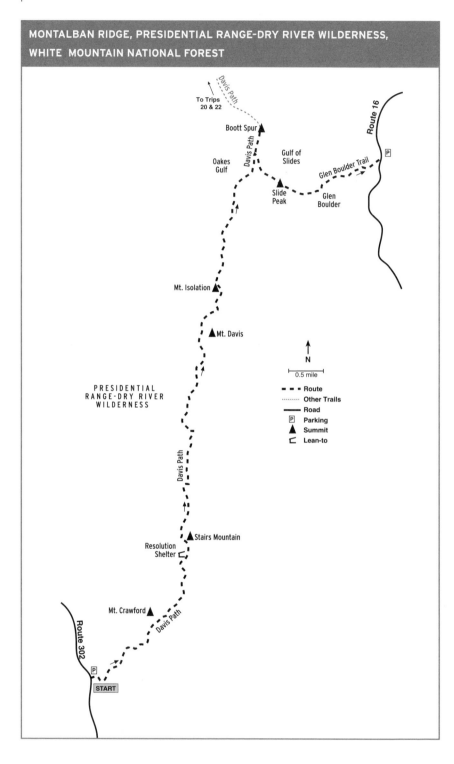

MONTALBAN RIDGE, PRESIDENTIAL RANGE-DRY RIVER WILDERNESS, WHITE MOUNTAIN NATIONAL FOREST

Davis Path

To Trips
20 & 22

Boott Spur

Davis Path

Oakes
Gulf

Gulf of
Slides

Route 16

P

Glen Boulder Trail

Slide
Peak

Glen
Boulder

Mt. Isolation

Mt. Davis

N

0.5 mile

- - - Route
.... Other Trails
——— Road
P Parking
▲ Summit
⊏ Lean-to

PRESIDENTIAL
RANGE-DRY RIVER
WILDERNESS

Davis Path

Stairs Mountain

Resolution
Shelter

Mt. Crawford

Davis Path

Route 302

P

START

The route's final leg descends the Glen Boulder Trail to Route 16, passing the impressive namesake stone en route.

Traffic is light on the Davis Path, though hikers become more common north of Mount Isolation, the only 4,000-footer on the ridge and a popular peak-baggers' destination. Water is scarce, with only a few sources along the ridge. Dogs are allowed.

Longer Variations. From Boott Spur, it is possible to connect with routes over the northern and southern Presidentials for a longer trip with sustained alpine scenery. Consult Trip 20 to connect south down the Dry River Trail or over the southern Presidentials. Review Trip 23 for a description of the route over the northern Presidentials, which ends at Pinkham Notch. These variations add many miles and at least one extra day.

OVERNIGHT OPTIONS

The Forest Service has established a series of designated campsites along Davis Ridge, each indicated by a small sign. Resolution Shelter is another option. Dispersed camping is permitted, but finding a site in the thick and uneven woods is difficult. Resolution Shelter is located near a reliable spring, but none of the campsites have water nearby—you'll need to pack it in whatever you need for the night. Campfires are permitted only at Resolution Shelter.

Resolution Shelter, 4.3 miles from the trailhead, tucks away at 2,920 feet on the slopes below Stairs Mountain. It sits flush against the ground, constructed from simple logs with gaps between. Limited views of the mountain flanks punctuate the otherwise thick forest. Water is available from a thin stream 30 feet below the shelter. Tentsites are scarce near the shelter, though a few marginal spots can be found. The shelter will likely be removed in the near future.

Designated campsites spread along the ridge and are highlighted in bold in the following text. They are generally small and not suited for larger groups. Three sites are located in close proximity to the shelter. The first perches high on Stairs Mountain, and the second and third ensconce themselves in saddles a few miles farther. For a longer first day (12.2 miles) consider using two sites near the end of the ridge, located in the trees just before the trail emerges in the alpine zone on Boott Spur. For late starters, there is also a site located 0.8 mile from the trailhead.

TO REACH THE TRAILHEAD

To Reach the Starting Trailhead. Follow Route 302 south of the Willey House Site in Crawford Notch State Park for 5.6 miles, or just over 6 miles north from

View from Stairs Mountain

Bartlett. The large paved trailhead lot is visible from the highway. A WMNF parking pass is required.

To Reach the Ending Trailhead. Head to the Glen Boulder Trailhead on Route 16, located a mile south of Pinkham Notch Visitor Center. A WMNF parking pass is required. You can also lengthen your trip by 0.6 mile to emerge directly at Pinkham Notch.

HIKE DESCRIPTION

From the parking lot (0.0/990), follow the dirt road signed CRAWFORD VAL-LEY WAY. The road quickly leads to the Saco River, where a suspension bridge crosses the watercourse. Known as the Bemis Bridge, it was completed in February 2001. A plaque provides additional background. Over the bridge you go, admiring the wide boulder-strewn river. Upstream you can see Frankenstein cliffs, a popular ice climbing destination; Mount Webster is the tallest peak behind it.

Once on the other side, the double-track trail passes a private residence on the right and then forks. Go right, respecting the private property signs to the left. Vegetation now encroaches the trail, and the narrower path crosses a swampy stream on a small bridge. The Davis Path was once a bridal path to the summit of Washington in the mid-nineteenth century, but fell into disuse around 1853. The AMC rehabilitated it as a footpath in 1910.

As you proceed, look for common members of the northern hardwood forest: white ash, red oak, yellow birch, hobblebush, striped maple, paper birch, and beech. You then cross into the national forest near an information sign and start a slow steady climb, traversing along a small brook shaded by hemlocks. You soon reach the posted boundary of the Presidential Range–Dry River Wilderness by a nice rock staircase and quickly reach the hike's first designated **campsite** (0.8/1,250), accessed via a short spur and tucked among hemlock, red pine, and spruce. From here, the trail begins a relentless climb up the mountain flanks. The route becomes rockier, spruce increase, and limited views behind you indicate the rising elevation. The burn, baby, burn goes on and on and on.

Views through the trees become more common as you climb, and Mount Willey appears beyond Frankenstein cliffs to the northwest. The vegetation around you transitions to spruce-fir forest, marked by the appearance of bunchberry underfoot and mountain ash overhead. The trail levels out briefly as you attain the ridge and then quickly resumes climbing for the final push to Mount Crawford. Views south open up, revealing the Sandwich Range (Trips 16 and 17) beyond the closer Moat Mountains.

A short distance farther, you reach some open ledges and the hike's first outstanding view south. To the southwest are the Attitash Ski Area and Moat Mountains; the tallest peak in the range is North Moat Mountain. Pointy Mount Chocorua peeks out behind Bear Mountain to the southeast. The two peaks west of Bear Mountain are Bartlett Haystack and Tremont. Below Tremont, trailing to the southwest, is the deep cleft of the Sawyer River Valley. Mount Carrigain looms above it.

Invigorated by the view, continue on the rocky trail and enjoy more views south and west. The first glimpse northeast appears shortly before you reach the spur to the summit of Mount Crawford (2.2/2,900). The continuing trail banks right to reenter the forest, but you should head left up the rock slabs on an indistinct pathway. Open ledges loaded with blueberries lead you to the summit and savory views north (2.5/3,119).

The view encompasses the entire Dry River drainage (Trip 20), extending north to the summit cone of Mount Washington and hemmed to the northwest by the southern Presidential peaks. Looking north along Montalban Ridge, you can spot the flat summit of Mount Resolution and the adjacent ledges and cliffs of Stairs Mountain. To the northwest, you can identify the deep gash of Crawford Notch; Mount Willey looms above it on the opposite side. In the western distance, you can discern the ridge of Mount Bond and Bondcliff in the Pemigewasset Wilderness (Trip 19). On a good day, you can spot Mount Lafayette on Franconia Ridge (Trip 18), 16 miles away.

Back on the Davis Path (2.8/2,900), you reenter the woods and make a mostly level traverse. Views behind you of Mount Crawford punctuate this stretch, as do a handful of larch trees on your right. North America's only deciduous conifer, larch, features small needle clusters and an overall lacy appearance. The trail then reaches the four-way junction (4.3/3,060) with the Mount Parker Trail (right) and the spur to Resolution Shelter (left). A steep 140-foot drop leads to the shelter and one of only two water sources found on the ridge.

The Davis Path next encounters the Stairs Col Trail on the right (4.6/3,060), makes a steep climb, and then levels. Becoming rockier, the path ascends directly and soon passes a sign for a DOWNLOOK on the right, which offers views south to Mount Crawford and beyond. The route returns to the ridgeline, where it encounters a spur on the right for Stairs Mountain (5.0/3,430). A worthwhile 0.2-mile side-trip takes you to the ledges and designated **campsite** atop Stairs Mountain. A nice flat tentsite in the trees provides ready access to outstanding views southwest.

Back on the Davis Trail, you make a slow gentle drop through spruce-fire forest. The trail then steepens before bottoming out in a boggy saddle. On the way back up, the trail passes another designated **campsite** (6.0/2,970) tucked into the woods on the right.

The route now becomes rough and uneven, and passes a few unreliable water sources. The trail steadily rises past rock-and-spruce formations, then levels out in a boggy section and passes an unremarkable designated **campsite** (7.3/3,480). There are two small sites, one near the trail in a rocky clearing, the other 50 yards back in a low-lying spot.

Your at-times boggy traverse continues, passing through a few clearings of dead fir with views toward the southern Presidentials. Marginal wood fern is common along the trail's edge. After a long traverse, you reach the Mount Davis Trail on the right (9.1/3,610).

Bear right and make the trip to the summit. It's a steep and bouldery climb that requires hand-over-hand scrambling as the path clambers over steep rock slabs. The surrounding terrain is steep until you reach the top (9.3/3,819), where there are many flat rocks for soaking in the views.

You're close to the center of the Whites. Mountains and ridges lance the sky in all directions. North, the alpine horseshoe of Mount Monroe, Mount Washington, and Boott Spur arcs around the upper Dry River Valley. The southern Presidentials line down the opposite ridge: Mounts Franklin, Eisenhower, and

Pierce. South is the entire Sandwich Range, from the distinctive pyramid of Mount Chocorua in the east to the summits of Mounts Paugus, Passaconaway, Whiteface, and Tripyramid to the west (Trips 16 and 17). In the distance, beyond and to the right of Chocorua, you can make out the Ossipee Mountains. Southwest, Mounts Carrigain and Hancock mark the southeast boundary of the Pemigewasset Wilderness (Trip 19). Below you to the southeast is the Rocky Branch drainage. East is Doublehead Mountain. Northeast are the Carter Range and the peaks of the Wild River watershed (Trip 24).

Back on the Davis Path (9.5/3,610), you descend to a small brook in the saddle between Mounts Davis and Isolation. Loaf-sized boulders dot the trail as it resumes climbing and curves around the east flanks of Isolation. You reach the spur to the summit on the left, just before the trail starts to descend (10.7/3,910).

To tag the summit of Mount Isolation, follow the spur and make a direct climb to open slabs with great views north of Mount Washington and Oakes Gulf at the head of the Dry River Valley. Good views west look toward the ridges of the Pemigewasset Wilderness—you can make out Zeacliff, the Bonds, and Lafayette.

Back on the Davis Path, you descend the north slope of Mount Isolation, make an undulating traverse along the ridgeline, and pass the first junction with the Isolation Trail on the right (11.6/3,850) and then the second junction

From Stairs Mountain

for the Isolation Trail on the left (11.9/4,150), which descends into the Dry River watershed. Now begins an almost continuous rise into the alpine zone.

The trail briefly crests in a young forest of fir and snags and comes to a clearing. A designated **campsite** is located nearby by the side of the trail (12.2/4,280). Onward, the trail quickly arrives at a viewpoint looking toward Boott Spur ahead. After a slight drop, you resume your ascent and reach the final designated **campsite** on the right (12.3/4,330), located in a secluded grassy clearing.

Bid the trees farewell. They thin and shrink as you climb the rocky route. Views open to the southern Presidentials. The climb is steady and sustained, but never radically steep, and you cross into the alpine zone around 4,700 feet. Regular cairns guide the way as you enter more open terrain. Views now sweep from southeast to southwest and include the long line of Montalban Ridge. The bald summits of Mounts Isolation and Davis are visible.

Continuing, you leave the Presidential Range—Dry River Wilderness and reach the Glen Boulder Trail on the right (13.5/5,170).

Drop your packs at the junction to complete the ascent of Boott Spur, a worthwhile 0.5-mile side-trip with just over 300 feet of elevation gain. Follow the Davis Path as it curves to the right of a rocky hump and soon rewards with motivating views of knobby Boott Spur ahead. At times, you climb parallel to a rocky outcrop on the left. Mount Washington reemerges from behind the ridge. As you crest the spur, upper Huntington Ravine comes into view to the north. From here, the trail drops to the Boott Spur Trail (14.0/5,420). The actual summit is accessible with some minor scrambling—walk on durable rock surfaces to avoid damaging the fragile alpine plants.

The views from the summit are the equal of any on the hike. The deep valley of Route 16 lies below. The ski runs of Wildcat trace down the Wildcat peaks on the opposite side. Looking south you can trace your entire journey along the ridge. The Sandwich Range punctures the southern horizon.

From here, you can connect with the southern Presidentials (Trip 20) by following the Davis Path and then the Camel Trail to reach Lakes of the Clouds Hut. To connect with the northern Presidentials (Trip 23), remain on the Davis Path for 1.4 miles, turn right on the Crawford Path, and follow it over the summit of Washington to the Gulfside Trail.

Back at the Glen Boulder Trail (14.5/5,170), trace your upcoming route toward Route 16 over Slide Peak. Head down the Glen Boulder Trail, quickly entering scrubby waist-high fir trees before returning to open terrain with views southeast. You can soon peer into the Gulf of Slides, the deep adjacent valley to the north. The trail bottoms out and then rises slightly to reach the summit of Slide Peak (15.1/4,806).

Enjoy your last look at the Boott Spur summit and ridges, the southern Presidentials, and Montalban Ridge. Downward you go, quickly entering overhead forest on a gradual descent. The views aren't over yet. Emerging from the trees, you reach a vista (15.7/4,410) of upper Huntington Ravine, Mount Washington, and the nearby Gulf of Slides, now on the far side of an unnamed ridgeline to your north. North is Pinkham Notch and the distant smokestacks of Berlin, located beyond the rocky outcrops of small Pine Mountain.

The trail descends over loose talus with clear views and then encounters the trail's namesake boulder (16.1/3,730). The dump-truck-sized rock perches precariously on the ridgeline, delicately placed here by the receding glaciers of the last Ice Age. The trail curves left below the boulder, briefly reenters the trees, and then emerges in the open for some final views.

You now begin a steep scrambling descent in the trees, aided at times by rock steps. Down, down you go. The sound of rushing water becomes audible; red maple, raspberries, and cinnamon fern appear as you approach and cross the stream (16.7/2,850). The trail gradient eases, yellow birch joins the forest mix, and the path crosses the Avalanche Brook Ski Trail (16.9/2,640), indicated by blue plastic diamonds.

The trail banks left away from the stream and the forest continues its transition to hardwoods—look for sugar maple, beech, and hazel. After a gradual descent, the trail makes one final steep drop, crosses a small brook flowing over little ledges, and reaches the Direttissima on the left (17.3/2,370). Remain on the Glen Boulder Trail for the final descent to the trailhead parking lot (17.7/2,010). Alternatively, follow the Direttissima left for 1.0 mile to reach Pinkham Notch, a level trail that runs parallel above Route 16 on rocky slopes.

INFORMATION

White Mountain National Forest, Saco Ranger District office, 33 Kancamagus Highway, Conway, NH 03818, 603-447-5448, www.fs.fed.us/r9/forests/white_mountain; Pinkham Notch Visitor Center, 603-466-2725, open daily 6:30 A.M.–10 P.M.

TRIP 22
THE GREAT GULF

Location: Great Gulf Wilderness and Northern Presidential Range, White Mountain National Forest
Highlight: A yawning chasm, an alpine ridge
Distance: 19.3 miles round-trip
Total Elevation Gain/Loss: 7,250/7,250
Trip Length: 3 days
Difficulty: ★★★★★
Recommended Map: Bradford Washburn's *Mount Washington and the Presidential Range*, Appalachian Mountain Club

The Great Gulf carves deep into the mountains, guarded thousands of feet overhead by the peaks of the northern Presidentials. The Peabody River is born here, tearing down a steep and boulder-strewn watershed. At the head of the ravine, tiny Spaulding Lake glistens in an amphitheater of cliffs. Come travel the Gulf to the very headwaters of the Peabody River, then journey high above it on the alpine spine of the Presidential Range.

HIKE OVERVIEW
The journey begins along the Great Gulf Trail, touring the powerful Peabody River and passing a series of designated campsites. The second leg of the trip is long and epic. After ascending the Great Gulf's formidable headwall—rising 1,700 feet in less than a mile—you travel along the open ridgeline of the northern Presidentials, passing over the summits of four 5,000-footers: Mounts Clay, Jefferson, Adams, and Madison. Descend north off the ridge for a night at the Valley Way Tentsite or Gray Knob or Crag Camp cabins, or remain on the ridge and stay at the AMC's Madison Hut. After tagging Madison's summit, the adventure concludes with a long rocky descent on the Osgood Trail.

Traffic is light in the Great Gulf, especially higher up near the headwall. The crowd factor increases markedly on the ridge—expect to see dozens if not hundreds of people. Above-treeline weather can get very nasty very quickly. Be prepared. Escape routes back into the Great Gulf—the Sphinx, Six Husbands, and Madison Gulf trails—are very challenging. Dogs are allowed.

GREAT GULF WILDERNESS AND NORTHERN PRESIDENTIAL RANGE, WHITE MOUNTAIN NATIONAL FOREST

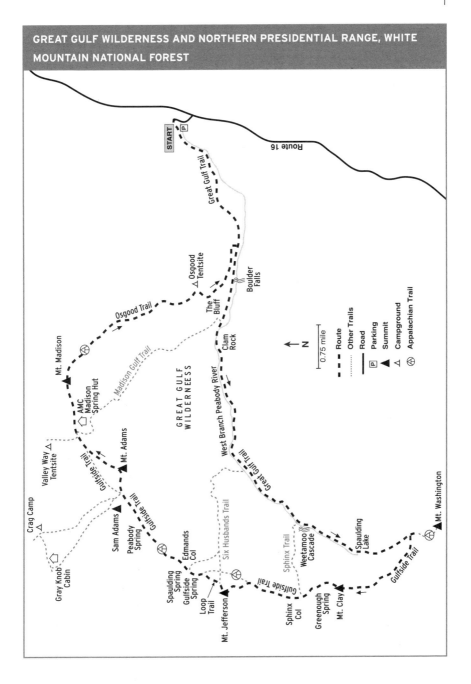

Route 16

START

P

Great Gulf Trail

△ Osgood Tentsite

Boulder Falls

The Bluff

Osgood Trail

Clam Rock

Mt. Madison

Madison Gulf Trail

AMC Madison Spring Hut

GREAT GULF WILDERNESS

West Branch Peabody River

Valley Way Tentsite △

Mt. Adams

Gulfside Trail

Crag Camp △

Great Gulf Trail

Sam Adams

Peabody Spring

Gulfside Trail

Gray Knob Cabin

Six Husbands Trail

Sphinx Trail

Spaulding Spring
Gulfside Spring
Edmands Col

Weetamoo Cascade

Spaulding Lake

Loop Trail

Gulfside Trail

Mt. Jefferson

Sphinx Col

Greenough Spring

Mt. Clay

Gulfside Trail

Mt. Washington

N

0.75 mile

- - - Route
.... Other Trails
——— Road
P Parking
▲ Summit
△ Campground
Ⓐ Appalachian Trail

OVERNIGHT OPTIONS

The Forest Service has established a series of designated campsites in the Great Gulf. Dispersed camping outside of designated sites is permitted, but you must be more than 200 feet from any trails. The rugged and overgrown terrain makes this difficult. No camping is permitted in the upper Gulf above the junctions of the Sphinx and Great Gulf trails. Campfires are prohibited.

Overnight options are limited once you attain the Presidential ridge. No camping is permitted above treeline, and most overnight locations require you to drop off the ridge for the night, climbing back up the following morning. They are also extremely popular. Try to complete this section on a weekday or after August, when Appalachian Trail (AT) thru-hiking traffic drops off.

The Bluff is the closest designated campsite, 2.6 miles from the trailhead at 2,280 feet. A large clearing offers space for several tents, and at least one smaller site tucks in the surrounding trees. The site's big attraction is the excellent view of the lower Great Gulf. Water is located 0.1 mile away in Parapet Brook.

Campsite #2, mile 2.8, sits atop a small bluff sandwiched between Parapet Brook and the Peabody River and has two good tentsites. There are no views, but you can scramble down to the river to enjoy rushing water.

Clam Rock Campsite, mile 3.1, is situated close to the river by its large namesake rock. The site has room for several tents. The big attractions are its proximity to the river and nearby swimming holes. Overhanging Clam Rock offers some shelter in rainy conditions, though water drips down the face.

Campsites #4 and 5, mile 5.0, are the farthest designated sites, located close to each other on opposite sides of the trail. Site 4 is situated in a grassy level clearing with good exposure to the sun and stars. Site 5 shelters in the trees. A number of other small sites have been established in the area. An adjacent brook provides water.

Crag Camp and Gray Knob are self-service cabins maintained by the Randolph Mountain Club. Crag Camp (capacity 20) perches on the lip of deep-cut King Ravine and provides a view into the abyss. Gray Knob (capacity 15) is located a short distance away in the trees and lacks views, though a full panorama north is located nearby. They are both situated near 4,300 feet in elevation on the northern slopes of Mount Adams, 1.2 miles and 1,200 feet below the ridgeline route, and 13 miles from the trailhead. They are both first-come, first-served facilities and cost $10 per night.

Madison Hut, mile 13.6, nestles in the saddle between Mounts Madison and Adams at 4,810 feet. It is the lowest-effort option—you don't have to drop off the ridge for the night—but it's also the most expensive. Weekends typically fill well in advance. Call 603-466-2727 or visit www.outdoors.

org/lodging/huts for reservations and more information.

The Valley Way Tentsite is free and quickly accessible from the ridge, 700 feet and 0.7 mile below Madison Hut. Located at 4,100 feet on the Valley Way, it offers two large tent platforms, the upper one has a view of Mount Madison's west face. It's a popular and often crowded destination. There is a reliable water source nearby.

Osgood Tentsite, mile 16.7, is one final possibility, though it's not well positioned for this hike. Located at 2,500 feet on the Osgood Trail, it's very far from the Great Gulf campsites and less than 3 miles from hike's end. The sites are located along the AT, which means regular use, especially during thru-hiker season (July–August).

TO REACH THE TRAILHEAD

Follow Route 16 to the Great Gulf trailhead, located 4.7 miles north of Pinkham Notch and 0.8 mile past Wildcat Ski Area. The turn-off is on the left. A WMNF parking pass is required.

HIKE DESCRIPTION

Head to the kiosk at the end of the parking area (0.0/1,380), where the Great Gulf Trail begins. The hike starts on a paved path, briefly travels along the Peabody River, and then curves left to cross the wide, shallow waterway on a substantial wooden suspension bridge. Notice the tall white pines just downriver. Shade-intolerant, they grow poorly in dense forest but the open river corridor provides them with good sun.

On the opposite bank, the wide dirt trail travels through mature hardwood forest punctuated by water-loving hemlock trees and some large red spruce. The Great Gulf Trail passes the Great Gulf Link Trail on the right (0.3/1,400) and then continues past a series of ski trail junctions, crossing several small creeks as it rises slowly. Substantial white pines and abundant sugar maple line the trail as it parallels the nearby Peabody River, which is audible but difficult to access. You pass the Hayes Copp Loop Ski Trail (1.6/1,750), cross into the Great Gulf Wilderness, and reach the Osgood Trail entering from the right (1.8/1,830)—your return route. A short distance farther is Boulder Falls, accessible by a short spur, where cascades funnel between three colossal rocks.

The trail now climbs steeply and parallels the river far below. Tiny bunchberry plants line the root-laced trail, yellow birch become increasingly common, and mountain ash appears—all signs of the transition to spruce-fir forest.

The trail briefly rejoins the river and then makes a steep climb over rock steps to reach the Bluff campsite (2.6/2,280) and its delicious view. Looking up the Gulf, the pyramidal hulk of Mount Adams (5,799) looms to the right, and Mount Jefferson (5,705) can be spotted farther in the distance to the left. The steep ridge falling into the Gulf from Jefferson's summit is known as Jefferson's Knee; the Six Husbands Trail twists up this steep ridge. The deep and trailless Jefferson Ravine lies between the two peaks. To the west, the Great Gulf curves out-of-sight behind Mount Washington's Chandler Ridge. You can spot the Mount Washington Auto Road snaking around the summit-like prow of the Horn.

Continuing, the trail quickly reaches the Osgood Cutoff (2.7/2,230), part of the AT. Bear left to remain on the Great Gulf Trail as it drops down and crosses strong-flowing Parapet Brook, a difficult crossing in high water. On the opposite bank, you encounter the Madison Gulf Trail on the right (2.8/2,250) and a spur to designated campsite #2 on the left.

From here, the Great Gulf Trail descends to the river and crosses it on a substantial bridge. The route winds along the river and soon encounters Clam Rock (3.1/2,380), an overhanging 12-foot-high boulder. The canyon palpably narrows at this point. The river gradient becomes much steeper. Pulsing rapids intermix with swimming holes as the trail continues across Chandler Brook and reaches the Chandler Brook Trail (3.9/2,760), which splits left to ascend steeply to the Horn.

You steadily ascend past brief views of looming Jefferson's Knee and reach the four-way junction with the Wamsutta and Six Husbands trails (4.5/3,100). Continue straight on the Great Gulf Trail as it alternately passes through young dense forest and then through an area of newly regenerating trees beneath bleaching snags—indications of a fir wave.

The trail maintains its steady grade, alternately climbing above and then winding alongside the river, which now starts to noticeably diminish in size. Pleasant pools and sluicing cascades are abundant. The route briefly levels and rock-hops the river (5.4/3,560), another potentially hazardous maneuver at high water. Mount Clay abruptly heaves into view ahead as the route continues upcanyon. You cross Sphinx Brook, and then immediately reach the junction with the Sphinx Trail (5.6/3,580).

Bear left to remain on the Great Gulf Trail as it re-crosses the Peabody River and encounters a sign that reminds you that there is NO CAMPING BE-YOND THIS POINT. You then reach Weetamoo Falls (5.8/3,660), a sluicing 20-foot cascade with an emerald pool at its base. Legend has it that Weetamoo, daughter of Chief Passaconaway, had six husbands. Her first, Wamsutta, was brother to Metacomet, or King Philip. Weetamoo drowned in 1675 during King Philip's War with the colonists.

Past the falls, the wild factor picks up considerably. The trail immediately begins a steep and rocky ascent that continuously flirts with the river corridor, passing impressive boulders and spews of foaming water. You eventually reach tiny Spaulding Lake by its outlet (6.5/4,230), where the mighty face of the Great Gulf headwall comes into view.

For the area's best view, continue to the head of the pond and scramble atop the prominent rock. From here, stare down the gullet of the Great Gulf as it plummets past Spaulding Lake. The northern Presidential Range is revealed in full profile, punctuated by the bulwarks of Mounts Adams and Madison. The headwall sweeps around behind you in an arc of bulging rock and alpine gullies.

Past Spaulding Lake, the trail follows a small flowing streambed. Trees rapidly diminish in stature and you soon pass a sign that welcomes you to the alpine zone (6.7/4,330). Now the vertical ascent begins. Views down the Gulf quickly become continuous. The trail closely follows the obvious flowing stream for most of the ascent, often traveling directly in the stream, and curving slightly left as it climbs. The path is generally apparent as it follows the most obvious route. Faint yellow blazes and small cairns help keep you on track.

Welcome to the Gulf

The stream disappears under the rocks as you crest 4,900 feet and enter a wide talus field. The route becomes indistinct in spots but remains near the audible stream burbling underground. At 5,400 feet, more distant peaks appear over the northern Presidentials. The trail becomes more defined, and you leave the trickling headwaters of the Peabody River. Follow the trail as it hugs solid rock on the edge of the talus field and then ascends a narrow gully to surmount the headwall.

As you crest the lip, the sense of untrammeled wilderness is abruptly shattered by the appearance of the nearby Sherman Adams Building atop Mount Washington's summit, as well as the Cog Railway tracks, which run past here a mere 75 yards away. You then immediately reach the Gulfside Trail (7.5/5,940), part of the AT. Bear right to follow the Gulfside Trail north. (If you are interested in visiting the crowds, cars, and structures atop Mount Washington, bear left on the Gulfside Trail and follow it 0.4 mile to the summit marker.)

The Gulfside Trail initially runs alongside the Cog tracks and features substantial cairns placed roughly 50 feet apart to aid navigation in low-visibility conditions. Chunks of coal litter the trailside, part of the debris exhaled by the Cog as it burns one ton of coal each round-trip up the mountain.

The trail wanders over to the edge of the Great Gulf, affording deep glimpses into the bowl and of Spaulding Lake far below. The views of Mounts Jefferson, Adams, and Madison are excellent. Passing the Westside Trail on the

Spaulding Lake

left (8.1/5,500), the Gulfside Trail descends to Clay Col. Here, the Clay Summit Loop splits right (8.2/5,390). Bear right on the Clay Loop to continue the view-riffic journey. (You can also continue left on the Gulfside Trail, an easier and slightly shorter route that skirts the peak to the west.)

The Clay Loop Trail undulates along the peak's long ridge, affording good views of the upper Great Gulf headwall, your earlier route. The southern Presidentials soon appear, lined up past the AMC's Lakes of the Clouds Hut. The trail crosses a grassy meadow, attains the summit (8.9/5,533), and then makes a much rockier and steeper descent. Careful footwork is required on the drop to the Gulfside Trail (9.4/5,100).

Greenough Spring—a reliable water source—is 0.2 mile south on the Gulfside Trail, located in scrubby chest-high trees. Continuing north, the Gulfside Trail descends to reach Sphinx Col and the Sphinx Trail (9.5/4,960), which drops back into the Great Gulf. Nearby, large rocks along the upper Sphinx Trail offer shelter from west winds. One outcrop is said to resemble the trail's Egyptian namesake. A reliable spring is located in a small boulder field a short distance farther down the Sphinx Trail.

Continuing on the Gulfside Trail, you immediately resume climbing. The summit of Mount Jefferson appears to the north, and views southwest encompass the rounded summit of Mount Eisenhower and the deep cleft of Crawford Notch. Huge cairns mark the route as it ascends past the Cornice Trail on the left (10.0/5,360). The terrain becomes rougher as the trail meanders through Monticello Lawn, an open meadow, to reach the Jefferson Loop Trail on the left (10.1/5,380).

The Gulfside Trail curves around Mount Jefferson to the east, but you should bear left and head for the summit on the Loop Trail. A scramble over loose rocks, including a glistening pocket of white quartzite, leads you atop the summit (10.4/5,705). Views southeast reveal a profile of the Great Gulf headwall that look considerably steeper than it is. North is the rocky pyramid of Mount Adams. The Jefferson Loop trail descends from the summit on a more mellow route. After a short section of talus-hopping, you pass through a krummholz corridor and rejoin the super-cairns of the Gulfside Trail (10.8/5,220).

Continue north on the Gulfside Trail as it drops past prominent Dingmaul Rock. The outcrop offers good views into the wild and trailless Jefferson Ravine, hemmed to the south by the distinctive ridge of Jefferson's Knee. After a steep and rocky descent through krummholz, you reach Edmands Col and the four-way junction with the Edmands Col Cutoff and the Castle Ravine Trail (11.0/4,940). There is a good flowing water source, Gulfside Spring, a short distance down the Cutoff. A less reliable source, Spaulding Spring, is located

0.1 mile down the Castle Ravine Trail near its junction with the Cornice and Randolph Path.

Remain on the Gulfside Trail as it climbs out of Edmands Col and returns to the ridgeline. This section is fully exposed to the elements. Even some of the boulders look windswept. Look northwest into the deep glacial cirque of Castle Ravine, bordered to the west by Castellated Ridge. The linear arête sweeps down the west edge of the ravine, punctuated by several gendarmes known as the Castles.

The trail levels out and next passes the Israel Ridge Trail on the right (11.7/5,250). Just past the junction on the left, a small pool known as Storm Lake can be seen after periods of wet weather. The Gulfside Trail now banks right through sheltered krummholz below the flanks of Mount Sam Adams, a satellite summit of Mount Adams, and passes thin Peabody Spring. Water can be accessed with the help of a filter; the best source is at the base of the largest trailside boulder. The trail slowly climbs, becoming loose and rubbly. A continuation of the Israel Ridge Path splits right just before the mountainous cairn that marks Thunderstorm junction (12.3/5,490).

Five trails converge on this point. The Great Gully Trail heads north to plummet down the headwall of King Ravine. Lowe's Path also leads north, down the ridge toward Gray Knob and Crag Camp. (For Gray Knob, remain on Lowe's Path for 1.2 miles and 1,000 feet of elevation loss. For Crag Camp, follow Lowe's Path a short distance and then bear right on the Spur Trail, which leads to the cabin in 1.1 miles.)

The rock pile of Mount Adams looms overhead here. The ascent to the summit is all rubble, all the time. To reach the peak, follow the final section of Lowe's Path upward. (To skip the summit, continue on the Gulfside Trail as it curves northeast around the base of Mount Adams, providing decent footing and good shelter from southerly winds.)

Small cairns mark the summit route as it scrambles over large piles of rocks. From the top of the peak (12.6/5,799), savor your first good views north. Mount Madison rises at the end of the ridge, with tiny Star Lake nestling at its base. You can trace your upcoming route on the Osgood Trail, which follows the alpine ridge on the far side of Mount Madison. The Mahoosucs (Trip 27) march off in the distance in line with Madison. The smokestacks of Berlin are visible in the valley below. The rolling mountains of the Pilot Range (see Trip 25) appear due north. Good views south stare into the Great Gulf, and the Carter Range, including the cleft of Carter Notch, can be spotted southeast.

Descend from the summit on the Air Line, which rubble-hops northeast and offers excellent views into King Ravine. A keen eye will discern

Crag Camp perched on the chasm's west ridge. Rejoining the Gulfside Trail (13.2/5,230), bear right and head toward Madison Hut, which quickly appears below. The trail descends a series of nice rock stairs to reach the hut and saddle (13.6/4,810).

Madison Hut sits on the edge of treeline, surrounded by stands of head-high trees. Even if you're not staying, definitely stop in to refill your water bottles and warm up. To access the Valley Way Tentsite, bear left and descend 0.7 mile and 700 feet on the Valley Way Trail.

The continuing route heads over Mount Madison on the Osgood Trail, which is very exposed to the elements. (If conditions are bad, you can also return to the Great Gulf Trail from Madison Hut via the Madison Gulf Trail. An adventure in itself, the 2.6-mile trail starts out by dropping 1,000 feet in less than a mile—good scrambling skills required—and then steadily descends to reach the Great Gulf Trail by Parapet Brook.)

The Osgood Trail strikes out from Madison Hut and immediately returns above treeline. A well-trod and rocky route steadily leads you upward to the summit (14.1/5,366), where the Watson Path joins from the north. Enjoy your last summit view, which encompasses the route of almost your entire journey. The final leg traces southeast along the long bare ridge before you.

It's all downhill from here. The Osgood Trail is a rocky and difficult path, much less traveled than the previous above-treeline section. You drop off the summit, pass the Howker Ridge Trail on the left (14.4/5,100), and then reach the four-way junction with the Parapet and Daniel Webster-Scout trails (14.7/4,830). Remain on the Osgood Trail, following the ridge over a series of steps, with more forgiving sections interspersed between steep drops. The views now look straight up the Great Gulf to the crown of Mount Washington.

The trail finally reaches the trees, curves right, and then begins a steady and direct descent along a root-laced path. You eventually reach the Osgood Cutoff on the right (16.7/2,500), where a spur leads left to the Osgood Tentsite. Follow the final section of the Osgood Trail to the Great Gulf Trail (17.5/1,830), turn left, and retrace your earlier steps to the trailhead (19.3/1,380).

INFORMATION

White Mountain National Forest, Saco Ranger District office, 33 Kancamagus Highway, Conway, NH 03818, 603-447-5448, www.fs.fed.us/r9/forests/white_mountain; Pinkham Notch Visitor Center, 603-466-2725, open daily 6:30 a.m.–10 p.m.

TRIP 23
KING RAVINE

Location: Northern Presidential Range, White Mountain National Forest
Highlights: Ravines, cliffs, ridgelines, alpine scenery, the second-highest summit in New England
Distance: 10.2 miles round-trip
Total Elevation Gain/Loss: 4,900/4,900
Trip Length: 2 days
Difficulty: ★★★★
Recommended Maps: Bradford Washburn's *Mount Washington and the Presidential Range*, Appalachian Mountain Club; *AMC White Mountain Guide, Map 1: Presidential Range*, AMC Books

A dense network of trails laces the flanks of Mount Adams, a mountain lined with rocky ridges and gouged by deep valleys. King Ravine cuts deepest, a giant bowl scooped from the mountainside. The densest collection of trails in New England extensively explores the surrounding area. This hike unravels the knot of possibility and guides you along the most dramatic combination of trails.

HIKE OVERVIEW

The hike follows a giant loop around King Ravine. It first winds along Snyder Brook, passes the Valley Way Tentsite, and then surmounts Durand Ridge to ascend the dramatic Air Line Trail above the King Ravine headwall. The route climbs to the top of 5,799-foot Mount Adams and then descends along the west edge of King Ravine to Crag Camp and Gray Knob, public cabins maintained by the Randolph Mountain Club (RMC). A descent down the brook-lined Amphibrach Trail returns you home.

The area is popular but the multitude of trails means that once you escape the main arteries, you will likely have sections to yourself. The limited number of overnight options can make for crowded experiences, especially on weekends. Water is abundant. Dogs are permitted.

OVERNIGHT OPTIONS

The Valley Way Tentsite and two RMC cabins are located directly along the route. The Perch, another RMC facility, is also a possibility, but requires a 2-mile detour. All of them are first-come, first-served. Dispersed camping

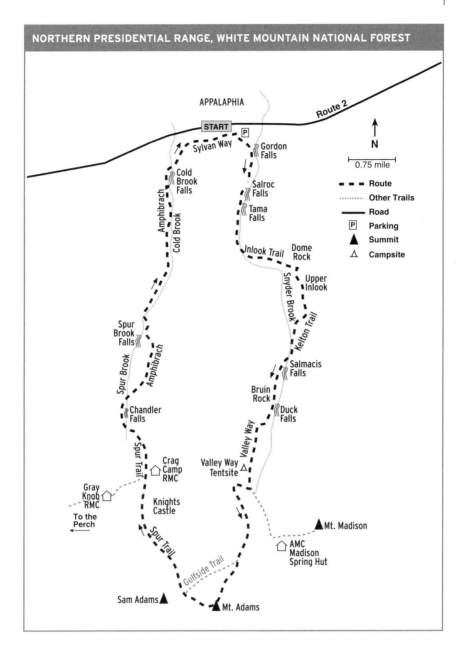

NORTHERN PRESIDENTIAL RANGE, WHITE MOUNTAIN NATIONAL FOREST

APPALAPHIA

Route 2

START

P

Sylvan Way

Gordon
Falls

N

0.75 mile

Cold
Brook
Falls

Salroc
Falls

- - - Route
.... Other Trails
——— Road
P Parking
▲ Summit
△ Campsite

Tama
Falls

Amphibrach

Cold Brook

Inlook Trail

Dome
Rock

Upper
Inlook

Snyder Brook

Kelton Trail

Spur
Brook
Falls

Spur Brook

Amphibrach

Salmacis
Falls

Bruin
Rock

Duck
Falls

Valley Way

Chandler
Falls

Spur Trail

Crag
Camp
RMC

Valley Way
Tentsite

Gray
Knob
RMC

Knights
Castle

To the
Perch

Spur Trail

Mt. Madison

AMC
Madison
Spring Hut

Gulfside Trail

Sam Adams ▲

▲ Mt. Adams

is permitted in areas below treeline (you must be 200 feet from any trail and a quarter mile from designated shelters and campsites, camping prohibited above treeline), but usable sites are nearly impossible to find in the steep, rugged, densely forested terrain. The weather may dictate where you choose to spend the night—take advantage of good weather for the above-treeline portion of the hike.

Valley Way Tentsite is located 3.4 miles from the trailhead at 4,100 feet along the Valley Way Trail. It consists of two large tent platforms and a privy. It is a good option if (1) you are starting late in the day, or (2) the weather higher up is disagreeable and you want to wait for better conditions the following day. The site receives heavy use and the limited space can make for crowded camping. Water is available a short distance from camp by

Above King Ravine in early October snow

the Valley Way Trail. Good views from the upper platform look out at the alpine flanks of Mount Madison.

Crag Camp perches at 4,250 feet on the lip of King Ravine's west headwall, 6.5 miles from the trailhead. Impressive views of the Ravine can be had from the front deck, as well as from the common area inside. The first-come, first-served RMC cabin has bunk space for twenty, split between two bunk-rooms of eight and one of four. The building is unheated and floor vents connect directly with the outside. A year-round caretaker collects $10 per person per night. Open year-round.

Gray Knob shelters in the woods at 4,370 feet, 0.5 mile from Crag Camp, and is an excellent overflow option if Crag Camp is full. The two-story cabin has a large upstairs area for sleeping and a common area replete with books, booth-style tables, and a cozier ambiance than at Crag Camp. No views are available from the cabin itself, but excellent vistas east are less than 0.1 mile away. It also costs $10 per person. The cabin is open year-round. An RMC caretaker fires up the cabin's wood stove only during periods of extreme winter cold.

The Perch is located 0.7 mile past Gray Knob in the upper reaches of Cascade Ravine, a prominent gorge immediately west of King Ravine. A small vintage shelter and four tent platforms are available. A shelter has stood at this site since J. Rayner Edmands built the first structure here in 1893. Built in 1948, the current cave-like incarnation looks its age and has a limited view north to the peaks of the Kilkenny. There are no views from the tentsites, though the uppermost platform offers glimpses north. The Gray Knob caretaker will visit to collect the $7 per person fee. Water is available from adjacent Cascade Brook. Campfires are prohibited.

TO REACH THE TRAILHEAD

Follow Route 2 to the Appalachia Trailhead, located in the town of Randolph approximately a mile west of Dolly Copp/Pinkham B Road. The large parking area is adjacent to the highway and has space for many cars, but often fills up on busy days.

HIKE DESCRIPTION

From the trailhead (0.0/1,310), head past the Appalachia trail sign. Young beech and red maple shade the trail as it immediately crosses a bike path, the Presidential Range Rail Trail. Bear left on the Valley Way, immediately cross a power line corridor, and then take your next left on the Maple Walk.

The path runs through a stand of sugar maples, joined by beech, yellow birch, and other hardwoods. The route slowly rises to reach Snyder Brook and

Gordon Falls (0.2/1,410), a sliding curtain of water over bedrock. Turn right here to follow the yellow-blazed Fallsway.

The Fallsway parallels the brook upward and winds below mature hemlocks, some greater than 2 feet in diameter. You next pass Lower Salroc Falls, a 10-foot bouldery cascade that drops into a deep swimming hole. Just above is 15-foot-high Upper Salroc Falls, another smooth sheet of water. The Fallsway then rejoins the Valley Way (0.6/1,630).

Bear left to head uphill on the blue-blazed Valley Way. Take the time to follow the Tama Fall loop on the left (0.7/1,650), which quickly rejoins the Valley Way past its staircase slab falls; there's a swimming hole just above the cascade. Back on the Valley Way, you steadily climb, pass the Beechwood Trail on the left, and then almost immediately reach the Brookside Trail, also on the left (0.8/1,950).

Bear left on the Brookside Trail to quickly reach Snyder Brook. A massive house-sized boulder guards the opposite bank. Rock-hop the stream to reach a triple junction where the Brookside Trail, Randolph Path, and Inlook Trail converge. Go straight on the yellow-blazed Inlook Trail, which narrows and steepens as it ascends a rocky staircase. Fir, spruce, and big-tooth aspens appear, as do blueberry bushes underfoot. The trail becomes less rocky as you go, the surrounding forest thicker and younger. Mountain ash and bunchberry join the spruce-fir community as the trail levels out and comes to an open slab with good views north up the Snyder Brook drainage (1.1/2,360). Lower Durand Ridge is visible on the southwest horizon. The Randolph valley runs off to the west.

Past the viewpoint, the trail clambers over open rocks and ledges with intermittent views of Madison Col at the head of the Snyder Brook watershed. The views become more frequent as the trail levels out, bears left, and attains Dome Rock (1.4/2,662). The view here is the best yet, with glimpses northeast to the Mahoosucs, including the distinctive cleft of Mahoosuc Notch (Trip 27). The town of Randolph is visible below. North above Randolph is the Crescent Range; Mount Crescent is due north. The Carter Range is visible east.

Continuing, the trail curves south to a similar view at the Upper Inlook—though this looks primarily to the northeast—where the Kelton Trail joins from the right (1.5/2,730).

Bear right on the Kelton Trail to begin a long, level stretch through dense spruce-fir forest. You cross a flowing creek where a massive yellow birch stands sentinel. The trail remains level and begins traversing along the slopes. The valley bottom and its rushing creek waters slowly rise up to meet you. The trail returns to Snyder Brook, rock-hops across, and rejoins the Brookside Trail (2.3/2,730).

Bear left and follow the Brookside Trail up the valley, soon climbing more steeply with the aid of rock steps. You next reach Salmacis Fall (2.4/2,830), another cascading bedrock sheet. Past the falls, the trail follows the brook, here almost nothing but sluicing whitewater. A steady and sustained rocky ascent brings you to the Watson Path (2.8/3,260).

Bear left on the Watson Path toward Mount Madison, quickly passing signed (but nondescript) Bruin Rock. Shortly afterward, you reach the junction with the Lower Bruin Trail (2.9/3,340). Here, the Watson Path crosses the creek to the left and ascends Mount Madison, but you should turn right up the Lower Bruin Trail. After making your first hand-over-hand scramble, you then follow the Lower Bruin Trail as it makes a steep, direct, and root-laced climb to reach the Valley Way (3.1/3,580).

Turn left and continue upward on the Valley Way, a rocky affair with a few glimpses of Mount Madison through the trees to the left. A steady climb brings you to the signed spur for the Valley Way Tentsite (3.4/4,100); a reliable spring is located a few feet toward the camping area.

Past the spur, the Valley Way encounters another stream and then reaches the Upper Bruin Trail on the right (3.6/4,150). Go right on the Upper Bruin Trail, commencing a direct, narrow, and rocky climb. The route curves right, back left, and reaches a sign indicating that you are entering the alpine zone. A few feet past the sign, you emerge onto open Durand Ridge and reach the Air Line (3.8/4,410).

The gaping maw of King Ravine opens before you. A jumbled pile of boulders sits at the base of its headwall. Across the ravine, almost due west, Crag Camp perches on the edge of this great divide. Good views also extend north; the Kilkenny Range now rises behind and above the Crescent Range. Turn left and ascend the Air Line, soon passing the Chemin des Dames (3.9/4,500) on the right, which plummets into the ravine.

The route now travels on the Knife Edge, a relatively narrow (though not precarious) open ridgeline. Impressive outcrops, balanced slabs, and good scenery deserve a slow pace. You next reach the junction with the Air Line Cutoff on the left (4.2/4,770), which leads over to Madison Hut, now visible in the col to your left. Looking north from here, you can identify the peaks of the Kilkenny Range. Mount Cabot is to the left; the Horn is the prominent peak to the right.

The final ascent of Durand Ridge leads you above Madison Col and passes the King Ravine Trail on the right (4.4/5,130), which drops into the ravine through a prominent cleft in the headwall. You then immediately reach the Gulfside Trail. Turn right on the Gulfside Trail—part of the Appalachian Trail

(AT)—and commence a slowly rising traverse below the summits of Mount Adams and its smaller, closer satellite, Mount John Quincy Adams. The trail is well traveled, though rocky, and marked by regular cairns. The Air Line quickly splits left (4.5/5,160).

Bear left to follow the Air Line and head toward the summit of Mount Adams. (To skip the summit, remain on the Gulfside Trail to curve around the mountain's flanks and reach Thunderstorm Junction in 0.6 mile.) The trail up Mount Adams is, well, not really a trail. It's a route indicated by blazes over loose rocks and boulders, a scrambling ascent where you'll want to watch your footing carefully. The reward is bagging the second-highest peak in New England (5.1/5,799), and enjoying one of its best views.

Mount Madison rises at the end of the ridge, with tiny Star Lake nestling at its base. The Mahoosucs (Trip 27) march off in the distance in line with Madison. The rolling mountains of the Pilot Range (Trip 25) appear due north. Good views south stare into the Great Gulf, and the Carter Range, including the cleft of Carter Notch, can be spotted southeast.

The northern flanks of Mt. Adams

Descend the equally rugged Lowe's Path down Mount Adams' west side to reach the giant mega-cairn of Thunderstorm Junction (5.4/5,490), where five trails converge. The jumbled slopes of Mount Adams are visible overhead to the east, the lower mass of Mount Sam Adams hulks to the east. Take a moment here to walk a short distance farther on the Gulfside Trail to an exceptional view south across the Great Gulf (Trip 22) to Mount Washington. The northern Presidential peaks are apparent in their entirety. Mount Jefferson is closest, the prominent ridge of Jefferson's Knee plunging into the Gulf. To the left of Washington's summit, you can spot the Auto Road snaking its way up the mountain.

Back at Thunderstorm Junction, follow Lowe's Path for less than 0.1 mile and then bear right on the Spur Trail. (If you are headed straight to Gray Knob, remain on Lowe's Path, which descends directly to the cabin in 1.2 miles.) The Spur Trail slowly descends below and parallel to the rocky bulges of Adams 4, offering views of your earlier route. The Knife Edge stands out in profile. Mount Madison rises beyond.

The trail passes below the promontory of Adams 4 and becomes rockier and more challenging. Crag Camp is visible ahead, a thousand feet below you, and soon the trail starts a more direct descent. As you go, enjoy the striking views of pyramidal Mount Madison. Views diminish as you reenter forest, drop down a wide corridor, and leave the alpine zone behind (6.1/4,750).

You next pass a spur on the right to Knight's Castle (6.3/4,590). This side-trip leads to a ledgy outcrop with excellent views into King Ravine and across toward Mounts Madison, John Quincy Adams, and Adams. From here, the steep rocky descent continues to the Gray Knob Trail (6.5/4,250). Turn right to immediately reach Crag Camp.

SIDE-TRIP TO GRAY KNOB

To reach Gray Knob from Crag Camp, follow the Gray Knob Trail west for 0.5 mile through dense spruce-fir forest. The trail passes the spring and water source for Crag Camp, rises briefly, then descends to reach a signed spur to another nearby spring. From here, the rocky route runs mostly level. You cross a water source beneath the rocks, pass another spring, and reach the cabin.

To visit the Quay, an open ledge with views west of Mount Jefferson's ridge-lined slopes, continue on the Gray Knob Trail a short distance past the cabin. Immediately below you to the west is the deep scoop of Cascade Ravine (the Perch shelters in its upper reaches). On the ravine's far side, Israel Ridge divides it from Castle Ravine to the west. The next ridgeline west is Castellated Ridge. It boasts some distinctive rock outcrops, especially along its upper lengths.

Farthest away is the Ridge of the Caps, easily identified by the gendarmes along its prow. To the north, you also have views of the Kilkenny Range (Trip 25) and the valley of Route 2.

SIDE-TRIP TO THE PERCH

If you're looking for more solitude than can be found at the cabins, consider heading over to the Perch. From Gray Knob (0.0/4,370), it's 1.4 miles round-trip with an elevation gain/loss of 600/600. Continue past the Quay on the Gray Knob Trail, crossing Lowe's Path and breaking out into chest-high trees with good views. A rising traverse with continuous vistas allows you to look deep into the heart of rushing Cascade Ravine. You next reach the Perch Path entering from the right (0.3/4,550). Bear right to follow it. The Perch Path makes a traversing descent along a narrow, lightly used trail, passes several rivulets, and then crosses the upper reaches of Cascade Brook to the Perch on the opposite side (0.7/4,310).

Back at Crag Camp (6.5/4,250), continue down the Spur Trail. (Those staying at Gray Knob can follow the Hincks Trail 0.7 mile down to reach the Spur Trail.) The forested Spur Trail begins as a steep and rocky drop along the ridgeline and soon passes a sign on the right for Lower Crag (6.6/4,210), your last opportunity to peer into King Ravine. The trail continues its plummet, aided by a wooden staircase, then moderates and curves left to head down into the gully of Spur Brook. You drop steeply to reach upper Spur Brook, rock-hop across it, and reach the Hincks Trail on the opposite side (7.1/3,440).

Continue down on the Spur Trail. The route remains in the gully but curves away from the stream, soon passing a posted spur on the right for Chandler Falls (7.2/3,180). A nice rest stop for the knees, the 30-foot falls hiss over bedrock and split into a triangular fan at the base.

Past the falls, hobblebush appears as the woods transition to hardwoods. The trail briefly mellows, steepens, descends some stairs, and returns alongside the stream to reach the Randolph Path (7.4/2,960). Go right on the Randolph Path, rock-hopping the brook and making a short traverse past large paper birch to reach a five-way junction with the King Ravine Trail, Randolph Path, and the Amphibrach Trail (7.5/2,930).

Follow the Amphibrach, which descends gently along a leafier trail. Yellow birch appears as the forest transition continues. You next cross the Cliffway Trail (7.9/2,500), remaining on the Amphibrach as it continues its mellow descent. Red and sugar maple soon appear, joined shortly by abundant beech. You return to the banks of Spur Brook by some pleasant cascades and then rock-hop across it to reach the Monaway Trail on the left (8.3/2,220). Here, a short spur leads right to the Cold Spur Ledges, a solid rock outcrop near the confluence of Spur Brook and an unnamed tributary, which combine to form Cold Brook.

Continue down the easy-cruising Amphibrach Trail, parallel to nearby Cold Brook. Shortly before the Amphibrach reaches the Link Trail (9.4/1,450), it passes pulsing Cold Brook Falls. The largest falls of the hike, the cascade rushes through a narrow rock gorge and can be approached from either side of the brook. At the Link Trail junction, turn right and cross over Memorial Bridge, held in place by stone foundations.

To return to the trailhead from here, follow signs to the Link. This last section of trail runs through an active sugar maple operation; sap tubing runs to and fro between the trees and numerous paths crisscross the area. Watch for trail signs, which lead you to the Link + Amphibrach trail. The single-track trail parallels the highway above the rail-trail and power lines. Turn left once you reach the Air Line Trail (10.1/1,330) to immediately cross the rail-trail and power lines and return to the trailhead (10.2/1,310).

INFORMATION

White Mountain National Forest, Androscoggin Ranger District, 300 Glen Road, Gorham, NH 03581, 603-466-2713, www.fs.fed.us/r9/forests/white_mountain; Pinkham Notch Visitor Center, 603-466-2725, open daily 6:30 A.M.–10 P.M.

TRIP 24
GO WILD

Location: Wild River Wilderness, White Mountain National Forest
Highlights: Streams, rivers, mountains, New Hampshire's newest wilderness area
Distance: 25.3–28.8 miles round-trip, depending on route
Total Elevation Gain/Loss: Full loop 7,900/7,900; shorter variation 6,100/6,100
Trip Length: 3–4 days
Difficulty: ★★★
Recommended Map: *AMC White Mountain Guide, Map 5: Carter Range-Evans Notch,* AMC Books

The Wild River Wilderness fills a broad valley in the east White Mountain National Forest. Hemmed by the Carter and Baldface Ranges, the watershed contains the second largest roadless area in New England and is much less traveled than the neighboring Presidential Range. Forest cloaks the watershed area, sheltering abundant wildlife and crystalline waterways. Great stands of paper birch dot the woods. View-rich mountains rise above it all.

Like much of the White Mountains, the Wild River area was intensively logged in the late nineteenth and early twentieth centuries. Railroad lines snaked up the valley to haul out timber. The entire drainage was felled. Vast amounts of woody debris littered the denuded terrain, which burned in 1903 in a massive conflagration that charred most of the watershed. Today, the Wild River Valley is a study of nature's resiliency, testament to what a century of regeneration can bring.

HIKE OVERVIEW

This journey makes a loop around the Wild River Wilderness. It first travels on the Appalachian Trail (AT) along the spine of the Carter Range and then drops back into the Wild River Valley to return either along the river or via the naked peaks of the Baldface Range. The hike begins along Moriah Brook, a small stream loaded with idyllic swimming holes, and then reaches Imp Campsite atop the Carter-Moriah Range. From here, a long ridgeline traverse on the AT leads over five 4,000-foot peaks en route to Carter Notch Hut, which nestles in the rocky cleft of Carter Notch. The trip then heads toward the remote and

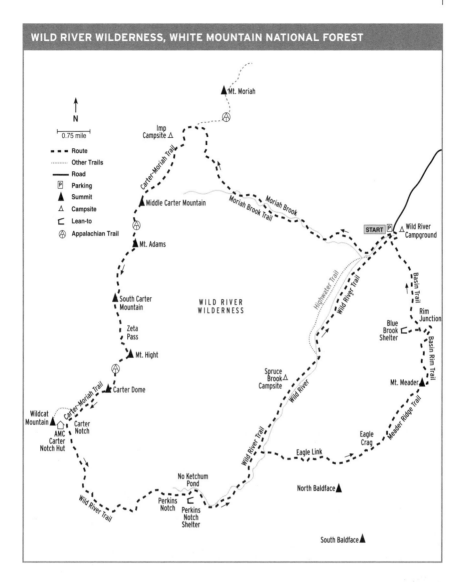

WILD RIVER WILDERNESS, WHITE MOUNTAIN NATIONAL FOREST

little-visited headwaters of the Wild River. At this point, you have two return options: You can either return to the trailhead along the Wild River (shorter variation), or ascend the Baldface Range and glory in views before returning to your car (full loop).

OVERNIGHT OPTIONS

Dispersed camping is permitted throughout the wilderness area. Good campsites are scarce along the ridgelines and mountain slopes, but there are numerous options early in the hike along the Moriah Brook Trail and later along the Wild River. As part of its management plan for the newly designated wilderness, the United States Forest Service (USFS) will likely remove the area's three backcountry shelters in the years ahead. Camping is permitted at the shelter sites. Note that the hike begins from the Wild River Campground, a good option for an evening arrival at the trailhead.

Imp Campsite, 6.5 miles from the trailhead, is located at 3,200 feet just below the Carter-Moriah Trail—part of the AT. The site features a cabin-like shelter and several tent platforms. Forest surrounds the location; a bench offers a limited view north. Water is available from an adjacent runnel of water. The site receives heavy use. Arrive early to snag a good spot, or visit mid-week and outside of thru-hiker season (roughly July and August). A caretaker is in residence during the summer and on fall weekends and collects an overnight per person fee.

Carter Notch Hut, mile 13.8, sits at 3,288 feet, below the rocky cliffs of Wildcat Mountain and Carter Dome. Front-porch views look out at the Ramparts, a debris field of massive talus. A giant stove, fully equipped kitchen, and running potable water make it a pleasant layover. Two bunkhouses are divided into four smaller bunkrooms of 4 to 6 beds for a total capacity of 40

Reflection of Wildcat Mountain in Carter Notch

guests. Carter Notch Hut is self-service (and more affordable) ten months of the year, full-service in July and August. Several heavily used campsites are located at the junction of the Nineteen Mile Brook and Wildcat Ridge trails, 0.3 mile from the hut (no water). Another site can be found along the Wildcat River Trail in a clearing of young spruce-fir, a 0.3-mile, 130-foot drop past the second bunkhouse.

Perkins Notch Shelter once hid near the headwaters of the Wild River, adjacent to a large boggy area known as No Ketchum Pond. The site is remote, more than 5 miles from the nearest trailhead, and feels like it. Carter Dome is partly visible from the shelter site, though better views of the mountain, plus the rocky prow of Mount Hight, can be had nearby from the edge of the pond/swamp. Tentsites are scattered in the area, including one large group campsite. The site lacks a good water source, though a trickle runs by the shelter—you'll need a filter. Water also flows near the bog outlet on the Wild River Trail; there is good camping potential downstream from this point.

Spruce Brook Shelter, mile 21.8, offers pleasant riverside camping along the Wild River Trail, 3.5 miles downriver from the Perkins Notch Shelter site. It's a pleasant option if you are exiting via the Wild River Trail, or want to take a detour off the full loop to camp close to the river. The shelter site gets good afternoon sun and offers several tentsites, including two platforms. The nearby river murmurs pleasantly and you can soak in waist-deep pools in both the river and adjacent Spruce Brook.

Blue Brook Shelter, mile 27.1, perches at 2,200 feet above its namesake stream, 2.3 miles from the Wild River campground and hike's end. Surrounded by forest, this site features a large group camping platform and numerous smaller tentsites. The nearby brook is readily accessible and offers a series of waist-deep pools for a refreshing soak.

TO REACH THE TRAILHEAD

Follow Route 2 east of the 113/2 junction for 3.1 miles and turn right onto unpaved, but easily navigable, Wild River Road. The road ends at the campground entrance in 5.7 miles. A hiker parking area is located on the left.

HIKE DESCRIPTION

From the parking lot (0.0/1,170), cross the entrance road and follow the Wild River Trail from near the outhouses. The path descends over a small brook and immediately reaches the Wild River by a large hemlock tree. Red oaks lean over the wide and rocky river. The route turns upstream and runs parallel to the river past hobblebush, spruce, and red and striped maple. You reach an old logging road above the campground; turn right to remain on the Wild River Trail.

After some easy cruising, you reach the posted Moriah Brook Trail on the right (0.3/1,180). A substantial red oak and yellow birch stand sentinel at the junction. Turn right to follow the wide Moriah Brook Trail as it heads down to the broad river and crosses it on a nice suspension bridge. Two trails diverge on the opposite side. They quickly rejoin and reach the Highwater Trail (0.4/1,220). Bear left on the yellow-blazed trail, winding past some exceptional hemlocks as you ramble along the river. You pass through a nice birch glade and then reach the junction where the Moriah Brook and Highwater trails divide (0.7/1,270).

Turn right to follow the blue-blazed Moriah Brook Trail, which follows an old railroad bed. Paper birch and sugar maples line the trail as you curve up and away from Moriah Brook, out-of-sight below. The path curves back left, and soon a rushing roar fills the woods. As the stream comes into view, glimpses of deep swimming holes and giant boulders tantalize.

The trail reaches Moriah Brook by a mini-gorge (1.7/1,540). The water-worn faces of giant boulders stare back at you. A good swimming hole—the first of many—invites you in. Cross the brook on a precarious rock-hop, potentially dangerous in high water.

The trail resumes a gentle climb, joined by moisture-loving white ash. As you proceed, watch the surrounding granite rocks for xenoliths, pieces of overlying rock that were not fully melted by the liquid magma that rose up and surrounded it.

The path briefly leaves the stream, quickly returns to it, and winds through a grove of substantial paper and yellow birch, interspersed with large aspen nearly 2 feet in diameter. The mellow trail continues, crossing a small tributary and climbing past big-leaf and quaking aspens, their large size a testament to their rapid growth habits.

You re-cross Moriah Brook in a clearing (3.1/1,770) and resume the ascent. The stream now rushes over extensive outcrops of solid bedrock and plunges into several ideal swimming holes. Reaching the confluence of two equally sized streams (3.5/1,940), the trail follows the branch to the left. You now pass the reach of the railroad bed. The trail becomes thinner and root-crossed.

The swimming hole parade continues along the increasingly steep terrain. The surrounding forest transitions to spruce-fir forest. Beech and hemlock disappear. Maples become less common. Blueberries line the trail, thriving in the acidic soil of the boreal woods. As you approach Moriah Brook's upper headwaters, the stream branches into numerous small tributaries; several pass underfoot.

The climb steepens and passes through thick stands of paper birch. Boulders increase around you, the route becomes rockier, and soon you pass a collection of giant stones. The creek has seemingly split one giant boulder in two. Others are as large as school buses.

The trail continues parallel to the brook, becoming boggy in spots. The Moriah Cliffs peek out ahead and above. You reach another confluence of small streams. From here, the trail goes directly up the rocks by the creek on the right—watch for the nearly overgrown blaze. The Moriah Cliffs loom overhead as you ascend a difficult section. The path then briefly levels, winds through alder bog, and then markedly steepens again for the final rise to the Carter-Moriah Trail, part of the AT (5.8/3,110).

Bear left to head south on the white-blazed AT. The AT quickly crosses bog bridging and immediately reaches the Stony Brook Trail on the right. Scattered glimpses through the trees look west and northwest toward the Kilkenny Range (Trip 25). Rocky and rough, the AT gradually rises, undulates along, and then climbs a steep rock staircase. You cross a flowing water source and continue steeply up, following a ribbon of rock through surrounding moss.

A sign indicates your arrival in the Forest Protection Area that surrounds Imp Campsite. Shortly thereafter, you reach an open view northwest. The twin summits of the Percy Peaks are evident, as are the mountains of the Kilkenny Range. The Androscoggin River drainage defines the ridge-lined landscape.

You next reach open rock slabs with dramatic views that extend to the rumpled terrain of far northern New Hampshire. The town of Gorham winds along the Androscoggin River as it curves north to Berlin. Northwest is the small massif of Pine Mountain; the Crescent Range rises beyond it, cut by a deep and obvious gash. Beyond are the peaks of the Kilkenny; Mount Cabot is just past the gash. Nearby to the south, along the ridgeline from closest to farthest, are Imp Mountain, North Carter, and then South Carter—your continuing route.

The rocky trail drops toward a small saddle and reaches the spur for Imp Campsite (6.5/3,360), located 0.2 mile down the hillside. Water is available from a small creek on the campground trail.

Onward, the AT resumes climbing over bedrock and commences a rising traverse over sloped, often wet, slabs. The trailless summit of Imp Mountain passes by on the right. The footing is challenging, but soon the trail levels out and travels over a long section of bog bridges by flowing water.

Views of North Carter Mountain appear. The mountain looks steep, as indeed it is—you'll be gaining 800 feet in the next 0.6 mile. The trail reaches a steep rocky rise, climbing 100 feet to reach some puncheon. You then resume the severely steep climb, clambering over slabs as you go. The route crosses flowing water, and then resumes its up, up, and up. As the elevation increases, views behind you peer into the Wild River drainage. You can spot your approach route along the Moriah Brook watershed, below the cliffs of Mount Moriah. On the northern horizon rise the Mahoosucs (Trip 27).

The route requires hand-over-hand scrambling as it rises above 4,000 feet and provides increasingly expansive views north. The entire Mahoosuc Range is now apparent, including its highest, most distant peak, 4,170-foot Old Speck. The cleft of Grafton Notch is to its right. The radical steep scrambles continue. The trail eventually becomes walkable and then eases to make a gradually rising traverse. As you wrap around the slopes, the first views appear of the upper Wild River watershed and your continuing route.

The broad gap at the head of the Wild River Valley is Perkins Notch. Mount Hight rises west of the notch, at the south end of the Carter Range. To the west (left) of Perkins Notch are the trailless peaks of Sable and Chandler mountains. The high round knob of North Baldface is apparent a few miles farther north.

You next reach a clearing on the summit of North Carter (8.1/4,530). A short distance farther, you reach a boulder and your first views of Mount Washington and the northern Presidentials. The deep gouge of the Great Gulf (Trip 22) pierces the range. Mounts Clay, Jefferson, Adams, and Madison march north from Washington.

The mellow trail now follows the ridge to reach the North Carter Trail on the right (8.4/4,470). Continue straight and remain on the AT as it winds through a short wind-blasted forest. Increasingly good views appear of the Presidential Range, from Boott Spur to Mount Madison at the northern end of the range. Views south also open up, encompassing Carter Dome ahead and Wildcat Ski Area to the southwest. You then crest the wooded summit of Middle Carter (9.0/4,610).

From here, the trail drops slowly, passing another great view; your continuing route over South Carter, Mount Hight, and Carter Dome lies out before you. After a long easy section, you begin the heart-pumping ascent of South Carter. The trail briefly levels, resumes its steady ascent, and then curves right to reach the wooded and viewless summit (10.3/4,430).

Past the summit, the trail drops steeply, then quickly moderates for an easier descent into Zeta Pass, where the Carter Dome Trail joins from the right (11.1/3,900). Two small trickles of water can be found here. Continuing on the AT, you next reach a fork in the trail (11.3/4,080). The Carter Dome Trail goes right, bypassing the summit of Mount Hight and saving you a few hundred feet of climbing and 0.4 mile of effort. But you miss the view! Go left instead to make a traversing ascent up Mount Hight, soon climbing directly uphill. A short distance from the top, you enter the alpine zone and scramble over boulders to reach a clearing on the summit plateau. Continue just past the clearing to reach the true summit (11.7/4,675).

The view looks east over the entire Wild River watershed. The prominent bald knobs of North and South Baldface are apparent. Below you is a tremendous bowl of paper birch, filling the Spruce Brook watershed. The Wild River itself is visible in the large marshy area near its headwaters. To the north, you can see Mount Moriah; farther down the ridge are the bald knobs of Shelburne Moriah Mountain. The Mahoosucs rise in the distance beyond it. To the south, the pointy summit of Mount Chocorua (Trip 17) is easily identified beyond the Moat Mountains. To the west are the Presidentials, including all of Montalban Ridge (Trip 21).

Carter Notch Hut nestles below the cliffs of Wildcat Mountain

Leaving the summit, you make a gradual descent and undulate along to reach the Carter Dome Trail on the right and immediately afterward the Black Angel Trail on the left (12.1/4,570). Continue on the AT as it rises upward on a steady cruise to reach the summit of Carter Dome (12.5/4,832). A large clearing here is dotted with the remains and foundation of an old lookout tower. A look north reveals your entire route thus far. The Rainbow Trail splits left here, providing a more direct route down to Perkins Notch (1.5 miles) through extensive paper birch stands. (This variation saves 2.2 miles of hiking, but skips impressive Carter Notch.)

Remaining on the AT, you begin a steady drop over a rocky path. The trail traverses left and soon you have your first glimpses into the approaching cleft of Carter Notch. Wildcat A looms on the far side, rising a thousand feet. The route traverses down to reach the start of a more serious drop. As you drop below 4,000 feet, the trail curves right and takes a direct line downward.

Soon you reach a view that looks into the notch, where Carter Notch Hut can be spotted by two small ponds. The steep trail switchbacks left and begins following large rock steps on a plummeting descent. The trail curves right and briefly eases before resuming its stair-aided descent. The descent eases as you approach the bottom and increasing paper birch and hobblebush appear alongside.

You reach the shore of a small idyllic pond and then encounter the Nineteen Mile Brook Trail on the right by the pond's outflow. Bear left to remain on the AT, passing a second small pond that reflects the cliffs of Carter Dome. The hut is just ahead (13.8/3,288).

Take a leisurely break and consider exploring the Ramparts, the talus field that fills much of the notch. A network of unmarked paths explores the boulders, best accessed by the posted spur just past the second bunkhouse. Once you're in the boulders, scramble as far as you care to go. Icy caves and views await.

The continuing route now leaves the AT (and crowds) behind as it journeys toward the Wild River headwaters. Follow the Wildcat River Trail past the second bunkhouse to begin a steady drop through the Wildcat River watershed, which ultimately feeds the Saco River to the southwest. Paper birch increase. Red maple, yellow birch, and sugar maple appear as you dip below 3,000 feet. The trail soon crosses a small brook and leaves the spruce-fir forest behind. The trail begins following an old road bed, briefly parallels a small inaccessible stream, and then traverses away to the left.

You next rock-hop across the Wildcat River, here still a stream. Red maple becomes increasingly common as you proceed toward the Wild River Trail

(15.7/2,390). Bear left on the Wild River Trail, making a level traverse over occasional rocks and boggy bits. Sugar maples line the trail, glorious in the fall. The route crosses a small tributary to Bog Brook, rises briefly, and then curves left to reach the Bog Brook Trail (16.8/2,420).

Bear left to stay on the Wild River Trail as it winds through a long stretch of young hardwoods. Spruce and fir reappear in some of the boggier areas, joined by red maple and blueberry. You then climb briefly, traverse the slopes just above Perkins Notch, and crest the height-of-land. The trail bends right and reaches the Rainbow Trail on the left (17.5/2,580).

Remain on the Wild River Trail, which soon crosses a flowing water source—fill up here if you are staying at Perkins Notch. After a short climb along a wet trail, you make a brief drop, enter the Wild River watershed, and reach the site of Perkins Notch Shelter (18.3/2,600).

To continue, follow the Wild River Trail, which leaves to the left of the shelter and is marked by blue plastic diamonds and faint yellow blazes. You quickly pass another spur down to the bog's edge and then hear the flowing headwaters. Soon the trail banks left, crosses the young Wild River, and drops gently to parallel the now rushing stream. This section offers good camping potential.

The route continues through a hardwood forest dotted with occasional spruce and fir, and then re-crosses the now rockier stream. The East Branch Trail joins from the right on the opposite bank (19.0/2,400). Downstream from the junction is a level brookside campsite, complete with fire ring. Remain on the Wild River Trail as it drops, parallels the stream, passes another streamside campsite, and then hops across boggy areas and a few rock staircases. The often-wet path winds through thick young spruce-fir forest, returns among hardwoods, and then descends to reach the Eagle Link on the right (20.5/2,050). You now decide between the shorter and longer versions of this hike.

Shorter Variation: The Wild River Trail. The hike's shorter loop returns to the Wild River Campground via the Wild River Trail. Initially thin, rocky, and root-crossed, the Wild River Trail winds through hardwood forest and makes a steady descent near the river, which is audible but not readily accessible. The route steepens as it drops into and crosses the Red Brook drainage (20.9/1,860), briefly running alongside the stream as it courses over bedrock and boulders. Several nice pools can be found at the confluence with the Wild River.

Keep your eyes peeled for relics of the logging era. Large metal spikes jut from the bedrock as the trail eases and starts cruising along an old railroad bed. You pass several nice campsites and soon begin to parallel the river, occasionally detouring around undercut banks. The trail becomes increasingly wide as you approach Spruce Brook, rock-hop across it, and immediately reach the site of Spruce Brook Shelter (21.8/1,650).

Past the shelter, the trail winds along the river and hemlocks begin to reappear. The going is easy along this section, which soon leads past the Black Angel Trail on the left (22.5/1,540). A short distance beyond it, the Highwater Trail splits left at the site of the old Spider Bridge. The bridge is no longer there, but the route crosses at a wide shallow spot; you can usually rock-hop across. (If the river is running dangerously high, follow the Highwater Trail instead. This slightly longer route climbs slopes and traverses several hundred feet above the river to eventually emerge at the Moriah Brook Trail in 2.9 miles.)

Once on the opposite side, continue downstream on the Wild River Trail, quickly passing the old bridge footings. The route cruises alongside the deepening river, and before long becomes a gravel road. From here on out, the hiking is easy and almost entirely level. The trail curves right as it approaches the campground, passes through a raspberry-laden meadow, and reaches the earlier Moriah Brook Trail junction (25.0/1,180). From here, either follow the single-track trail you started on, or remain on the road to emerge in the campground (25.3/1,170).

Full Loop. To complete the full Wild River circuit, head right on the Eagle Link. You quickly pass another large camping area and then cross the diminutive Wild River. The yellow-blazed trail next rock-hops a significant tributary and begins a steady traversing rise through young hardwood forest along a gentle path. Carter Dome occasionally peeks through the trees behind you. Roughly halfway up the slopes, you cross another large tributary (21.8/2,490) where a nice campsite nestles in a paper birch grove.

The steady rise continues. Occasional glimpses northwest reveal Mount Moriah and Shelburne Moriah Mountain. After traversing steeply over rockier terrain, the trail begins a level traverse and slowly descends to cross several water sources. The forest transitions back to spruce-fir as you start the final rise over solid rock slabs (slippery when wet). As you approach the ridge, views south appear of nearby North Baldface. You pass one final water source, briefly pass through a flat boggy section, and then attain the ridge and four-way junction with the Baldface Circle and Meader Ridge trails (23.2/2,990).

For a jaw-dropping view of the area, drop your pack and head south on the Baldface Circle Trail for 0.1 mile (130 feet of elevation gain) to the junction with the Bicknell Ridge Trail. You can see adjacent Eagle Crag to the north along a long ridge. Mount Meader drops abruptly off the end of the ridge.

Beyond Meader are the upper Basin Cliffs, then West Royce Mountain on the left (in New Hampshire) and East Royce Mountain to the right (in Maine). Evans Notch lies below these two massifs. In the distance, directly in line with the Notch, are the twin peaks of Caribou (south) and Gammon (north) Mountains. To the west is the entire Carter-Moriah Range, from Carter Dome on the left to Shelburne Moriah on the right. Mount Washington peeks over the top of the range; the Mahoosucs are visible on the horizon to the north. To the south, the rounded symmetrical summits of North and South Baldface tantalize. A line of naked exfoliating granite runs down the lower ridge of South Baldface. (If you're motivated, you can head south to tag the Baldface summits via the Baldface Circle Trail. It's 1.2 miles one-way to North Baldface, 2.4 miles to South Baldface.)

Back at the previous junction (23.2/2,990), head north on the Meader Ridge Trail. The trail proceeds along the ridgeline and next encounters the small bump of Eagle Crag, another exceptional viewpoint. The large forested massif of Speckled Mountain (Trip 26) rises to the east for the first time.

The trail descends the east side of the crag—watch for cairns—and makes a brief traverse over solid rock with continuing views. You then enter thick spruce-fir woods and begin an undulating section, passing a tannin-brown water source. The trail passes two posted spurs to more viewpoints; the first looks south, the second offers good views of the Mill Brook headwall below. The trail continues its undulating ramble, passes several trickling springs, and then comes to an open rock dome and the Basin Rim and Mount Meader trails (25.2/2,710).

Continue along the ridgeline on the Basin Rim Trail, which immediately leads to open ledges with excellent views north into the heart of Evans Notch. The cliffs of the upper Basin rise below. West and East Royce mountains loom beyond. Speckled Mountain is visible on the opposite side of the notch.

From here, the Basin Rim Trail winds over slabs before dropping steeply over roots and rocks. You pass a large flat boulder sheltering a dry bivy site and then abruptly enter a grove of pure paper birch. The route crosses a stream, mellows, and traverses past increasing yellow birch. A few restricted views look northwest. You then wind through an older copse, highlighted by some large yellow birch snags and straight spruce trees, and pass near the summit of Ragged Jacket Mountain.

The trail now commences its steep descent toward the Rim Junction. The deep ravine lurks palpably to your right. You pass occasional glimpses into the Basin as you steadily drop into a saddle, curve right, and reach the lip of the Basin (26.2/1,880), where open slabs peer at Ragged Jacket and Mount Meader.

You curve back into the woods, cross a glacially polished outcrop, and then reach a steep sloping slab with views straight down into the Basin below. To the southeast, the low-elevation Deer Hill complex sits across the state line in Maine. Continuing, you quickly encounter more slabs with equally good views (and better seating) and then reach the Rim Junction, where the Basin, Black Angel, and Basin Rim trails converge (26.6/1,970).

To head toward Blue Brook Shelter site, make a 150-degree turn to your left and head down the Black Angel Trail, reaching the shelter after an easy 200-foot descent. To return directly to the Wild River Campground, bear left (west) on the Basin Trail, which gently drops and reaches a short spur that connects it with the Blue Brook Shelter site in 0.3 mile (26.8/1,810).

From this trail junction, continue down the Basin Trail as it rambles past dense young hardwoods, crosses a small brook, and then runs parallel to rocky Blue Brook itself. Suddenly the trail passes below vertical cliffs of solid stone, towering nearly 100 feet above the opposite bank. Enjoy the spot by a large swimming hole at the cliff base (27.1/1,560).

The trail continues past several more swimming holes, briefly curves away from the rushing brook, and then rejoins it by a final swimming hole at the base of a bedrock water sluice (27.5/1,390). The route crosses the stream and makes an easy descent through hardwood forest, curving away from the stream beneath sizeable hemlocks. You cross a tributary, pass over a long stretch of bog bridging, parallel a small tributary 20 feet down to the left, and then reach a fork. Go right here as indicated by an arrow sign (a left turn leads into the campground). The trail curves back toward Blue Brook, nearly reaching it, and then emerges at the trailhead parking area (28.8/1,180).

INFORMATION

White Mountain National Forest, Androscoggin Ranger District, 300 Glen Road, Gorham, NH 03581, 603-466-2713, www.fs.fed.us/r9/forests/white_mountain; Pinkham Notch Visitor Center, 603-466-2725, open daily 6:30 A.M.–10 P.M.

TRIP 25
THE KILKENNY

Location: Pilot Range, White Mountain National Forest
Highlight: The wild and empty northern White Mountains
Distance: 16.1 miles round-trip
Total Elevation Gain/Loss: 4,600/4,600
Trip Length: 2 days
Difficulty: ★★
Recommended Map: *AMC White Mountain Guide, Map 6 North Country-Mahoosuc,* AMC Books

A mountain range in miniature, the Pilot Range rises above the Great North Woods of northern New Hampshire. Known as the Kilkenny, the surrounding region is set apart from the rest of White Mountain National Forest, a landscape of roaming moose, bald summits, looming ledges, and few people.

HIKE OVERVIEW

The hike approaches the Pilot Range from the east, looping counter-clockwise up and along the highest points of its mountain spine. Along the way, you visit some of the region's best highlights, including open cliff-top views from Rogers Ledge, reflections in Unknown Pond, a 360-degree vista from the summit of the Horn, and a small cabin atop Mount Cabot, one of New Hampshire's 4,000-footers. This hike is a good option on busy summer weekends and holidays, when other areas in the Whites may be overrun, and in late September, when the forest here blushes with peak color—earlier than anywhere else in the Whites. Dogs are allowed.

OVERNIGHT OPTIONS

The hike travels past two designated tentsites, Rogers Ledge and Unknown Pond, as well as a small and somewhat dilapidated cabin atop Mount Cabot. Dispersed camping is permitted throughout the hike but good sites are hard to find in the densely forested terrain. Campfires are permitted.

Rogers Ledge Tentsite is located in a clearing at 2,450 feet, 3.8 miles from the trailhead, surrounded by a forest of paper and yellow birch. A few level tentsites are scattered about. Water is available from a nearby brook, a short distance north on the Kilkenny Ridge Trail. A privy and fire ring complete

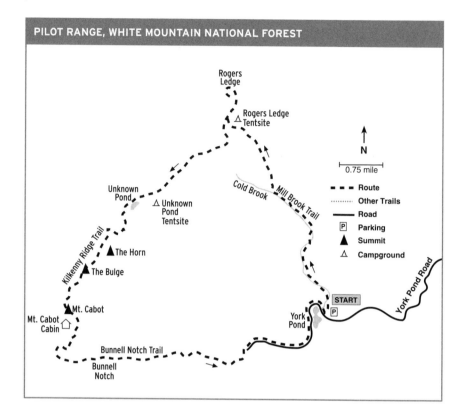

PILOT RANGE, WHITE MOUNTAIN NATIONAL FOREST

Rogers
Ledge

Rogers Ledge
△ Tentsite

N

0.75 mile

Unknown
Pond

△ Unknown
Pond
Tentsite

Cold Brook

Mill Brook Trail

— — — Route

.... Other Trails

———— Road

P Parking

▲ Summit

△ Campground

Kilkenny Ridge Trail

▲ The Horn

▲ The Bulge

▲ Mt. Cabot

Mt. Cabot
Cabin ⌂

Bunnell Notch Trail

Bunnell
Notch

START

P

York
Pond

York Pond Road

the amenities. The site makes a convenient base for a sunset visit to Rogers Ledge, 0.6 mile north on the Kilkenny Ridge Trail.

Unknown Pond Tentsite shelters at 3,200 feet by its namesake lake, 5.9 miles from the trailhead. Several established sites cluster beneath spruce-fir forest; the uppermost offers glimpses through the trees toward the northern Presidential Range. Water is obtained from the pond. (A filter is useful for removing the inevitable floaters.) This is the most popular overnight location in the area and is one of the few spots in the region that may attract a crowd. A privy is located nearby. A variety of heavily–used sites are scattered near the pond as well—not the most environmentally friendly options.

Cabot Cabin perches at 4,080 feet just below the summit of Mount Cabot, 8.7 miles from the trailhead. The small, dilapidated structure once accompanied an adjacent fire tower (built 1924, abandoned 1946, and dynamited by the United States Forest Service in 1965). The tiny green-shingled building offers four small bunks free of charge on a first-come, first served basis. A propane stove may be set up for use in the cabin, fueled by an outside tank, but shouldn't be relied on. Water is obtained from a small spring 200 feet down the mountainside—head toward the summit to find the posted spur. A filter is recommended. Good views from the cabin's small deck look west toward the distant Green Mountains. A privy and small fire ring are available.

TO REACH THE TRAILHEAD

Follow Route 110 north from Berlin for 7 miles and turn left on York Pond Road. In 1.5 miles, you reach the Kilkenny Guard Station (usually unmanned) and Bog Dam Road on the left. Continue straight on paved York Pond Road for another 3.3 miles to reach a gate and small parking area on the left by the entrance to the Berlin Fish Hatchery. The trailhead is a short distance farther up the road, but you'll want to leave your vehicle here. The Hatchery is open 8:30 a.m.–4 p.m. and the gate may be locked after closing time.

HIKE DESCRIPTION

From the parking area (0.0/1,480), start walking down the road toward the hatchery, passing a small pond on your left. Big-toothed aspen line the road, joined by red and striped maple, and you quickly pass an information sign that provides background on the hatchery's trout-raising efforts. You next pass the covered Foster's Raceways and another sign detailing the trout life cycle. Shortly thereafter, you reach a fork in the road. A trail sign points you right (uphill) toward your starting path, the Mill Brook Trail. As you approach the trailhead, you pass the Fire Warden headquarters and raceways full of hundreds of squirming fish. A circular pool holds some particularly large specimens.

The trail begins to the right of the Fire Warden building (0.2/1,530) on an old dirt road, briefly following Cold Brook before curving right and away from a WATER SUPPLY, NO TRESPASSING sign. The route then quickly turns sharply left onto a single-track path by a picnic table. Passing beneath spruce trees, the obvious trail soon bears left at a fork—follow the yellow and blue blazes. Rejoining Cold Brook, the hike is now accompanied by an understory of blueberry, hobblebush, and bunchberry.

The gentle trail slowly climbs along the gurgling creek. In spots, grass grows directly in the trail, which slowly becomes rockier as the creek valley narrows. Soon you begin traversing along the adjacent slopes, at times rising a short distance above the stream.

The trail returns along the placid stream then once again climbs the slopes. Watch for pink lady's slippers as the forest becomes increasingly dominated by

Rogers Ledge

spruce and paper birch. The trail then levels, curves away from the creek, and crosses a trickling tributary. The route now runs roughly parallel to this small watercourse, climbing slowly and steadily, and then levels out to undulate gently past abundant paper birch and hobblebush. You then drop through a dense young forest to reach a four-way junction with the Kilkenny Ridge Trail (3.8/2,400). Turn right on the Kilkenny Ridge Trail to immediately reach the Rogers Ledge Tentsite and the start of the highly recommended side-trip to Rogers Ledge, 1.2 miles round-trip with 550 feet of elevation change.

SIDE-TRIP TO ROGERS LEDGE

Head north on the Kilkenny Ridge Trail, winding past bracken fern, paper birch, and sugar and red maple. The route is intermittently indicated by yellow blazes and soon a view appears of Rogers Ledge and its naked rock face. The route steadily climbs, curves right past a large boulder, and then ascends a series of rock steps to reach a flat clearing atop Rogers Ledge. Open slabs along the cliff's edge are readily accessible. The panorama overlooks a mix of hardwoods and conifers, in fall a painted mosaic of foliage. To the west, the rolling summits of the northern Pilot Range are capped by 3,730-foot Hutchins Mountain.

Back at the earlier junction with the Mill Brook Trail (5.0/2,400), head south on the Kilkenny Ridge Trail to immediately cross the flowing headwaters of Mill Brook. The trail undulates over roots and rocks beneath spruce and fir trees and passes tiny Kilback Pond, a shallow and boggy beaver pond. A few small rocks along the shore provide options for a moment of relaxation. Just past the pond, look northeast for a view of Rogers Ledge.

The path crosses the pond outlet and starts to climb, soon offering better views of Rogers Ledge. The trail then levels and begins a slow rising traverse through groves of paper birch and spruce-fir. Wood ferns proliferate in the understory. The trail crests (6.7/3,320) and then makes a gentle descent, widening as it approaches the Unknown Pond Trail and adjacent Unknown Pond Tentsite (7.1/3,190). Savor views across the water toward the Horn's distinctive summit.

Continue on the Kilkenny Ridge Trail, which soon begins undulating away from the pond. You drop briefly to cross a rivulet and then begin a rising traverse up the Horn's west flanks. The rocky trail attains the saddle between the Bulge and the Horn (8.2/3,680), where an unsigned spur heads left toward the summit of the Horn, a rewarding excursion (0.6-mile round-trip with 250 feet of elevation gain).

The Horn offers the hike's best views. Follow the spur trail to the open summit knob, scrambling up some large boulders to reach the top. The view encompasses all of northern New Hampshire. To the south, the rounded dome of nearby Mount Cabot is apparent, and farther away and to its left are the northern flanks of the Presidential Range. The prominent bowl of King Ravine gouges deeply into the slopes below Mount Adams (Trip 23), and Mounts Jefferson and Washington, and the rounded hump of Mount Eisenhower can be seen trailing away to the south. To the southeast, the Carter Range and prominent cleft of Carter Notch are apparent (Trip 24). Northeast, the rugged Mahoosucs straddle the Maine–New Hampshire border (Trip 27). The smoking mills of Berlin lurk in the valleys below the Mahoosucs, fed by the many clear-cuts visible on the landscape.

Continuing from the saddle (8.8/3,680), you make a direct ascent to the viewless summit of the Bulge (9.0/3,950), situated in a forest of snags. The trail narrows as it descends the opposite side to reach an easy-cruising section. Now you begin the hike's final climb. As you ascend toward the summit of Mount Cabot, the surrounding slopes become lumpy moss gardens of boulders and fir trees. The trail gradient eases as it approaches the summit and then tops out in a clearing. A short spur leads to the actual summit (9.9/4,170).

Views in the area look south toward more near peaks, including the adjacent summits of Mounts Waumbek (left) and Starr King (right), and beyond to the Presidential Range. Descending from the summit, you pass a posted spur to a nearby spring and then make a momentary rise to reach a clearing on the lower summit with views east. You pass Bunnell Rock on the left—another good viewpoint—shortly before reaching Cabot Cabin.

From the cabin, the trail drops steadily over sharp basketball-size rocks. A series of switchbacks soon leads to a more direct descent over rocky terrain, including some large slabs. As you descend, watch for a spur that leads to an open rock ledge with more views south. Soon paper birch and hobblebush reappear in the spruce-fir mosaic. The trail then traverses east to reach the Cabot Trail on the right (11.3/2,970).

Bear left to remain on the Kilkenny Ridge Trail as it curves past sugar maple, blackberry, and raspberry to reach Bunnell Notch and the Bunnell Notch Trail (11.6/3,030). Turn left to head down the yellow-blazed Bunnell Notch Trail and begin your return down to the trailhead. The path is initially level, but soon starts to descend above a small gully. A creek flows audibly below, and the forest transitions back to hardwoods. Beech appears first, followed by paper birch and striped and sugar maple.

Abundant springs flow out of the adjacent hillside, creating numerous boggy sections, many bridged by rock steps. The gradient steepens, the trail

Cabot Cabin

narrows, and soon the route leads you alongside the pretty stream as it cascades over mossy stones.

The route eventually eases and runs level through a lush forest of sugar maple and yellow birch. You then rise above the creek and pass through a dense stand of saplings—the first signs of recent logging activity in the area. Soon the trail widens, descends slowly past more stick forest, and then banks right to encounter a logging road. The continuing route bears right (don't continue uphill to the left) and returns to single-track, winding along an old road overgrown with raspberries and blackberries

The trail returns to the creek (13.1/1,770), rock-hops its crystalline waters, and then crosses a gully to pass through a clearing with two large slash piles. Past the clearing, the single-track trail winds along a grassy road and reaches another logging road. An arrow sign here indicates the continuing trail direction to the right. Look up the road to spot pyramidal Terrace Mountain (3,655).

The trail now rambles through older forest and reaches the York Pond Trail on the right (13.8/1,700). Glance up the York Pond Trail to spot Mount Weeks. Go left to continue on the road—now the York Pond Trail—crossing the creek on a footbridge and reaching a metal gate (14.0/1,660). Just beyond is the dirt hatchery road by a small parking area. From here, it's a 2.1-mile road walk to the trailhead (16.1/1,480). As you go, look behind you for views of the Horn, Bulge, and Mount Cabot.

INFORMATION

White Mountain National Forest, Androscoggin Ranger District, 300 Glen Road, Gorham, NH 03581, 603-466-2713, www.fs.fed.us/r9/forests/white_mountain

4

MAINE

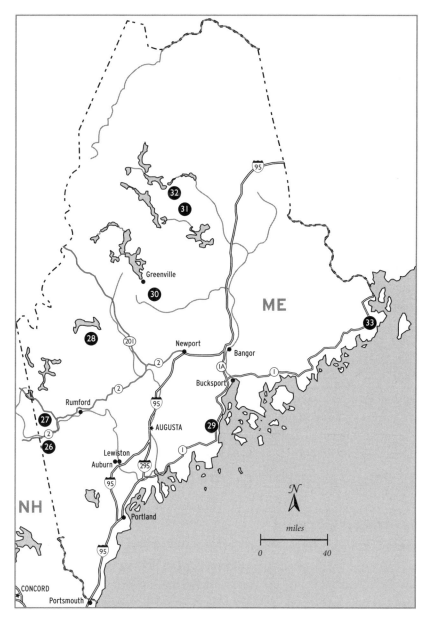

TRIP 26
SPECKLED-TACULAR

Location: Caribou-Speckled Mountain Wilderness, White Mountain National Forest
Highlight: Maine's White Mountains
Distance: 8.6 miles round-trip
Total Elevation Gain/Loss: 2,500/2,500
Trip Length: 1–2 days
Difficulty: ★★
Recommended Map: *AMC White Mountain Guide, Map 6: North Country-Mahoosucs,* AMC Books

Speckled Mountain hides in the east Whites. Secluded east of the Baldface Range, over the Maine state line, and invisible from elsewhere in the Whites, it offers a quiet ledge-walking escape with good views. Speckled Mountain is part of the 12,000-acre Caribou-Speckled Mountain Wilderness, designated in 1984.

The Brickett Place awaits you at the trailhead, undoubtedly the quietest visitor center in the White Mountains. Built in the early nineteenth century, the unusual brick building has had a diverse life: farmhouse, Civilian Conservation Corps regional headquarters, Boy Scout facility, even an AMC hut. Today, it's a sleepy wayside.

HIKE OVERVIEW
This short loop uses the Bickford Brook and Blueberry Ridge trails to ascend 2,906-foot Speckled Mountain. After passing a series of small cascades—the Bickford Slides—the route sticks to the mountain ridges, which offer several exceptional views. Most of the trip is dry and without water—the slides are your only reliable source. Carry what you need for the night. The hike is described counter-clockwise, but can easily be done in the opposite direction. Opt for the Blueberry Ridge Trail (and its views) on whichever day has better visibility.

OVERNIGHT OPTIONS
Dispersed camping is permitted throughout the Caribou-Speckled Mountain Wilderness, though good campsites are hard to find on the wooded slopes of this hike. Small bivy sites and the occasional tentsite scatter along a few ledges

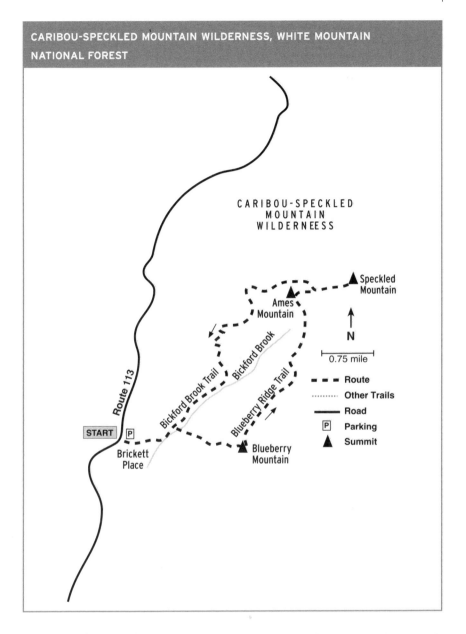

CARIBOU-SPECKLED MOUNTAIN WILDERNESS, WHITE MOUNTAIN NATIONAL FOREST

CARIBOU-SPECKLED
MOUNTAIN
WILDERNEESS

Speckled Mountain

Ames Mountain

N

0.75 mile

- - - Route
.... Other Trails
——— Road
P Parking
▲ Summit

Bickford Brook Trail

Bickford Brook

Blueberry Ridge Trail

Route 113

START P

Brickett Place

Blueberry Mountain

on the Blueberry Ridge Trail. Bedrock exposures on the summit also provide several options.

TO REACH THE TRAILHEAD

Take Route 113 north from Fryeburg for 20 miles. The trailhead is on the right and signed for the Brickett Place, 0.3 mile past the Basin Recreation Area turn-off and immediately across the Maine state line. A WMNF parking pass or daily permit is required to leave your vehicle here.

HIKE DESCRIPTION

From the trailhead parking lot (0.0/640), head out on the single-track Bickford Brook Trail. You immediately pass through woods of paper birch, beech, white ash, and sugar and striped maple—common members of the northern hardwood forest. Red oak appear in the mix as the trail quickly rises. The gradient soon eases, and you reach an old woods road (0.3/860) where the route bears right on a wider path. Snags punctuate the boulder slopes. The trail crests, the creek below becomes audible, and you cross the wilderness boundary. After a brief rise, you reach the Blueberry Ridge Trail (0.7/1,010). Look for an old CTA sign here.

Bear right on the yellow-blazed Blueberry Ridge Trail and descend the single-track path to the brook (0.8/940), where signs indicate the nearby presence of upper and lower Bickford Slides.

SIDE-TRIP TO BICKFORD SLIDES

Head downstream to reach the Lower Slides, where the creek sluices through a smooth foot-wide channel before sheeting over a two-tiered waterfall and into a sliver of head-deep water. The riparian corridor is lush, cool, and full of hemlocks. The slides continue downstream past this point, spilling over exposed bedrock, but access becomes increasingly challenging.

To visit the Upper Slides—and a nice swimming hole—head upstream to immediately cross the brook and follow the Slide Trail along the right (east) bank. You pass some stately yellow birch and sugar maples and cross a few small streams. The trail then switchbacks twice to climb above a spilling ramp of water that drops into an emerald pool. From here, the trail climbs steeply and runs parallel to the creek, which sluices below through deep and inaccessible grooves in the bedrock. The route drops to cross the creek and then cuts left up the opposite slope to reach the unposted junction with the Bickford Brook Trail, 0.5 mile from the Blueberry Ridge Trail. (Coming down the Bickford Brook Trail, look for the prominent yellow blaze on a yellow birch that marks the junction.)

Back on the Blueberry Ridge Trail (0.8/940), rock-hop the stream and bear right at the junction with the Upper Slides Trail. The rocky trail climbs steeply, quickly gaining elevation. Occasional glimpses through the trees reveal the adjacent Rattlesnake Brook drainage to the east. The trail's namesake berry bushes make an appearance as you climb, soon encountering open slabs (1.1/1,330). Views look north to East and West Royce mountains. The bare ridgeline continues to an open clearing with views west. North and South Baldface mountains rise on the far side of the Cold River, connected by a long ridge that extends north to Mount Meader, above The Basin and its cliffs, and then ends at West and East Royce mountains on the far side of Evans Notch. Peeking over the Baldface Range are the more distant summits of the Carter Range (Trip 24).

The route continues upward on a granite highway interspersed with patches of vegetation. Small white pines, spruce, and fir grow from green clumps. The trail levels and reenters spruce-fir forest, where blueberry bushes, pin cherry, bunchberry, and Indian cucumber are common in the understory. Numerous pink lady's slippers bloom here in June.

The trail soon returns to open ledges where sun-exposed blueberry bushes produce abundant fruit. Red pines cling to the sparse granite slabs. You next reach the White Cairn Trail on the right (1.4/1,730). Continue straight on the Blueberry Ridge Trail and quickly reach the junction for the Outlook—an old sign marks it.

The worthwhile side-trip to the Outlook follows a 0.5-mile loop to open views south from atop the Blueberry Mountain cliffs. From this vantage point, you can look below at Shell Pond, with Harndon Hill just beyond it and Deer Hill behind it to the right. East of Shell Pond are the twin bumps of Palmer and Adams mountains. South Baldface is visible to the southwest. Complete the loop by following small cairns and the occasional blaze to the Blueberry Ledge Trail.

Back at the Blueberry Ridge Trail, you can see the low ridge rising above you to north—your continuing route. The summit of Speckled Mountain rises to the right. Continue across the open slabs to reach the Stone House Trail (1.6/1,770), remaining on the Blueberry Ridge Trail as it makes a gentle drop to the base of the upcoming ridge.

The route soon begins traveling through the forest along a ribbon of solid rock. You pass abundant blueberry bushes and quickly reach another open ledge with views west; Mount Chocorua (Trip 17) can be spotted to the southwest. The open slabs continue, many with bivy potential but few with flat tentsites. The trail encounters a small alpine bog populated with larch and laurel, able to survive in the highly acidic soil. The steady ascent continues. Views west now reach as far as Mount Washington, which peeks out just to the right of Mount Hight in the southern Carter Range.

A series of giant rock steps lead to a level clearing near the summit of Ames Mountain (3.7/2,660). The trail curves right and briefly descends to reach the

Bickford Brook Trail (3.8/2,620). Your return route heads left, but definitely visit the top of Speckled Mountain before heading back (1.0 mile round-trip, 300 feet of elevation gain). To tag the summit, turn right on the double-track Bickford Brook Trail, which cruises along a duff-covered path, winds through a clearing full of blackberries and elderberries, and then attains the summit (4.3/2,906).

The footings from a long-gone fire tower crown the summit. Open views look north for the first time, revealing the long line of the Mahoosucs marching toward the horizon; Goose Eye Mountain is the prominent peak at the northern end of the range. To the west, Mounts Washington, Adams, and Madison peer over the Carter Range. To the northwest, Mount Moriah rises behind West and East Royce mountains. Due north, and much closer, Caribou Mountain rises beyond Haystack Notch and the cliffs of Haystack Mountain. To the east is Red Rock Mountain near the edge of the wilderness area.

Back at the earlier junction with the Blueberry Ledge Trail (4.8/2,620), head west on the Bickford Brook Trail. The route follows an old woods road and easily descends through nice spruce-fir forest. A few gnarly, century-old yellow birch punctuate the scenery. The trail makes a long level traverse, then resumes its descent and passes the Spruce Hill Trail on the right (5.5/2,410).

The trail steadily drops and returns to northern hardwood forest. As you descend below 2,000 feet, a pair of broad switchbacks leads you toward a small stream. The trail switchbacks down several more times and then crosses the creek. The path then becomes more road-like as it descends into woods of beech and maple.

The trail mellows around 1,500 feet, and you can hear Bickford Brook rushing out-of-sight below. You soon pass the junction for the Upper Slides trail (7.5/1,300) and then return to the earlier junction with the Blueberry Ridge Trail. Follow the Bickford Brook Trail back to the trailhead (8.6/640).

INFORMATION

White Mountain National Forest, Evans Notch Information Center, 18 Maryville Road, Bethel, ME 04217, 207-824-2134, www.fs.fed.us/r9/forests/white_mountain

TRIP 27
THE HARDEST MILE

Location: Mahoosuc Notch, Mahoosuc Range, the Appalachian Trail
Highlights: Rugged mountains, alpine bogs, summit views, the hardest mile on the AT
Distance: 15.1 miles one-way
Total Elevation Gain/Loss: 6,200/6,200
Trip Length: 2–3 days
Difficulty: ★★★★
Recommended Map: *AMC White Mountain Guide, Map 6: North Country–Mahoosuc Range,* AMC Books

The Mahoosuc Range straddles the Maine–New Hampshire border northeast of the White Mountains. Even by New England standards, these mountains are remarkable for their ruggedness. Mahoosuc Notch slices through the heart of the range, a deep cleft filled with enormous boulders and traversed by the Appalachian Trail (AT). It is one of the most challenging sections of trail in New England and readily earns its moniker as the AT's Hardest Mile.

Only a narrow corridor of land is protected within the mountain range, including the AT corridor in New Hampshire and a slightly broader swath of state land in Maine. The remaining area is unprotected, owned largely by logging companies. Clear-cuts and other intensive logging practices are common sights in the area.

HIKE OVERVIEW

This hike can be done either as an overnight trip or as a leisurely three-day excursion that takes time to relax and savor the scenery. The trip begins and ends at trailheads located 4.8 miles apart on unpaved Success Pond Road. To return to your starting point, you'll need to shuttle cars, bring a mountain bike, or gird yourself for a long road walk.

The journey begins on the Speck Pond Trail, which climbs from Success Pond Road through active logging areas to reach Speck Pond and the ridge-line. The route then heads south on the AT, traveling along the ridgeline for 9.5 miles. Past Speck Pond, the hike quickly descends into adventure. It scrambles through Mahoosuc Notch and then rises steeply back to the ridgeline. Five very long miles south of Speck Pond, you reach Full Goose Campsite.

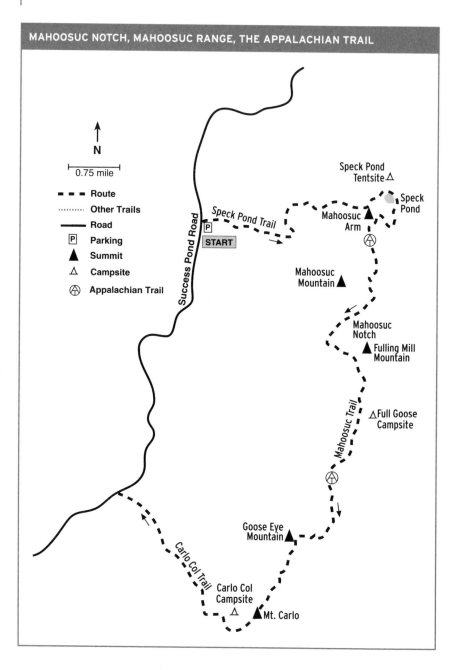

MAHOOSUC NOTCH, MAHOOSUC RANGE, THE APPALACHIAN TRAIL

N

0.75 mile

- - - Route
.... Other Trails
——— Road
P Parking
▲ Summit
△ Campsite
Ⓐ Appalachian Trail

Success Pond Road

Speck Pond Trail

P

START

Speck Pond Tentsite △

Speck Pond

Mahoosuc Arm ▲

Ⓐ

Mahoosuc Mountain ▲

Mahoosuc Notch

▲ Fulling Mill Mountain

Mahoosuc Trail

△ Full Goose Campsite

Ⓐ

Goose Eye Mountain ▲

Carlo Col Trail

Carlo Col Campsite

△ ▲ Mt. Carlo

From here, the route continues on the AT for another 4.4 miles, passing open views atop Goose Eye Mountain and Mount Carlo before reaching Carlo Col Campsite. An easy descent down the Carlo Col Trail returns you to Success Pond Road.

OVERNIGHT OPTIONS

Stick to the three established camping areas located along this hike. The approach trail crosses private land and the ridgeline is not a good place to camp.

Speck Pond Campsite is located at 3,400 feet near the shore of its namesake pond, 3.6 miles from the trailhead. A shelter sleeps eight to ten comfortably, and there are six tent platforms, three doubles and three singles. From Memorial Day through late September, and on weekends in October, a caretaker is on hand to collect an overnight per person fee. Though the site receives moderate use compared with many locations in the Whites, it is still busy in July, August, and on most weekends. A seasonal spring provides water or you can obtain it from Speck Pond.

Full Goose Campsite sits at 3,000 feet in dense spruce-fir forest, 8.2 miles from the trailhead. There is a shelter and four tent platforms. Water is available from a spring a short distance down the mountainside; a thin seasonal stream also flows nearby.

Carlo Col Campsite and Shelter is also located at 3,000 feet, 12.7 miles from the starting trailhead and 2.4 miles from hike's end. Its best feature is the enclosed cabin-like shelter. Four tent platforms complete the nicely maintained site. Rock-lined paths lead to a few restricted views north. Please use the provided bear box to store your food at night.

TO REACH THE TRAILHEAD

Take Route 16 north toward Berlin. Turn east off Route 16 to cross the Androscoggin River on the Cleveland bridge, located 4.5 miles north of the east Route 2/16 junction in Gorham. Turn left on Unity Street and proceed through a stoplight. The road then curves right, crosses the railroad tracks, and becomes Hutchins Road. Follow Hutchins Road 1.2 miles past the stoplight to reach unpaved Success Pond Road on the right.

Success Pond Road is the main artery for logging operations in the region and is usually dusty, muddy, or heavily washboarded. It is passable, albeit slowly, in a low-clearance vehicle. Be watchful for high-speed logging trucks and always give them the right-of-way. From the start of Success Pond Road at Hutchins Street, proceed 8.0 miles to the turn-off for the Carlo Col Trail and parking area—your ending trailhead—on the right. Continue another 4.8

miles to reach the start of the Speck Pond Trail on the right. There is a small parking area adjacent to the road on the left. Be watchful—trail signs are small and difficult to spot.

HIKE DESCRIPTION

From the roadside parking area (0.0/1,750), cross the road to the posted Speck Pond Trail trailhead. A few young denizens of the forest can be identified at the trailhead: balsam fir to your left, yellow birch on your right, and big-tooth aspen overhead. The single-track trail initially runs parallel to Sucker Brook, a small trickling stream, and passes through young northern hardwood forest. Paper birch and red, striped, and sugar maples are all present. You cross a small tributary, leave the brook, and begin hiking parallel to the audible stream below.

The trail slowly rises, returns along the boulder-strewn brook, and cruises past extensive pink lady's slippers on the forest floor, blooming in May and June. You steadily climb through a shady riparian corridor and pass a nice spa-sized soaking pool in the brook. The route then steepens markedly and switchbacks left. Mature yellow birch line the rocky and root-laced path as it traverses up the slopes. Other trees are young and small, an indication of past logging efforts that selectively removed the most valuable trees but left less precious species like birch behind.

You then encounter evidence of very recent logging activity. The first of several skid roads crosses the trail corridor, a broad linear cut running straight up the mountain slopes that provides access for harvesting equipment. The trail is obliterated where it crosses such cuts, but usually can be located easily on the opposite side. Be watchful and prepared for the unexpected.

The trail starts climbing more steeply and eventually bears right to take a more direct line upslope, using several nice rock staircases en route. The gradient briefly eases as the trail passes through stands of paper birch and the surrounding woods transition to spruce-fir forest. The route then resumes a long rising traverse, slowly gaining altitude. The gradient increases markedly as the trail passes 3,000 feet. It becomes progressively steeper near the top, where a log staircase and some scrambling are necessary before you can proceed. You top out just below the summit of Mahoosuc Arm and reach the May Cutoff (3.1/3,710), which bears right to reach the AT in 0.3 mile. Follow it to skip Speck Pond and shave 1.1 miles off your hike.

Otherwise, remain on the Speck Pond Trail as it begins a steep drop. Old Speck Mountain looms ahead. Speck Pond shimmers in the basin below. A rocky descent deposits you at the lakeshore. Speck Pond Campsite is just ahead

(3.6/3,400). From here, you can make the side-trip up Old Speck Mountain, Maine's fourth highest peak. To tag the summit— and its unparalleled views of the surrounding landscape—follow the AT north for 1.4 miles, gaining 770 feet of elevation.

The hike continues south from Speck Pond on the AT, wrapping around the east shore, where there is a view of Mahoosuc Arm across the water. The trail crosses the pond outlet and then climbs steeply via rocks, slabs, and rock staircases, passing a restricted view of Old Speck Mountain en route. After topping out, the route travels over some bog bridging and then undulates along the top of Mahoosuc Arm. Views look southeast into the Androscoggin River Valley and northeast to the peaks beyond Grafton Notch.

The trail then reaches an open viewpoint looking south toward the deep cleft of Mahoosuc Notch, shadowed beyond by Fulling Mill Mountain, North Peak, and Goose Eye Mountain—your continuing route. Sunday River drains the slopes below you to the east, namesake for the nearby ski resort. To the north, you can make out the fire tower atop Old Speck.

Looking south toward Mahoosuc Notch

Continuing south, you next reach the May Cutoff on the right (4.5/3,680), which you can follow a short distance to reach the summit of Mahoosuc Arm and views southwest. Heading south on the AT, you soon start the descent into Mahoosuc Notch, visible ahead. You pass a rock slab offering unobstructed views into the notch and then begin to plummet over solid rock. Conditions are slick in spots and scrambling is often required to safely navigate the drop. The trail descends several hundred feet and then eases somewhat. Though still steep, most of the rock slab sliding is now behind you.

Giant boulders begin to appear as you approach the notch and soon the trail starts a traversing descent. The notch comes into view, as do the flanks of Mahoosuc Mountain to the north. Leveling out, the trail bears right among increasing yellow and paper birch and encounters a brook. Water emerges from mossy boulders, sluices over rock slabs, and fills a few small pools to a depth of about 2 feet—nice for a refreshing soak.

The rocky trail resumes its descent, winding past mature spruce and yellow birch. The trail passes a large sugar maple, and curves right to reach the foot of the notch (5.6/2,150). The environment now becomes very lush. Mats of polypody ferns crown boulders. Multitudes of ferns, mountain maple, and false Solomon's seal fill the understory. Fulling Mill Mountain looms above you to the south.

You then encounter the first boulder field and begin the Hardest Mile. The moss-covered rocks come in all sizes, from microwaves to semi-trucks. The trail drops through a crevice and squeezes through a small cave. It reaches a high point and then goes underneath a large boulder. It passes through a crack so narrow that you must remove your pack, feeding it behind you.

The stream flows directly underneath you, occasionally audible but always invisible underneath the boulders. The rock-hopping gymnastics continue. Sheer rock cliffs rise above you to the left. The trail passes under another giant boulder. The section concludes with a final scramble through a dark cave crevice. Misty smoke emerges from nearby cracks as hidden ice slowly melts away.

The trail now rises steeply beneath overhanging cliffs along a boulder-free route. You surmount a few more boulders and undulate along to reach the height-of-land and the Notch Trail (6.7/2,460).

Turn left to remain on the AT, which immediately starts going up, up, and up. Slabs, rock staircases, and a pair of log ladders lead straight up the flanks of Fulling Mill Mountain. After gaining more than 500 feet of elevation, the route bends right and the gradient eases. The trail now gradually rises, makes a level traverse, and then resumes its gentle climb to enter the unique alpine bogs of the Mahoosuc Range.

The trail travels along puncheon through a low-lying alpine garden of blueberry, leather leaf, Labrador tea, cranberry, and sheep laurel. Keep an eye out for small larch trees, deciduous conifers able to tolerate the extremely acidic soils found here. You next reach the rocky summit of South Peak (7.7/3,395), where vistas sweep north once again toward Old Speck. North Peak is nearby to the south. Goose Eye peeks over its shoulder. To the west is the Kilkenny Range; Mount Cabot is the highest peak (Trip 25). The Presidential Range rises to the southwest; Mounts Washington and Madison are visible (Trip 23).

The AT descends from here, passing a few restricted views west, and then begins a steeper drop. The descent is steady but at first not radically steep. But the gradient soon increases as the trail descends stone stairs and crosses a creek. A wooden ladder on the opposite shore immediately brings you to Full Goose Campsite (8.2/3,000).

Continuing south, the AT descends more wooden steps, runs briefly level, and then climbs a bouldery slab. The level traverse resumes, offering glimpses northwest through the trees toward Success Pond. The trail bears right and slowly climbs through an interesting forest that diminishes in size to near-pygmy stature. You then encounter an open slab with more views north and east.

The views continue as you steadily rise along the blueberry-dotted ridge. The trail then reenters the trees, levels briefly, and resumes a more direct ascent. You reach the lower summit of North Peak, where views north look first to South Peak, then the Notch, Mahoosuc Mountain, and the long ridge that leads to Old Speck Mountain. Looking south you can see the bald hump of Goose Eye Mountain—your final ridge-top destination.

Continuing south, the AT immediately reaches the true summit of North Peak (9.2/3,675), where views west reveal the Kilkenny Range. The Presidential Range juts to the southwest. Looking north, you can see the mountains of northern New Hampshire, including the distinctive twin humps of the Percy Peaks.

From the summit, you briefly drop among trees before entering another open alpine bog. The trail slowly descends, bottoming out in a narrow gulch before rising to another mostly bald plateau. A final brief drop deposits you at the Wright Trail (10.2/3,480), which heads off to the left down the range's little-visited east flanks.

Remain on the AT as it begins a real-life version of chutes and ladders. Dozens of wooden ladders and stairs traverse up and along the slopes. The amount of trail work that went into this section is staggering. You eventually reach the summit of Goose Eye Mountain's East Peak (10.4/3,790). Goose Eye itself looms just ahead, with Mount Carlo beyond. Views north encompass the long ridgeline of the Mahoosucs.

Continuing south, the AT makes a steep but quick drop to reach the Wright Trail South Fork on the left (10.5/3,640). From here, a steady climb leads through the trees to an open view. The Goose Eye Trail joins from the right (10.8/3,840).

To tag the summit of Goose Eye Mountain, follow the Goose Eye Trail less than 0.1 mile to more great views. Looking north, you can see the cleft of the Notch and all the peaks leading up to it. Mount Carlo is next up on the ridge heading south, followed by the bald peak of Mount Success in New Hampshire. (Note that you can return to Success Pond Road via the 3.2-mile Goose Eye Trail. This variation reduces the overall hike by a mile, but is steeper and rougher than the easy-cruising exit via the Carlos Col Trail.)

Proceeding south on the AT, you make a steep ladder-aided drop, then level out and head gently down to the last alpine bald. This is the final section of low-lying trees and stunted vegetation. You then leave it all behind and steadily wind down through thick spruce-fir forest, bottoming out in the saddle between Goose Eye Mountain and Mount Carlo (11.6/3,180).

The trail climbs steadily though the trees, tops out on the summit plateau, and then undulates along it to reach the actual summit, indicated by a marker (12.2/3,565). Limited views reach north to Goose Eye Mountain and

The boulder-strewn trail through Mahoosuc Notch

Wright Peak and south to Success Mountain. The route then descends through spruce-fir forest and reaches the Carlo Col Trail on the right (12.4/3,190).

Bear right on the Carlo Col Trail to begin your descent off the ridge. The rocky path drops slowly at first, but soon steepens as it follows a bouldery streamcourse downward. As you pass below 3,000 feet, you cross a thin stream, rise up the opposite bank, and reach Carlo Col Shelter (12.7/3,000).

Past the shelter, the trail continues down the watercourse over slippery rocks. Yellow birch appear as the trail leaves the streambed, bears left, and then returns to the creek and crosses it. This point marks the state line and your passage from Maine into New Hampshire. The path traverses steadily downward to the right, accompanied by increasing paper and yellow birch, and reaches the main branch of the creek (13.3/2,350). Cross and enter an increasingly lush forest that transitions steadily to hardwoods. Soon it's almost all ferns, sugar maples, and yellow and paper birch.

You then begin a long, gradual descent, an easy-cruising rock-free section that soon enters thicker, younger forest. The creek reappears by the trail and big-tooth aspen flutter overhead. After an easy rock-hop over the stream, the trail follows an old woods road surrounded by encroaching vegetation. The trail next enters a clearing and rambles past prolific blackberry and raspberry bushes, which offer nice end-of-the-hike refreshment in late summer. You then emerge in the Carlo Col parking area, where the Goose Eye Trail joins from the right (15.1/1,680). Shuttle back around, or drop your pack and walk the 4.8 miles back along Success Pond Road to retrieve your car.

INFORMATION

Grafton Notch State Park, 1941 Bear River Road, Newry, ME 04261, 207-824-2912, 207-674-6080 (off-season), www.maine.gov/doc/parks/programs/index.html; www.outdoors.org/conservation/wherewework/mahoosucs

TRIP 28
GO BIGELOW

Location: Bigelow Mountain, Bigelow Preserve Public Reserved Land
Highlight: A mountainous ridge with maple-cloaked flanks
Distance: 12.7 miles round-trip
Total Elevation Gain/Loss: 4,000/4,000
Trip Length: 2 days
Difficulty: ★★★
Recommended Map: *AMC Maine Mountain Guide, Map 2: Rangeley-Stratton Region,* AMC Books

Bigelow Mountain creases the landscape of western Maine, a long, rocky ridge dotted with peaks and far-reaching views. At lower elevations, enriched soils create habitat for abundant sugar maples. In fall, they blaze in leaf-peeping glory. Come experience the full spectrum of 3,000 feet of elevation change, climbing from the mountain's base to its dramatic high point atop 4,145-foot West Peak.

HIKE OVERVIEW

The hike uses the Fire Warden, Appalachian, and Horns Pond trails to loop up Bigelow Mountain's steep slopes and along the highest 4 miles of ridgeline. En route, the trail passes three designated camping areas and some of the best views in Maine. Dogs are permitted but must be leashed at designated campsites.

OVERNIGHT OPTIONS

Two of the three designated camping areas—Avery Memorial Tentsite and Horns Pond Campsite—are located along the ridgeline and next to the Appalachian Trail (AT). They consequently receive heavy use. The recommended overnight spot is Moose Falls Campsite, especially on weekends and during thru-hiker season (August and September). There are also several campsites located less than a mile from the trailhead, good options for a late-day arrival at the trailhead. Campfires are permitted at designated sites.

Moose Falls Campsite perches at 2,470 feet, 3.6 miles from the trailhead. Surrounded by sugar maples, the site is located 1,300 feet below Bigelow Col and the AT, and consequently receives minimal thru-hiker traffic. Two platforms and two other established sites spread along the slopes. Sugarloaf

BIGELOW MOUNTAIN, BIGELOW PRESERVE PUBLIC RESERVED LAND

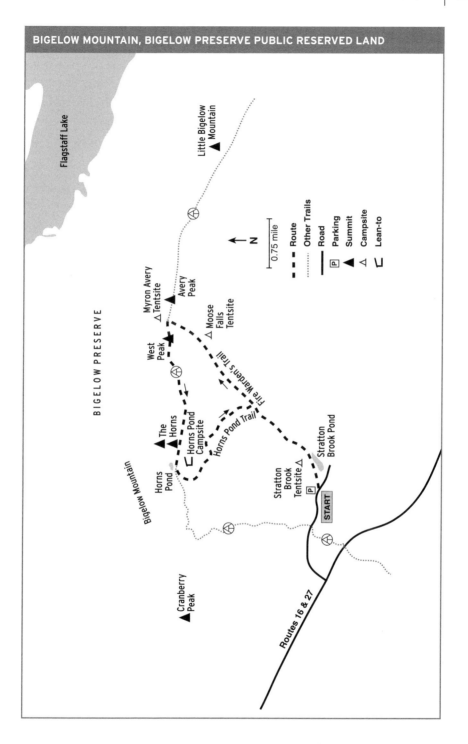

Mountain peeks through the trees; the lights of the ski resort are visible at night. Water is located a short distance uphill along the Fire Warden Trail.

Avery Memorial Tentsite, 4.6 miles from the trailhead, hunkers down at 3,800 feet in Bigelow Col, a narrow cleft sandwiched between Avery and West peaks. Four tent platforms are tucked among balsam firs; one has a decent view south toward Sugarloaf Mountain and Crocker Mountains. A larger group platform is also available. Two unreliable springs are located nearby; a filter is usually necessary to suck up any water.

Horns Pond Campsite is situated 3.2 miles from Avery Memorial Shelter near the shores of its namesake pond, which nests atop the ridge at 3,170 feet. It is one of the highest bodies of water in the state. The overnight area is a substantial complex that receives heavy use. Four tent platforms, two group tentsites, a general tenting area, two privies, a day-use lean-to, and two overnight lean-tos are all located here. Views to the south and east are available from a few spots, especially the privies. Water is readily accessible from the pond. Fishing is permitted, and the shallow pond is stocked annually with brook trout. Metal garbage cans are scattered around for food storage *only*; pack out all your trash.

TO REACH THE TRAILHEAD

Follow Route 27/16 north from Kingfield to the Sugarloaf Ski Area entrance on the left. Continue 3.3 miles farther to Stratton Brook Road, a small and easily-missed dirt road on the right. A small brown sign for Bigelow Preserve helps indicate the turn-off. Stratton Brook Road is readily navigable for low-clearance vehicles and leads in 1.6 miles to a small parking area. Coming from the north, Stratton Brook Road is located 4.6 miles south of the Route 27/16 split in central Stratton.

HIKE DESCRIPTION

From the trailhead (0.0/1,250), the blue-blazed route heads out past an information kiosk and down a wide woods road. Young forest surrounds you, highlighted by the fluttering leaves of quaking and big-tooth aspen. The white trunks of these trees superficially resemble paper birch, but do not peel in sheets. A pioneer species, aspen grows rapidly in disturbed areas with good sun exposure. Tell the two aspens apart by their leaf margins.

Continue on the road as it cruises atop a small levee, passes a small two-car parking area, and then descends toward Stratton Brook Pond, intermittently visible to the right. The trail soon encounters an excellent view of Bigelow and Little Bigelow mountains. Above you to the north, the central spine of Bigelow

Atop Avery Peak

Mountain can be spotted stretching from the Horns to West Peak—your upcoming hike. To the east, you can see the rocky cliffs of lower-elevation Little Bigelow Mountain, the AT's continuing route north.

The trail crosses an inflow to Stratton Pond, where you can take in a view of Bigelow Mountain's west front, from Cranberry Peak to the Horn. The mass of 4,250-foot Sugarloaf Mountain bulges to the south. Though the shore is reedy, Stratton Pond has swimming potential. A designated campsite, complete with privy, is located by the lakeshore on the opposite side of the creek (0.5/1,230).

The route continues along the woods road, passing red spruce, balsam fir, and the occasional cedar. As you proceed, keep an eye out for a big larch tree on the right near the water's edge. The only deciduous conifer in North America, larch is characterized by clusters of small radiating needles, a fine pattern on its bark, and glowing yellow foliage in fall. A water-loving tree, it often grows near ponds, bogs, and other wet areas.

You next reach a fork by a designated trailside campsite and privy (0.7/1,240). Several other tenting areas are scattered among the nearby trees. Bear left at the fork, passing a beaver pond and a brief view toward the deep saddle overhead between West and Avery peaks. Sugar and striped maples start to appear, and you quickly come to a posted sign for the Fire Warden Trail (1.0/1,240), which turns left. Follow the Fire Warden Trail as it slowly ascends through increasingly rocky terrain. Sugar maple and paper birch fill

Looking toward South Horn

the deciduous forest. As the trail abruptly steepens, watch for some large red oaks, growing here at the upper limits of their range.

The trail narrows and commences a steady ascent up rocky slopes, at times traveling over rock slabs. The path then levels, dances over sections of bog bridging, crosses a tiny stream, and reaches the Horns Pond Trail on the left (2.3/1,740)—your return route.

Remain on the Fire Warden Trail, which stays level and crosses a few rivulets. Hobblebush, yellow birch, and even a few large white pines appear in the forest mix.

You then begin a rising traverse, aided by occasional rock steps, and cross a boulder-strewn brook. The ridgeline is palpable overhead and occasionally peeks through the trees. Sugar maples remain abundant as the trail climbs, eventually curving left to ascend a steep rock staircase and reach the spur to Moose Falls Campsite (3.6/2,470).

Past Moose Falls, the trail climbs 1,300 feet in just under a mile. It's an ascent that keeps getting steeper . . . and steeper . . . and steeper. Water is scarce and at times unreliable between here and Horns Pond Lean-to, a distance of 4.2 miles—fill up at Moose Falls before you start the ascent.

Sugar maples accompany you to 2,800 feet, at which point the woods abruptly transition to spruce-fir forest. Mountain ash and paper birch become common. Large boulders sprout from the slopes. The trail eventually curves around to ascend almost directly up the mountainside, aided by extensive rock staircases. The gradient eases as you approach the saddle and curve right to make a gradual rise to the Avery Memorial Tentsites, located to the right just below Bigelow Col. You then reach the col and junction with the AT (4.6/3,800).

SIDE-TRIP TO AVERY PEAK

Make the recommended side-trip to 4,088-foot Avery Peak, 300 feet up and 0.4 mile east. To tag the summit, bear right and head north on the AT. Initially level, the trail passes a caretaker's cabin (closed to the public) and then reaches a boulder field. Views north appear for the first time as you ascend the rocky slopes and reach the summit, crowned by an abandoned fire tower.

The view north reveals a seldom-visited New England landscape, rolling in furrowed waves to the Canadian border. Flagstaff Lake spreads out below you, formed by the damming of the Dead River. Smaller Spring Lake is visible due north beyond it. Between Spring Lake and the northeast arm of Flagstaff Lake rises 2,225-foot Blanchard Mountain. Slightly to the left of Blanchard, prominent Coburn Mountain (3,718) rises in the distance. The long ridge of Flagstaff Mountain (2,497) rises west of Spring Lake. The Canadian border runs along the many peaks to the northwest; the low gap in the range marks the Route 27 border crossing. On a clear day, Katahdin is visible far to the northeast, 85 miles away as the crow flies and 180 miles on the AT. White Cap Mountain (3,644) rises just to the right of Katahdin, near the center of the 100-Mile Wilderness (Trip 30).

Return to Bigelow Col (4.6/3,800) and head south along the AT. The white-blazed trail climbs steadily, remaining entirely within the trees until it nears the summit of West Peak. The trail bears left at some rock outcrops, revealing views across the col toward Avery Peak and then traverses toward the summit, reaching the top among krummholz (4.9/4,145). Savor sweeping views north one more time. Look west along the ridge, where you can see the approaching twin summits of the Horns. You can also pick out your starting point at Stratton Pond far below. Farther south, the more distant massif of Crocker Mountain neighbors Sugarloaf Mountain.

From the summit, the trail descends a narrow rocky ridge and quickly reenters the trees. It then drops through dense fir forest, offering an occasional glimpse west toward the Horns. The trail then undulates along the ridgeline on a duff-covered track, providing intermittent views east toward West Peak and west toward the Horns ahead. The trail slowly descends to reach a low point, gradually rises, and then slowly steepens as it approaches the summit of South Horn (7.0/3,805).

From the summit, look down at Horns Pond and its adjacent lean-tos. Farther west is the continuation of Bigelow Mountain, including Cranberry Peak (3,213) and the isolated summit of East Nubble (2,439) just beyond. Little Bigelow Mountain marches away to the east. Nearby is the slightly higher summit of North Horn, another worthwhile side-trip. To visit it, remain on the AT as it descends South Horn and reaches the posted spur to North Horn (7.1/3,710). A steady ascent along the spur leads to the top (3,820), where a nice boulder provides another 360-degree view.

Shimmering Horns Pond and its guardian cliffs intermittently appear as you continue south on the AT. You descend on a rocky trail and reach the col and the large covered awning of the site caretaker (7.8/3,170).

After checking out the pond, privies, and other area sights, return to the AT, where a massive mileage sign indicates distances north and south. Next to the sign is a vintage lean-to, built by the Civilian Conservation Corps in the 1930s as the site's original shelter. Briefly head south on the AT to reach the Horns Pond Trail (7.9/3,170) on the left.

Leave the AT behind and follow the blue-blazed Horns Pond Trail as it descends rock staircases, passes several boulder fortresses—including a huge 20-footer—and then levels out to wind through stately spruce-fir forest. Glimpses of South Horn accompany you on the descent, which leads through an open grassy field (a filled-in bog) that offers full, and final, views of the Horn massif more than a thousand feet above.

The trail becomes rockier after crossing the bog outlet. Red maples appear for the first time, followed shortly by sugar maple. The route descends parallel to a pleasant brook for a period, then turns away from it to quickly reach a short spur that leads to a good view south of Sugarloaf and Crocker.

As you continue down, sugar maple once again burst forth in profusion, dominating a forest that also includes balsam fir, yellow birch, and big-tooth aspens. Beech and the occasional large white pine appear farther down. A steady traversing descent takes you through this rustling broad-leaf forest and across several small brooks to return to the earlier junction with the Fire Warden Trail (10.4/1,740). Bear right and retrace your route on the Fire Warden Trail to the trailhead (12.7/1,250).

INFORMATION

Maine Bureau of Public Lands, 25 Main Street, Farmington, ME 04938, 207-778-4111, www.maine.gov/doc/parks

TRIP 29
COASTING

Location: Camden Hills State Park
Highlights: Coastal mountain views, forest diversity
Distance: 3.4 miles round-trip direct to shelter, 12.4 miles round-trip via scenic route
Total Elevation Gain/Loss: Shelter Direct 800/800, Scenic Route 3,000/3,000
Trip Length: 1–2 days
Difficulty: ★ for direct ★★ for scenic
Recommended Maps: *AMC Maine Mountain Guide, Map 4: Camden Hills* AMC Books; *Camden Hills, Maine: Hiking and Biking Map,* Map Adventures

The lofty lumps of the Camden Hills rise as the highest coastal promontories on the Eastern seaboard south of Acadia National Park. Most people zoom straight to the top of 1,385-foot Mount Megunticook, the highest summit in the range, for its excellent ocean vistas. Far fewer explore the park's remaining network of trails, which tour a diversity of forest types and a handful of surprise views. Bald Rock Mountain hides out in the park's northern tier, offering two lean-tos near ocean panoramas.

The ecological diversity of 5,500-acre Camden Hills State Park is exceptional. Low-elevation, high-elevation, southern, northern, and coastal species all grow here. A short stroll around the park campground passes more than a dozen tree species, including black cherry, choke cherry, yellow birch, paper birch, red maple, striped maple, white ash, balsam fir, red spruce, red oak, beech, white pine, basswood, dogwood, and quaking aspen. Find them all on the park's trails as well.

HIKE OVERVIEW

There are two variations of this hike. The first provides direct access to the Bald Rock Mountain shelters from the northern corner of the park, a mini-loop on easy trails. The second is a longer 12.4-mile loop that tours all the park highlights, including the views atop Mount Megunticook and the sugar maple-cloaked Jack Williams trail. The two variations can be combined by approaching from the north, setting up camp, and day-hiking from there.

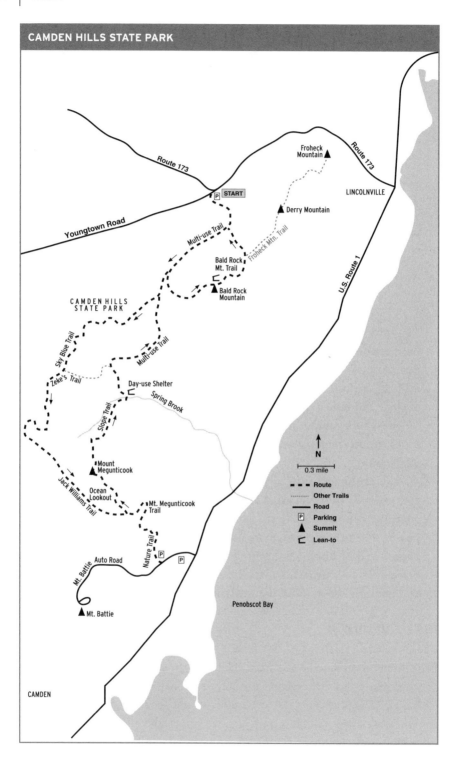

CAMDEN HILLS STATE PARK

Route 173

Froheck Mountain ▲

Route 173

LINCOLNVILLE

P START

Youngtown Road

Multi-use Trail

Derry Mountain ▲

Froheck Mtn. Trail

U.S. Route 1

Bald Rock Mt. Trail

Bald Rock Mountain ▲

CAMDEN HILLS STATE PARK

Sky Blue Trail

Multi-use Trail

Zeke's Trail

Day-use Shelter

Slope Trail

Spring Brook

Mount Megunticook ▲

Ocean Lookout

Jack Williams Trail

Mt. Megunticook Trail

N
0.3 mile

- - - Route
.... Other Trails
——— Road
P Parking
▲ Summit
⌐ Lean-to

Nature Trail

P   P

Mt. Battie Auto Road

▲ Mt. Battie

Penobscot Bay

CAMDEN

OVERNIGHT OPTIONS

Backcountry camping is permitted only at two shelters atop 1,100-foot Bald Rock Mountain. Located just below the summit, the three-sided lean-tos are cave-like, leak in the rain, and have space for roughly six people each. They are free and available on a first-come, first-served basis. The first is located just below the summit slabs, has a huge fire pit, and is surrounded by an un-usual mix of spruce and red oak. Open views southeast over the ocean are a few steps away. The second is a short distance north of the summit near some large boulders. There is no water at either shelter. Bring what you need before you arrive or obtain it from the stream just past either trailhead. The shelters generally receive light use, though they appear to be popular with locals.

There is also a nice drive-up campground at the main park entrance. Hik-ing trails emanate directly from the campground, providing walk-from-your-site access to the trail system. It is full most weekends in summer, but you can make reservations by contacting the park.

TO REACH THE TRAILHEADS

Follow Route 1 north from Camden to the signed entrance for Camden Hills State Park, where the scenic variation begins. For the direct shelter route, con-tinue 4.1 miles farther on Route 1 to Route 173. Turn left and follow Route 173 for 2.3 miles to Youngtown Road. Turn left again; the trailhead lot is located immediately past the intersection, with space for about two dozen cars.

SHELTER HIKE DESCRIPTION

From the trailhead (0.0/270), head down the wide multi-use trail. Sensitive fern, interrupted fern, red oak, white ash, aspen, paper birch, beech, white pine, sarsparilla, and striped maple all line the broad trail, used in winter as a snow-mobile route. The path slowly rises, crosses a flowing stream, and then passes the Frohock Mountain Trail on the left (0.5/420)—your return route. Continue straight on the multi-use trail, which levels out, cruises past a few larger oaks, and then reaches the Bald Rock Mountain Trail on the left (1.3/610).

The longer scenic route joins here and the unsigned Cameron Mountain Trail heads right, but you turn left (right if you're joining from the scenic varia-tion) to follow the Bald Rock Mountain Trail and immediately enter a clearing shaded by white pine. Initially wide and root-laced, the trail soon narrows and becomes rockier as it ascends, aided by a nice stone staircase. Dogwood and maple leaf viburnum appear.

The trail curves up the mountain's southwest flanks and becomes steeper, climbing among increasing softwoods, over abundant roots, and past a good tentsite as you approach the top. The trail diverges just below the summit. Follow the blue-blazed trail left to reach the first shelter or continue straight to reach the open summit slabs (2.1/1,100). From here, the shimmering ocean is only 1.5 miles away. Dotted with islands, it bends and blends with the horizon on clear days.

From the shelter, continue north on the blue-blazed Bald Rock Mountain Trail, which drops and reaches the second shelter. Red maple, choke cherry, and striped maple shade the lean-to. A pile of adjacent rocks offers a restricted view south-southeast.

From here, the trail drops steeply, then eases and slowly curves left to reach the Frohock Mountain Trail (2.6/720). The Frohock Mountain Trail leads 1.8 miles over 777-foot Derry Mountain to reach its namesake peak (454 feet), a pleasant and little-traveled side-trail. To return to the trailhead, bear left to continue down the Frohock Mountain Trail, which widens as it descends past nice oaks to the earlier junction with the multi-use trail (2.9/420). Bear right and return to the trailhead (3.4/270).

SCENIC HIKE DESCRIPTION

This longer loop begins from the main park entrance. After paying your entrance fee at the gatehouse, follow the Mount Battie Auto Road 0.3 mile to the trailhead parking area on the right. If the lot is full, park in the lot near the gatehouse.

From the trailhead (0.0/270), begin beneath white pines and pass a NO CAMPING SIGN (this does not refer to the shelters). The heavily trod trail is rocky, loaded with roots, and immediately travels over some bog bridging near an audible creek. You quickly reach the Nature Trail (0.1/310)—turn right toward Mount Megunticook. The trail crosses the small creek and then traverses beneath a canopy of oaks and beech. Most of the beech is badly diseased with the nectria fungus, as evidenced by the canker-like sores that dot their trunks. The path rises to reach the Megunticook Trail on the left (0.3/440)—follow it toward the Ocean lookout. (A right turn leads to the campground.)

The trail now widens and passes extensive sarsparilla and yellow clintonia (also known as blue-bead lily) on the ground. Two gently curving switchbacks bring you to some nice rock stairs, after which the trail curves right to resume a level traverse past abundant maple-leaf viburnum.

The trail becomes rockier. Hobblebush appears. Soon after, you catch your first glimpses of the ocean through the trees behind you. You then reach the Adams Lookout Trail on the left (0.8/800). Follow the Adams Lookout Trail, which soon encounters open slabs with limited views southeast. You can see the town of Camden and a few islands in Penobscot Bay. The single-track trail then slabs upward and reaches the Tableland Trail (1.1/1,020).

Go right on the Tableland Trail and ascend to a view framed by red oaks, this one of Camden harbor and Mount Battie Auto Road. Just above this point is a better view, overlooking the open waters and islands of Penobscot Bay, including the large mass of Vinalhaven Island in the distance and Isleboro Island closer in. Glacial striations from the last ice age are evident in the bare rock underfoot, tracing the movement of the ice sheet to the south-southeast.

Sugar Maple forest on the Jack Williams Trail

Continue up the Tableland Trail, passing along the top of some cliffs with good views south to Camden, Battie, and the Megunticook River. Your return route—the Jack Williams Trail—runs along the base of these cliffs.

You then reach the Mount Megunticook Trail on the right (1.3/1,220). Proceed straight to continue along the cliff edge. The path now becomes the Ridge Trail, which soon bears right into a forest of spruce, blueberry bushes, and laurel. The trail slowly rises, crosses some puncheon, and reaches the Slope Trail on the right (1.7/1,380). Just past the junction, a summit cairn sits in a small viewless clearing.

Head down the Slope Trail and leave the trafficked portion of the park behind. The lightly used single-track trail drops past a pair of nice yellow birches, steadily descends, and crosses several small brooks on little bridges. Halfway down, the trail widens and becomes wet and muddy in spots. You enter a shady hemlock grove, where rushing Spring Brook appears to your left. The route runs parallel to the stream and then crosses it on a new bridge, emerging at an old Civilian Conservation Corps ski shelter (3.2/560). Renovated in 2006, the substantial structure makes a pleasant rest stop.

From here, bear left (north) and follow a wide dirt road through dense spruce-fir forest. The route rises slowly, passes Zeke's Trail on the left (3.7/660), and then levels out, passing the posted Clay Brook Trail on the right. Bald Rock Mountain peeks out ahead as the trail curves left near a swampy area and passes the Sky Blue Trail (4.6/630)—your return route—on the left. To continue to the shelters, remain on the road as it drops down to cross a flowing brook, briefly rises, and then reaches the four-way junction with the Cameron Mountain and Bald Rock Mountain trails (4.9/610). Head right and proceed as earlier to the shelters (5.7/1,070).

To return to the park entrance, retrace your steps to the earlier junction with the Sky Blue Trail (6.8/630). Follow the Sky Blue Trail west as it initially cruises on an old woods road but quickly splits right at a posted fork. Trillium and wintergreen are abundant along the single-track trail. Lady's slippers soon appear as the path steadily rises through a forest of spruce, fir, and abundant beech. Overgrown in spots, the trail seems lightly used. You undulate along, passing prolific lady's slippers and blueberry bushes. Small cairns mark the route, which winds through several stone walls. The trail rolls along to reach the Cameron Mountain Trail on the right (8.3/980). Continue straight to reach Zeke's Trail (8.4/960), where you turn right on the wide woods road.

Zeke's Trail rises slowly up a grassy corridor along an old woods roads buttressed by stone embankments. The trail crests briefly, becomes muddier and rockier, and then resumes climbing to reach a clearing on the right with no views but good blueberry potential. You next reach the Ridge Trail (9.3/1,160). Turn right and follow the Ridge Trail as it steeply drops across a creek and runs along its streambed over roots and rocks. The gradient eases, and you traverse a slope with restricted views south-southwest. You soon resume the descent, curve left through a hemlock grove, and reach the Jack Williams Trail (9.6/910).

Turn left and follow the single-track Jack Williams Trail past continuing hemlocks. After a short drop, you encounter a spur on the right signed for Chuck's Lookout. A bald eagle roosted here one June afternoon. There are views southwest over Lake Megunticook and to the hills beyond.

From here, the trail descends to cross a boulder-lined creek and begins a level traverse through occasionally muddy terrain. The woods abruptly transform from beech, red oak, and striped maple to a lush forest of sugar maple. The trees thrive in the enriched soils that collect at the bottom of cliffs and talus fields, such as those intermittently visible to the left. Some nice stands of white ash are interspersed.

The trail meanders through this exceptional forest, eventually crossing a brook on a footbridge near a small pool. A younger forest then thickens around the trail. Softwoods reappear, and the cliffs become visible through the trees to your left. The route winds through denser forest and closer to the looming cliffs. You then reach the Tableland Trail (11.2/980).

Go left and follow the Tableland Trail up a talus-rock staircase to quickly reach the earlier junction with the Adam's Lookout Trail (11.3/1,030). Turn right and retrace your steps to the trailhead via the Adam's Lookout, Mount Megunticook, and Nature trails (12.4/270).

INFORMATION

Camden Hills State Park, 280 Belfast Road, Camden, ME 04843, 207-236-3109, 207-236-0849 (off-season), www.maine.gov/doc/parks

TRIP 30
THE 100-MILE WILDERNESS

Location: Appalachian Trail, Northern Maine
Highlight: The most remote section of the Appalachian Trail
Distance: 99.4 miles one-way
Total Elevation Gain/Loss: 18,000/18,500
Trip Length: 5–10 days
Difficulty: ★★★★★
Recommended Maps: *The Appalachian Trail Guide to Maine, Maps 1–3*
Appalachian Trail Conservancy, *Southern Piscataquis Regional Recreational Map and Guide* AMC Books

The 100-Mile Wilderness encompasses the longest section of the Appalachian Trail (AT) that does not cross a paved road. It is a legendary stretch of trail, a rugged and challenging adventure deep in the Maine woods. The journey travels through a range of elevations, crosses rivers and streams, climbs mountains, lounges by lakeshores, and visits mature hardwood and conifer forests. It is an endless parade of ever-changing scenery and one of New England's most challenging hikes.

HIKE OVERVIEW

The journey follows the AT from the town of Monson to Abol Bridge on the edge of Baxter State Park, a one-way 99.4-mile trip.

The hike first travels through a lush low-elevation hardwood forest and crosses numerous streams and rivers that cut through wild terrain. The trail then ascends the Barren-Chairback Range, traversing the mountain spine for 15 miles before descending to cross the West Branch of the Pleasant River and reaching the slate gorge of Gulf Hagas. From here, the journey climbs over the alpine summit of 3,644-foot White Cap Mountain, the highest point on the hike.

After steeply descending Whitecap, the AT leaves mountainous terrain behind and makes an undulating journey toward Crawford Pond, the hike's midpoint. The route then follows Cooper Brook along an easy-cruising section of trail, passing idyllic Cooper Brook Falls en route. The adventure next enters the land of large lakes and more level walking, touring the shore of substantial Jo-Mary and Pemadumcook lakes and then traveling alongside Nahmakanta Stream to emerge at Nahmakanta Lake. After a steep climb over Nesuntabunt

Mountain, the final leg of the hike travels beside rushing Rainbow Stream and then cruises the long length of Rainbow Lake. A final rise over the Rainbow Ledges leads to hike's end at the southwest edge of Baxter State Park.

Many people underestimate the rigors of this hike. Overall, the trail is rugged, intensively laced with roots and rocks, and occasionally boggy. There are no resupply points. The longer you go, the more food you'll need to carry—and the slower you'll hike. Achieving the right balance of speed, pack weight, and enjoyment time is a challenge. AT thru-hikers often complete the 100-Mile Wilderness in only five days, an average of 20 miles per day. But keep in mind that thru-hikers are in top physical condition by this point in their journey, and inspired by the approach of their journey's end atop Katahdin. Also, moving this quickly allows little time for relaxing at the many beautiful locations on the way.

A more relaxing, but still steady, pace would be a seven- or eight-day itinerary. Even then, you will need to cover an average of 12 to 14 miles per day. A trip of nine to ten days is a more leisurely journey, with plenty of time for fishing, swimming, and view-savoring, but you'll have to pack a lot of food. No matter how long you take, the trip requires a high degree of fitness. Dogs are allowed.

OVERNIGHT OPTIONS

Thirteen shelters and three designated tenting sites line the route. Many other campsites are scattered throughout the hike as well. Campfires are permitted in fire rings at designated sites only.

Leeman Brook Lean-to, mile 3.0, perches on the slopes above rocky Leeman Brook at 1,100 feet. Surrounded by cedars and campsites, the shelter has ready access to water from the brook.

Wilson Valley Lean-to, mile 10.4, is located at 1,070 feet near a small brook. Two large hemlocks guard the eight-person shelter. Ample tentsites are available uphill.

Long Pond Stream Lean-to, mile 15.1, sits at 940 feet and is washed by the sounds of Long Pond Stream boiling over rocks several hundred feet below. The adjacent water source can be thin at times and you may need a filter to obtain it; the next closest source is Long Pond Stream, 0.8 mile south on the AT. Several campsites are located uphill behind the shelter.

Cloud Pond Lean-to, mile 19.7, sits adjacent to its namesake pond at 2,440 feet. The shelter receives heavy use. Cloud Pond is the highest body of water in the 100-Mile Wilderness and an excellent swimming hole. An ephemeral spring is nearby, or you can collect water directly from the pond.

Chairback Gap Lean-to, mile 26.0, is situated on the east (northern) end of the Barren-Chairback Range at 1,980 feet. The small shelter perches between

100-MILE WILDERNESS NORTHERN MAINE

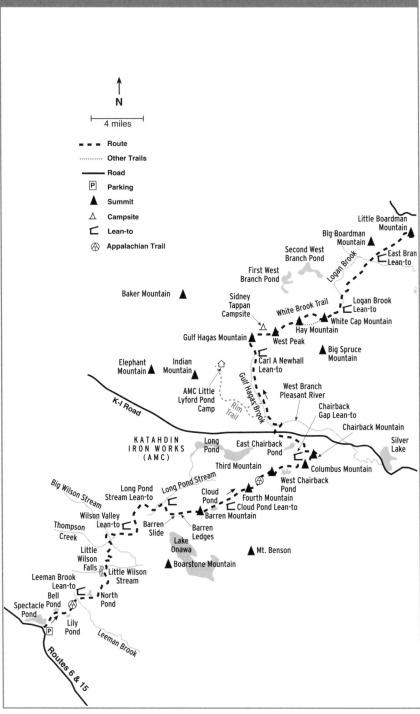

N

4 miles

- - - Route
.... Other Trails
—— Road
P Parking
▲ Summit
△ Campsite
⊏ Lean-to
Ⓐ Appalachian Trail

Little Boardman Mountain

Big Boardman Mountain

Second West Branch Pond

First West Branch Pond

Logan Brook

East Bran Lean-to

Logan Brook Lean-to

Baker Mountain

Sidney Tappan Campsite

White Brook Trail

White Cap Mountain

Hay Mountain

Gulf Hagas Mountain

West Peak

Big Spruce Mountain

Carl A Newhall Lean-to

Elephant Mountain

Indian Mountain

AMC Little Lyford Pond Camp

Gulf Hagas Brook

West Branch Pleasant River

Rim Trail

Chairback Gap Lean-to

Chairback Mountain

K-I Road

KATAHDIN IRON WORKS (AMC)

Long Pond

East Chairback Pond

Silver Lake

Third Mountain

Columbus Mountain

Long Pond Stream Lean-to

Long Pond Stream

Big Wilson Stream

Cloud Pond

Fourth Mountain

West Chairback Pond

Cloud Pond Lean-to

Wilson Valley Lean-to

Barren Slide

Barren Mountain

Thompson Creek

Barren Ledges

Little Wilson Falls

Lake Onawa

Mt. Benson

Little Wilson Stream

Boarstone Mountain

Leeman Brook Lean-to

Bell Pond

North Pond

Spectacle Pond

P

Lily Pond

Leeman Brook

Routes 6 & 15

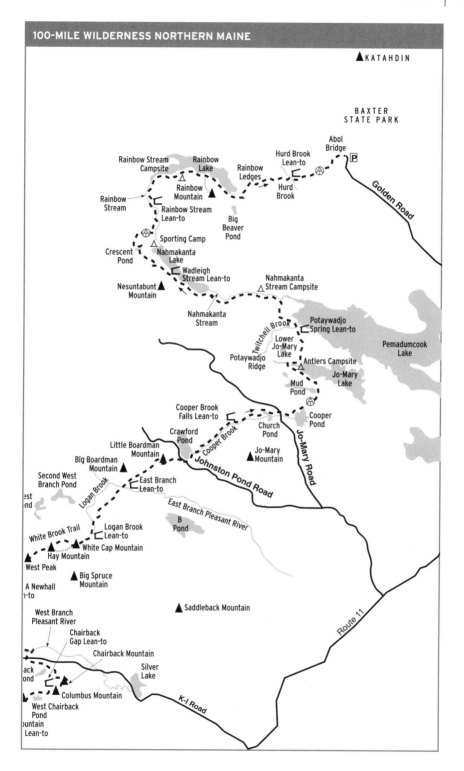

100-MILE WILDERNESS NORTHERN MAINE

Columbus and Chairback mountains and offers some nice nearby tentsites among spruce and rocky outcrops. Water can be a problem here later in the season; a small spring in the saddle can get pretty thin and green during dry conditions.

Carl A. Newhall Lean-to, mile 35.9, sits on the flanks of Gulf Hagas Mountain at 1,900 feet, just above gurgling Gulf Hagas Brook. The small basic shelter is a popular layover because of the shortage of campsites to the south. (Camping is prohibited along the 2 miles of the AT north of the West Branch of the Pleasant River that lead to this lean-to.) A large open clearing on the opposite side of the brook has room for multiple tents.

Sidney Tappan Campsite, mile 37.7, rests in the saddle between Gulf Hagas Mountain and West Peak. Several open grassy tentsites provide a quieter respite from the shelter crowds. A good spring can be found a short distance down the slopes.

Logan Brook Lean-to, mile 43.1, nestles in a grove of paper birch at 2,400 feet on the east (northern) flanks of White Cap Mountain. The namesake brook rushes adjacent to the shelter, splashing crystal clear. There are four or five established tentsites around the basic shelter, plus one more about 100 yards down the trail.

East Branch Lean-to, mile 46.7, features a new shelter and a basic picnic table and benches. The East Branch River flows audibly nearby and provides water. Big Boardman Mountain can be spotted from the riverbanks. Cedars,

Let the adventure begin

spruce, red maple, and a few white pine surround the camp. A few tentsites scatter among the trees.

Cooper Brook Falls Lean-to, mile 54.8, is one of the more idyllic. Situated at the bottom of its namesake waterfall, it offers views of foaming sheets falling into a deep swimming hole. The rushing noise of water is omnipresent, boulders dot the area, numerous tentsites tuck among them, and a diverse forest surrounds the site.

Antlers Campsite, mile 62.7, is located at 500 feet on a small peninsula surrounded by Lower Jo-Mary Lake. The large camping area spreads out in a red pine grove. A few boulders protrude from the water. A lake breeze often cools the site and helps keep bugs at bay. Rock-lined paths lead to plentiful sites, and there are several good lake access points. Views from the peninsula look northwest toward the open slabs of Potaywadjo Ridge.

Potaywadjo Spring Lean-to, mile 66.2, tucks in the woods near its namesake spring, a large pool of crystal-clear water that emerges from the hillside as a flowing stream. The log-cabin-style shelter has a rough and uneven floor that may cause a lumpy night's sleep. Extensive tenting areas can be found nearby beneath hemlock and beech trees.

Nahmakanta Stream Campsite, mile 70.5, features an open tenting area under hemlocks, 50 to 75 yards from Nahmakanta Stream. The waters riffle pleasantly past numerous boulders, and there is easy access to the shore. Numerous sites dot the area, some well established. Fires are limited to the one central fire ring. Droves of mosquitoes frequent the area in season!

Wadleigh Stream Lean-to, mile 76.3, is a small shelter next to the trail, shaded by large sugar maples and adjacent to Wadleigh Stream. An old yellow birch stands sentinel on the opposite bank. Tenting areas are limited near the shelter, though there is a small tenting area near the brook past the shelter on the right. A sandy beach on Nahmakanta Lake is only a few minutes' walk away.

Rainbow Stream Lean-to, mile 84.4, sits 20 feet from the riffling brook and features an uneven corduroy wood floor that can make for an uncomfortable night's sleep. Several tentsites rest in needle-covered clearings uphill—the best is above the stream right behind the shelter on a big rock. A small totem pole next to the shelter keeps you company.

Rainbow Spring Campsite, mile 88.2, is located on the southern shore of massive Rainbow Lake near its namesake spring. Situated just inland from the lakeshore, it offers three established sites in young hardwood forest. The refreshingly cool spring emerges right by the lake and the top of Katahdin peeks above the hills on the far shore. Swimming opportunities in the lake are excellent.

Hurd Brook Shelter, mile 95.9, is your final overnight option. Shaded by hemlocks, it is located within earshot of Hurd Brook, which flows through a rocky garden of roots and stones. It emerges from a big marshy pond just upstream—be diligent about treating or filtering water from the brook. The shelter features another uneven corduroy floor. Campsites strew about the area.

OVERNIGHT OPTIONS: LODGES/HOSTELS

The AMC's *Little Lyford Pond Camps* is located 2.2 miles beyond the head of Gulf Hagas on the River Trail, which can be accessed from the AT at mile 31.7 via the Rim Trail (3.0 miles) or Pleasant River Tote Road (2.2 miles). The sporting camp features cabins and a bunkroom for overnight lodging, as well as hot showers and some basic supplies for purchase. Meals are included with an overnight stay. Little Lyford is not equipped to accommodate last-minute walk-in guests; advance reservations are required (603-466-2727, www.outdoors.org/lodging/).

White House Landing Wilderness Camps is located a mile off the AT on the shores of Pemadumcook Lake. Access it via a muddy road that crosses the AT near mile 70 and leads to a boat landing and water shuttle to the camps. Cabins and a bunkroom are available for overnight use and limited supplies are available for sale. Hot food can also be purchased; their burgers are legendary (207-745-5116, whlcamps@aol.com).

Nahmakanta Lake Wilderness Camps is located at the north end of Nahmakanta Lake and is the most accessible sporting camp along the trail. Reach it via a short road walk that diverges from the AT at mile 83. Built in 1872, the camp's cabins and lodge are the only structures on the 4-mile-long lake and cater more toward affluent overnight visitors than thru-hikers. It is often booked solid during the summer; advance reservations are recommended (207-731-8888, www.nahmakanta.com).

TO REACH THE TRAILHEAD

To Reach the Starting/Southern Trailhead. Follow Route 15 north of Monson for 3.5 miles. The trailhead parking area is located on the right by a significant curve in the road. The turn-off can be hard to spot—be watchful.

To Reach the Ending/Northern Trailhead. Follow Route 11 west of Millinocket to the Route 11/157 junction by the First Congregational Church. Turn right and proceed 8.7 miles to a confusing intersection by the Big Moose Inn and pool. Bear left here onto the Golden Road and follow it 10.1 miles to the Abol Store, located just before Abol Bridge. You can leave your car without charge on the far side of the Abol Store's shed—touch base with store staff before you go.

Shuttle Services. You will need to coordinate transportation between the starting and ending trailheads. Shaw's Lodging in Monson offers a shuttle service throughout the 100-Mile Wilderness, though it can be pricey for small groups (207-997-3597, www.shawslodging.com).

Other Trailheads. Several major unpaved roads intersect the AT in the 100-Mile Wilderness and can provide alternate access points. Note that most of these roads lie within the KI Jo-Mary Multiple Use forest, which charges a daily access fee to use the privately maintained road network. The KI Road crosses the AT 29.9 miles from the trailhead and connects the towns of Greenville and Brownville. The West Branch Ponds Road intersects the AT at mile 44.7 and approaches from the West Branch Ponds area to the northwest (a very confusing area to navigate). The Kokadjo-B Pond Road crosses the AT at mile 51.6 and the Jo-Mary Road at mile 58.5; both are accessed from the Jo-Mary checkpoint on Route 11, located 15 miles south of Millinocket. The Jo-Mary Road also connects with access roads to Nahmakanta Lake, which cross the AT at miles 73.7, 79.4, and 83.1. You'll need a good map to navigate these roads—a network of logging roads makes for confusing travel. Consult Delorme's Maine Atlas or the *Southern Piscataquis Regional Recreation Map and Guide County Recreational Map* (AMC Books).

HIKE DESCRIPTION

The 100-Mile Wilderness adventure begins from the edge of the parking area (0.0/1,220), where you can identify several of the trees and plants that you'll see throughout the hike. Raspberry bushes grow to the left of the trailhead, recognized by the white undersides of their leaves. The pointy leaves of red maples flutter overhead on both sides of the trail. The needles of aromatic balsam fir join the forest mosaic. To the right of the trailhead, the scaly bark of young black cherry trees can be spotted in the understory.

Heading out, you quickly encounter some wet sections and meet the first bog bridging of the hike. Spectacle Pond is visible to the left through the trees, and you soon rock-hop across the pond's flowing outlet. Northern cedar trees line the lakeshore, though you can spot a larch tree across the inlet about 100 yards away; recognize it by its tall stature and droopy foliage.

The trail follows a root-laced track underlain by black shale. The dinner-plate leaves of hobblebush and 5-needled clusters of white pine appear, joined by small blueberry bushes underfoot. As the trail slowly rises, the woods transition toward spruce-fir forest. The fluttering leaves of big-tooth aspens mix

Little Wilson Falls

in with balsam fir and red spruce. You next encounter the old Stage Road (0.7/1,270), a woods road that marks the route followed by stage coaches to Greenville in the nineteenth century.

Continuing, views of Bell Pond soon appear to the left. Several spur trails approach the water, but none provide good shore access. The AT curves right past the pond, and crests a small rise. It then descends, traversing toward Lily Pond and passing some nice sugar maples. An obvious spur soon goes down to the overgrown lakeshore (1.9/1,130).

Past the pond, the trail makes a slow traversing rise through lush sugar maple forest. Diseased beech afflicted with the nectria fungus join the forest—look for the canker-like sores on their otherwise smooth trunks. The route crests and then heads downhill, providing the journey's first long-distance view of the Barren-Chairback Range—your upcoming route. Notice the exposed rock faces of the Barren Ledges and Slide. To their right is Borestone Mountain, easily identified by its bald summit.

You now make the steepest descent yet and drop into the mini-gorge of Leeman Brook (3.0/1,080). The stream incises through solid slate here, leaving 20-foot-high cliffs and calving rock-bergs. Hemlocks shade the tumbling watercourse. Boulders fill the streambed—one large slab creates a grotto where you could sit under the showering water. The Leeman Brook Lean-to perches just above the brook.

Undulating onward through rocky terrain, you next reach the shores of North Pond. The trail parallels the lake and offers good views, including glimpses of a tempting island nearby. You skirt the pond's small south arm, cross the outflow stream (3.8/1,030), and make a gradual ascent. The route crosses a woods road and then passes restricted views northwest toward the rolling mountains. You then begin an undulating descent, reaching an open view of small Mud Pond, which is slowly filling in to become a bog.

The AT climbs past several mature spruce and crests atop Bear Pond Ledge. Banking left, the trail descends steeply through an older forest punctuated by large sugar maple, yellow birch, and hemlock. You cross trickling James Brook at the bottom (6.3/990), lined by the lacy foliage of hemlock trees.

The dull roar of Little Wilson Falls soon becomes audible as you continue. You climb briefly, cross a woods road, and soon descend to this rushing landmark (6.6/880). The falls hiss down a staircase of fractured stone. Walls of cracked slate enclose the narrow ravine, precariously balanced like a deck of cards on its side. Above the falls, interrupted ferns line shallow placid pools.

Past the falls, the trail runs along the gorge's edge and passes a giant fin of slate protruding into space, plus nice hemlocks, white pines, and cedar. Rock-hopping Little Wilson Stream at a tranquil confluence (6.8/800), you next ascend a beech-covered hillside and reach a small shallow pond. The trail crosses the outflow on puncheon and then curves around the pond to reach a dirt road.

The AT turns left, follows the road for about 100 yards, and then turns right and returns to single-track. You climb to open ledges with views southwest, and emerge atop an open and rocky prow. Borestone Mountain highlights the terrain to the southeast. A few red pine inhabit the thin soil here; recognize them by their needles in clusters of two.

The trail drops through spruce-fir forest and makes a slow U-turn, then traverses steadily and descends through a moss-carpeted forest and into the valley of Big Wilson Stream. Hardwoods reappear, the flowing stream becomes audible, and you soon encounter a wide woods road near the water's edge (8.9/620).

Turn left and follow the road as it parallels the river-like stream and reaches its confluence with Thompson Creek. This spot provides your first easy access to the creek. Moisture-loving white ash and hemlock line the riparian corridor. The AT rock-hops across Thompson Creek and continues on the easy-walking road. Big Wilson Stream weaves in and out of sight, then the route turns right to cross it by an obvious sign (9.7/620). The stream is wide here, and usually deep enough to require a ford.

Once on the other side, the trail immediately starts climbing, passes some nice white pines, and then crosses active railroad tracks. Beyond the tracks, the trail levels and traverses to reach a small brook. Turning uphill to follow it, you soon reach the junction for the Wilson Valley Lean-to (10.4/1,030) on the right.

Shortly past the shelter, the trail crosses the brook and parallels it before curving right to begin a long level section. You cross another woods road and make a gradual climb through hardwood forest, cresting atop an open outcrop (11.2/1,280) with tantalizing views of the fast-approaching Barren Mountains. On the steep descent, Barren Slide, Barren Ledges, and substantial Lake Onawa appear intermittently through the foliage. The trail switchbacks twice, winds over talus, and then crosses the base of a large rock slide. After hopping over a few small streams, the trail bends right and starts the final descent into the Bodfish Intervale.

You pass a grassy road just before reaching Wilber Brook (13.5/630). The AT rock-hops the creek and then quickly reaches Vaughn Stream by a pretty 20-foot waterfall. A nice waist-deep pool lies at the base of the falls, shaded by big-tooth aspens and cedars. Also notice the rock, a fine-grained and grayish stone much different than the Monson Slate, without obvious cleavage and what looks like some granite inclusions.

Continuing, the muddy trail runs level and reaches a wide dirt road. Turn right, proceed 50 yards on the road, and then turn left to remain on the AT. From here, the route quickly descends to reach rocky Long Pond Stream (14.3/630). The river-like stream can be rock-hopped with care—be careful at high water. Resume your journey on the opposite bank by a large big-tooth aspen, but fill your water bottle before continuing—this is the last good source until you reach Cloud Pond Lean-to 5 miles ahead. The trail climbs a rock staircase and winds above the rushing stream and its many rapids and pools. You eventually turn steeply uphill and climb to reach the spur for Long Pond Stream Lean-to (15.1/940).

Past the shelter, the trail begins its ascent of the Barren-Chairback Range. The route is gradual at first, crossing an overgrown woods road and slowly traversing upward. Then the trail abruptly steepens and becomes rockier as it climbs through spruce-fir forest. You traipse through a grassy clearing flush with pin cherry and restricted views west, and then take a direct line up a rocky draw. The route then bears left and the gradient eases. The trail crests onto the ridge, but continues a slow rise to reach the spur for Barren Slide on the right (16.3/1,980).

The spur trail leads you 60 feet down to a jumble of giant rocks. Carefully scramble to the edge and look down a tumble of talus that stretches far down the mountainside. Lake Onawa is visible below. Borestone Mountain rises lumpily to the south. To the west and southwest, the broad valley of Bodfish Intervale is apparent; your route here follows the ridge bordering the Intervale to the west.

Return to the trail and continue a few hundred yards to reach the spur for Barren Ledges, another worthwhile side-trip. The ledges offer large flat areas better suited for lounging and view-savoring, and the vistas peer a bit farther west than from the Slide. Lake Sebec is visible in the distance beyond Lake Onawa to the southeast. Peaks dot the west horizon, including a prominent twin pyramid peak—the Bigelow Range (Trip 28), some 50 miles away. To the east, the rounded summit of 2,660-foot Barren Mountain is visible for the first time, crowned by the remains of an old fire tower. If you sit quietly, you may hear the call of loons wafting up 1,500 feet from the lake below.

Back on the AT, continue on the mellow path as it travels along the north side of the ridge. The trail slowly rises, then cuts right, and begins a steep ascent toward the summit of Barren Mountain. This section is nicely maintained, and features a quality rock staircase. After climbing a final rocky gully, you reach the summit of Barren Mountain (18.2/2,660) and its all-encompassing views north. The rusting framework of the old tower still stands, but the structure that once stood on top is scattered debris on the ground. If you are feeling adventurous, clamber up the ladder to enjoy sweeping views north.

To the northwest is the long prominent ridge of the Whitecap Range—your continuing route—topped by the bald summit of Whitecap itself. Below you to the north is linear Long Pond. Beyond its west arm is the low rise of Indian Mountain, which is in turn shadowed by Baker Mountain. Elephant Mountain is to the north-northwest, beyond the end of Long Pond. Northwest in the distance, you can spot portions of Moosehead Lake, including the distinctive profile of Mount Kineo.

Most of the immediate area to the north, including all of Long Pond and Indian Mountain, are part of the Katahdin Iron Works Property, a 37,000-acre parcel purchased by the AMC in December 2003 as part of its Maine Woods Initiative, a long-term effort to create a protected corridor of land from Moosehead Lake to Baxter State Park.

Continuing past the tower, the route makes a gradual descent to reach the spur for Cloud Pond Lean-to (19.3/2,490), located 0.4 mile off the main route. To visit the shelter, bear right and follow the narrow and rough spur trail down toward the pond's edge. Shortly before reaching the shelter, you pass a large tenting area on a small point near the shore. Spruce-fir forest surrounds the site; several nice specimens complement the bouldery landscape.

Back on the AT, you continue along an almost perfectly level section of trail for the next half mile. The trail then abruptly starts a steep descent, aided by a nice rock staircase. You encounter a small sag—a thin trickle provides a limited water source—and continue down through mature spruce-fir forest. A few sugar maples and gnarled yellow birch join the forest mix shortly before you bottom out and cross a more substantial brook (20.5/1,920).

After a short easy stretch, you reach one of the ecological highlights of this hike: Fourth Mountain Bog. The bog sits in the saddle below Fourth Mountain, a wetland complex that harbors many unusual plants, including two carnivorous species: pitcher plant and sundew. As the sign indicates, please stay on the bog bridging in this section. The spongy ground is easily damaged by boot prints.

As you proceed past abundant cedars, look for the meat-eating flora. For sundews, keep an eye out for tiny red-haired globes. These sticky appendages trap flies, where they are slowly absorbed for their nitrogen—essential for survival in a nitrogen-poor soil environment. Pitcher plants grow in clusters and in season sport a wild and distinctive flower. The plant's "pitchers" are roughly 3 inches high, lined on the inside with downward-pointing hairs, and emit a smell similar to rotting flesh. Flies attracted to the odor crawl inside and are led inexorably downward. Eventually they tumble into a small pool of water at the bottom, where they drown and are absorbed by the plant.

After the bog, the AT returns to dry spruce-fir forest. The broad hump of Fourth Mountain is visible ahead and the trail begins a direct ascent. After cresting atop the undulating summit plateau, you pass a restricted view north to Baker Mountain and then reach the signed summit (21.3/2,378). Good views extend east to Columbus Mountain—your continuing route—with Saddleback Mountain beyond. The full spine of the White Cap Range is visible to the northeast. The watershed of the West Branch of the Pleasant River watershed is visible north; Baker, Indian, and Elephant mountains are all visible.

The trail then plummets down the opposite side. The gradient eases somewhat as you drop, but the descent is steady until you reach beech trees in a saddle between Fourth and Third Mountains.

Undulating past several gullies—some with the occasional trickle of water—the trail then climbs again, soon reaching an open slab with views west to Fourth Mountain. As you continue, the trail passes along open slabs. Watch the rocks for parallel scratches, or striations, evidence of the former ice sheet that once ground over these mountains. You top out on slabs offering views south toward Caribou Bog and the nearby east ridge of Mount Benson.

After a few short undulations, the trail drops to make a long traverse on the northern flanks of Third Mountain, slowly curving to the right. After a gentle ascent, the route makes an abrupt, short, and very steep climb to the summit of Third Mountain (23.6/2,060). The open summit slabs provide restricted views north, but continue briefly along the uneven summit plateau to reach another open pinnacle. This one looks west down Long Pond and along the spine of the Barren Range; the fire tower atop Barren Mountain is visible past Fourth

Clouds track across the Maine sky

Mountain. But the best views are still to come at Monument Cliff, a flat ledge a short distance farther. Views sweep 180 degrees north across the landscape, including the White Cap Range and nearby Columbus Mountain, your next destination. You can also spot East Chairback Lake for the first time to the northeast.

Continuing, the trail makes a steady traverse and then drops to reach the outflow from West Chairback Pond and the posted junction for the lake (24.3/1,760). To visit the shore, turn right and follow the spur 0.1 mile to a heavily used area near the water. Spruce, fir, and white pines border the quiet lake. The fishing must be good here; local residents have hauled numerous small boats here and chained them to trees. Tenting areas are limited and close to each other. The area would feel crowded with more than two groups here.

Back on the AT, cross the pond's rocky outflow stream, slowly ascend through dense forest, and then climb steeply again as the trail rises up the slopes of Columbus Mountain. The gradient eases, and you pass a posted viewpoint and then a small signed spring by the trail. Fill up here if you are staying at Chairback Gap Lean-to, which often has a dry or stagnant water source. From here, a gradual ascent leads to the posted summit (25.6/2,342).

The level trail passes two restricted views north, then drops steeply to reach the Chairback Gap Lean-to (26.0/1,980). Continuing down past the shelter, you immediately reach the saddle below Chairback Mountain, where a trail sign indicates your progress. After crossing a boggy morass on single-plank puncheon, you begin a steady ascent to the open ledges of Chairback Mountain's summit (26.5/2,180).

It's another exceptional 180-degree view north. East Chairback Lake is visible below to the northwest. The long line of the Katahdin Ironworks Road traces northwest across the landscape toward Greenville. Looking up the watershed of the West Branch Pleasant River watershed, the cleft of Gulf Hagas is apparent in the landscape—your next destination. Baker Mountain and its identifying slide can be spotted on the northwest horizon. Due north is the round summit of White Cap. Big Spruce Mountain is closer, almost directly in line with White Cap, and Little Spruce Mountain rises to its right.

Views expand east as you descend from the summit, and Silver Lake can now be seen below Saddleback Mountain. The route drops over loose talus and heads diagonally to the left—watch for blazes—departing the talus before reaching the bottom of the slide. After a steep drop, the trail then mellows and undulates through several rocky clearings that offer views behind you of Chairback Mountain's steep cliffs.

You now leave views behind as the trail reenters taller spruce-fir forest and winds downward. The woods soon transition back to hardwoods. Sugar maple and beech appear as you steadily descend, ramble along a long undulating section, and reach the junction for East Chairback Pond (28.7/1,690).

To visit the pond, turn left on the spur trail and head 0.2 mile and 170 feet down. The pond is nicer than its eastern cousin, with a rockier and more open shore, fewer boats, and less used tentsites. The ledges of Chairback Mountains can be seen from shore, as can Columbus and Third mountains.

Back on the AT, you drop quickly and then begin a more gradual descent through mature spruce-fir woods. The forest slowly transitions to hardwoods and large big-tooth aspens begin to predominate, easily identified by their platy bark and fluttering leaves. The abundance of big-tooth aspens—a fast-growing species that thrives in disturbed areas—indicates that a large-scale disturbance, most likely a clear-cut, took place on this hillside sometime in the past 100 years or so. Near the bottom, large white pines appear alongside hemlock trees shortly before you reach the wide KI Road (29.9/780).

The AT crosses the road and becomes a wide track as it briefly parallels Henderson Brook. The stream soon joins the West Branch of the Pleasant River by a substantial camping area. The trail turns downriver, crowded by hazel and blackberry bushes, and reaches a major thoroughfare. A right turn leads to the Gulf Hagas parking area (30.4/650).

At this point, you'll need to ford the wide, shallow river. It's an ankle- to shin-deep crossing in normal conditions, though heavy rains may make it more difficult or even dangerous. Once on the other side, put your shoes back on beneath the spreading branches of red oak. Note that there is no camping for the next 2 miles along the AT, because of the area's heavy visitation.

Past the crossing, the wide trail parallels the river beneath nice hardwoods and reaches the junction with the KI Trail, which enters from the right. The AT next enters the Hermitage, a rare grove of old-growth white pine. As you pass the first specimen—a large pine 3 feet in diameter—look left into the stand of old-growth forest. Perfectly straight white pines dominate, with a younger understory of paper birch and striped and red maples.

The AT slowly ascends, curves right, and leaves the stand behind. The route begins to run parallel to the river and you can hear the water murmuring below. The slopes of the Chairback Range peek through the trees. The trail becomes rockier as it turns uphill and continues to curve right, passing a restricted view into the deepening gorge below and then crossing a flowing brook. The slow rise leads you to the Gulf Hagas Trail (31.7/930) on the left.

In Gulf Hagas, the West Branch of the Pleasant River tumbles over multiple waterfalls as it races through a narrow slate gorge. The scenery is striking and well worth the side-trip. To see it all, follow the Gulf Hagas Trail to immediately reach the Rim Trail, a rugged path that winds along the edge of the gorge for 3.0 miles. Return via the easy-cruising Pleasant Valley Tote Road for a 5.2-mile round-trip. Alternatively, follow the Rim Trail 0.9 mile to a short connector and then return along the Tote Road, a 1.5-mile round-trip that provides a good sample of the experience.

To reach the AMC's Little Lyford Pond Camps, located 2.2 miles past the end of Gulf Hagas, proceed to the farthest intersection of the Rim Trail and Pleasant River Tote Road where a single-track path, signed for LLPC, continues past the Gulf. About halfway to Little Lyford, you encounter a dirt road. Turn left on the road, cross the bridge, then take an immediate right to resume the single-track route to the camps.

Past the Gulf Hagas Trail junction, the AT immediately narrows to single-track and becomes more overgrown. The trail steadily rises, then levels out in a maturing second-growth spruce-fir forest. You descend briefly, then traverse near audible Gulf Hagas Brook to reach the Gulf Hagas Cutoff Trail on the left (32.4/1,060). This point marks the end of the no-camping zone.

The root-laced trail steadily climbs, running parallel to the invisible brook 30 feet below. As you continue, the stream becomes intermittently visible as the route crosses several small tributaries and undulates through diverse hardwoods. You resume a steady rise through spruce-fir forest, and soon the gradient increases. The trail curves right, away from the brook, and levels out, offering glimpses east of lower Gulf Hagas Mountain. After a rough level stretch, the trail bends back toward the creek, mellows, and passes a tenting area on the right just before reaching Gulf Hagas Brook. Rock-hop the clear water and reach the short spur to the Carl A. Newhall Lean-to (35.9/1,890).

Past the shelter, the trail rambles past a swampy beaver pond on the right; the rounded summit of West Peak—your continuing route—is visible beyond. The gradient increases as the trail passes through spruce-fir forest and encounters an enriched site at the base of a cliff, where sugar maple proliferates and some nice yellow birches fill in a mature canopy. The trail now steepens markedly, making half a dozen switchbacks as it climbs, then traverses left and becomes a grassy track lined with hay-scented ferns, blackberry vines, and hobblebush. The route levels, curves right, and offers a few glimpses of Whitecap Mountain ahead. You then reach the signed and viewless summit of Gulf Hagas Mountain (36.8/2,683).

The trail undulates along the summit ridge, passing extensive bracken fern and thick hobblebush. As you begin to descend, brief views to the north-northwest look toward Mount Baker. The trail winds along the north side of the ridge and makes a steep drop toward the saddle. After a momentary rise, you descend through a dense green tunnel to reach the Sidney Tappan Campsite (37.7/2,450). A nice flowing spring is available nearby, located 70 feet down a posted blue-blazed trail.

Past the site, the path immediately enters a young spruce corridor and widens as it begins a steady traversing rise. The trail switchbacks right and then markedly steepens, ascending some nice rock stairs. Views peek west behind you on the sustained climb, which ascends through dense spruce-fir woods. The gradient eases as you crest 3,000 feet and make a more gradual rise to reach the signed summit of West Peak among dense firs (38.4/3,181).

You now descend steeply though more thick forest. As the trail approaches the gap below Hay Mountain (which peeks out intermittently ahead of you), it curves right, levels, and then makes a slower descent to reach the muddy saddle. Dense forest continues as you resume climbing up a rocky trail. Dead snags are abundant, likely caused by fir waves. As you crest 3,000 feet, the trail mellows briefly and then resumes a steady ascent to reach the broad summit plateau of Hay Mountain. The trail undulates along, entering a skeletal forest of snags just before reaching the posted summit in dense woods (40.0/3,244).

The rocky trail descends once again. As you drop, watch for glimpses of Whitecap Mountain ahead and Big Spruce and Chairback mountains to the south. The route levels out in a final saddle and encounters the White Brook Trail on the right (40.6/2,960), a challenging backdoor access route to White Cap Mountain. The desperately thirsty can find water 0.6 mile down this side trail, though a much better source awaits 2 miles ahead, shortly before Logan Brook Lean-to.

You pass a small trailside tentsite immediately past the junction and then climb toward White Cap. The trail briefly eases as it approaches the summit ridge, then resumes a steady ascent and curves slightly to the right. The route runs level for 0.2 mile to reach the White Brook Trail Spur on the right (41.4/3,480), which joins the White Brook Trail a short distance down the mountain.

The trail now resumes a slow rise, enters a smaller forest with loose rocks and talus underfoot, and emerges atop the summit (41.7/3,644). A broad field of talus composes the summit and offers expansive views south. (The rocky terrain makes pitching a tent here a lumpy proposition.) The rounded summit of Big Spruce Mountain is visible nearby, due south. Greenwood Pond sits in the bowl between Big Spruce and Little Spruce mountains. To the west are Hay Mountain and West Peak. Along the horizon, you can trace your previous route along the Barren-Chairback Range.

Head to the north side of the summit for more views. Third West Branch Pond shimmers down below, and Big Boardman Mountain—near your continuing route—is apparent to the northeast. On a clear day, Katahdin itself is visible on the horizon 29 miles away. Thick diminutive firs crown the summit. Some alpine plant species can be spotted, including cranberry, crowberry, and Labrador tea.

Continuing north, the AT hops over talus and krummholz and then begins its descent down the mountain's east ridge. There are views east of large B Pond before the trail reenters the trees and starts heading down, down, and down,

View from Barren Ledges

aided by long sections of excellent rock steps. Just before dropping below 3,000 feet, you encounter a water source, the first since Sidney Tappan Campsite.

The trail levels out briefly on its continued descent, offering glimpses left into the deep drainage of Logan Brook. You encounter an open ledge with views over the sheer drainage; water rushes down below, White Cap rises above. To the northeast, your continuing route heads across the East Branch River and toward Big Boardman Mountain. The trail soon banks left, leaves the ridge, and begins a steady side-hilling traverse. You enter an almost pure stand of paper birch just before the brook and encounter the Logan Brook Lean-to (43.1/2,420).

Past the shelter, the trail cruises nice and steady. The nearby creek remains audible but inaccessible. The extensive paper birch stands continue and are slowly joined by other hardwoods, including all the maples: red, striped, mountain, and sugar (at around 2,000 feet). The trail crosses a small tributary, curves right, and then runs level for some time. You eventually make a steep drop, curve left, and begin side-hilling downward. Beech appears and some mature sugar maples punctuate the forest. Just before you reach West Branch Ponds Road, a major dirt thoroughfare (44.7/1,590), you pass a small covered spring on the left, which is channeled through a convenient PVC pipe.

Cross the road and continue your descent past granite boulders in an increasingly buggy area. The trail crosses a trickle and levels out in a hemlock-spruce forest loaded with pink lady's slippers. Cedars appear intermittently as the surroundings fill with nice spruce trees and occasional white pines. A long level walk weaves through the dense lumpy woods. You eventually start a slow descent, abruptly enter dense foliage, and cross a section of puncheon over ale-colored water. Alders and irises line the banks. The route winds across another flowing brook and reaches the spur for the East Branch Lean-to on the left (46.7/1,340). Boulders protrude from the ground all around, a living rock garden.

Past the shelter, the trail runs parallel to the hidden East River and then rock-hops across it. The route travels through a wet area and then begins climbing the slopes of Big Boardman Mountain. You slowly gain elevation, crossing an old woods road in rocky spruce-fir woods. The gradient increases, the trail switchbacks left, and you ascend a remarkable tree talus field; tree roots seemingly hold the rocks in place. You switchback right, make a steady uphill traverse, and eventually curve left. Restricted views look south as you traverse through young forest.

The trail continues to rise, bends right, and then begins a level traverse to soon enter hardwood forest highlighted by nice sugar maples and yellow birch. You undulate through an area of selective harvesting—only spruce remain after past logging activity selectively removed other species—and then drop back into hardwood forest and reach Mountain View Pond (48.6/1,600). The AT crosses the pond outflow by an old beaver dam and then parallels the placid, but inaccessible, shoreline. Just before the route turns away from the lake, an unposted spur on the left leads to a number of tentsites and chained-up canoes. A sign indicates that no campfires are permitted here.

The route follows the flowing pond outlet along a boggy creek bed and soon encounters a posted spring, located a short distance off the trail. Sweet, cold, and refreshing water pours out of the rocks here, an easy fill-up. You now cruise on an overgrown woods road past young hardwoods and abundant diseased beech. The trail eventually bears right off the old roadbed, drops briefly to cross a boggy area, and then makes a quick rocky climb to begin a level section through dense spruce-fir forest. The route slowly rises, turns right to begin a more direct ascent, switchbacks left to resume a more gradual climb, and then turns right once again to head straight up the slopes.

A few tantalizing glimpses through the trees motivate you onward, and you soon reach an open view west-southwest toward the Whitecap Range and nearby Big Boardman Mountain. On White Cap, you can identify your route down from the summit and through the Logan Brook watershed. Past this vista, the trail curves to the top of Little Boardman (50.2/2,010). The trail runs level past red maple, sugar maple, and the occasional red oak before entering a rocky area full of blueberry bushes.

You then begin a descending tour through a magnificent sugar maple grove. It's a gorgeous stand, full of mature twisting trees, standing snags, and only a handful of beech and yellow birch—one of the best groves of the hike. Beech and yellow birch slowly increase and eventually the gradient eases. Crawford Pond becomes visible ahead through the trees. You pass some impressive spruce and a few final sugar maples, then emerge on Kokadjo B Pond Road (51.6/1,260).

The AT continues across the road and immediately crosses a small wash gully, which leads to a small nearby beach and some good tenting possibilities. The trail then rises and traverses the slopes past spruce and cedars, staying roughly 50 feet above the water with little to no access. You then drop to cross a small feeder brook and encounter a posted sign for SAND BEACH (52.0/1,240). A spur trail quickly leads to another small beach with several good tenting areas.

The AT soon merges with an old woods road for some easy walking, then leaves the road and continues to parallel the lake, just visible through the trees. The trail rambles closer to the water, passes a few access spots, and then crosses the lake outflow (Cooper Brook) over the remains of an old dam (52.5/1,220). Look for recent beaver activity in this area.

On the far side of the brook, the trail turns right and begins following an old roadbed through a young forest of paper birch, fir, spruce, red maple, and beech. This marks the start of the longest easy stretch in the entire 100-Mile Wilderness. You slowly descend parallel to nearby Cooper Brook, audible but seldom seen. The route travels over intermittent puncheon, crosses a few small streams, and passes a few nice white pines and hemlocks. Sugar maple and ash slowly join the forest mosaic. Eventually the roadbed begins a series of minor but pronounced drops. After crossing the largest tributary thus far, the trail widens and makes a final descent to reach Cooper Brook Falls Lean-to on the right (54.8/980).

Past the shelter, Cooper Brook once again disappears from sight as the AT remains on the old road and crosses a more substantial tributary. The walk is delightfully easy as it rolls past lush and diverse hardwoods, slowly descends, and crosses another brook. Bugs increase, as does the diversity of trees—ash and hickory appear in increasing numbers. The route slowly turns away from Cooper Brook, passes through stately hemlock groves, and enters increasingly soggy terrain; slippery puncheon and bugs increase. You cross another stream and soon Church Pond becomes faintly visible through the trees ahead. After a few brief rises, Cooper Brook reappears on the right and the trail runs right alongside it, passing several good campsites in hemlock forest. You then emerge on Jo-Mary Road (58.5/690).

The AT crosses the road and briefly parallels Cooper Brook in young woods, punctuated by the appearance of big-tooth aspens. The trail bends away from the brook, returns to dense spruce-fir forest, and reaches an unposted, blue-blazed trail on the right leading to nearby Cooper Pond (59.3/660). The five-minute side-trip passes a nice campsite en route to the lake's outflow, where there are good views south of nearby Jo-Mary Mountain.

The AT continues through spruce-fir forest and past occasional red pines, readily identified by their flaky scaly bark and distinctive branch structure. Cooper Brook reappears on the right, now a calm and wide waterway. The trail leaves the roadbed and returns to single-track for the first time in many miles. Roots crisscross the path as it winds near placid Cooper Brook. After turning away briefly, the route returns to the brook at a dirt road, which crosses the stream on a bridge.

Cross the road and follow a wider trail across a smaller woods road. You now enter a noticeably drier upland area populated by young conifers. The route crosses a small brook, a larger one on a puncheon bridge—the outflow from nearby Mud Pond (61.4/500)—and then another small one via well-placed rocks. Now the route tours above the shore of Mud Pond; Jo-Mary Mountain is visible to the south.

The trail winds through a red pine forest carpeted with needles and filled with abundant huckleberry bushes. The single-track trail passes through the hike's driest section before slowly curving to reenter a lusher environment. The woods transition back to mossy softwoods. Lower Jo-Mary Lake begins to appear north through the trees and the route is lined with evidence of an old communications line that was once strung through the trees.

The trail winds just inland from the lake, passing some nice white pines near the shore, and leads you to the signed junction for Antlers Campsite (62.7/500). Turn left, away from the lake, to continue north on the AT, quickly passing an amusing privy dubbed FORT RELIEF. The single-track trail heads away from the lake through young forest and then bends back toward the shore and crosses a small stream. The trail touches a tiny sandy beach at the far end of the lake, which offers a long view across the water. Continuing, you cross another small stream, return inland to lush hardwood forest, and reach the posted junction for Potaywadjo Ridge on the left (64.2/540).

SIDE-TRIP TO POTAYWADJO RIDGE

This detour is one of the hike's best, though it does involve 650 feet of elevation gain in under a mile. From the junction, the blue-blazed trail steeply climbs the slopes to reach open slabs that offer views down the entire length of Lower Jo-Mary Lake. Mud and Cooper ponds are also visible, and the White Cap Range can be spotted in the distance. Nearby is the low hulking mass of Jo-Mary Mountain; Cooper Brook flows below it. But the best parts of this side-trip are the prolific blueberries that cover the open ledges. They get lots of sun, ripen in mid- to late July, and produce more fruit than you'll have time to enjoy!

Back on the AT, you follow a rocky path past some enormous boulders and reach a posted spur for SAND BEACH (64.4/500), which quickly leads to a small beach with views across the lake toward the hump of Jo-Mary Mountain. The AT turns away from the lake, begins climbing, and quickly crosses a small stream. You slowly rise and curve left through a young forest of birch, beech, and big-tooth aspen. The trail steepens and parallels a rivulet, passing more giant rocks as it climbs.

The route levels and then makes a gradual descent, passing extensive patches of Indian cucumber near the top. (Identify them by their two-tiered whorls of leaves and tiny flowers dangling beneath the upper whorl.) After a steady descent, the trail abruptly levels off, the forest thickens with conifers, and you reach the Potaywadjo Spring Lean-to (66.2/600).

As you continue past the lean-to, you quickly encounter its namesake spring—an impressive pool—and cross a stream beneath abundant hemlock.

The trail next crosses a dirt road, enters a hemlock-cedar forest, and reaches Twitchell Brook, crossing it on a puncheon bridge. Pemadumcook Lake appears ahead through the trees, and you soon encounter a posted sign for a VIEW OF KATAHDIN. The mountain is just visible from the lakeshore; you can scramble over nearby driftwood and rocks for better views.

Beyond this point, the AT follows extensive bog bridging over another stream and begins traveling along an easy-walking path through dark forest. The trail becomes boggy as you pass near a swampy wetland on the left. The level trail runs over several long stretches of puncheon, crosses a muddy seldom-used road, and then enters the land of super bog.

The next section is extremely wet and washed out, requiring careful travel to avoid soaking your boots. The delicate bog-hopping act leads you to a super muddy road. (Head right here to reach the landing for White House Lodge in about a mile.) Successfully navigate the muck and follow the AT north. A stream soon appears on the right, and you next rock-hop across Tumbling Dick Stream, a moderately tricky crossing.

Nahmakanta Stream appears on the right, the trail quickly crosses another small tributary, and you then begin your journey along broad, shallow, and quietly riffling Nahmakanta Stream. Before long, the route splits. A high water route branches left to rejoin the main trail in 0.2 mile, but unless the stream is running exceptionally high, choose the regular route; it's in much better condition.

The route winds directly along Nahmakanta Stream atop steep cutbanks, a pleasant level walk past many flat areas with good camping potential, though accessing the stream can be a challenge in many spots. A young forest of hemlock, beech, spruce, and fir surrounds the trail, which eventually leads you to Nahmakanta Stream Campsite on the left (70.5/600).

Past the campsite, you quickly pass another established tentsite and then turn inland a short distance from the stream. Roots and mud increase, and both the trail and river become increasingly rocky. After more than a mile of steady level progress, the stream widens into a broad placid pool and the slopes to your left become perceptibly steeper. The trail crosses several small brooks and then heads inland on an intensely root-laced path. You cross the largest tributary yet, rise briefly, and begin a rising traverse along sheer slopes above the broad river visible below.

A rock staircase leads you down quickly, where you meet a dirt road and bridge (73.5/700). The AT crosses the road and returns along the river, passing a giant knobby white pine as it goes. You then pass a series of campsites by a small carry-in boat launch on the edge of Nahmakanta Lake

A white pine laden with
morning dew in the
100-Mile Wilderness

(73.7/650). The trail turns left, then quickly right off the area's wide main path, and cruises level past softwoods. The lake is nearby, just to the right through the trees.

The trail touches the shore at one point and offers views north of approaching Nesuntabunt Mountain—your continuing route—on the left side of the lake. The route then crosses a small brook, runs directly along the rocky shore, and encounters a small sandy beach. A short distance later, you turn inland, climb briefly, and then drop back to the lakeshore and rock-hop over Prentiss Brook. The trail now undulates near the shore through a young forest of cedar and yellow and paper birch.

The going is generally mellow, and eventually the trail returns to the water by a small beach. Alder and small hickory trees line the lakeshore. The trail turns inland again, climbs around a small point, and rises nearly 200 feet. You drop quickly past some large granite boulders and then switchback left to begin a traversing descent among rock boulder chaos. Once near the lake again, the path resumes its easy-cruising demeanor and reaches the water by a posted white sand beach. A campsite and trickling spring are located just inland from here.

The trail heads inland once more, weaves through lush deciduous flatlands, and crosses a clear-flowing stream emerging from the Wadleigh Valley. Several large sugar maples line the route as you continue inland; standing snags and downed trees indicate the age and maturity of this stand. You then encounter Wadleigh Stream Lean-to on the left, located adjacent to the trail (76.3/690).

Past the shelter, you immediately start climbing through hemlock forest on a soft and needle-covered path. The trail rises atop a steep outcrop with restricted views of the lake and then swings right to begin traversing the slopes on an easier grade. Century-old white pines and fern-topped boulders accompany you on the traverse, which curves over a rise and then descends. Abundant huckleberry lines the trail as it passes good lake views, turns back inland, and visits a car-sized boulder balanced atop two others. The route briefly rises and then descends past more large boulders as the forest transitions to a deciduous mix of sugar maple and beech.

The trail crosses a flowing brook, makes a slow traversing rise, and then markedly steepens. You cross a trickling brook and then climb up a broad fissure in the bedrock alongside the trickling flow. The trail crosses the stream, banks left, and briefly levels. You next curve right to ascend another broad cleft of large rocks. The route crosses the creek again, passes more cliffs, and continues its ascent through the rock fortress.

After a brief flat section, the trail climbs rock stairs up, up, and up, still running alongside the same trickle of water. The route curves left at one point, then rises through a young sugar maple grove via another broad cleft in the mountainside. More rock steps lead to a saddle, where the trail curves right and continues its rise to finally reach the posted summit in a stand of spruce (78.2/1,560).

From here, a short side trail leads 250 feet to an exceptional view from a small outcrop. The entire massif of Katahdin reveals itself. All of Nahmakanta Lake unfurls below you; Nahmakanta Lake Wilderness Camps is visible at the lake's northern edge. The Rainbow Stream watershed—your continuing route—flows into the north end of the lake; your previous route past Pemadumcook Lake is visible south.

The trail drops steeply from the summit, traverses by more rock fortresses, descends more rock stairs, and then curves left. The route levels, passes over a rock ledge with another view of Katahdin, and then resumes a slow drop to reach a dirt road (79.4/1,000). Cross the road and follow the AT as it slowly rises and then falls through younger hardwood forest. Crescent Pond soon appears through the trees. The trail wraps over to the far side of the pond, where smooth granite ledges slide into a perfect swimming opportunity (80.6/1,030). Good southern exposure here means lots of sun for drying out. Locals have tied up a few boats here.

The route winds around the shore, passes a nice boat-free shoreline spot near the middle of the lake, and then heads through spruce-fir forest. Curving right, you now begin the descent toward Rainbow Stream and enter a short stretch of old-growth forest amid a chaotic garden of rock and deadfall. As you undulate through this rough terrain, take time to admire the massive white pines that punctuate the woods. Far below in a deep ravine, Pollywog Stream, the outflow from Crescent Pond, can be heard rushing downward.

You soon pass an unposted viewpoint overlooking the sheer slopes of the ravine. The trail briefly rises, traverses through dense woods, and heads slowly down. The gradient becomes steeper as you go and footing is tricky at times, but eventually you reach the bottom, where a nice campsite can be found to the right.

The route now parallels wide Pollywog Stream, which riffles in a shallow streambed. The rough and rocky trail passes through a diverse forest and then emerges on Nahmakanta Road (83.1/680). Turn left, cross the bridge, and go straight on the road past the NLC sign on the right. Fifty yards later, across from several nice white pines, the AT bears to the right off the road and enters a young forest. You quickly cross an icky-looking stream and enter young forest, though a few massive white pines still lurk by the trail.

Before long, rushing Rainbow Creek becomes audible ahead. The trail quickly reaches the racing stream and begins to run parallel to it. The water rushes over solid rock, sheeting, sliding, sluicing. As you ascend alongside, you encounter a small tributary and follow it to the left for a few hundred yards, then cross it to return to the main creek.

The trail runs directly alongside Rainbow Stream, which booms and tumbles continuously over rapids and drops. Water chokes itself in raging chutes. Eventually the rapids end and the trail levels out. You now turn away from the stream for nearly half a mile, crossing a small tributary before returning to the now placid brook. A level and easy-going stretch leads you to Rainbow Stream Lean-to (84.4/980) by the water.

To continue, you must now cross Rainbow Stream. This may require either fording the shin- to knee-deep brook or delicately balancing across on thin logs, depending on conditions. Once on the other side, the trail continues parallel to the stream and quickly reaches the first of the Rainbow Deadwaters. The trail runs just inland from the placid water through softwood forest. The stream flow resumes on the far side of the pond, the occasionally muddy trail runs close to the water, and you next reach the second deadwater. The path now becomes all roots and mini bogs, which makes it hard to develop a hiking rhythm.

The trail remains close to the second deadwater and then turns inland near its far end. You rise briefly through increasing hardwoods and reach the signed junction for Rainbow Dam (86.4/1,100), a worthwhile side-trip. This easy five-minute detour leads to a small dam and two nice campsites at the end of massive Rainbow Lake, though only a small arm of the lake is visible from here. Katahdin looms ahead, looking closer than ever. Signs indicate that campfires are allowed here by permit only.

Back on the AT, you descend momentarily to cross a tributary and then begin a long level stretch through hardwood forest. The path is generally easygoing, though there are regular patches of mud and bog and the bugs can be bad. Rainbow Lake is occasionally visible through the trees on the left as you make your way to Rainbow Spring Campsite (88.2/1,070) on the right. The spring is down by the lake's edge. Its cool waters bubble into a small clear pool and then immediately pour into the lake. Loons call from the lake, which is shallow for some distance from shore.

From here, the trail winds inland, climbs slowly, then winds back toward the water, crossing a few small brooks as it goes. You can catch glimpses of the lake to the left through a young forest of ash, red maple, sugar maple, and other hardwoods. You may hear the sound of boat motors and other human activity along this section, emanating from a nearby sporting camp. After passing among softwoods for the first time in a while, you pass the posted Rainbow Mountain Trail on the right (90.2/1,120).

The brief 1.0-mile one-way side-trail leads to the top of Rainbow Mountain, and as the sign says, offers EASY GREAT VIEWS of the surrounding lake and rumpled terrain—a worthwhile excursion.

The trail now returns to the lake's edge and passes several nice spruce trees and good access points. Steeper slopes run upward to your right, populated by fern-topped granite boulders. The root-laced and rocky trail makes for slower going, though the forest is pleasantly mature; enjoy some nice sugar maples. The route rises among boulders and spruce-fir forest, passing a handful of 3-foot-plus diameter white pines before winding down to a shallow cove at the far end of the lake (91.6/1,050), where you can find a pair of nice campsites.

The AT crosses a small inflow stream and almost immediately encounters the posted spur to Big Beaver Pond on the right (91.7/1,060). The side trail leads in 0.7 mile to a big beaver pond, which is as exciting as it sounds.

Continuing onward, the trail undulates through a mature forest of white pines, spruce, and paper birch. You then leave this older stand and enter thicker and younger woods with more red maple and beech. The trail descends to cross a boggy area on puncheon and then starts to steadily rise, entering young softwood forest. The ground underfoot becomes increasingly rocky as you ascend toward Rainbow Ledges. Before long, you're climbing a solid ribbon of bedrock. The forest diminishes on the sparse soil. Blueberries and lichens become common. As you climb, views southwest begin to peek out; you can spot Jo-Mary Mountain and the White Cap Range in the distance. The trail crests at 1,500 feet and runs level along the ridge top, a pleasant stretch on solid rock. Huckleberry bushes become as prolific as blueberries.

The trail then encounters a striking view of Katahdin, here only 9 miles away, before dropping back into a mossy and root-chocked spruce-fir forest. The trail undulates through the dense woods, slowly rises, and then starts descending into the Hurd Brook watershed. The route drops quickly at first, aided by rock stairs, then tapers off and descends more gradually. As you approach the bottom, the needle-covered trail eases and winds among woods that become increasingly lush. The trail resumes a steep descent and reaches the valley floor, where you'll find Hurd Brook in a maze of roots, rocks, yellow birch, and cedar. Hurd Brook Shelter sits on the other side (95.9/700).

Past the shelter, the AT continues its rocky root-hopping journey through softwood forest, passing a spring 0.3 mile beyond the shelter by some stone steps. The route slowly rises, drops, and passes over more roots and more rocks in a hemlock forest. Mossy boulder humps are everywhere. The trail makes a slow rising traverse through young beech, and descends a very rocky section as it undulates along. Beech, paper birch, and sugar maples eventually appear in green profusion as the trail begins its final descent.

The rocky drop leads through a mixed forest and then eases a bit before reaching an extended section of puncheon—the longest of the entire hike. The final section of trail cruises through thick spruce-fir forest to emerge onto the paved Golden Road. Turn right to follow the road, cross Abol Bridge, and reach this long journey's end by the Abol Store (99.4/660).

INFORMATION

The Maine Appalachian Trail Club maintains the AT through the 100-Mile Wilderness and is your best source of information for current trail conditions. P.O. Box 283, Augusta, ME 04332-0283, www.matc.org; email: mrbeanat96@verizon.net. For more information on the AMC's Maine Woods Initiative and additional recreation opportunities around the Barren-Chairback Range, visit www.outdoors.org/mwi.

TRIP 31
KATAHDIN

Location: Chimney Pond, Baxter State Park
Highlights: New England's grandest alpine amphitheater, base camp for climbing mile-high Katahdin
Distance: 6.6 miles round-trip to Chimney Pond; 4.0 to 4.4 miles round-trip from Chimney Pond to climb Katahdin
Total Elevation Gain/Loss: 1,600/1,600 to Chimney Pond; approximately 2,500/2,500 to climb Katahdin from Chimney Pond, depending on route
Trip Length: 1–3 days
Difficulty: ★★ (climbing Katahdin: ★★★★★)
Recommended Maps: *Maine Mountain Guide, Map 1: Baxter State Park/Katahdin,* AMC Books, *Katahdin, Illustrated Map & Guide,* Wilderness Map Company

Surrounded on three sides by soaring granite cliffs, Chimney Pond sits in the mountainous heart of Baxter State Park. Overhead looms mile-high Baxter Peak—northern terminus of the Appalachian Trail—which is connected to neighboring Pamola Peak by a mile-long arête known as the Knife Edge. From the pond and its adjacent campground, wild and adventurous trails scrape their way up the mountain flanks. Come enjoy the view. Come enjoy the challenge of Maine's mightiest mountain.

HIKE OVERVIEW
The hike is an out-and-back journey to Chimney Pond on the Chimney Pond Trail. It is an easy day trip, or a longer multiday base-camping adventure for summiting Katahdin. The journey steadily ascends a well-trod path—the most heavily used in the park—through pleasant forest with occasional views. Crowds are common throughout the summer season. Dogs are prohibited in Baxter State Park.

Park staff will be watching you. Follow the rules.

OVERNIGHT OPTIONS
Camping in Baxter State Park is permitted only in designated areas. They are usually in high demand, especially Chimney Pond Campground. Reservations are required, an effort that takes some significant advance planning (see later).

CHIMNEY POND, BAXTER STATE PARK

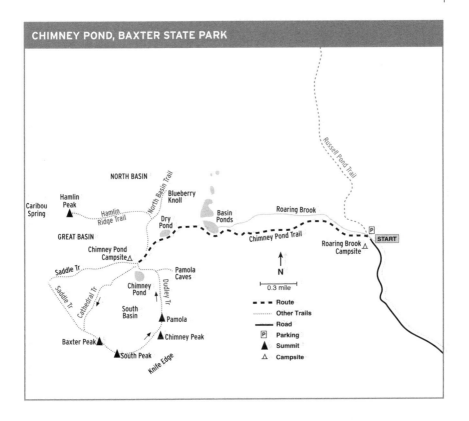

Chimney Pond Campground consists of a 10-person bunkhouse and nine lean-tos scattered among the trees on the east side of Chimney Pond. This area is extremely popular, and you'll need to plan well in advance to secure a site here, especially for any weekend excursion. You can request a preferred lean-to when making a reservation.

Lean-to 1 is located by the main trail and offers views of Hamlin Ridge to the northwest. *Lean-to 2* is tucked away on a side trail and offers an unobstructed view of Pamola. *Lean-to 3* is a larger shelter with restricted views of Pamola and Katahdin's main headwall. *Leant-to 4* also sits by the main path, offering views northeast back down the valley. *Lean-to 5* is closest to the pond and has a view of Pamola, but is close to the main path. *Lean-tos 6, 7, and 8* cluster near each other in the trees, offering no real views, but are removed from the campground bustle. Lean-to 6 is the smallest of the bunch. *Lean-to 9* is the most isolated of the sites and offers glimpses of Pamola's cliffs through the trees. The lean-tos cost $9 per person (minimum $18 per night), the bunkhouse $10 per person. A maximum of four people are allowed per site. Note that the park has established specific cutoff times for hikers traveling to Chimney Pond, generally about three hours before sunset. You will not be allowed in after this point.

Reservations. To reserve a site at Chimney Pond (or anywhere in Baxter), first visit the park's website, www.baxterstateparkauthority.com, which details the reservation system and the park's myriad rules and regulations. Reservations can be made as much as four months in advance, and if you're planning a weekend trip to Chimney Pond, it is recommended that you send in your reservation as early as possible. Print out the reservations form, fill it out, and mail it in with a self-addressed, stamped return envelope. Your request may arrive one week before the day they open reservations for four months later; earlier than this and they will return it to you. As of 2007, no phone or online reservations were possible, though an online reservation system is rumored to be in the works. You can also make reservations in person at park headquarters in Millinocket. *Don't forget to bring your reservation with you when you come.* It might as well be your passport.

TO REACH THE TRAILHEAD

Head to Millinocket and follow Route 11 west to the Route 11/157 junction by the First Congregational Church. Turn right on Millinocket Road and follow it to the park boundary, where the road becomes unpaved. You soon reach Togue Pond Gatehouse—the park entrance—where you will need to show your reservation form and pay an entrance fee. From the gatehouse, bear right toward Roaring Brook and proceed 8.1 miles over the unpaved road to the trailhead parking area. The designated parking area for overnight users is on the right.

HIKE DESCRIPTION

From the parking area, proceed to the Roaring Brook Ranger Station and trailhead (0.0/1,500). Sign in at the register, and notice the young striped maple, balsam fir, paper birch, and red maple near the building, all common companions on your upcoming hike. Past the ranger station, the double-track trail immediately encounters the Russell Pond Trail on the right. Bear left to remain on the Chimney Pond Trail, which quickly reaches crystalline Roaring Brook, a good spot for obtaining water. The trail initially runs parallel to the inaccessible brook, remaining double-track and very rocky. Some of the granite shows scars from early path-clearing efforts. You soon reach the Helon Taylor Trail on the left (0.2/1,540).

A few sugar maples and the golden peeling bark of yellow birch appear alongside the trail. Hobblebush becomes increasingly common. The trail briefly touches Roaring Brook, providing access, and then crosses a small feeder stream on a plank bridge. The route follows some puncheon, curves away from the brook, and steepens. You steadily rise on the rocky track, crossing Pamola Brook on another plank bridge (1.0/1,800). Pamola itself peeks out upstream above its namesake waterway. Mountain ash, yellow birch, and paper birch shade the burbling stream.

The trail ascends some nice rock stairs, eases somewhat, and then steepens again to remain at a sustained grade. Occasional steps moderate the rocky route. The trail then passes Halfway Rock on the left in a small clearing (1.6/2,320), the midpoint of your journey to Chimney Pond. The route drops momentarily, offers a view down the trail corridor toward the North Basin, and quickly reaches a posted spur on the right to a nearby viewpoint. Make the short side-trip, which leads to a rocky clearing surrounded by wind-sheared spruce and fir. Views look west toward the North Basin and its headwall, topped by Hamlin Ridge. You can also see the saddle between Hamlin Peak

The Knife Edge rises above Chimney Pond

and Baxter Peak. There are two saddles actually—the Saddle Trail ascends the slightly higher one to the right. South Turner Mountain is visible east behind you. A few larch trees can be spotted in a small bog below.

Back on the Chimney Pond Trail, you pass through a paper birch grove and briefly enjoy a level stone-free path before rising to reach the posted spur to Lower Basin Pond (1.9/2,460). The short side-trip leads you to the pond's south shore. The water is clear and deep, a good swimming spot. From here, views look toward the North Basin, Hamlin Peak, the Saddle, and Pamola. Chimney Pond is up ahead, just out-of sight to the left.

Continuing on the Chimney Pond Trail, you skirt around the pond on a rocky but level path and cross a stretch of bridge-like puncheon. Keep an eye out for cedar, which appear for the first time. You then mosey along a long boardwalk shaded by the curving branches of mountain ash. You cross above a much-diminished Roaring Brook in a marshy area, resume climbing, and quickly encounter the North Basin Cutoff Trail on the right (2.3/2520).

Continue straight on the Chimney Pond Trail, crossing a dry streambed on a guardrail-protected bridge. Looking down the gully, you can spot Lower and Upper Basin Ponds. The trail climbs again, but soon levels as it passes diminutive Dry Pond on the right; the North Basin headwall is visible across the water. Cross Saddle Brook—the inflow to Dry Pond—on a plank bridge and enjoy the easiest section yet. Katahdin's headwall looms over the trees ahead. You pass the North Basin Trail on the right (3.0/2,820), cross a dry gully on a final plank bridge, and emerge at the Chimney Pond bunkhouse and start of the campground area (3.3/2,890).

SHORTER EXCURSIONS FROM CHIMNEY POND

North Basin, 2.0 miles round-trip with 600 feet of elevation gain/loss. The North Basin is easily accessible from Chimney Pond via the North Basin Trail, which starts from the Chimney Pond Trail 0.3 mile below Chimney Pond. The path ends at Blueberry Knoll with a 360-degree view of the bare alpine landscape. To the east, you can see Sandy Stream Pond, South Turner Mountain, and Katahdin Lake. Pamola and the Knife Edge are visible.

Pamola Caves, 1.4 miles round-trip with 400 feet of elevation gain/loss. Located at the base of Pamola's slopes, these crevices provide opportunities for wriggling through small passages. To reach them from Chimney Pond, follow the Dudley Trail toward Pamola for 0.3 mile and then bear left on the posted 0.4-mile spur trail.

Hamlin Peak, 4.0 miles round-trip with 2,000 feet of elevation gain/loss. The climb up Hamlin Peak follows the airy Hamlin Ridge Trail along a narrow, treeless ridge with superlative views of the North Basin and Katahdin massif. It is much less used than routes up Katahdin. To reach the Hamlin Ridge Trail, follow the North Basin Trail 0.4 mile past its junction with the Chimney Pond Trail.

KATAHDIN AND THE KNIFE EDGE

The Knife Edge is the only true mountain arête in New England. Unlike all other peaks in New England (even Mount Washington), Katahdin was not overtopped by ice during the last Ice Age. Instead, glaciers scoured its lower flanks, gouging the mountain from both sides to create a narrow ridgeline along its crest: the Knife Edge. Today, you can hike its entire length, a thrilling adventure that requires strong footwear, good balance, good fitness, and good scrambling abilities. The crux of the Knife Edge is the Chimney, a cleft in the ridge just below Pamola that requires the route's most difficult scrambling.

The park's premier hike is the loop over Baxter Peak, the Knife Edge, and Pamola—the primary goal for most hikers heading beyond Chimney Pond.

The Knife Edge

To complete the loop from Chimney Pond, you can either hike counterclockwise—up Baxter Peak, over the Knife Edge to Pamola, and then down the Dudley Trail—or complete the loop clockwise by ascending the Dudley Trail, crossing the Knife Edge to Baxter Peak, and then descending the Saddle Trail. The former is more popular because the Dudley Trail provides the least hair-raising descent. (The Saddle Trail has a lot of scree and loose rock on its upper reaches. The Cathedral Trail is extremely steep and not recommended for descent.)

If making the recommended counter-clockwise loop, your ascent options are the Saddle and Cathedral trails, which create loops of 4.6 and 4.0 miles respectively. The Saddle Trail is more popular, winding through forest to reach the Great Basin's headwall and then ascending the Saddle Slide—a scar of loose scree and talus—to attain the ridge at 4,300 feet. From there, it's another mile and thousand feet of elevation gain to reach Baxter Peak.

The Cathedral Trail ascends the prominent ridge that divides the Great and South basins. Three large bulging rock promontories protrude from the ridge. From bottom to top, they are dubbed First, Second, and Third Cathedral. The route scrambles steeply over talus and solid rock and is well marked by blue blazes. It is an exciting adventure and provides the most direct route to the top, climbing 2,300 feet in just 1.4 miles. Only in New England would this route be called a trail—it is not for the faint of heart.

INFORMATION

Baxter State Park, 64 Balsam Drive, Millinocket, ME 04462; 207-723-5140; www.baxterstateparkauthority.com. For detailed route descriptions beyond Chimney Pond, consult the AMC's *Maine Mountain Guide.*

TRIP 32
BIG BAXTER

Location: Baxter State Park, Russell Pond Loop
Highlights: Ponds, peaks, the grandeur of Maine
Distance: 19.8 miles round-trip
Total Elevation Gain/Loss: 4,500/4,500, plus side-trips
Trip Length: 3–4 days
Difficulty: ★★★★★
Recommended Map: *Maine Mountain Guide, Map 1: Baxter State Park/ Katahdin,* AMC Books

Leave behind the trod and trammeled trails of Katahdin for a landscape as hauntingly wild as anywhere in New England. It is a land of alpine plateaus, remote ponds, rushing rivers, and hidden valleys. Come experience all that Baxter State Park has to offer.

HIKE OVERVIEW

The hike loops through the heart of Baxter State Park. The journey begins from Roaring Brook Trailhead, where a short, well-traveled ascent leads you to Chimney Pond and the sheer headwall of Katahdin. You then scramble up the mountain on the Saddle Trail and head north across the Northwest Plateau, a little-visited alpine landscape. A steep descent deposits you in the remote Northwest Basin, a small cirque occupied by cliffs, a waterfall, and Davis Pond. Spend your first night at Chimney Pond campground or the lonely Davis Pond Lean-to.

From Davis Pond, the journey continues down the Northwest Basin Trail and through the Wassataquoik Stream valley to reach boulder-studded Russell Pond. Adjacent Russell Pond Campground makes an ideal base camp for exploring the surrounding terrain; myriad day-trips head off in all directions. You return to the trailhead via the Russell Pond Trail, which first fords substantial Wassataquoik Stream before cruising south to return to the trailhead.

Dogs are prohibited in Baxter State Park. Crowds are common around Chimney Pond and Katahdin, but diminish once you reach the Northwest Plateau. There are good fishing opportunities at Russell Pond and its surrounding streams and ponds.

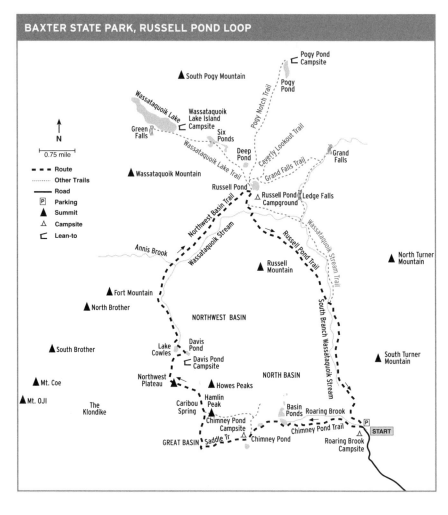

BAXTER STATE PARK, RUSSELL POND LOOP

OVERNIGHT OPTIONS

Camping is permitted only at designated overnight areas in Baxter State Park, and they are usually in high demand. Reserving a site requires some effort and advance planning (see later).

Chimney Pond Campground, 3.3 miles from the trailhead, consists of a 10-person bunkhouse and nine lean-tos scattered among the trees on the east side of Chimney Pond. This area is extremely popular, and you'll need to plan well in advance to secure a site here, especially for any weekend excursion. *Lean-to 1* is located by the main trail and its many travelers, but offers views of Hamlin Ridge to the northwest. *Lean-to 2* is tucked away on a side trail and offers an unobstructed view of Pamola. *Lean-to 3* is a larger shelter with restricted views of Pamola and Katahdin's main headwall. *Lean-to 4* also sits by the main path, offering views northeast back down the valley. *Lean-to 5* is closest to the pond, though not next to it, and is close to the main path with a view of Pamola. *Lean-tos 6,7, and 8* all cluster near each other in the trees, offering no real views, but are removed from the campground bustle. Lean-to 6 is the smallest of the bunch. *Lean-to 9* is the most isolated of the sites, and offers glimpses of Pamola's cliffs through the trees.

When making a reservation you can request a specific site, which will be assigned depending on availability. The lean-tos cost $9 per person (minimum $18 per night), the bunkhouse $10 per person. A maximum of four people are allowed per site. Note that the park has established specific cutoff times for hikers traveling to Chimney Pond, generally about three hours before sunset. You will not be allowed in after this point.

Davis Pond Lean-to is located 7.7 miles from the trailhead, tucked away at 2,900 feet on the floor of the rugged Northwest Basin and a short distance from its namesake pond. There is only one site here—a single lean-to— which means that once you book the spot you'll have it entirely to yourself. The lean-to is within 30 yards of the pond, but trees hide the water from sight. A small waterfall slaps against the rocks on the basin's headwall and provides a soothing background murmur. Water is readily available from the pond's inflow stream, and a three-sided privy—THE NEW THRONE OF THE THUNDER GODS—provides relief a short distance from the shelter. A maximum of four people can spend the night here. Tenting and campfires are prohibited.

Russell Pond Campground, 12.8 miles from the trailhead, lines three sides of Russell Pond, a circular lake ringed by boulders and low bluffs. There are five lean-tos and three tentsites. *Lean-to 1* is located closest to the lakeshore, offering limited water views from the shade of a battered white pine. *Lean-to 2* is the least private, located near the canoe racks, dock, and main trail. *Lean-to 3* is farthest from the lakeshore and near the main path, but still reasonably private. *Lean-to 4* features decent lake views and water access from the pond's northwest corner. *Lean-to 5* is the most isolated, located by the south shore in a bouldery landscape. *Campsite 16* features a large immaculate tent platform but no direct lake access. *Campsite 17* has two small tent platforms located well away from the lake and plainly visible from the main trail. *Campsite 18* is the smallest of the bunch, with one small platform and better privacy. Campfires are permitted at all sites, though you will need to travel far afield to find usable dead and downed wood. Canoes are available for rent by overnight guests ($1/hour, $8/day).

Water can be obtained from the north shore, where a pipe redirects water near the ranger station, or you can fill up from the lake.

Reservations. To reserve a site at Chimney Pond (or anywhere in Baxter), first visit the park's website, www.baxterstateparkauthority.com, which details the reservation system and the park's myriad rules and regulations. Reservations can be made as much as four months in advance, and if you're planning a weekend trip to Chimney Pond, it is recommended that you send in your reservation as early as possible. Print out the reservations form, fill it out, and mail it in with a self-addressed, stamped return envelope. Your request may arrive one week before the day they open reservations for four months later; earlier than this and they will return it to you. As of 2007, no phone or online reservations were possible, though an online reservation system is rumored to be in the works. You can also make reservations in person at park headquarters in Millinocket. *Don't forget to bring your reservation with you when you come.* It might as well be your passport.

TO REACH THE TRAILHEAD

Head to Millinocket and follow Route 11 west to the Route 11/157 junction by the First Congregational Church. Turn right on Millinocket Road and follow it to the park boundary, where the road becomes unpaved. You soon reach Togue Pond Gatehouse—the park entrance—where you will need to show your reservation form and pay an entrance fee. From the gatehouse, bear right toward Roaring Brook and proceed 8.1 miles over the unpaved road to the trailhead parking area. The designated parking area for overnight users is on the right.

HIKE DESCRIPTION

From the parking area (0.0/1,500), proceed to the Roaring Brook Ranger Station and trailhead and follow Trip 31 to Chimney Pond (3.3/2,890). From Chimney Pond, strike out on the Saddle Trail. A steady rocky climb leads past glimpses of the Katahdin headwall and Cathedral Trail but soon breaks out in more open terrain. Snags jut out of the forest, and you soon see the Saddle Slide ahead of you in the col to the left—your route up! The route eases and heads straight toward the slide, passing through a green corridor of spruce-fir forest.

The trail crosses a brook (4.1/3,520) and then immediately transforms into a scrambling route up a narrow rockfall. Dense and scraggly paper birch line the path. As you climb, views behind you appear of Pamola, the Chimney (the cleft in the ridge below Pamola), and Katahdin Lake in the eastern

The upper Wassataquoik Stream Valley

distance. The route now cuts directly up toward the left, steepens further, and passes through a tunnel of birch branches growing horizontally from the hillside.

You reach the slide proper (4.3/3,810) where the terrain becomes more open, and views look down toward Chimney Pond and the trail corridor below. The slide widens as you climb over loose rocks and scree. The potential for rockfall is high—be aware of hikers above and below you. The slide returns to solid rock as you approach the top, becoming more of a staircase for the final ascent to the top and the Northwest Basin Trail (4.5/4,300).

To the south, you can see the continuing route of the Saddle Trail, which winds up the bare flanks of Baxter Peak. Chimney Pond shimmers below. Beyond it is Pamola's north ridge, route of the Dudley Trail. To tag the summit of Baxter from here, drop your pack here and follow the Saddle Trail 1.0 mile and 1,000 feet up. Also at the junction, an unsigned path heads straight to reach Saddle Spring in less than a quarter mile, a small unreliable source located in a rock pile near the edge of the krummholz.

Leave behind the trammeled trails and continue your journey by turning right (north) and following the Northwest Basin Trail. You descend briefly to reach the Saddle itself, and then proceed on a nice level path through an open alpine tableland. Views now peer westward to the cache of mountains in the park's west area. From north to south, they include North and South Brother, Mount Coe, and Mount O-J-I, beyond which is the distinctive summit ridgeline of Doubletop Mountain.

As you proceed across the waving grasslands of the alpine zone, watch for crowberries, Labrador tea, dense clumps of diapensia, and other denizens of this harsh above-treeline environment. The trail cruises along, then makes a slow rise and enters a talus field; blazes and cairns mark the way through the boulders. The trail eases as you crest 4,500 feet, levels off, and then drops slightly to reach the Hamlin Ridge Trail on the right (5.5/4,630). Caribou Spring flows strongly from nearby rocks, a reliable water source.

To ascend Hamlin, a recommended 0.2-mile side-trip, bear right on the Hamlin Ridge Trail and talus-hop your way to the flat-topped, 4,756-foot summit. The vista encompasses the Knife Edge, Baxter Peak, most of the Katahdin massif, and the disk of Chimney Pond below. The Dudley, Chimney Pond, and Saddle trails vein the mountain slopes. From Hamlin Peak, the North Peaks Trail continues northeast above treeline to visit the Howe Peaks. The North Peaks Trail once connected north to Russell Pond, but today is no longer maintained and closed below treeline.

Back heading north on the Northwest Basin Trail, you quickly pass the North Peaks Cutoff Trail on the right and head toward the ridge before you. Beyond the open ridgeline are 4,151-foot North Brother (on the right) and 3,970-foot South Brother (left). Textbook fir waves line both peaks, gray lines of dead trees that resemble arching eyebrows.

The path becomes fainter and less traveled as you walk across the plateau; waving grasses make it seem almost prairie-like. Views of Baxter Peak behind you continue along the open route, which briefly passes through a section of head-high krummholz. You can espy the Saddle Trail snaking up the peak and the deep gouge of Witherle Ravine is apparent on Baxter's west flanks.

The trail reaches a knob at the end of the Northwest Plateau (6.6/4,410), which offers deep views into the Northwest Basin itself. Striking cliffs loom on the opposite side. To the north and northeast is the Wassataquoik Stream drainage—your continuing route. The watershed leads toward adjoining Russell and Deep ponds, visible in the distance. The cliffs that hem in out-of-sight Wassataquoik Lake are apparent almost due north.

Starting your descent toward Davis Pond, you drop over loose scree and quickly enter waist-high krummholz. The route follows ankle-breaking talus down through thickening krummholz, a steep and rocky drop that soon travels through a corridor of trees. Intermittent views continue as the trail starts following a flowing streamcourse and descends through taller forest. You follow the water down for nearly 300 feet, leave it briefly, and then re-cross it a short distance farther. Views of the vertical cliffs in the basin peek out before the trail abruptly steepens.

Lake Cowles, companion to Davis Pond, appears straight below you. Davis Pond is just visible to the right. For the next 300 feet of descent, it's a steep scrambling drop over roots and boulders of all sizes. The plummet finally ends, you bank right through a forested boulder field, and blueberry bushes proliferate. Views of the basin open up as the trail finally levels, curves left, passes a marshy area with larch trees, and reaches Davis Pond Lean-to (7.7/2,920). A path leads from the shelter down to the pond's inflow, where good views look over the pond and toward the upper headwall; a waterfall tumbles down the rock face.

After enjoying this wild place, head out on the trail again and climb quickly to an open clearing, which offers expansive views of the Northwest Basin. To the northwest, you can peer down your continuing route, which runs through the narrow gap ahead. Nearby Fort Mountain earns its name from the rocky redoubt that crowns its summit. Larches populate the rocky bald and dot the surrounding cliffs. The trail travels over several rocky clearings with continued views down the U-shaped valley ahead. Lake Cowles briefly appears to the left, and then the trail crosses extensive puncheon through a boggy area to reach the lake's north shore.

Evidence of old beaver activity is abundant and gnawed branches are scattered about. You cross the lake outflow on an abandoned beaver dam, which offers a nice view of the water and surrounding ridges and cliffs. The route then descends a narrow single-track path into the valley ahead of you. Rocks, roots, and a section of wet sloping slabs make the descent tricky at times.

You approach the main stem of the stream that emerges from the basin—a tributary of Wassataquoik Stream—and hike parallel to it on rock slabs, boulders, and roots. The trail then reaches the rocky waterway by a small pool and begins traveling directly along the streambed itself. The water disappears beneath the rocks underfoot and soon the trail crosses the streambed above a mossy slab. You next enjoy the first level stretch of trail since the Northwest Plateau as the route cruises parallel to the stream.

Young paper birch and mountain ash surround you as the trail passes intermittent views of the looming nameless cliffs overhead. The route crosses a small tributary, remains parallel to the main rushing watercourse, and winds gently through young forest. Though still rocky, the path is free of giant boulders and is a delightful contrast to sections preceding it. You cross another small tributary, pass a few cedar trees, and continue on a mostly level route to reach Wassataquoik Stream (9.2/2,120).

The trail rock-hops the 10- to 20-foot wide stream over boulders. Once on the other side, enjoy nice views nearby of the cliffs. Continuing, the trail passes through a boggy area on puncheon and then widens to become a level double-track corridor through spruce-fir forest. A large slope of talus peeks through the trees to your left as you pass near the stream again in a floodplain area. As you cross an old beaver dam, look for views of the talus field behind you. The route then winds briefly through a boulder field and returns to the stream by some massive car-sized boulders. A chest-deep swimming hole here may lengthen your stay. You continue parallel to the extremely rocky stream, pass quaking aspen, bracken fern, and blueberries, and then cross Annis Brook (10.3/1,890) by a pile of rusty logging artifacts.

Past Annis Brook, the trail winds above the stream. The water soon disappears from sight, though it remains audible. The route now cruises slowly and steadily downward through a forest of increasing hardwoods, especially yellow birch. Beech soon appears in abundance as the environment rapidly transitions to northern hardwood forest. Sugar maple joins the mosaic overhead and hazel and elderberry bushes soon fill in the understory. A long level section then leads to an abrupt transition back to spruce-fir forest, which slowly mixes with hardwoods as the easygoing trail continues.

The trail then steepens noticeably and curves left to pass a swampy boulder-studded pond. Views across the water look north to North and South Pogy mountains. At the outlet, views expand south to include the nearby massif of Russell Mountain. Cross the outlet on an easy rock-hop, and then travel over puncheon to reach the Russell Pond Trail (12.7/1,320). Bear left to visit Russell Pond Campground in 0.1 mile (12.8/1,320).

A primitive scale has been constructed at the campground entrance. Complete with marked stones for weight, it provides the opportunity for some pack-weighing diversion. Next to it, the outline of a moose has been painted on a nearby rock. A diversity of trees surrounds the lake, including larch, cedar, white pine, red pine, spruce, fir, red maple, and paper birch. Larch are particularly common along "Ankle Knocker Bridge" on the lake's west shore. A profusion of boulders dots the lake.

EXCURSIONS FROM RUSSELL POND

Russell Pond sits at a nexus of trails. Nearly half a dozen routes emanate from here and it makes a great base camp for exploring the surrounding landscape.

The Caverly Lookout Trail leads to good views south from the low hill north of the pond. Formerly the Lookout Ledges Trail, it was renamed to honor long-time park director Buzz Caverly, who retired in 2005 after 24 years in the position. The walk is a 1.3-mile one-way journey with 400 feet of elevation gain and leads you through spruce-fir forest to a series of three viewpoints looking south to southeast, including Russell Mountain (right) and the Turner Mountains (left). Your return route to Roaring Brook traces between the two as it travels up the watershed of South Branch Wassataquoik Stream.

Wassataquoik Lake is a long, wild body of water located 2.2 miles from Russell Pond via the Wassataquoik Lake Trail. The hike from Russell Pond requires 450 feet of elevation gain/loss as it travels over undulating rocky terrain, passing Deep Pond at 0.5 mile and Six Ponds at 1.1 miles, where canoes are available for use. Hemmed by steep bluffs, Wassataquoik Lake features a small canoe launch at its east end where canoes, paddles, and personal floatation devices are located for hiker use. Wassataquoik Lake Island Campsite hides on the small island just opposite the canoe launch (do not visit if the site is occupied). Green Falls, a rushing cascade, is located on the lake's south shore, near its midpoint, 1.1 miles past the canoe launch on the Wassataquoik Lake Trail.

Grand Falls is located 2.5 miles from Russell Pond via the Grand Falls Trail, which splits off near the start of the Lookout Ledges Trail. The substantial cascade chutes over naked granite walls and is located near Inscription Rock, a massive boulder marked by loggers in the late nineteenth century. It is possible to make a 6.4-mile loop to the falls and back by returning via the Ledge Falls and Wassataquoik Stream trails, which pass by Ledge Falls and near the Wassataquoik Stream Campsite.

Pogy Pond is located in a broad flat area 3.7 miles north of Russell Pond via the Pogy Notch Trail. Isolation is the big attraction of this viewless and little-traveled hike, which descends slowly from Russell Pond and crosses the headwaters of Pogy Brook en route to the pond and adjoining campsite, located on the pond's northeast shore.

Once you're done exploring, begin your return journey to Roaring Brook by heading south along the Russell Pond Trail. Russell Mountain occasional peeks through the trees ahead as you undulate over a mix of dirt and rocks, drop briefly, and cross flowing Turner Brook on slippery puncheon. On the far side of the brook, you reach the Wassataquoik Stream Trail on the left (13.3/1,300), which follows the area's original logging route back to Roaring Brook. It is a slightly longer and wetter return option, but provides an alternate route if Wassataquoik Stream is unfordable on the Russell Pond Trail.

Remain on the Russell Pond Trail to quickly reach Wassataquoik Stream. The trail continues on the other side but to reach it you need to undertake the most difficult river crossing of the trip. The stream is 10- to 20-feet wide and can easily reach above the knees (or higher during wet conditions). A walking stick or trekking poles are recommended.

Once on the opposite bank, the trail rises and begins traversing the slopes of Russell Mountain. Sugar maple, beech, and paper and yellow birch line the route; glimpses look east through them toward North Turner Mountain. You traverse along a thin single-track path, cross numerous small brooks, and then make a slow, steady rise to rock-hop across a rushing tributary. The trail continues to rise and then levels near a boulder field and several good-sized sugar maples.

The route then descends a rocky staircase and passes glimpses of South Turner Mountain across the valley. You then emerge before an RV-sized mega-boulder. The trail winds underneath an overhanging bulge of this "colossalith," which offers dry shelter in wet weather. This monster calved from the cliffs above you to the right. Beyond the rock, the trail gently descends, reenters spruce-fir forest, and crosses a clear-flowing brook.

The route takes a more direct line down the mountain, then curves right, levels, and descends to meet audible Wassataquoik Stream below (16.4/1,450). You now must re-cross the stream, here a bouldery rushing waterway approximately 20 feet wide. It is substantially reduced in volume from the earlier ford, but can still require a shin- to knee-deep ford or an exciting rock-hop.

Once on the other side, the trail turns right to head upstream and immediately reach the Wassataquoik Stream Trail entering from the left (16.5/1,460). Big-tooth aspen, spruce, and fir line the trail as you continue upstream parallel to the creek on the Russell Pond Trail. The route rises above it again and begins to offer glimpses of Katahdin peeking out toward the southwest; the cliffs of Russell Mountain are visible beyond it.

The trail levels, crosses a tributary, rises briefly, and then winds over several small brooks in a young, diverse forest. The single-track path undulates gently along and winds past another nice boulder. It then enters denser spruce-fir woods, where views peek west toward Hamlin Ridge and Blueberry Knoll in Katahdin's North Basin. The trail encounters a section of bog bridging and reaches a short puncheon spur down to the marshy shore of Whidden Pond on the right (18.4/1,640). Head to the water's edge for a final view of the Katahdin massif. Going from north to south (right to left), the distinctive features are the Little North Basin, Blueberry Knoll in the North Basin, Hamlin Ridge, and finally the Great and South basins, including Baxter Peak, Pamola, and the Saddle Trail.

The trail next crests the height-of-land and leaves the Wassataquoik Stream drainage. The path continues through dense spruce-fir and reaches the Sandy Stream Pond Trail on the left (18.7/1,600). This marks the start of the popular Sandy Stream Pond Loop from Roaring Brook; the odds of encountering other hikers increase.

Remain on the Russell Pond Trail as it slowly descends over roots, steepens, and becomes rockier. Leveling briefly and becoming muddy in spots, the trail crosses some puncheon and passes a glimpse of nearby South Turner Mountain. You cross a stream on more bog bridging, then rise and drop briefly to rock-hop the rushing brook that feeds Sandy Stream. The trail runs level, then ascends briefly through a paper birch grove and attains a small ridge of beech and other hardwoods. You can hear Roaring Brook ahead and soon descend to reach the Sandy Stream Trail and rushing brook. Cross the bridge and return to the trailhead (19.8/1,500).

INFORMATION

Baxter State Park, 64 Balsam Drive, Millinocket, ME 04462; 207-723-5140; www.baxterstateparkauthority.com

TRIP 33
THE END

Location: Cutler Coast Public Reserved Land
Highlight: Coastal backpacking
Distance: 9.8 miles round-trip
Total Elevation Gain/Loss: 1,600/1,600
Trip Length: 2 days
Difficulty: ★★
Recommended Map: *Cutler Coast Map,* Maine Department of Parks and Lands

Located at the farthest end of Maine's coast, the Cutler Coast is a very long drive away. It is also often muddy, foggy, and wet. The only payoff is the opportunity to backpack through a spongy cedar forest along the rockbound hide of New England's northern coast.

HIKE OVERVIEW
The hike first follows the Coastal Trail south along the ocean for 4 miles, passing cliffy promontories and coves. It then returns via the Inland Trail, where soggy cedar forest drapes the landscape. The trail is often muddy and travels across extensive sections of slick bog bridging. Available water sources are mostly brown and tannin-soaked. Carry a filter or bring all your water.

OVERNIGHT OPTIONS
There are three primitive backcountry campsites located midway through the hike. Perched in the forest immediately inland from the coast, the sites are available on a first-come, first-served basis. Camping is prohibited elsewhere. The area receives light use, and a site is usually available. If they are all taken, please look for a flat rock ledge near the ocean rather than establish a higher-impact (and illegal) site inland. The boggy, rooty, and mossy forest would make camping difficult anyway. Campfires are prohibited.

The sites are described from north to south in the order you encounter them. The closest water source for all three sites is located just past site 3, a funky brown stream.

Site 1 is located in a small clearing just inland from the coastal rocks, offering a lookout point over the water and space for two small tents. The most primitive privy you'll ever see is located here.

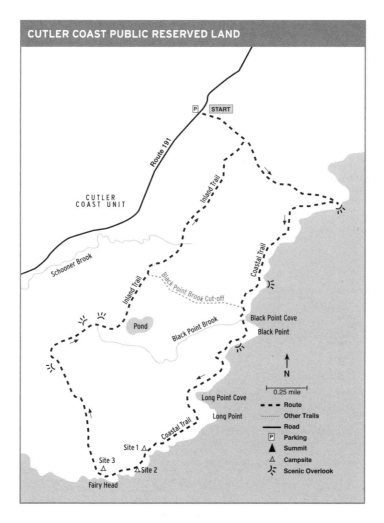

Site 2 shelters in a larger clearing surrounded by spruce, with ready access to the rocks and good spots for cooking and lounging. Good views extend south along the coast to a classic lighthouse and its red-roofed buildings.

Site 3 tucks farther back in the trees and provides more shelter in inclement weather. Ringed by spruce, alder, and mountain ash, the site has a limited view. Nice open ledges are accessible down below, and there are several flat areas for cooking and relaxing.

TO REACH THE TRAILHEAD

Take Route 191 to the town of Cutler. From the flagpole and bell in the town center, continue on Route 191 for 4.0 miles to reach the signed parking lot and trailhead on your right.

HIKE DESCRIPTION

From the trailhead (0.0/140), survey the surrounding trees. Yellow birch, spruce, red maple, and young black cherry ring the parking area. More interesting is the presence of Atlantic white cedar, a common tree along Maine's east coastline, but rare on most Northeast hiking trails. Recognize it by the vertical ribbons on its trunk and flat splays of needles.

Sign in at the information kiosk—free maps are usually available—and head out past a nice spruce tree. Yellow clintonia (a.k.a. blue-bead lily) grows below it. You immediately encounter the first bog bridging, a slick foot-sliding

The Cutler Coast

balance exercise, and cross a boggy area on a small footbridge. Paper birch mixes in with the surrounding spruce trees. A few roots and rocks protrude in the blue-blazed trail as it rises briefly, makes a slow drop, and reaches the Inland Trail entering from the right (0.4/120)—your return route.

Continue straight on the Coastal Trail, which quickly passes a flowing water source and winds through increasingly dense woods. Understory plants fade away beneath the drunken stick forest. The trail undulates along, passes a big gnarly yellow birch on the left, and travels over much bog bridging. The trail then widens and passes through a few clearings before beginning a noticeable descent. Ocean blue appears through the trees ahead, and you soon reach the coast (1.5/50).

Paths provide ready access to clifftops rising vertically from the ocean 50 feet below. Get as close to the edge as you dare. Looking south from the clifftops, Black Point—part of your continuing route—juts into the sea. A gravelly cove is visible to the north, but be aware that the coastline becomes private property only a few yards north of this access point. (Don't worry, the scenery in that direction isn't as grand.) Take a look down at the water below you. The tides here are extreme, rising and falling between 12 and 20 feet twice each day.

Back on the Coastal Trail, head south along the cliff's edge and past intermittent views. Alders and wood ferns line the single-track path as it navigates roots, climbs briefly via a rock staircase, and then steeply descends. You pass views into a rocky cove. Ocean glimpses are intermittent but regular, and you next peer down at whitewashed boulders littering the coast below.

The trail then winds close to the cliff's edge, offers extensive views, and passes above a deep cove where small waterfalls tumble. Slowly descending, you pass through a field of spruce and abundant laurel. The trail then drops down to sea level, crosses flowing water, and runs right along the coastal rocks. Blue paint and a few cairns mark the route. The seaweed-coated rocks are evocative of matted Chewbacca hair.

Raspberry bushes are common and now blueberries appear as well. The trail climbs briefly and then drops into the Black Point Brook watershed. Just before reaching the stream, you come to the signed junction with the Black Point Cutoff Trail (3.0/20), which leads north to the Inland Trail in 0.8 miles. Remain on the Coastal Trail as it heads to the adjacent cobblestone beach.

Leaving the beach, you climb a long ladder, reenter the forest, and curve away from the water to bypass Black Point. Winding through a spruce-cedar forest, the trail soon emerges at more views of the cliff-studded coast. The trail rambles along the clifftop, passes another small cobbled beach, and then rises more than 100 feet over rocks and slabs. The route curves right and soon emerges by a broad valley dotted with stands of cedar and spruce.

The trail bends right and then left to meander above the meadow. Abundant blueberries line the path, which soon dips to cross the brook draining the valley. You next descend to another placid cobblestone cove, a horseshoe beach accessed by a short flight of stairs. The trail resumes climbing, switchbacks left, and makes a steep ascent via rock stairs. You then ramble downward along a rocky path and past an offshore mega-boulder. The route undulates along, crosses a bridge, and reemerges on the open coastline by a rocky outcrop. The trail returns inland, travels just above the cliffs, and then quickly drops back down next to the shoreline and returns to the rocks. Campsite #1 is just ahead, indicated by a small sign (5.0/30). A log ladder leads up to it.

Past the site, the trail continues along the open rocks and then turns inland to climb up a small ravine and reach the posted junction for site #2 (5.1/40) by a log ladder on the left. From here, the continuing route passes through a boggy section and returns to the shoreline rocks. You crest the sloping promontory of Fairy Head, where views look south toward a major antenna array poking above the hills. The Navy operates a very low frequency (VLF) installation nearby, which consists of 26 1,000-foot high antennas spread over 2 square miles.

Purple irises, wild pea, and yarrow are common in the small patches of vegetation that dot the rocks. You turn a corner and reach the posted junction for site #3 (5.3/30). Immediately past it is a meadow and small pond, fed by flowing brown water—the only nearby water source. The route continues past one final cove and then turns inland, leaving the coast behind for good.

The single-track trail immediately returns to the sponge forest. After rising briefly, you level off and follow an easy-cruising, not-too-wet path. The trail curves back and forth as it resumes a slow rise, aided at times by small log steps, and then again winds downward. After encountering some puncheon, you start up a rocky hill, enter a nice yellow birch grove, then cruise along to a posted rock overlook. A short spur leads to a view southwest over a sea of conifers.

After a brief descent, you reach a fork in the trail, signed INLAND TRAIL TO FERRY HEAD (sic). Go right to remain on the Inland Trail, which now cruises down an old woods road. The route slowly descends, crosses a tributary of Black Point Brook, and then passes through birch groves. Red maple mixes in. You next rise to reach another posted overlook, this one peering northeast. A hundred yards farther, another signed spur leads to a bald rock with views east and southeast. The trail returns to single-track, drops again, and crosses more puncheon. It forks roughly 200 yards past the second viewpoint—follow the path to the left. Skirting a wet area, you pass through a stand of red maple and begin a level section.

The hike next reaches the edge of a large pond, headwaters for Black Point Brook. Larch trees ring the shore, some of them substantial. Blackberry is abundant. The trail runs near the pond, offering numerous glimpses of the water. You then climb atop open boulders for an overlook of the entire scene, a spot that captures the essence of the region.

From here, the trail returns to spruce-fir sponge-land. The route is mostly level and then rises briefly over open rocks to intersect the Black Point Brook Cutoff Trail (7.9/190), which reaches its inland end here by a cairn.

Continue on the Inland Trail and drop steeply over a talus-like section. The single-track path then levels and rambles past extensive spruce. You eventually cross an open marshy meadow; houses to your left indicate the approximate location of the highway. This section is particularly wet and several portions of bog bridging almost float in the underlying water.

You wind for some distance through a small bog forest of aspen, alders, azalea, laurel, and larch, interspersed with a few dry rock outcrops. After crossing the hike's longest stretch of bog bridging, the trail reenters the matchstick forest of cedar, spruce, and fir. The final section of the Inland Trail winds through a chaotic forest of tilting trees and deposits you at the earlier junction with the Coastal Trail (9.4/120). Turn left and head back to the trailhead (9.8/140).

INFORMATION

Maine Bureau of Parks and Lands, P.O. Box 415, Old Town, ME 04468; 207-827-1818, www.maine.gov/doc/parks

REFERENCES AND RECOMMENDED READING

NATURAL HISTORY

Bell, Ritchie C., and Lindsey, Anne H., *Fall Color and Woodland Harvests.* Laurel Hill Press, 1990.

Cronon, William, *Changes in the Land: Indians, Colonists, and the Ecology of New England.* Hill and Wang, 1983.

Eastman, John, F*orest and Thicket: Trees, Shrubs, and Wildflowers of Eastern North America.* Stackpole Books, 1992.

Jorgensen, Neil, *A Sierra Club Naturalist's Guide to Southern New England.* Sierra Club Books, 1978.

Kricher, John, and Morrison, Gordon, *Peterson Field Guides Eastern Forests.* Houghton Mifflin, 1998.

Marchand, Peter J., *North Woods: An Inside Look at the Nature of Forests in the Northeast.* Appalachian Mountain Club, 1987.

Newcomb, Lawrence, *Newcomb's Wildflower Guide.* Little, Brown, 1977.

Skehan, James W., *Roadside Geology of Massachusetts.* Mountain Press, 2001.

Stack, Nancy G., and Bell, Allison W., *Field Guide to the New England Alpine Summits.* Appalachian Mountain Club, 1995.

Steele, Frederic L., *At Timberline: A Nature Guide to the Mountains of the Northeast.* Appalachian Mountain Club, 1982.

Symonds, George W. D., *The Tree Identification Book.* William Morrow, 1958.

Symonds, George W. D., *The Shrub Identification Book.* William Morrow, 1963.

Van Diver, Bradford B., *Roadside Geology of Vermont and New Hampshire.* Mountain Press, 1987.

Wessels, Tom, *Reading the Forested Landscape: A Natural History of New England.* Countryman Press, 1997.

GENERAL NEW ENGLAND

Chazin, Daniel D., *Appalachian Trail Data Book 2005.* Appalachian Trail Conservancy, 2005.

Emblidge, David, *Exploring the Appalachian Trail: Hikes in Southern New England.* Stackpole Books, 1998.

Hooke, David (editor), *Appalachian Trail Guide to New Hampshire-Vermont,* 10th edition. Appalachian Trail Conservancy, 2001.

Kodas, Michael; Condon, Mark; Scherer, Glenn; and Weegar, Andrew, *Exploring the Appalachian Trail: Hikes in Northern New England.* Stackpole Books, 1999.

Stier, Maggie, and McAdow, Ron, *Into the Mountains: Stories of New England's Most Celebrated Peaks.* Appalachian Mountain Club, 1995.

Taylor-Miller, Cynthia (editor), *Appalachian Trail Thru-Hikers' Companion 2006.* Appalachian Trail Conference, 2006.

Waterman, Laura and Guy, *Forest and Crag: A History of Hiking, Trail Blazing, and Adventure in the Northeast Mountains.* Appalachian Mountain Club, 1989.

SOUTHERN NEW ENGLAND

Burns, Deborah E., and Stevens, Lauren R., *Most Excellent Majesty: A History of Mount Greylock.* Berkshire Natural Resources Council, 1988.

Connecticut Walk Book East, 19th edition. Connecticut Forest and Park Association, 2006.

Connecticut Walk Book West, 19th edition. Connecticut Forest and Park Association, 2006.

Leary, Joseph, *A Shared Landscape: A Guide and History of Connecticut's State Parks and Forests.* Friends of Connecticut State Parks, 2004.

Sills, Norman, and Hatton, Robert (editors), *Appalachian Trail Guide to Massachusetts-Connecticut,* 11th edition. Appalachian Trail Conservancy, 2000.

Smith, Charles W. G., *Massachusetts Trail Guide,* 8th edition. Appalachian Mountain Club, 2004.

VERMONT

Gange, Jared, *Hiker's Guide to the Mountains of Vermont.* Huntington Graphics, 2001.

Green Mountain Club Long Trail Guide, 25th edition. Green Mountain Club, 2003.

Johnson, Charles W., *The Nature of Vermont,* 2nd edition. University Press of New England, 1998.

Plumb, Sylvia L. (editor), *Green Mountain Club Day Hiker's Guide, 4th edition.* Green Mountain Club, 2002.

Scofield, Bruce, *Hiking Green Mountain National Forest, Southern Section.* New England Cartographics, 2000.

NEW HAMPSHIRE

Belcher, C. Francis, *Logging Railroads of the White Mountains.* Appalachian Mountain Club, 1980.

Daniell, Gene, and Smith, Steven D., *Mount Washington and the Presidential Range Trail Guide,* 7th edition. Appalachian Mountain Club, 2003.

Daniell, Gene, and Smith, Steven D., *White Mountain Guide,* 28th edition. Appalachian Mountain Club, 2007.

Flanders, John E., *Wapack Trail Guide.* Friends of the Wapack, 1993.

Howe, Nicolas, *Not Without Peril, 150 Years of Misadventure on the Presidential Range of New Hampshire.* Appalachian Mountain Club, 2001.

Julyan, Robert and Mary, *Place Names of the White Mountains,* Revised edition. University Press of New England, 1993.

Nilsen, Kim Robert, *The Cohos Trail: The Guidebook to New Hampshire's Great Unknown.* Cohos Trail Association, 2004.

Pinder, Eric, *Life at the Top: Tales, Truths, and Trusted Recipes from the Mount Washington Observatory.* Down East Books, 1997.

Randolph Paths, 8th edition. Randolph Mountain Club, 2005.

Reifsnyder, William E., *High Huts of the White Mountains,* 2nd edition. Appalachian Mountain Club, 1993.

Scudder, Brent E., *Scudder's White Mountain Viewing Guide, 2nd edition.* High Top Press, 2005.

Smith, Steven D., and Dickerman, Mike, *The 4000-Footers of the White Mountains: A Guide and History.* Bondcliff Books, 2001.

MAINE

Maine Mountain Guide, 9th edition. Appalachian Mountain Club, 2005.

Neff, John W., *Katahdin: An Historic Journey.* Appalachian Mountain Club, 2006.

Pinder, Eric, *North to Katahdin.* Milkweed Editions, 2005.

Ronan, Ray, *Appalachian Trail Guide to Maine.* Maine Appalachian Trail Club, 2005.

INDEX